LIBRARY OF MONEY AND BANKING HISTORY

THE COMMERCIAL CRISIS
1847-1848

Also Published in

<u>Reprints of Economic Classics</u>

by D. Morier Evans

Facts, Failures and Frauds [1859]

The History of the Commercial Crisis of 1857-1858 [1859]

Speculative Notes and Notes on Speculation [1864]

THE

COMMERCIAL CRISIS

1847 - 1848

BEING

FACTS AND FIGURES

ILLUSTRATIVE OF THE EVENTS OF THAT IMPORTANT PERIOD
CONSIDERED IN RELATION TO THE THREE EPOCHS OF

THE RAILWAY MANIA, THE FOOD AND MONEY PANIC & THE FRENCH REVOLUTION

BY

D. MORIER EVANS

Second Edition

REVISED AND ENLARGED

[1849]

REPRINTS OF ECONOMIC CLASSICS

AUGUSTUS M. KELLEY · PUBLISHERS
NEW YORK 1969

First Edition 1848

Second Edition 1849

(London: *Printed & Published by* Letts, Son & Steer, *8 Royal Exchange*, 1849)

Reprinted 1969 by

AUGUSTUS M. KELLEY · PUBLISHERS

New York New York 10010

FROM A COPY IN THE COLLECTIONS OF

THE NEW YORK PUBLIC LIBRARY

ASTOR, LENOX AND TILDEN FOUNDATIONS

SBN 678 00515 X

Library of Congress Catalogue Card Number

68-24163

PRINTED IN THE UNITED STATES OF AMERICA

by SENTRY PRESS, NEW YORK, N. Y. 10019

THE

COMMERCIAL CRISIS,

1847–1848.

THE COMMERCIAL CRISIS, 1847–1848;

BEING

FACTS AND FIGURES

ILLUSTRATIVE OF THE EVENTS OF THAT IMPORTANT PERIOD,
CONSIDERED IN RELATION TO THE THREE EPOCHS OF

THE RAILWAY MANIA, THE FOOD AND MONEY PANIC,

AND

THE FRENCH REVOLUTION.

TO WHICH IS ADDED;

AN APPENDIX,

CONTAINING AN ALPHABETICAL LIST OF THE

ENGLISH AND FOREIGN MERCANTILE FAILURES,

WITH THE

BALANCE SHEETS AND STATEMENTS,

OF THE MOST IMPORTANT HOUSES.

Second Edition,
REVISED AND ENLARGED.

By D. MORIER EVANS.

London:
PRINTED AND PUBLISHED BY LETTS, SON AND STEER,
8, Royal Exchange.

1849.

TO

CHARLES BARKER, ESQ.

THIS VOLUME IS INSCRIBED, AS A SMALL TRIBUTE

OF RESPECT AND ESTEEM, BY

THE AUTHOR.

PREFACE TO SECOND EDITION.

The unequivocal success attending the appearance of the First Edition of the Commercial Crisis, 1847-48, and the unanimous testimony of the Press that it was not to be regarded as an ephemeral publication, are circumstances which will readily account for the issue of a Second and enlarged Edition.

In preparing the new Edition, the author has availed himself of many kind suggestions made by personal as well as by unknown friends, and while acting upon them, has, at the same time, paid due regard to the spirit and intention of the volume, as expressed in the Preface to the First Edition.

To render the "Commercial Crisis, 1847-48," complete in every respect, it was considered essential to bring down the narrative to the end of the latter year, and in arranging the Appendix on a more comprehensive plan, space has been afforded for the insertion of balance-sheets and statements of several important mercantile establishments, which it was found almost impossible to procure at the period when the undertaking was first entered upon. The table of dividends, immediately following the alphabetical list of failures, will, doubtless, prove a feature of some importance, and to the labour and expence incurred in making this and various other additions, must be attributed the necessity of increasing the price of the work.

To the public, who have so liberally patronized him, and to the press, who have so warmly supported him in his endeavour to trace the progress of the remarkable financial and commercial events during the years 1845 and 1848 inclusive, the author desires to tender his most grateful acknowledgments.

LOMBARD STREET,

April 25th, 1849.

PREFACE.

The title of this volume may be fairly considered to describe its contents, and whatever defects may appear in the compilation, they must not be attributed to any desire on the part of the author to misrepresent the events which have come under his notice, but to the want of a proper appreciation of them as they may have been exhibited to other persons' view.

Confessing that the only motive actuating him in the arrangement of the following pages was to put into shape, for reference, "a plain unvarnished tale" of circumstances which, either regarded as of present or future interest, cannot fail to engross attention, he presumes he stands absolved from the charge of meditating a daring intrusion into the arena of Currency debate.

Studiously avoiding attempts at dissertation, and strictly eschewing theories, he has endeavoured to confine himself to a description of "Facts and Figures," which while they may prove serviceable to most parties connected with mercantile pursuits, can be looked upon as offensive by few.

The notion prompting the author to divide the volume into the separate Epochs of the Railway Mania, the Food and Money Panic, and the French Revolution, originated in the conviction that, whereas the first and second periods were in a material degree identified with each other, the third so closely following, and producing a commercial revulsion abroad of great severity, might likewise be advantageously introduced, and its prominent characteristics recorded.

Objection may be taken to the manner in which most of the failures occurring during the progress of the Second Epoch have been treated. Distinctly naming each establishment, their locality and trading, and placing them in the order of the several months in which the disasters were announced, no allusion is made to debts and liabilities or assets, except when properly authenticated by a published account, and then only in the shape of reference to the Appendix. The reason for this mode of arrangement, however, is obvious. In the height of the panic, such incorrect *data* appeared respecting the position of a number of firms that, when their affairs were investigated, it was found little reliance could be placed upon these statements; for, apart from the exaggeration occasionally indulged in, so multifarious were the changes they underwent, through the continuous recurrence of suspensions, that their character, in the majority of cases, was ultimately wholly metamorphosed. Besides, the intent of the writer was not to give the actual result of every failure, but simply to sketch, in a general and intelligible manner, the career of the crisis.

A few words respecting the Appendix. Great care has been taken so to class the balance-sheets and statements as to make them readily available for examination, which, assisted by the notation given in the body of the book, will at once point to their place in that collection

The alphabetical arrangement of the failed firms, it is also presumed, will prove of utility, and their accuracy in description has been tested as far as possible, by consulting the various Directories, English and foreign, at immediate command.

Finally, then, craving the reader's indulgence for errors of omission or commission, the author would merely wish to conclude by stating, that any inaccuracies which may be deemed worthy of correction, shall receive his best attention, should his present attempt be rewarded with success, and a second edition of the "COMMERCIAL CRISIS 1847-48" be at a future date demanded.

LOMBARD STREET,

November 9th, 1848.

CONTENTS.

EPOCH THE FIRST.

Page

The Railway Mania and its Effects .... 1 to 52

EPOCH THE SECOND.

The Food and Money Panic.. 53 to 108

EPOCH THE THIRD.

The French Revolution .... 109 to 129

BANK RETURNS, 1845, 1846, 1847, 1848 .... 130 to 133

PRODUCE PRICES, 1845, 1846 1847, 1848 .... 134 to 155

INDEX TO APPENDIX, &c.

BALANCE SHEETS AND STATEMENTS.

	Page
Alexander & Co.	lxxii
Barclay, Brothers, & Co.	xxv
Bensusan & Co.	lxxx
Birley, Corrie, & Co.	li
Boyds and Thomas	lv
Braine, G. T.	xxx
Castellain, Sons, & Co.	lvi
Cockerell, Larpent, & Co.	v
Cruickshank, Melville, & Co.	lii
Fraser, W. T.	xlviii
Fry, Griffiths, & Co.	lxvi
Gower, Nephews, & Co.	xxvii
Giles, Son, & Co.	lxxv
Harman & Co.	i
Hastie and Hutchison	lxxvii
Hughesdon and Mackay	lxxxvii
Johnson, Cole, & Co.	xli
Kingston, John, & Co.	lxxx
Lackersteen, A. A.	xxxviii
Lackersteen, Crake, & Co.	xxxix
Leaf, Barnett, Scotson, & Co.	lxxxiii
Lyall, Brothers, & Co.	xxix
Lysaght, Smithett, & Co.	l
Morley, James and William	lxxxv
Nevins and Allen	lxxviii

INDEX TO APPENDIX, &c.

Page

Perkins, Schlusser, and Mullins xxxiv

Phillips, Laurence, and Sons xxxvi

Phillips, Samuel, & Co. xxxv

Reay and Reay lxxix

Reid, Irving, & Co. xxi

Rougemont, Brothers lxxi

Rickards, Litttle, & Co. xxxiii

Robinson, W. R. & Co. lxxiv

Ryder, Weinholt, & Co. xlix

Sanderson & Co. lviii

Sargant, Gordon, & Co. lxx

Scott, Bell, & Co. xlv

Tanner and Ward lxxxvi

Thomas, Son, and Lefevre lv

Thurburn & Co. xl

Trueman and Cook lix

Usborne and Son lxxvi

Woodley, W. & J. lxxvi

ALPHABETICAL LIST OF FAILURES from August, 1847 to December, 1848 lxxxix

TABLE OF DIVIDENDS cii

EPOCH THE FIRST.

THE RAILWAY MANIA AND ITS EFFECTS.

Remarkable periods, like remarkable men, are seldom suffered to fade from memory for want of an historian. It is the fate of great events, however saddening their impression, to scatter in their track something in the shape of information, which if judiciously selected and stored, may hereafter be usefully administered and found serviceable, humble though the agency through which it may pass.

Popular narratives of popular movements appeal to the fancy and carry with them all that is pleasing to the public taste, but unfortunately it too frequently happens, that the sober realities with which they abound lose much of their practical importance when served in this guise.

Amusing and instructive as these histories usually are, they frequently fail in defining those connecting links in the general chain of circumstances, a knowledge of which is deemed indispensable by the studious enquirer for arriving at correct results, and which links themselves become in reality more a matter of statistical detail or condensed and running commentary, than of lengthened description.

The events of the last three years have acquired especial notoriety. Fraught with the highest interest to all associated in business their career must have been watched with deep, and in the majority of cases, most painful anxiety. The temporary prosperity generating the railway mania, the relapse occasioned by the subsidence of that gigantic speculation, the subsequent food and money crisis, and lastly, the French revolution, have each contributed to incite and aggravate the devastation by which we have been surrounded.

"The history of the railway mania of 1845," it has been said,* "is not the least remarkable among those delusions which from time to time arise to throw aside legitimate trade and paralyse national commerce. From 1842 discounts had been easy and money plentiful, the funds maintained a high rate; low interest only could be obtained. In 1844, it was remarked that there had been a larger continuance of a plentiful supply of money than had occurred in the memory of the oldest capitalists. A desire to speculate grew out of these circumstances, and England was seized with her ancient phrenzy. For some time it was legitimate and confined within its proper sphere, but the desire spread; the contagion passed to all, and from the clerk to the capitalist the fever reigned uncontrollable and uncontrolled."

The extension of the railway system, which in reality commenced in 1844, was not plainly perceptible until the early part of the following year. Then there was no mistake respecting it. The great trunk lines occupied the field with branches. The public were for the while apathetic spectators. Only those who possessed original shares could obtain an interest in the new issues, and dividends standing well with a prospect of increase, fresh projects at length made their appearance.

In November, 1844, the state of the Money-market, serving as an index, may be taken as representing the position of capital. The bullion in the Bank was £14,300,000; the notes in circulation amounted to £21,000,000. The rate of interest in Threadneedle-street was 2½ per cent. Consols were above par; Exchequer Bills (at 1½d. per diem) 60 premium: some

* Francis's History of the Bank of England.

impulse this to speculation. The fever made rapid advances. The abundance of money, together with the absence of profitable channels of employment, soon exerted its wonted influence. Projectors mapped out undertakings, engineers patronised them, the schemes were advertised, and applications inundated the committees.

The year 1845 opened, and in the course of January, sixteen new companies were registered. These did not materially augment the speculation, but they gave fresh zest to business. The Share-market was becoming more than ordinarily active, and in the succeeding three months, the number of projects registered had increased from sixteen to fifty-two for the month of April. In the meanwhile, railway progress, and the prospect of a large consumption of iron, created an immense demand for that article—so that with the combined action of cheap capital, and the formation of these undertakings, a wild rage existed for an adventure in the various descriptions of the staple.* Thus encouraged confidence soon gained ground, and the primary and legitimate movement resulted in an overwhelming and destructive mania.

The position of the markets for public securities for January and May inclusive, accurately distinguishes the course of the speculation. All that was done by the Bank was to give a new form to their notice relative to the discount of bills and notes. Instead of adhering, as previously, to one fixed rate, a *minimum* was named, ($2\frac{1}{2}$ per cent. being the minimum in this instance,) leaving it, under such circumstances, at the option of the directors to raise their terms according to the character of the paper

* *Highest and lowest prices of Scotch Pig Iron in* 1845.

	per Ton.				per Ton.		
January	60s.	to	68s.	July	60s. 0d.	to	67s. 6d.
February	65s.	,,	90s.	August	60s. 0d.	,,	70s.
March	105s.	,,	120s.	September	77s. 6d.	,,	85s.
April	95s.	,,	115s.	October	82s. 6d.	,,	97s.
May	70s.	,,	80s.	November	70s. 0d.	,,	85s.
June	60s.	,,	77s. 6d.	December	70s. 0d.	,,	80s.

presented to them. The stock of bullion at the same time was steadily increasing.

GOVERNMENT SECURITIES.

	JANUARY, 1845.				MAY, 1845.			
	Price on the 1st.	Lowest Price.	Highest Price.	Price on the 31st.	Price on the 2d.	Lowest Price.	Highest Price.	Price on the 31st.
Consols, Money	Shut	99⅞	100¼	100	98⅝	98¼	99½	99⅝
Do. Account....	100¼ ex.d.	99¾	100¼	100⅛	98¾	98⅜	99¾	99½
Exchequer Bills, 1½d.	63/ pm.	56/ pm.	67/ pm.	63/ pm.	58/ pm.	54/ pm	63/ pm.	61/ pm.

RAILWAY SECURITIES.

	JANUARY, 1845.						MAY, 1845.						
	Amount per Share.	Amount paid.	Price on the 1st.	Low-est Price	High-est Price	Price on the 31st.	Amount Paid.			Price on the 1st.	Low-est Price	High-est Price	Price on the 31st.
	£	£					£	s.	d.				
Brighton	50	50	52	50¼	53	53	50	0	0	63¾	62¼	68¼	68⅛
Caledonian	50	5	4½	4⅜	6⅝	6	5	0	0	11¾	8½	12	9¾
Eastern Counties ..	25	£25 nom	15¼	15	19½	17½	14	16	0	20¼	17⅞	22	20½
Great Western	100	75	155	152½	178	175	80	0	0	186	184	210	207
London & N.Westn.	Stock.		228	227	236	233	Stock			234½	233	253½	251
Midland Counties..	Stock.		116½	115	134	128½	Stock			156½	152	190	188½
South Eastern	Av. £33 : 2 : 4		40¾	40⅜	49½	48½	Av. 33	2	4	39¾	39¼	45	44¾
Do. Western . ..	Av. £41 : 6 : 10		75	73	82	77½	Av. 41	6	10	79¼	76½	82	81¾
York & N. Midland	£50	£50	104	104	113	108	50	0	0	102	102	118	117
Boulogne & Amiens	20	2	5	4⅜	5⅛	4⅞	4	0	0	9¾	8¼	10½	9¼
Northern of France	20	4	5¾	5½	6	5¾	4	0	0	5⅜	5¼	6⅛	5⅝
Paris and Lyons ..	20	2	3½	3⅜	3⅞	3¾	2	0	0	2½	1⅞	3⅛	2½

Incontestable evidence is furnished by these figures that "the delusion which had seized the public" was working actively by influencing the value of all classes of railway property. There was no check, no impediment to the improvement, and the concourse of operators daily and hourly augmented. The Board of Trade having assumed the power of issuing decisions as to the particular schemes which would first meet attention at the hands of Government, furnished another potent incentive to adventure. Such was the excitement then among the speculators, that bargains were made in the favorite shares at the coffee-houses and other places of resort in the City, long after the conclusion of business at the Stock-exchange. The appearance of the *Gazette* was impatiently looked for, and its contents eagerly perused. "This form of the prevailing mania" it was observed, "is beyond the reach, of course, of all caution or control, and as all concerned have access to the important information sought exactly at the same time, this is a matter of secondary consequence. It is only those who are upon the spot, and witness its violence, and the general infection arising from it, both within and without the walls of the Stock-exchange, who can form an idea of the perilous task undertaken by the Board of Trade in putting forth these decisions, and which are the fuel for this fire."

Between the months of May and June the increase of speculation was fearful. The papers teemed with advertisements unrestricted to the limits of ordinary announcements. Columns scarcely sufficed to give the world a knowledge of each scheme. Lists of provisional committee-men, which in the beginning of the year had seldom exceeded a dozen or twenty names, now extended their length to ten times that number. Earls and Marquises struggled with London capitalists and rustic landowners to add attractiveness by the sanction of their names; the needy barrister professed affection for a seat at the councils of boards, which seemed likely to bring more profit than the law, and was as importunate as most persons to be ensured that position.* Numberless M.P.'s, with a few Aldermen, made a traffic on their presumed responsibility; the plurality churchman and the ill-provisioned curate also were not behind in the general scramble, and the lifesome sketch of the country being engaged

---

* A letter characteristic of the desire which prevailed to get appointed a director is here appended, the authenticity of which the Editor vouches. He could produce scores of the kind but does not think it necessary. *Ex uno disce omnes.*

"Dear ———, "Do you want a director of your railway? as I have lately been dealing rather extensively in such commodities, and am a director of the 'Direct * * * * * *,' advertised in the '———' and other papers. I am also a director of a Jamaica line, which will be advertised next week, and as I find railways much more profitable than law, I have cut the latter. If you can put my name down as director I shall be obliged.

"Your's faithfully,
"——— ———

"Regent-street. "——— Club."

"P.S. As I am intimate with several leading and influential directors, I might bring some with me if requisite."

in one universal game of hazard was without the least exaggeration realized. Never before were "such times or such prospects." The fortunes made in some few cases maddened their gainers; their success soon spread, rich and poor were alike susceptible; and the "great chance" was not neglected. It was a golden moment for the "alley-man," the jackall of the Stock-exchange—his perceptive faculties were sharpened, and he pushed his vocation assiduously.*

The railway market had at this period become the grand focus both of legitimate and speculative operations. The attractions of scrip lavishly distributed, far outvied the steady dividend paying 3 per cents., and these, with other favorite securities, were at once abandoned. Nothing under 8 or 10 per

* "A third class of dealers, who may be said to exist on the skirts of the Stock-markets, are the 'little-go,' or 'alley-men.' They are a description of people including the lowest of the low among the outside speculators trafficking in the letters and shares of railway, or any other joint-stock company that may happen to fall into their hands. They frequent the purlieus of Capel-court, the Auction-mart, and the adjoining lanes and alleys, and principally consist of broken-down merchants' clerks, decayed tradesmen who have lost money by speculation, and others, whose pretensions to honesty and character it would be difficult to describe. Visit Bartholomew-lane at any time in the year, and you will be sure to find several people of shabby exterior holding converse at the entrance of Capel-court, or on the steps of the Auction-mart. These are 'alley-men.' You will see one, perhaps, take from his pocket a goodly-sized parcel of dirty-backed letters, all arranged, and tied round with string or red tape, which he sorts with as much care and attention as if they were bank-notes. That parcel is his stock in trade; perhaps those letters may contain the allotment of shares, in various companies, to an amount, if the nominal capital were paid, of many hundreds of thousands of pounds. They, doubtless, in his hands, are scarcely worth as many farthings: yet he makes a living on them, and is as busy as the most opulent broker in finding a buyer for his 'securities.'

"To describe fairly the 'alley-man,' we must take him from the first of his career. He is generally, as we have said before, some broken-down clerk or tradesman, who, having lost every prospect in life, chooses this description of business as a *dernier ressort*. First started in his calling, he associates with the loiterers at the Stock-exchange, where, by mixing with them, and, perhaps, making an acquaintance through the introduction of Mr. John Barleycorn at the tap of the Auction-mart, he is initiated, by degrees, into the secrets of the business, and, before long, becomes as great an adept in the sale or purchase of letters as the oldest man on the walk. When he has acquired the necessary information respecting dealing, he can commence letter-writing for shares. This is effected at the expense of a penny only for

cent. was recognised as a fair return for investment. That rate would most surely be obtained when the various undertakings arrived at completion. Hence it was observed, "capital among the daring city speculators has been of little consideration. Men without houses or homes, clerks at small salaries in banks and merchants' establishments, have as openly proclaimed themselves buyers and sellers of the favorite shares, as if they represented their employers. The work has not only been confined to London, but it has also extended itself to Manchester, Leeds, Liverpool, Glasgow, Dublin, Hull, Edinburgh, and Bristol, in all which towns markets have been established, and as much, if not more, business transacted than in London. Indeed the whole circle of society is so entangled in the mania,

---

postage, pen and ink being always obtainable, either in the tavern-parlour or coffee-house he frequents. When a new company comes out, and is advertised in the daily papers, he immediately calls for a form of application, fills it up, and despatches it, with the moderate request to be 'allotted' one hundred or two hundred shares, the amount of call or share being quite immaterial to him, as he never intends to pay upon or keep them, his only aim being to increase his valuable stock of letters, so that he can make a 'deal,' and pocket the profit should they have a price among the fraternity. In this manner the whole of the 'alley-men' write to the companies for shares, and do not hesitate to adopt all kinds of fraud and trickery to gain success. From the numerous applications which directors in these projects receive from this class of people, the names of the greater number are already known, and discarded accordingly, it being well ascertained that they only seek the shares for the temporary profit they yield. In order, therefore, to lull the suspicion of the directors, they, with their confederates, write in fictitious names, imitating influential city firms in Christian and surname, and giving false and fraudulent addresses, with assumed references of the highest respectability. Should the 'alley-men' be fortunate enough to get an allotment, he goes among his brethren and learns the price, if any, for the shares. If there are but few among them, and the letters are in demand, he may, perhaps, get as good a market as ten shillings per share, which, upon twenty, a number not unlikely to be allotted when two or three hundred are applied for, will give him ten pounds. Thus, if fortune attend his applications, he may make some little money; but yet, as the love of speculation is strongly allied with this description of business, he may, on the other hand, lose what he makes in the purchase of letters of less note and value. It is, however, not very often that this description of dealer realizes the large sum of ten shillings per share. The more current price for letters ranges from one shilling to three shillings per share; and cases have been known where sales have been effected at as low as one penny and one halfpenny per share."—*The City, or the Physiology of London Business.*

that when one link goes, the weight of responsibility will be found vastly embarrassing to those who possess property that may be jeopardized by such a crisis."

Again, there was no end to the employment of the brokers. The increase of business was so great, that the "accounts" formerly occupying not more than one or two days, nearly exhausted the week before differences could be paid, transfers made, and books regularly adjusted. Day and night clerks were engaged in arranging sales and purchases, and conducting the required correspondence. Extra assistants were in most cases secured; the sabbath even brought no rest. At home or abroad relief was impossible from the wearing pressure of the excitement, and the result was that "the denizens of the Stock-exchange, instead of complaining as they did two or three years previously at the dearth of business, were now impatient for time, and opportunity to perfect their clients' commissions."

The feasibility of a number of schemes encouraged the example of starting competing lines, while in addition foreign undertakings of the most questionable description were advocated, and it was boldly declared that the "railway reformation" was at hand. "Verily railways," it was said, "are the wonder of the world! Nothing during the last few years has created so marvellous a change as the great iron revolution of science. Beneath it the features of old Christendom have become changed, and its wealth and physical grandeur augmented. Other revolutions have scattered luminous influences over the world, peopling it with the precious things of the present and the past; but it remained for the new generation of railways, aided by the presence of universal peace, to bring about one of the mightiest moral and social revolutions that ever hallowed the annals of any age. Railways unquestionably form the greatest discovery in what has been termed the century of science. They are the mightiest of all modern motive powers, and have continued triumphantly to reproduce themselves in spite of every opposition, so that we may shortly expect to hear of the great steam automaton sweeping by means of the undeviating rail, from the steppes of the Cossack to the Indian's home. England, Europe, and the world will soon be too small for their marchings. Omnipresence is one of the principles of their progress. Not content with making Liverpool their lineage-home, and many-sounding Manchester marked mistress of their choice, they are throwing a girdle round the globe itself, and rearing measureless dominions throughout its circuit. Far off India woos them over its waters, and China even listens to the voice of the charmer. The "ruined hills and broken altars" of Old Greece will soon re-echo the whistle of the locomotive, or be converted into shrines sacred to commerce, by the power of those magnificent agencies by which rivers are spanned, territories traversed, commerce enfranchised, confederacies consolidated: by which the adamantine is made divisible and man assumes a lordship over time and space."

Such was the fever height that north, east, south, and west, the "socializing influence" of the system was sought to be extended. Whether a town in the United Kingdom, a foreign or a colonial possession, it mattered not—the name, the locality were alone wanting to usher before the world, the desirableness of the enterprise. "London was to be tunnelled, that the train might pass under her mighty heart; and colonnades were to be formed in the air, that the engine might pass over the path of the pedestrian." St. Kitt's, described in the "Gazetteer" as "fifteen miles long and four broad, with mountains in the middle, whence rivulets flow, and between the high mountains dreadful rocks, horrid precipices, and thick woods, and in the S. W. parts, hot sulphureous springs at the foot of them," was to be benefited by a line, the advantages of the site, though proportionately colored, being prominently eulogized in the published prospectus. Comparisons made respecting the "spirit of speculation" which prevailed, pronounced the mania to bear "some affinity to the bubble period of 1825—26," and its progress was described as following under almost similar circumstances. "Between 600 and 700 projects for railways" it was remarked,* "have appeared before the public for support within the last twelvemonths closely identified with English interests, while foreign schemes have

---

* *The City, or the Physiology of London Business.*

poured in from all quarters. The English, Irish, Scotch, and Welsh lines, included in this list, require upwards of £600,000,000 to carry them out; and the progress of the mania is so rapid, that it is unsafe to give any estimate of the nominal amount of capital the new projects involve. Every day fresh schemes are appearing,* and millions upon millions are required to support the plans proposed.

"The great difference between the speculation of 1845—46, and 1825—26, appears to be that in the one period the general principle of joint-stock companies was advocated, and in the other, the principle being well ascertained, is applied to the extension of the railway system.

---

* Before the railway mania set in with full force, only three railway papers existed. As speculation progressed, others were called into life. In the course of the year 1845, as many as twenty publications identified with the railway interest had made their appearance. Of these, fourteen were professedly hebdomadal—but in the height of the fever, they were issued semi-weekly—two others came out daily, one morning and one evening, and several were monthly publications. The morning paper dignified with the title of the "Iron Times," flourished prodigiously for months, securing vast patronage, from advertisements, some, so it is stated, being paid for at the rate of 2s. a line, when honoured by a position immediately following the leading article. Bankruptcy finally extinguished its struggles in the panic period, and the proprietors eventually appeared before the commissioners in Basinghall-street. Many of these publications lived little longer than a few weeks. Started expressly to get advertisements, the proprietors principally directed their attention to that source of profit, and when advertising began to decline, suddenly discontinued them. Among the multitude that sought patronage at the hands of promoters and secretaries were Railway Expresses; Railway Worlds; Railway Examiners; Railway Globes; Railway Standards; Railway Mails; Railway Engines; Railway Telegraphs; Shareholders Advocates; Railway Directors; Railway Registers; Railway Reviews, &c. The surviving railway papers are—the Railway Times; the Railway Chronicle; the Railway Record; Herapath's Railway Journal; and the Railway Gazette.

The daily press was thoroughly deluged with advertisements; "double" sheets did not supply space enough for them; "double-doubles" were resorted to, and then frequently insertions were delayed. It has been estimated that the receipts of the leading journals averaged at one period £12,000 and £14,000 per week from this source. The railway papers on some occasions contained advertisements that must have netted from £700 to £800 each publication. The printer, the lithographer, and the stationer, with the preparation of prospectuses, the execution of maps, and the supply of other requisites, also made a considerable harvest. The upholsterer was not without his portion of business. Furnishing board-rooms and secretaries' offices promoted his views, and as payment was derived from deposits, economy was not closely studied.

" In 1825—26, the number of companies brought out for the suffrages of capitalists was about 300, involving a nominal sum of £180,000,000. They included companies for the construction of railways and metal mining, canals and locks, gas companies, insurance companies, banking companies, sugar companies, fishing companies, early milk delivery companies, and others of every conceivable denomination. The excitement of this period is well comparable to the rage of our own day, when exclusive of the large sum of money necessary to carry out British schemes of railway, an amount of nearly £70,000,000 or £100,000,000 is asked in contribution, towards foreign projects. We trace again the same features in the present period as those manifested in 1825—26; an advance in the value of iron; an increased demand for manufactures, better prices for sugar and other articles of consumption, and an overwhelmed and an abundant Money-market. These were all the symptoms of the speculative era, 1825—26, they are again the symptoms of the speculative era, 1845—46."

" In its different phases" the railway mania was also said to manifest " much of the excitement and superstition of the previous bubble period. If in the great days of Spanish-American mining companies it was considered a fortune to possess a friend, who held an interest in the Real del Monte Association, there is a parallel case with respect to those who have now any influence with the successful patrons and supporters of railways. If in 1825—26, the individual claiming acquaintance with a Kinder was expected to realize the imagined wealth of an Eldorado, he that in 1845—46, can command the nod of a Hudson, may be supposed to reckon upon unlimited premiums in all kinds of lines, whether on the broad or narrow gauge, and only find the happy phantasy dissipated after a three months anxious longing. Every one connected with railways must have made money is the cry of the public—and so it was in the rage of 1825—26. The truth was only discovered when the panic came, when right and left the infatuated dupes were cut down as grass under the mower's scythe."

In July the number of projects registered was considerably

augmented. These registrations however did not determine the career of the "rash spirit of speculation" abroad.* Hundreds of schemes sanctioned and advertised by provisional committees, and committees of management were never registered at all. Deposits and premiums were alone sought,—these if they came were extravagantly disbursed or appropriated for personal benefit, as occasion served, and the deluded subscribers left to relieve themselves as best they could.

As determining the point to which prices of securities had advanced, the annexed comparative table may be referred to.

GOVERNMENT SECURITIES.

	JUNE, 1845.				JULY, 1845.			
	Price on the 2d.	Lowest Price.	Highest Price.	Price on the 30th.	Price on the 1st.	Lowest Price.	Highest Price.	Price on the 31st.
Consols, Money	99⅞	99⅝	100⅛	Shut	Shut	98½	99¼	98½
Do. Account....	100⅜	98⅞	100⅝	99 ex d.	98⅞ ex d.	98½	99¼	98½
Exchequer Bills, 1½d.	61/pm.	55/pm.	63/pm.	57/pm.	54/pm.	51/pm.	58/pm.	52/pm.

RAILWAY SECURITIES.

	JUNE, 1845.						JULY, 1845.						
	Amount per Share.	Amount Paid.	Price on the 2d.	Lowest Price	Highest Price	Price on the 30th.	Amount Paid.			Price on the 1st.	Lowest Price	Highest Price	Price on the 31st.
	£.	£.					£.	s.	d.				
Brighton	50	50	70½	69	76	75¼	50	0	0	75½	74½	80½	80
Caledonian	50	5	10¾	10¼	12⅝	11⅜	5	0	0	11½	10¼	12⅛	10⅜
Chester & Holyhead	50	10	17¼	15½	18½	15¾	10	0	0	15¾	15½	22¼	22
Churnet Valley	20	2	5½	4¼	5¾	4½	2	0	0	4½	4⅛	6	—
Croydon	Av. £13 : 15 : 9		19¼	18¼	22	22¾	Av. 13	15	9	21½	21	28½	26¾
Eastern Counties ..	25	£14 6	21¼	19¼	22	21¼	14	16	0	21¼	19½	22	21¼
Edinb. and Glasgow	50	50	74½	66	75¾	75¼	50	0	0	75	74	85½	84½
Great Western	100	80	205	197	217	206	80	0	0	206	203	225	224
Hull and Selby	50	50	108	104	109	106½	50	0	0	106½	105½	108½	106½
London & N. Westn.	Stock.		251¼	236	252	242½	Stock.			242½	241	246	245
London and York..	50	2 10	3¾	2⅞	4⅝	3¼	2	10	0	3¼	2⅞	7¾	6½
Manchester & Leeds	100	73	160	157	185	164	73	0	0	171	158	196	195
Midland	Stock.		190	180	193	187	Stock.			188	185	195	181
North Kent........	50	2 15	6	3⅝	6¼	4¼	2	15	0	4¾	2⅜	5	2⅞
South Eastern	Av. £33 : 2 : 4		47¼	44½	48½	47¾	Av. 33	2	4	47¾	45½	49	45⅝
Do. Western	Av. £41 : 6 : 10		83½	80½	85	80	Av. 41	6	10	80	77	82½	81½
Trent Valley	£20	£2	19¼	18¼	20	—	2	0	0	—	17¾	18¾	18¼
York & N. Midland	50	50	117½	105½	120	110½	50	0	0	110½	108	114½	—
Boulogne & Amiens	20	4	9¾	8⅜	10½	8¾	4	0	0	9	8⅝	11⅝	10¾
Northern of France	20	4	5⅝	5	5¾	5¼	4	0	0	5¾	5	6⅝	6
Orleans & Bordeaux	20	2	11⅛	8	11⅝	10¼	4	0	0	10¾	10¼	11½	11
Paris and Lyons ..	20	2	2½	1¼	3¼	2¾	2	0	0	2¾	1¾	3	3
Sambre and Meuse.	20	4	11¼	8	11⅝	8¼	4	0	0	8¼	6¼	8½	6¾

* Those who remember the perpetual excitement in the Money-market during the

It was not until a lengthened course of adventure, verging upon desperation, and characterised by every species of fraud human ingenuity could devise, that any bold attempt was made to expose this national folly. The opportune admonitions of The *Times*, supported by the sober reasoning of The *Economist*, were scornfully disregarded; all who countenanced their views, had to maintain themselves against a battery of the most poignant ridicule; and the "oracular wisdom of the alarmists" became for a time a sort of by-word and a reproach.

The country had witnessed the notable exhibition of a prime minister having "cut the first sod" of the Trent Valley railway, had listened to the congratulations of the Government on the quantity of labour employed, and had solaced itself with the belief that the prosperity of the hour was to remain for ever undisturbed. How then could arguments involving the consideration of the chimerical notions of a rapid conversion from "floating" into "fixed" capital—and of "the impossibility of expending more upon public works than the surplus of the nation's wealth," expect to receive attention? So long as shares bore a high premium, so long as the guage question brought profit to its supporters, so long as direct lines were pregnant, with prospects of certain 10 per cent. dividends, and so long as "short and sure guides" were published which promised to carry speculators "over the long threatened crisis should it

---

continuance of the last war, and the sudden fluctuations in prices, which then became a perfect barometer of the state of public feeling, look upon the present long continued state of the public funds as a financial miracle! It was thought a great thing some few months back, that Consols had reached *par*, but that they would continue at that rate, and even increase in value, was hardly contemplated as a possibility. And yet there seems no prospect of any interruption to this state of affairs. The Exchanges are all in our favour; money becomes more and more abundant, and the amount of bullion in the Bank increases day by day. Those who look beyond the present, naturally enquire what will be the probable results of this long continued financial prosperity? and there is little difficulty in indicating some of them, even without laying claim to any superior discernment or sagacity. There will be a large supply of bubble companies; enough already are in the field; but, like the fabled monster, the destruction of one seems to give existence to innumerable others.—*The Banker's Magazine, June* 1845.

arrive," so long "the public sympathised with a philosophical government,"* and interference was not contemplated.

It was shortly subsequent to this date, the ranks of promoters having gained an accession from all classes, that a fierce crusade against the public was commenced, and which partook of so much dishonesty, as to call forth the severe reprehension of the press. The fashion was then first brought into vogue of securing applications for share allotments, in order to protect the committees from liability, but no chance of distribution existed, while the project was marketable at a premium.

Still the contagion spread, and the passion of the public was stimulated by the most daring species of stock gambling that ever darkened the page of history. One authority† did not hesitate to brand many of the advertised undertakings as "fraudulent," adding "there is too much reason to fear that during the last three months, but especially during the last five or six weeks the real object of the concocters of railway schemes has not been to devise desirable and good lines of railway, or to start a scheme with which they really intended to go to Parliament, but, in plain language, to rob and delude the public by getting their scrip into the market at a premium, and to rob and swindle their subscribers in particular by squandering and embezzling the deposit-money. Pettifogging attorneys and rejected engineers are the true authors, 'for a consideration,' of three-fourths of the railway schemes before the world at this moment."

Perceiving the marked alteration in the course of events, every day conversation among the active co-operators in the movement did not now turn upon the probable result of an application for shares; it was solely directed to enquiries as to the terms of premium upon which the directors meant to bring them out. It was considered little better than a formal proceeding to write to any of the companies unless supported by strong personal influence. Senators proved stags,‡ anecdotes were freely circu-

* Vide Mr. Disraeli's Speech in the House of Commons, April 1846.

† The Bankers' Magazine, Sept. 1845.

‡ "The Stock-exchange is a sort of menagerie, which, like the Zoological-gar-

lated of the large profits made by directors and committee-men, and every expedient was adopted, by high and low, to participate to some extent in the "golden vision" of the day.

Wonderful as was the excitement that prevailed, there were many who predicted that the system of fraud, which the mania had engendered, would ultimately prove a severe blow to confidence so illimitedly placed in all kinds and species of projects. Absurd as a number of the schemes were, long lists of provisional committees seemed sufficient to satisfy the public of the soundness of their origin, and it was not until they were distinctly apprised of the character maintained by many of their promoters, that any permanent impression was made. The press steadily proceeded with its warnings. Exposures were also continuously published respecting the trickery adopted in the emission of shares. City bankers even did not hesitate to connect themselves with undertakings that promised a large share of premium when brought into the open market. The name of the Railway King was likewise freely used as a stepping-stone to profit by railway adventurers. The accession of Mr. Hudson to a director's seat in any particular company immediately gave a value to the line; the shares were soon in demand, and, save a small distribution among immediate friends, those who desired to possess them were obliged to purchase considerably above par.

All this time there was no restraint. The Government having

---

dens, is every now and then adding to its collection; but it must be confessed, the variety of animals it exhibits is not so numerous, though the total number be greater. Bulls and bears, and lame ducks, have long flourished there; but of late, a whole herd of stags have invaded the place, of whom there exists at this moment an extraordinary amount of somewhat indefinite terror. The stag, in a state of nature, is a harmless, timid, graminivorous animal, whose appetite is small, and easily satisfied; whereas there is no end to the voracity of the carnivorous railway stag; who is always in search of those premiums which constitute the very flesh and blood of railway speculators. The railway stag has only one characteristic in comcom with his antlered namesake; he is very shy of being seen, and the most experienced hunters find great difficulty in tracing him to his lair. He is, in fact, more cunning than a fox, by which cognomen he would have been more appropriately designated."—*British and Foreign Railway Review.*

originally encouraged the movement, took no active steps to avert its consequences. An increase in the deposit from 5 to 10 per cent. on shares allotted, did not in the least repress the ardour of the speculators. What was this increase compared with the prospect of gain from high and rapidly-advancing values?

A remarkable feature in the state of the mania that grew out of these circumstances, was the inordinate desire for amalgamation and leases, exhibited by the larger companies. They bought or took under management smaller undertakings promoted by rivals, at a high per centage, and guaranteed dividends varying from 4 to 6 per cent. An augmentation of capital to the extent of millions was thus permanently effected; but strange to say, that, accompanied by the delusive bait of issues of new shares, which, for a few weeks or months brought considerable premiums, these arrangements were unanimously approved; and, contrary to all law or precedent, prices went up in proportion to the amount of incurred liability.* Such, therefore, was the preference for railway investment, that Consols, it was said, were daily sold to be replaced by their formidable compeer Railway Stock. The bullion in the Bank between January and June had risen from £14,800,000 to £16,600,000.

In July and August, the number of registered schemes again increased. The latter month decided the fate of the bills brought before Parliament. September was extremely prolific. The projects then registered were 457, making altogether for the year a registration of 1,035. The *Times* more potently than ever descanted upon the "nation's madness." Consols, all along well maintained, at last showed some tendency to weakness. The stock of bullion in the Bank began to decline, having fallen to about £15,000,000. There was an increased demand for money. October was less fertile in schemes than the preceding month, then only 363 were registered. The Bank it was said would raise the rate of interest, and the Government was almost

* The third railway panic which occured in October, 1848, has since shown the effect of these issues upon the value of share property in general.

suspected of risking the responsibility of such advice, with the view of checking the hitherto uncurbed violence of the mania. The railway press caught up the rumour, but professed to feel no apprehension that any measure of the sort would be carried out.

One journal said—" The conduct of the Bank of England, since the new system of banking has been in operation, must be admitted to have been unexceptionable. Many have allowed themselves to imagine that, acting upon some sinister hint of the Government, the directors might have been induced to make money scarcer by the adoption of a higher rate of interest; but this would appear to have been an idle and merely speculative notion. Sir Robert Peel having declared in his place in Parliament, that it was the intention of Government to give every encouragement to the extension of the railway system, and the declaration of the minister having been responded to in the manner witnessed, any interference on the part of the Bank of the nature of that alluded to, could only be justified by a pressure of circumstances that is not at present to be recognised, and of which, if the same prudent course be persevered in, there can be no reasonable apprehension. The directors have only to proceed upon the principle that they have done, and no difficulty will result. But if, indeed, it should be their pleasure, or rather the pleasure of our Government, that the various railway schemes which have been set on foot shall be strangled by a curtailment of the circulation just as they are advancing to maturity, a heavy responsibility will be incurred. Nothing of the kind is, however, to be expected. The Bank coffers are full to overflowing of metallic treasure. The establishment has fifteen millions of gold and silver bars and coin, and, all alarm with regard to the harvest having passed away, the enormous mass will remain undisturbed where it now lies, not an idle and useless body as some political economists would pretend to say it is, but in the most efficient state of vitality, since its paper representatives are spread over the whole face of the country, and in all respects better perform its active functions than it could do itself."

These sanguine expectations however were not fulfilled. The influx of adventurers into the public market was more than ever apparent. In the early part of October no doubt was entertained of the increasing value of money, and on the 16th, the Bank directors advanced their rate to 3 per cent. In Lombard-street higher terms were demanded. There the more current quotation on first class paper was $3\frac{1}{4}$ to $3\frac{3}{4}$ per cent.

Although the great host of share speculators at first treated the Bank's advance with indifference, it was not long before the price of securities underwent considerable change. In prospect of the amount of capital to be deposited with the Government under legislative enactment, it was seen that a continuous demand for money would in all probability ensue, and hence arose a cause for substantial anxiety.

The latter end of October, 1845, will be ever memorable for the commencement of the panic in the Share-market. The animation of speculators was suddenly arrested; Consols, which towards the end of September were quoted at $98\frac{1}{4}$ had gradually declined to $96\frac{1}{2}$; and Exchequer Bills from 47s. premium had fallen to 38s. premium, the markets generally presenting an unsatisfactory appearance. At this period the leading journal again addressed its best energies to the exposure of the "hazardous delusion" which had fallen upon the country, and a prophetic voice advised "a shortening of sail as the storm was at hand." Speedily this ominous prediction was verified—many of the schemes dropped as if by fell enchantment to a discount, and the prices of all kinds of shares hourly became further depressed.

The anxiety to "get out" had not then taken the form of that indiscriminate and spasmodic rush known as panic, but nevertheless it had reached a point sufficiently intense and general to create serious alarm for the future. As was naturally the case, London experienced the first effect of the revulsion; but Liverpool, Manchester, Bristol, Leeds, Edinburgh and Glasgow, soon evinced sympathetic action. At all these great marts,—where share speculation had been encouraged to an extent vastly disproportionate to the means of the parties engaging in it, the failure of confidence was immediately responded to by a heavy declension in prices.

When the question of the Government deposit presented itself in its true light the shock was most terrific. Calculated at a sum which fortunately it never realized, the multitude took alarm—since even the most prudent then saw, making allowance for over estimates, that an enormous amount of capital would be temporarily withdrawn from active circulation.

The event so long prognosticated had come to pass. From one end of the kingdom to the other the tocsin of alarm resounded. The panic shout was scarcely universal, but terror nevertheless palled the hearts of the stoutest and boldest. Danger was apparent, and every one sought safety from the ruin which it was evident must fall somewhere. Indefinite as was the belief respecting the course the crisis would take, it was clearly foreseen that an enormous depreciation would occur in the value of all shares. August marked a high advance in the prices of the various descriptions.* October, in comparison with that period showed

---

* In the month of August, the period when railway prices generally saw what is technically called "the top of the market," the rage for gambling was enormous. The responsibility incurred by parties signing deeds of subscription attracted universal notice. At this particular date, the *furor* was so great, that those who were engaged in railway share business, found a large portion of their time occupied in keeping the necessary appointments for perfecting these documents, which were of vital importance to the existence of the companies. Parliamentary returns shortly afterwards published, gave a list of subscribers who had affixed their names to deeds. Signatures were common for amounts averaging from £20,000 to £60,000. Mr. George Hudson, M.P., stood highest on the public list. He represented subscriptions for £818,000. Other parties were set down for £300,000 and £400,000 each. Earls, Privy Councillors, Baronets, Knights, M.P.s, Colonels, Captains, Lieutenants, Clergymen, Bankers, Barristers, Merchants, Lawyers, Directors, Secretaries, Promoters, Projectors, Stock-brokers, Tradesmen, and Clerks, were all alike centred in the vortex of speculation, and figured for the amount of their assumed liabilities. The number of clergymen who signed was 257. Of these the greater number were comparatively for small amounts, of from £2,000 to £5,000. Some however went into the speculation more extensively. Thus one was a subscriber for £26,000, one for £27,500, three for £20,000 and upwards, six for £15,000 and upwards, ten for £10,000 and upwards, fifty-three of from £5,000 to £9,000 each. Members of Parliament were subscribers for much larger sums, and reckoned 157 in number, being

on the average a startling fall as demonstrated by the subjoined figures. The bullion in the Bank was further declining; the stock in both departments on the 25th of the last mentioned month having receded to £14,000,000.

GOVERNMENT SECURITIES.

	AUGUST, 1845.				OCTOBER, 1845.			
	Price on the 1st.	Lowest Price.	Highest Price.	Price on the 30th.	Price on the 1st.	Lowest Price.	Highest Price.	Price on the 31st.
Consols, Money	98½	98⅜	99⅜	98⅞	98	96⅝	98⅝	97
Do. Account	98¾	98⅝	99⅜	99⅛	98	96½	98⅝	97⅛
Exchequer Bills, 1½d.	52/ pm.	46/pm.	53/ pm.	47/pm.	46/ pm.	37/ pm.	54/ pm.	38/ pm.

RAILWAY SECURITIES.

	AUGUST, 1845.						OCTOBER, 1845.				
	Amount per Share.	Amount Paid.	Price on the 1st.	Lowest Price	Highest Price	Price on the 30th.	Amount Paid.	Price on the 1st.	Lowest Price	Highest Price	Price on the 31st.
	£	£					£. s.				
Brighton	50	50	80	76	80½	78½	50 0	70½	60	72	64
Caledonian	50	5	10⅝	10	12⅝	12¼	5 0	15¾	8½	16¼	12¼
Chester & Holyhead	50	15	22	20¾	22¾	21⅛	15 0	20¾	17	21½	17½
Croydon	Av. £13 : 15 : 9		26¾	22¾	27¼	26¾	Av. 13 : 15 : 9	24½	20½	25¾	22¼
Direct Northern ..	50	2 : 10	2	1⅞	2¾	2⅜	2 10	2⅝	2½	3⅞	2¾
Eastern Counties ..	25	14 : 16	21¼	19	21½	20½ ex. d.	14 16	22½	19¼	24¼	22¾
Edinb. & Glasgow..	50	50	84½	83½	91	90 ex. d.	50 0	74½	68	79½	—
Great Western	100	80	224	175	236	176 ex. new	80 0	161	141	167	154
Hull and Selby	50	50	106½	102½	109	104 ex. d.	50 0	104	98	105½	102½
London & N. Westn.	Stock.		245	214	254	223 ex. d. & ex. new	Stock.	219	214	222	220
London and York ..	50	2 : 10	6½	4½	7⅝	7⅛	2 10	6⅞	4½	7	5¾
Manchester & Leeds	100	73	195	194	219	217½	76 0	—	146	154	—
Midland	Stock.		181	170	183	175 ex. d.	Stock.	170½	152	176½	155½
North Kent........	50	£2:15	2⅞	2⅝	5½	5	2 10	4⅛	2¾	4⅝	3½
South Eastern	Av. £33 : 2 : 4		45⅝	44¾	48½	48	Av. 33 : 2 : 4	43¾	35½	44	37½
Do. Western	Av. £41 : 6 : 10		81½	77	84	78¼	Av. 41 : 6 : 10	80	70	81	75
Trent Valley	£20	£2	18¼	18	20¼	20	2 0	—	15¼	18¾	16¼
York & N. Midland	50	50	—	106	112	108½	50 0	118	106	119	106
Boulogne & Amiens	20	6	10¾	10⅜	11⅛	11¼	8 0	13	10	13¾	11
Dutch Rhenish	20	3	9	7½	10	9¾	5 0	12¼	8¼	12¼	9½
Northern of France	20	4	6	5¾	7⅜	7	4 0	6¾	6¼	7	6¾
Orleans & Bordeaux	20	4	11	10¾	14⅜	14¼	6 0	—	9¼	13¾	12
Paris and Lyons....	20	2	3	1⅞	4⅛	3½	2 0	2½	1¾	3½	2½
Paris and Rouen ..	20	20	—	40¾	43¼	42½	20 0	—	38	42½	39½
Sambre and Meuse .	20	4	6¾	5½	9	8⅞	6 0	8½	5½	8½	6⅝

nearly one-fourth of the entire House of Commons. This fact clearly indicated the strength of the railway interest in Parliament, and the sums subscribed for by individual members were in many cases very heavy.

The active progress of share gambling may be said to have received the first efficient check at this date. New schemes were no longer regarded with favour; the registration of projects, reckoned by hundreds, sensibly declined and were at the end of the year altogether suspended; promising undertakings which feebly supported a premium, soon gave way and were placed at a discount; and the whole fabric of speculation found itself shaken to its very centre.

The month of November brought an additional increase in the value of money. Its worth at the Stock-exchange was about $4\frac{1}{2}$ per cent. Difficulty was experienced in obtaining accommodation by parties who were supposed to have engaged in share operations; credits were limited throughout the kingdom; and the stock of bullion continued to decrease. The Bank of England again raised their *minimum* rate to $3\frac{1}{2}$ per cent.

Preparatory to the arrangements made for lodging plans and sections according to notice with the Board of Trade at the end of November, The *Times* appeared with an immense array of figures, the compilation of Mr. Spackman, which exhibited in a general synopsis, the position and responsibility of the country in connexion with railway works. Overcharged as this statement was alleged to be in some minor respects, it afforded ample testimony of the wild and extravagant theories of the day which spurned all reasoning adverse "to the entire concentration of England's wealth and England's credit in these national undertakings." No admission could be gained from the advocates of the system as to risk ultimately accruing; obstinate against conviction, they expressed not the least concern for the manner in which trade would be pinched by this drain of capital; "Spackman's data and calculations" were quietly dismissed as "illusory," and most share tricksters sought to denounce the journal that gave them currency.

Mr. Spackman's table furnished, as will be seen, much food for comment.

RAILWAYS COMPLETED.

	£
On account of which the shareholders have paid up	48,043,563
The shareholders have borrowed on debentures, loan-notes, and mortgages	22,637,314
47 Companies completed	£70,680,877

RAILWAYS IN COURSE OF CONSTRUCTION,

AND FOR WHICH ACTS OF PARLIAMENT HAVE BEEN OBTAINED.

	£
On account of these the shareholders have paid up	6,432,155
And to complete the same according to the estimates, will have to pay the further subscribed sum of	44,927,170
Parliament having in all cases given the power to borrow one-third more, this will probably be further increased by the sum of	16,000,000
118 Lines and Branches in course of execution	£67,359,325

RAILWAYS PROJECTED.

Of 218	of these the amount of deposit stated in the prospectus is 5 per cent., and a per centage for expenses. A large proportion of this class received their deposits before the resolution of the Lords was passed, and others since, amounting to	11,171,727
	To comply with the resolution of the Lords, a further payment of 5 per cent. must be made, amounting to about	9,595,464
402	A deposit of 10 per cent. is required, which many of them have received,—the whole, if paid, will amount to	38,369,109
643	Have not registered their prospectuses.	
1263	Companies. Total of deposits required	£59,136,300

Being 10 per cent. on £563,203,000, and 5 per cent. for parliamentary expenses.

CAPITAL.

Capital actually paid up and invested in railways completed	48,043,563
,, Paid up on railways in course of execution, and sanctioned by Parliament	6,432,155
,, Required to pay the deposits on new projects	59,136,300
Total capital invested	£113,612,018

LIABILITIES.

Borrowed on the security of railways completed	22,637,614
Incurred in respect of railways in course of execution	60,927,170
To carry out the new projects, deducting the amount of deposits paid or required to be paid	506,882,706
Total liabilities	£590,447,490

"But if," said The *Times*, criticising these figures, in its leading article of the 17th Nov., "six millions a-year (alluding to the previous annual rate of railway expenditure) has been a difficulty, and twenty-two millions a-year (in addition to an immense amount of foreign engagements) is almost a four times greater difficulty, what are we to say to the enormous—the stupendous—the infinite sums,—if infinity can be summed up,—that appear in our synoptical view? Here we have 1,428 railways, with an estimated capital of £701,243,208, with a deposit of £49,592,816. Take away £140,000,000, for railways completed, or in progress, exclude the most extravagant items, such as the £40,000,000 for "Cooke's National," and divide the remainder by ten;—can we add a tenth of the vast remainder?—can we add £50,000,000 to the railway speculation we are already irretrievably embarked in? *We cannot*, without the most ruinous, universal, and desperate confusion.

"The mischief has gone too far already. With so fearful a testimony to the speculative madness of our countrymen as that which we this day display to our readers, we may apprehend almost anything. It may be said these 1,263 projects are nearly all smoke. But where there is smoke there is also fire. Though not a quarter of the schemes here enumerated have come into the Share-market, still they have all, more or less, had their knaves or their dupes, and, moreover, a considerable waste of money. The luxuriant crop of absolute weeds affords an indication of the favour which merely unprofitable schemes have met with. It is the ridiculous amount of premium on worthless scrip, and the gullibility, or rather the voracity, of the multitude, which have prompted a crowd of adventurers to bait their hooks and cast out their nets for the prey. If there was not a very promising shoal of flats, you would not see so many fishermen abroad.

"From the month of July we have kept up one even tenour of warning, one consistent line of advice, against rash speculation, against the folly and sin of railway gambling.* If any-

* The *Times* was never, perhaps, more eloquent than on the subject of the rail-

body is concerned to be assured of our consistency on this point, the articles are before us, and we only hesitate to inflict on our readers the tedium of extracts from calculations and cautions which months ago we apologised for reiterating. It was not for us to attempt a decision between the multitudinous applicants. That is neither in our place nor our power. We proceeded on the simple fact that the limited capabilities of the country and its many other demands only allowed of a certain expenditure in railroads. Early in September we reckoned that limit at thirty millions as the very outside. We always urged the ruinous absurdity of hundreds of schemes at a premium, when only a few could be ultimately realized. We did all we could to expose the craft of provisional committees, and to recommend the utmost inquiry into the conditions under which the unitiated shareholders bought their shares and paid their deposits. We spoke of the practical impossibility of the parliamentary deposits being paid on so vast a mass of schemes, and the consequent certainty of the greater part being indefinitely postponed. As far as we are concerned we should have the greatest pleasure in reprinting all our leaders and city articles from July to this day. We might then leave our cause in the hands of the public. On the 1st of July the ominous question 'Whence is to come all the money for the construction of the projected railroads?' is thrice repeated—at the beginning, the middle, and the end, of an article on the subject. This was on the 1st of July, and on the last day of that month we gave utterance to a deep presentiment, the whole truth of which time has yet to show, but which has been so far verified that we consider ourselves called on to repeat the words, perhaps more seriously felt than expressed."

The month of November progressed. The time drew nigh for compliance with the orders of the Board of Trade. Strenuous exertions were made by the various companies to achieve

way mania, commencing from the period of its first exposure of that speculation down to the latest predictions respecting the effect of railway calls upon the commerce of the country.—ED.

the desired end; and expense was not spared to procure the required aid for completing the necessary plans.

From this date forward serious obstacles interposed to a resuscitation of the mania. Sanguine as had been the anticipations entertained on this point by the majority who had engaged in share dealing, little time elapsed before it was clearly apparent that the state of business was past immediate hope of recovery. It was not only the present difficulty experienced in arriving at a perfect condition for the authorities of the railway department, but also the prospective one, even should compliance in that respect be effected, of lodging the deposit-fund with the Accountant-General in Chancery, as an earnest of the *bonâ fide* character of the undertaking. Attention being much directed to this latter circumstance, and money gradually becoming scarcer at higher rates, the value of Consols and Exchequer Bills declined. Already operated upon by what had been considered a kind of preferential investment, viz. guaranteed railway stocks and railway bonds and debentures, these securities felt strongly the effect of the apprehended call for capital, to make good the large amount payable in the early part of 1846, on behalf of new companies seeking parliamentary sanction.

Notwithstanding it was soon ascertained that a considerable number of the undertakings were lost, at least for the next session, owing to non-compliance with the regulations of the Board of Trade, "that incubus—the question of railway deposits," continued to be described as "weighing heavily upon the public mind." The amount of these deposits originally calculated at between £20,000,000 and £30,000,000 on the number of schemes promoted, underwent a sensible reduction, when, out of the 1,263 companies which made an attempt to arrive at that position, not more than half were successful. Of course it was not for one moment imagined, taking these enormous figures, that the whole of the schemes would be prepared to give in their plans and sections as stipulated; but nevertheless, regard being had to the safety of trade, it was considered a triumph, particularly by those who had ranged themselves under the banner of the "alarmists," to know that the proceedings of a large proportion had signally failed in their first essential stage.

Between November and December the stock of bullion in the Bank underwent some change. From about £14,000,000 it declined to about £13,000,000, but again slightly increased towards the end of December, when it stood at £13,325,000. The fluctuations in public securities, it will be perceived, had mainly occurred, as already stated, in the cases of Consols

GOVERNMENT SECURITIES.

	NOVEMBER, 1845.				DECEMBER, 1845.			
	Price on the 1st.	Lowest Price.	Highest Price.	Price on the 29th.	Price on the 1st.	Lowest Price.	Highest Price.	Price on the 31st.
Consols, Money	97	94¼	97⅝	94½	94⅞	93¼ with d	95	Shut
Do. Account....	97⅛	94¾	97⅛	95	95⅛	91⅞ ex d.	95⅜	94⅞
Exchequer Bills, 1½d.	38/pm.	19/pm.	39/pm.	22/pm.	20/pm.	11/pm.	28/pm.	27/pm.

RAILWAY SECURITIES.

	NOVEMBER, 1845.						DECEMBER, 1845.				
	Amount per Share.	Amount Paid.	Price on the 1st.	Lowest Price	Highest Price	Price on the 29th.	Amount Paid.	Price on the 1st.	Lowest Price	Highest Price	Price on the 31st.
	£.	£.					£. s. d.				
Brighton	50	50	62½	57	65	60	50 0 0	60	60	70	69
Caledonian	50	5	11½	6¾	12½	7⅛	5 0 0	7⅛	6¾	16¼	15½
Chester & Holyhead	50	15	18¼	12¾	19	13¾	15 0 0	13¾	13	17¼	17
Croydon	Av. £13 : 15 : 9		21½	18	23	18½	Av. 13 15 9	18½	18¼	24	23¼
Direct Northern ..	50	£2 10	2¾	1½	4¾	1¾	2 10 0	1¾	1½	2½	2¼
Eastern Counties ..	25	14 16	22	18¼	23	18⅞	14 16 0	18⅞	18½	23¼	22¾
Edinb. and Glasgow	50	50 0	74	62	74	63½	50 0 0	63½	62	77	77
Great Western	100	80 0	157	140	160	144	80 0 0	144	140	166	163
Hull and Selby	50	50 0	102¾	98	103½	99	50 0 0	99	98	105	104
London & N. Westn.	Stock.		219	204	222	207	Stock.	207	205	224	221½
London and York..	£50	£ 2 10	5½	2½	6	2¾	2 10 0	2¾	2½	4⅞	4⅝
Manchester & Leeds	100	76 0	143½	126	146	130	76 0 0	130	123	138	135½
Midland Counties..	Stock.		152	132	156	136	Stock.	136	135	158	155
North British	£25	£15 0	24	19	24½	20¾	£17 10 0	20¾	19	27	25¾
North Kent........	50	2 10	3¾	2¼	3¾	2½	2 10 0	2½	2½	3½	3¼
South Eastern	Av. £33 : 2 : 4		37½	32	38	33¾	Av. 33 2 4	33¾	33	40	39½
Do. Western	Av. £41 : 6 : 10		74½	70	77	73	Av. 41 6 10	73	72	77½	77¼
Trent Valley	£20	£2	16⅝	13	16½	14½	2 0 0	14½	13½	21¼	20¾
York & N. Midland	50	50	109½	102	110	102	50 0 0	102	101	108	—
Boulogne & Amiens	20	8	10½	7	11	7⅝	8 0 0	7⅝	7	13	12½
Dutch Rhenish	20	5	8⅞	6½	9½	6⅝	·5 0 0	6⅝	6¼	8¾	8⅛
Northern of France	20	4	6½	6	15	10½	5 0 0	10½	10¼	16¼	14¾
Orleans & Bordeaux	20	6	11½	8½	11¾	9⅛	6 0 0	9⅛	9	12¼	11¾
Paris and Lyons ..	20	2	3	1⅞	3¼	2¼	2 0 0	2¼	1⅞	3¼	9¾
Do. and Rouen	20	20	38½	34	39	35¼	20 0 0	35¼	35	41	40½
Sambre and Meuse .	20	6	6⅝	3½	6¾	4⅛	6 0 0	4⅛	3¾	6	6

and Exchequer Bills. A number of the most ephemeral schemes had been swept from existence; the horde of petty gamblers usually infesting the alleys of the Stock-exchange had dwindled into insignificance, and much of the distracting madness which so alarmingly characterised the autumn of the year had altogether passed away. Original undertakings once more held up their heads. Henceforward it was to be their day. A sudden reaction in most of these shares was considered indicative of the favor they maintained; and it was prognosticated that the market when relieved from the superabundant mass of rubbish which inundated it, would shortly be restored to a proper condition.

No sooner had the first effects of the panic subsided than a movement, as startling as it was novel, commenced. At the time the October reaction brought down, with unprecedented violence, the value of all railway securities, a number of companies had been but recently brought into existence. These having issued their prospectuses, were receiving in return applications for shares. Acting upon the widely disseminated principle of watching the turn of the market, whether favourable or otherwise, the committees anxiously delayed allotments. With the cupidity distinguishing persons placed in their position, they desired not honestly to set their undertakings afloat by subscribed capital from the public, but to increase their own share of profit from the premium which their several projects might command. The result of their patience was suicidal. The revulsion came and their market was irretrievably lost.

The struggle for allottees at length arrived. In the full assurance of enduring stability in prices, numbers had unhesitatingly made application for a portion of the supposed distributable shares. Knowing the large reserves made by committee-men, &c., for themselves and their friends, applications were generally tendered for a considerable quantity, in order that, if the shares were distributed at all, some allotments might be secured.

In the period intervening between the close of 1845, and the commencement of 1846, the majority of embryo companies seeing it was useless to look for any revival, and "discounts" being more frequently quoted in the share lists than "premiums," abandoned all further reservation, and letters of allotment poured in upon the unsuspecting applicants in the most liberal manner. Suddenly availing themselves of the power vested in their hands by the terms of applications which bound the allottee to accept whatever number might be appropriated to him, and also to pay deposits upon and sign the deed for the same, the various committees endeavoured to shift all personal risk from their own shoulders to those of their unfortunate victims. Persons therefore who perchance had written and pledged their responsibility for 200 shares in a particular company, with the expectation of getting twenty or ten shares, or as had been previously the case, not more than five shares, were without further prelude, honoured with the whole number first applied for.

The principle adopted in the early progress of the mania, of "cutting down" applications to one tithe of what were sought, and which had been rigidly recognised throughout its preceding stages, was now altogether discontinued. Deposits were demanded, and legal proceedings threatened, if they were not paid. Allottees in most instances refused to comply on any terms. It was much questioned whether the committees could enforce these claims, and their various attempts to cajole the public, were valiantly resisted. Companies who had failed from non-payment of deposits only asked for small subscriptions in liquidation of expenses. Others less matured, pledged themselves so to economize expenditure, as to deduct but a small amount from deposits when paid, and proposed even to restrict outlay in some cases to 3s. and 4s. per share. But even these alluring promises were unavailing, and schemes continued to disappear.

Concurrently with these events the "deposit question" occupied the attention of capitalists. February* was the period fixed

* Mr. Samuel Gurney, before the Committee on Commercial Distress, alluding to the payment of railway deposits, said—"In February, 1846, the operation of the Bank Act of 1844 was sensibly felt. The pressure of 1846 arose from the excitement that had occurred upon the subject of railways for the previous two years, and more particularly from a regulation of Parliament, that a certain amount of deposit on each

for the payment, and since the reactionary spirit had worked out numbers of projects, between £12,000,000 and £14,000,000 was the sum which it was estimated would pass to the account of the Accountant-General in Chancery for that purpose. The latter amount approximated nearly to what was paid in England, Ireland, and Scotland. Of this sum upwards of £11,000,000 was deposited directly through the Bank. The current value of cash then was 5 per cent. This grand difficulty surmounted, more ease was experienced in the Money-market, and rates again declined.

But while in this respect less fear was exhibited by those more immediately connected with the financial concerns of the country, on the other hand new cause of alarm arose in consequence of the active litigation carried on between directors, provisional committee-men, and shareholders. Cases were argued and verdicts given for and against the several parties interested. Woolmer *v.* Toby, a cause tried at Exeter, settled the liability of allottees.* Then came the one known as Walstab *v.* Spottiswoode,

---

company's scheme should be paid into the Bank, on account of the Court of Chancery, within a certain number of days of the meeting of Parliament; before the payments took place it was impossible to ascertain the exact amount of what the payment might be, but it was presumed that it would range from ten to twenty-five millions sterling. The payment was to be made in Bank-notes; so very large a sum to be taken out of the circulating medium then existing, was a very severe operation; the Bank being under the restriction of this Act, instead of giving increased accommodation to the monied interest, which, were it not for this Act, they would have done, acted upon a very marked system of limitation; the usual accommodation that we had had, had been by the discount of bills having less than ninety days to run, or loans on the security of bills for the same period, of ninety days or less; the Bank were alarmed in consequence of the effect of this Act, and limited the period first to sixty days, then to thirty and to twenty, and at last to only ten days; the effect of which was, that the money-dealers were wholly disinclined to take money for such short periods, and to accommodate the mercantile community with it, and very great stagnation and pressure took place for a fortnight or three weeks."

* "Can Government" said the *Railway Times* in March, 1846, "be ignorant of what is at this moment doing throughout the country by a set of scoundrels whose only object is plunder, who conduct their proceedings with the most barefaced and brazen audacity, and who, in defiance of the plain and recognised law, seek to extort large sums of money from thousands and tens of thousands of people, by threatening

in which it was decided subscribers could demand a restitution of deposits, if the undertaking they supported was not proceeded with; and the confusion then became desperate. In addition, engineers, tradesmen, &c., who had been employed by the companies were striving for an arrangement of their accounts,

---

them with legal proceedings! Some of the bubble companies we have heard have sold the whole number of their letters of applications to speculative attornies who have at once proceeded to issue threatening notices, and who, in some instances, have reaped a rich harvest; others have conceived that this course was too good a thing for the attorney, and they have entered into an agreement with one or more lawyers to allow a per centage on the sums they can extort from parties worth "powder and shot." Nay, we have heard of one instance in which a capitalist was applied to by a needy attorney who had been promised the refusal of the whole batch of allotment letters of a bubble company, for an advance of money at an enormous interest, in order to cover the expense of issuing somewhere about one thousand speculative writs. In order to give a slight insight as to what is going on, we here present a few instances of the different ways in which the promoters of abortive companies seek to obtain money from the public. It must be borne in mind that the pertinaceous reliance on the Toby case is at once disposed of by recent decisions of eminent judges, who have declared that 'the promoters of projects are liable for the whole of the preliminary expenses of those projects which prove from any cause abortive, and that they must return the deposits without deduction to the subscribers.' In the teeth of this plain statement of the law, we find a Mr. ———, who describes himself as attorney-at-law, demanding the immediate payment, on behalf of an alleged railway company, termed the Grand Junction, Great Western, and South-Western Railway Company, not of a proportion of alleged expenses, but of the whole number of shares allotted! The Liverpool and Derby Direct defunct project employ a Mr. ———, attorney, to demand 3s. per share, with the expense of lawyer's letter, 3s. 6d., on pain of an action-at-law. On behalf of the Manchester, Southampton, and Poole line, Messrs. ——, of ——, require 5s. per share to be paid, otherwise they threaten proceedings against parties for the full amount of their deposit. The Bristol and English Channels Railway directors demand 4s. per share as the price of the allottee's letter of application, and intimate in case of non-compliance they will proceed for the whole of the deposit. The Hon. and Reverend ——, in the name of his co-directors, requires 2s. 6d. per share to be paid towards defraying the expenses incurred by the Staffordshire and North Midland Junction Railway Company. The Hon. and Rev. gentleman significantly refers to the case of Woolmer *v.* Toby, in the event of refusal. The Cheltenham, Oxford, and London Junction project has peculiar features of its own. In order to induce allottees to pay the deposit, the committee, by circular dated from their offices, inform the allottees that 'in the event of their not being enabled, from any unexpected deficiency of deposits,' to go before Parliament in the next session, the whole sum which the allottee shall have paid shall be returned,

and getting impatient and annoyed by decamping directors, and the reported irresponsibility of provisional committee-men,* sought redress by legal interference, and so increased the current of commotion. "The time is come," it was jocosely remarked, "for the practice of that equivocal recommendation conveyed in the words 'every man his own lawyer.' What was once a satirical idea must soon become a serious reality, or else we are all undone. Unless the public will learn the terms of art and plumb the deep profundities of legal form, master the mysteries of rules *nisi* and absolute, and understand the difference between verdict and judgment—unless they will give themselves up to the study of Tomlin's Dictionary, or spend a few pleasant months within a lawyer's office—why, it seems to us, that this poor public is lost, quite lost." And the truth of this could not be denied, since what with conflicting decisions and the undefined state of the law, perplexing difficulties were started at every fresh step.

---

without any deduction whatever! And yet, in the face of this compact, we find that on the 4th of April they issued a circular, signed '———,' demanding 3s. per share expenses. The Dorking, Brighton, and Arundle Atmospheric scheme has also some remarkable features. Two attornies, Mr. ——— and Mr. ———, have issued threatening circulars to numerous persons, calling on them to pay the sum of 7s. 6d. per share as the condition on which the letter of application would be parted with, and hinting in case of refusal, the commencement of reprisals at law." The names of the several parties were inserted in the *Railway Times*, but the Editor of the Commercial Crisis does not deem it essential to enter into those particulars.

* "October, 1845, ushered in the panic in all its terror, the golden dreams of the committee-men vanished, and many of those very gentlemen fled to foreign lands, to avoid the responsibilities they had incurred. Who were the sufferers? The tradesmen, engineers, &c. The secretary had obtained credit of those parties on the strength of the solvency and acknowledged respectability of those whose names appeared on the list of the provisional committee. The day of reckoning came at length; those very gentlemen who had perhaps realized large sums by their connexion with the project, repudiated all liability; the parties who gave them credit, and who had paid away large sums of money on their behalf, in the full belief of their solvency and honour, were set at defiance, and the only means left to the unfortunate creditor was to bring actions, and to plunge into a doubtful litigation in order to recover the amount of his fair demands."—*Judge-made law—versus the Law of the Land*—an able pamphlet published on the question of the liabilities of railway committee-men.

The appended table of the markets for public securities from January to March, 1846, shews the fluctuations that occurred in that period. A number of the abortive lines were then attempting a liquidation but without any great success. Shares in the old lines of railway were for the time pretty steady, though the prospect of permanent improvement was remote.

GOVERNMENT SECURITIES.

	JANUARY, 1846.				MARCH, 1846.			
	Price on the 1st.	Lowest Price.	Highest Price.	Price on the 31st.	Price on the 2d.	Lowest Price.	Highest Price.	Price on the 31st.
Consols, Money	Shut	93¾	95½	94⅞	96⅜	95	96½	96⅜
Do. Account....	94⅞ ex.d.	94⅛	95¼	95⅛	96⅞	95⅜	97	96⅝
Exchequer Bills, 1½d.	28/ pm.	10/ pm.	32/ pm.	27/ pm.	35/ pm.	21/ pm	37/ pm.	29/ pm.

RAILWAY SECURITIES.

	JANUARY, 1846.						MARCH, 1846.						
	Amount per Share.	Amount paid.	Price on the 1st.	Low-est Price	High-est Price	Price on the 31st.	Amount Paid.			Price on the 2d.	Low-est Price	High-est Price	Price on the 31st.
	£	£					£	s.	d.				
Brighton	50	50	69	66¾	70	68¾	50	0	0	65	60½	65¾	62¼
Caledonian	50	10	15½	13½	16¼	14⅝	10	0	0	13⅜	7	13½	8
Chester & Holyhead	50	15	17	15¼	22	21½	20	0	0	21¼	16½	21¼	17½
Croydon	Av. £13 : 15 : 9		23¼	92	24	22¾	Av. 13	15	9	22⅛	19	22¼	20½
Direct Northern ..	50	£2 : 10	2	1⅞	2¼	2⅛	2	10	0	2¼	1½	2¼	1½
Eastern Counties ..	25	£14 : 16	22¾	21¾	23¼	22⅛	14	16	0	21¾	19¾	22	21
Edinb. and Glasgow	50	50	77	74	80	76⅜	50	0	0	72	71¾	73¼	—
Great Western	100	80	163	159	170	168	85	0	0	149	140	151	143
Hull and Selby	50	50	104	103	106	106	50	0	0	104¼	99	105	106
London & N. Westn.	Stock.		221	219	230	229	Stock			222	214	224	217
London and York ..	50	2 10	4⅝	3⅞	4⅞	4⅜	2	16	0	3⅝	1½	3¾	1¾
Manchester & Leeds	100	76	135	133	138	136	82	0	0	—	116	131	116
Midland	Stock.		155	148	158	152	Stock			148¼	139	149	141½
North British	25	£17 : 10	25¾	23½	27	24⅜	20	0	0	27⅛	22½	27¼	24
Do. Kent	50	£2 : 16	3⅜	2¾	3½	2⅞	2	16	0	2¾	1	2⅞	1¼
South Eastern	Av. £33 : 2 : 4		39½	38	40½	38¾	Av. 33	2	4	38	34	38¼	34¾
Do. Western . ..	Av. £41 : 6 : 10		77¼	76	79	78½	Av. 41	6	10	77½	73	78	75
Trent Valley	£20	£5	20½	20	21¼	21	5	0	0	26⅜	26	28	27½
York & N. Midland	50	50	—	100	114	102½	50	0	0	99¾	94	100	96
Boulogne & Amiens	20	10	12⅜	11½	13	10¾	10	0	0	11½	10¼	12⅞	12⅛
Dutch Rhenish	20	5	8	7¼	8½	7½	5	0	0	6⅝	5¼	6⅞	5¾
Northern of France	20	5	14¾	14	15½	14¾	5	0	0	16	14⅞	16½	15½
Orleans & Bordeaux	20	6	11¾	10¾	12½	11½	6	0	0	12¼	11¾	13¼	12⅛
Paris and Rouen ..	20	20	40½	38½	41	38¾	20	0	0	42	40¼	42½	40¼
Sambre & Meuse ..	20	6	6	5½	6½	5⅝	6	0	0	—	3¾	4¾	3½

Besides the litigation encouraged, the meetings of expiring companies afforded scenes rarely witnessed in well ordered society. Directors and committees were found in their collective character to have forfeited all claims to honesty, illegal traffic in shares proved in several instances the least reprehensible part of their conduct; and frauds and forgèries became, in some cases, subjects of criminal investigation. And thus they not only pandered to their own selfish appetites, but they also suffered the costs of lawyers and other professional attendants, to make so great an inroad upon shareholders' deposits, as to leave but little for subsequent distribution.

Under the attractive title of the "Progress of Exposure," one of the railway papers,* rendered weekly an account of the reckless proceedings of the bubble companies, and unflinchingly held up to public odium, the adventurers who had profited by their existence. Share gambling having been wholly arrested, the hollowness of the system was shortly made manifest. Some directors and committee-men finding the prosperity of the mania at an end, sought to avoid responsibility by advertising themselves as unconnected with any undertakings; others judging this plan inexpedient, and considering "responsibility and payment" were not terms synonymous with "fees or premiums," quitted for the Continent, with the proceeds of their operations; while some, compelled by the pressure of circumstances, and inability either to pay or take flight, willingly submitted to individual incarceration, with the anticipation of the friendly interference of bankruptcy or insolvency, to free them from liability.

A report, issued about this time from the Board of Trade, demonstrated in the most palpable manner the fertility of invention among the promoters of joint-stock companies. Railways, patronized as they were, had not been suffered to occupy an exclusive monopoly.† "This mirror of national hallucination"

---

* *Railway Gazette*, 1846.

† "Among the most 'amusing nondescripts' the report gave the following:—

The People's Colliery Co.
Melides Anglo-Franceza Mining Co.
Biographical Dictionary Society
St. Marylebone and Paddington Joint-stock Building and Trading Co.
Agricultural Cattle Insurance Co.
Tehuantepec Colonization and Canal Co.
Greenwich Bath Co.
York-street Flax-spinning Mill Co.
Bury Athenæum Co.
Patent Concentrated Tea Co.
Tollesbury Oyster Co.
National Land-draining Co.
Patent Fuel Co.
Rotherham & Masbrough Public Bath Co.
National Joint-stock, Loan & Discount Co.

(as the document was described*) "when every bubble was invested with a value as the true offspring of English joint-stock genius, shows the progress of the evil of a plethoric speculation,

Quartertown Cotton Joint-stock Co.
Economic Draining Tile and Brick Co.
General Oceanic Telegraph Co.
Church of England Cemetery Co.
Highbridge Market-house Co.
Lancashire £100 Money Co.
New Protecting Society
Norfolk & Suffolk Ramoneur Association
Mercantile Bill of Exchange, Discount and Loan Co.
Fidelity Guarantee Society
Patent India Paper Manufacturing Co.
Marine Glue Co.
Wenham Lake Ice Co.
Patent Cork-cutting Co.
Hull Worsted Mill Co.
Wylam's Steam Fuel Co.
Practicable Gen. & Invalid Assurance Co.
Burnley Cotton Twist Co.
Defender Co., now called Property Protection and Insurance Co. against Fraud and Robbery
Craig Dhu Slate Co.
Patent Timber Co.
Great British Advertising Co.
Railway Club House, Chambers, and General Goods Depot Co., now called Bank Approaches Improvement Co.
British Class Journal Co.
National Glass Co. of Ireland
General Commercial Telegraph Co.
Railway Carriage Building Co.
Prosser's Patent Wooden Railway Guide-wheel Co.
British and Colonial Provident Life Assurance Annuity Endowment, and Freehold Investment Co.
Liverpool Joint-stock Railway Bank Co.
Burnley Building Co.
Manchester Auxiliary Investment Co.
Bridlington Quay and Public Rooms Co.
Fitzroy Investment Association
Hull Sugar Refining Co.
Royal Irish Glass Co.
New Share and Stock Exchange Co.
Westminster&Charing-crossBuilding Co.
Chorley Cotton Twist Co.
General Canal Steam Haulage Co.
Metropolitan and Brighton Sea-Water Conveyance Co.
Provincial Sewage Manure Co.
Great City Shambles Co.
Nova Scotia and New Brunswick Transit and Colonization Co.
Universal Railway Contracting Co.
Joint Stock Newspaper Co.
Railway and General Gas Co.
Railway Land Investment Co.
Victoria Aqueduct Co.
Inland Ports and Sea Ports Union Ship Railway and Goods Traffic Co.
Isthmus of Darien, Atlantic, and Pacific Junction Railway, Harbour and Dock, and Steam Packet Co., now called Isthmus of Darien, Atlantic, and Pacific Junction Railway Harbours, Docks, Canal and Steam Packet Co.
Northampton General Cemetery Co.
Necropoli, or Grand Eastern and Western Cemeteries Co., now called Metropolitan Necropolis, or Grand Eastern and Western Cemeteries Co.
Sheffield Coal Consumers' Co.
Bradford Sanatory Building Co.
Atmospheric Rapid Mail Conveyance Co.
United Iron and Railway Extension Co.
Dublin Coal Ship Co.
Railway Contracts Co.
Royal Irish Railroad Carriage Co.
East of England Locomotive Engine Building Co.
Patriot Association
Somersetshire Lighting Co.
Devonshire Lighting Co.
Law Chambers Society of Ireland
Norwich Church of England Burial Ground Co.
British Patent Naphtha Co.
Union Joint-stock Building Co.
Hibernian Coal and Peat Consumers' Co.
Liverpool Stock Exchange Building Co.
Great Metropolitan Artesian Water Co.
England Life and Invalid Hazard Assurance Co.
Grand European Mining and Manufacturing Iron Co.
Miniature World, or Grand National Association
Grand National Association for the Profitable Employment of Capital, Skill, and Labour, in Trade, Commerce, and Agriculture
South London Newspaper Co.
Patent Fibre Manufacturing Co.
National Investment and Benevolent Land Association, for the Encouragement of Agricultural Labourers and Small Farmers
West Kent Hop Co.
Hereford Cottage Association
Litherland Land Co.
National Philanthropic Investment Co.

* *Morning Chronicle, April,* 1846.

without at all unveiling the disastrous and uncalculated consequences of the period—consequences, which can only be thoroughly arrived at by visiting Whitecross-street and other debtors jails, half peopled with projectors and speculators, who have sported in the late railway game." This assertion did not long remain unexemplified. Proceedings in bankruptcy and insolvency every now and then disclosed striking facts connected with the ravages of the mania, and the majority of balance sheets and schedules filed in the respective courts contained heavy accounts of "losses by railway shares."*

And now we approach the important period when the Legislature found it necessary to interfere for the relief of the public, and to adopt measures for at once determining the dissolution of

---

* A bankrupt named Charles Collins, described as of Adelaide-place, London-bridge, and Kidderminster, Commission-agent, when he appeared before the Court, showed by his balance-sheet that he had been largely connected with many of the projects started during the mania, and in giving an account of his liabilities as provisional committee-man or director, included the subjoined choice selection:—

"1. Pilbrow's Atmospheric Railway and Canal Propulsion Company—liabilities none. 2. Jamaica Western—they are winding up, and I expect they will meet all their engagements. 3. Jamaica Southern, Eastern, and Northern—the same. 4. Oxford and Thame—winding up. 5. North Devon (Bridgewater to Portlock)—winding up. 6. Avon and Severn Valley—never attended a meeting, and don't know the state of affairs. 7. Dutch Hanoverian—no liability. 8. London and Gravesend Direct—winding up. 9. London and Dublin Direct—winding up. 10. Irish West Coast—liabilities transferred to the Irish Directory. 11. Railway Guarantee Company—Irish liability of about £14 balance. 12. Railway Banking Company—joint liability of about £120. "13. Widow's Insurance Company—balance of about £100 owing, to be divided between five persons. 14. Great Welch Junction Railway—winding up. 15. Holborn-hill Improvement Company—all paid. 16. Concentrated Essence of Tea and Coffee Company—liability ceased. 17. Panama Company—all paid. 18. A proprietor of the British and American Steam Navigation Company—all paid but £53 and costs."

Numerous other cases could be adduced, *vide* Tanner's and Ward's balance-sheet in the Appendix. Mr. Commissioner Holroyd, in June, 1848, refused altogether the certificate of J. G. Moon in the East India trade, on the ground of reckless trading. His losses in railways during nine months of the "celebrated speculative year 1845" amounted to £7,500. The decision on the certificate of Lyon Samuel, by Mr. Commissioner Fonblanque, in August, 1848, also brought out the fact that losses on railway shares in that instance, were put down by the bankrupt at £13,400.

the numerous companies left as the great wreck of this speculation. From the commencement of the session continued appeals were made to the ministers as to the course they intended to pursue.

It was in April, 1846, that Lord Sandon from his place in the House of Commons determinedly called the attention of the then Premier, Sir Robert Peel, to the question.—" The present condition of the Money-market " said the noble Lord, alluding to railways, " is very different from what it was when these companies first came forward, and there is now a great desire on the part of those who have embarked in these projects to retire ; but, notwithstanding this desire, it is a question whether, by the rules of the house, they are enabled to fulfil their wishes. Not only is the question of importance to the few shareholders concerned, but every one is either directly or indirectly concerned, even though he may have been unconnected in any way with railways. The present state of things affects every branch of trade and commerce. In the first place, there is injury from the mere blocking up of the deposits ; in the next place, there is the apprehension of success, for success is no longer wished for but apprehended ; and in the next place the whole of the railway projects which have already received the sanction of Parliament are affected, and the directors are unwilling to make calls for their completion whilst the market remains in its present condition." And in support of his assertions he quoted the circulars of Messrs. Trueman & Cook, of London, and Messrs. Collman and Stolterfoht, of Liverpool.*

* The extract from Messrs. Trueman & Cook's circular ran thus :—

" The various branches of commerce are severely depressed; there is not only a continual fall in prices, but great difficulty in realizing goods at any sacrifice. The India and China trade is particularly suffering. Tea, indigo, silk, cotton, &c., forming the principal imports from thence, have all been reduced to a scale of prices unusually low. In the manufacturing districts stocks of goods are accumulating, and a general absence of all enterprise in trade is evident. The principal cause of this stagnation unquestionably is the enormous amount of railway undertakings, which are gradually absorbing a large portion of the capital of the country hitherto devoted to trading purposes. This evil is already very severe, but if it be increased by the success of many of the numerous projects now before Parliament, the inevi-

The discussion once pertinently raised, the subject was entered into without delay, and Sir Robert Peel, in propounding the measures which Government proposed to effect a dissolution of abortive schemes, entered into details.—" I find " said the Right Hon. Baronet, " that in 1844 the number of railway projects which received the sanction of the Legislature was 37; that the capital authorized to be raised by those acts amounted to £13,981,000; that the amount of loan capital, as distinguished from share capital, authorized to be raised, amounted to £4,006,000, being a total amount of share and loan capital authorized to be raised by the bills passed in 1844 of £17,987,000. Then I find in 1845 the number of railway bills passed was 118; and the share capital authorized to be raised by those acts amounted to not less than £45,849,000, whilst the amount authorized to be raised by loan, in addition to the share capital, is £14,635,000, making a total amount of capital authorized to be raised by the acts of

---

table embarrassment which must ensue can hardly be magnified. Public attention has recently become more awakened to this important subject, and Government has been urgently called upon to interpose by an unflinching determination to defer for a time most of the schemes now before Parliament. It has been urged, however, that the subscribers themselves have the power of withdrawing the undertakings if they find them beyond their means, and this is certainly true; but although many would gladly exercise the power, it would be difficult to procure a general consent to do so, while a parliamentary interference to relieve what is now admitted to be a serious impending difficulty, would be hailed with universal satisfaction. The little progress made with the important measures now before Parliament excites much anxiety, and aggravates the depression under which trade lingers."

Messrs. Collman & Stolterfoht advised their correspondents as follows:—

" We have still to repeat our former reports of a languid business, and of an uneasy feeling in the mercantile world, as a consequence of the late excessive railroad speculation, and from the dread of the serious effects which must arise if the numerous projects for the further construction of railroads which are now seeking the sanction of the Legislature be persevered in. It is easily to be understood, that if the railroads now in the course of construction will require about £20,000,000 per annum for the next three years, and will thus absorb most of the available capital of the country which can be spared from other pursuits, an additional demand of about £40,000,000 per annum, which the new projects would require, must be fraught with the most ruinous consequences, for it is utterly impossible that so rapid a conversion of floating into fixed capital, and a diversion of such immense sums from the industrial pursuits of the country, should not deprive them of their very life-blood."

1845, and applicable to railway enterprise, of £60,484,000. I have called for a return of the number of railway bills which, on the 11th of April last, were under the consideration of this or the other house of Parliament, and I find that the number of English bills amounted to 369; of Scotch bills, 107; and of Irish, 43—making a total of 519 bills, which, so far as the public records can be relied on, are bills in respect to which the decision of Parliament must be given. I find by the English bills that capital to the amount of £184,700,000 would be raised, supposing all those bills received the sanction of Parliament, and that in addition, under the same bills, loans to the amount of £58,000,000 might be raised. By the Scotch bills, capital stock to the amount of £28,500,000 might be raised, and loans to the amount of £9,500,000; whilst by the Irish bills, £18,104,000 capital stock could be constituted, and loans to the amount of upwards of £5,000,000 would be sanctioned, making a total of capital stock authorized to be raised by the bills for England, Scotland, and Ireland, respectively, of £231,302,000, and of capital to be raised by loans of £72,781,000, being a total of capital authorized to be raised by bills pending in this session, independently of the unpaid capital of the acts sanctioned by Parliament in 1844 and 1845, of £304,000,000. I know it would be quite illusory to rely upon that as the amount of capital which would be actually required. Many of these are competing railways, and many are bills the passing of which would be quite unnecessary for the public interests; and therefore, although I state £304,000,000 to be the total amount of capital which, if all these bills were sanctioned, would be authorized to be raised, yet a very great deduction must be made for many of them which Parliament would reject, and many of them which would not go on; but still, make what deduction you will, the total amount of capital, were there no interference at all on the part of Parliament,—if we are entirely passive,—that will be sanctioned in the present session, will be much greater than that which I think it would be essential for the public interests should be raised for railway speculations."

Three considerations, Sir Robert said, he thought should have weight with the House and induce the members to concur in the suggested plan.* These were—First, the enormous amount of capital, which, with whatever deduction might be made from the number of bills, must be pledged to railway engagements in the course of that session,—secondly, the increased cost of articles required for the construction of railways,—thirdly, the difference in the current value of shares from that which they bore when the undertakings were originally projected. Of the desire of the large body of subscribers to incohate schemes to release themselves from responsibility, he said, he was perfectly cognizant, and regarding with consideration the fact, that their liabilities in the aggregate were enormous, and that the powers of directors and provisional committee-men were great, unaccompanied by effectual controul—a circumstance which had led to the commission of great abuses, he believed that some interference on the part of Parliament was required.

That Sir Robert possessed good information relative to the practices of the governing bodies is amply proved when he quoted a communication which he had received disclosing their unprincipled manœuvres.—" One of the great deceptions of the new companies," that is, schemes formed by provisional committees, inviting persons in all districts of the country to commit themselves as partners of companies hereafter to be established, "has been the holding back of large portions of the shares for the purpose of rigging the market, and pocketing premiums at the expense of the public. I will instance a few out of the countless number of the railway rigs that have been played. In the ——only 42,000 out of 50,000 shares, I understand, were issued, the other 8,000 being kept back, though the shares were at a high premium, and applications out of number for them. In——

* The terms of the Bill were, that three-fifths of the scrip-holders of any undertaking that had not obtained its act, could determine whether the scheme should be carried forward or not: and resolutions were also passed in connexion with the standing orders of the house, enforcing proof of such an affirmative or negative vote before the third reading of any railway bill was allowed.

10,000 out of the 100,000 were reserved by the directors above the number paid on. —— had only 55,000 out of 100,000 shares issued, though the shares were also at 1½ to 2 premium. There are some facts connected with this line I could not trust on paper. The —— reserved an enormous number of shares, notwithstanding hundreds of thousands more than the whole number of shares in the company were applied for. In the —— about one-half the shares were kept back, the market rigged to £6 or £7 premium, and then certain of the directors sold to their friends, as favours, shares at, I believe, 3 or 4 premium; a part of which premium they were compelled to give back on the breaking up of the company." But the last is the most extraordinary of all:—" In the —— several thousand pounds of the deposits were taken out of the bankers' hands to rig the market. These are a few of the cases. That is to say,—the shareholders and scrip-holders in these schemes having paid £10 per cent. there was a sum of £20,000 paid into the bankers, and I am told that that money was taken out and invested in the purchase of shares wherever shares could be got,—that, in consequence, the shares rose to very high prices, and then the reserve shares were sold in the market at higher prices—that higher price having been obtained in consequence of the application of the deposits, and the directors having pocketed the premiums. I was told this day that this was a fact—that a gentleman, and, to my surprise, a lawyer, applied to a certain committee for some shares; that he was told by the company all the shares were gone—there was not a share left; but upon further inquiry he ascertained that not a single share had been issued, and yet the answer universally returned was, that all the shares were bought up, and that was for the purpose of taking advantage of the impression on the part of the public that the shares were in such requisition, and then the shares were issued."

The addresses of Earl Dalhousie in the House of Lords were equally convincing, if any person required additional testimony to his own experience. Unfortunately few of the public desired more than such knowledge to satisfy them that it was imperatively necessary for Government to interfere. If any had themselves wholly escaped the meshes of the general ensnarer, the lamentations of relatives and friends soon brought home conviction.

"It is hardly necessary for me" said Earl Dalhousie, "to recall to your lordships' recollection the state of railway business within the last twelve months and to the number of bills which were introduced at the close of 1844. In the last session of Parliament 248 railway bills were introduced, and at that time this was looked upon as a number utterly unprecedented, and every member of Parliament held up his hands and thanked his stars that such a number of bills was not likely to occur again. Speculation, however, waxed more hot and fiery every day; it pervaded every class, high and low, rich and poor, young and old, and I am sorry to be obliged to say that it exerted its influence upon one sex as much as upon another. The result was, as shown in the report which I have laid before your lordships, that, before the 31st of December last, there had been provisionally registered upwards of 1,400 schemes. I will not say what was the amount of capital; that is another question. On the 30th of November there had been deposited with the Board of Trade upwards of 800 plans. By the 31st of December that number was in some slight degree diminished; but nearly 700 had been deposited in the office at that date. The attention of the Government had been at an early period directed to this subject; but it was impossible, before the meeting of Parliament to have taken any course of proceeding. It was not in the power of the Government to have come down to Parliament with any definite plan till the facts necessary to guide us were in our possession."

On the subject of the relief prayed, a case in point was thus stated. A company had subscribed a capital of £100,000, which was deposited; the directors saw reason not to press this project, and they desired to wind up their affairs. An opinion was taken to ascertain if that were possible. Of the £100,000 there had been spent about £10,000, and consequently there would have remained to be divided £90,000, which would have given them £2 : 5s. on the £2 : 10s. shares. The proposition was very generally agreed to; but it was objected to by some; and it was found impossible to divide, or to come to the desired arrangement.

"With respect to the general state of feeling throughout the country on this subject, we know," said Lord Dalhousie, "the progress of a railway bill through Parliament has always been watched with anxiety; has been the means of stimulating the hopes of those directly engaged in such a bill, and the expectations of others desirous of being connected with it; consequently that invariably for that period the value of the stock has increased. But precisely the contrary is the fact now."

"Formerly," said Lord Dalhousie truthfully, "when a bill was going through committee, with so intense an interest was its fate awaited, that expresses of every description were daily sent off from the House of Commons to convey information to the Stock-exchange; and many of your Lordships may have observed, and no doubt all have heard, that it was no uncommon thing for carrier-pigeons to be let loose outside the doors of Parliament to wing their flight to different parts of the country, in order to give a chance to some one or other to operate successfully, and with the advantage of early information, in railway schemes. But, now, I have been distinctly informed by parties whose information is to be relied upon, and whose interests are affected by the results, that this session, so altered are the circumstances,—just in proportion as railway schemes appear to be favourably progressing through Parliament, and as they have a prospect of success, exactly in that proportion does the value of the stock fall in the market. In Scotland, in my own country, I know that not only is this description of railway affairs correct, but it is also the fact that there is a most earnest desire on the part of all those engaged in these undertakings to free themselves from them—to disconnect themselves together, for the present, from railway enterprise. I myself read in a Scotch paper of three—I know of two—railways which had already passed through several of the stages in the House of Commons, which had gone through committee, met with no impediment, and floated unrestrainedly down the stream, but which, the very moment they had got through committee, had had their subscribers called together in Scotland, with a view of enquiring how and when they could wind up their affairs, and into the mode by which they could put a stop to the undertaking."

But Earl Dalhousie saw further. It was not only the difficulty to be experienced by young companies that filled him with apprehension: it was something more. He saw trade would be endangered by the increasing demand for money. And he was also aware that "even the old-established companies, fully invested with power, and in active operation, found themselves, when desirous of increasing their influence, and adding to their wealth, by the construction of new branches, encompassed with difficulties."

The views enunciated by Lord Dalhousie were received with the same attention as those expressed by Sir Robert Peel, and notwithstanding the Government did not wholly escape from blame,* for the want of proper vigilance in restraining the general current of the speculation, still the act they proposed to bring into force was hailed with satisfaction, as one tending to put in course of arrangement outstanding differences between parties respectively interested in the numerous suspended companies. The Scotch had the credit of giving the first indication of the approaching distress in the railway world; and they were fully entitled to it. None were more eager, in the early days of the mania, to profit by the inflation of prices; but as soon as the reaction came, they manifested much apprehension for consequences, and made every possible attempt to unshackle themselves from their enfettered condition. The Act, since universally known as "Lord Dalhousie's Dissolution Act," was then passed, and its provisions were immediately brought into effect.

The subjoined table of prices from April to June inclusive does not present any astonishing alteration. The markets, ge-

---

* *Vide* the speeches of Lord Monteagle and Mr. Disraeli in Parliament, April, 1846.

nerally considered, exhibited steadiness if not firmness. Consols had advanced "on the prospect of an early dissolution of many of the abortive railway schemes, and the consequent distribution of a considerable amount of capital." Exchequer Bills were quoted in decline, principally caused by sales on behalf of companies arranging for a partial return of deposits. The better classes of railway shares, although scarcely strong, even at the prices quoted, were in a less fluctuating position than at any time since the previous October.

GOVERNMENT SECURITIES.

	APRIL, 1846.				JUNE, 1846.			
	Price on the 1st.	Lowest Price.	Highest Price.	Price on the 30th.	Price on the 1st.	Lowest Price.	Highest Price.	Price on the 30th.
Consols, Money	96⅜	95⅜	96½	96⅛	96½	96⅜	97	Shut
Do. Account....	96⅜	95¾	96½	96⅜	96⅞	96¾	97¼	95½ ex.d.
Exchequer Bills, 1½d.	27/pm.	18/pm.	29/pm.	2/pm.	15/pm.	5/pm.	22/pm.	12/pm.

RAILWAY SECURITIES.

	APRIL, 1846.						JUNE, 1846.				
	Amount per Share.	Amount Paid.	Price on the 1st.	Lowest Price	Highest Price	Price on the 30th.	Amount Paid.	Price on the 1st.	Lowest Price	Highest Price	Price on the 30th.
	£.	£.					£. s. d.				
Brighton..........	50	50	62¼	61¾	66⅜	65½	50 0 0	65¼	64½	65⅞	65¼
Caledonian........	50	10	8	5½	8	7	15 0 0	11¾	9¼	12	9½
Chester & Holyhead	50	20	17½	17	22¼	21¾	22 10 0	—	19½	21¼	20½
Croydon	Av. £13 : 15 : 9		20½	20	23½	23	Av. 13 : 15 : 9	22	21½	22⅞	22½
Direct Northern ..	50	£2 10	1½	1⅛	2⅛	2	2 10 0	1⅞	1¼	2	1⅜
Eastern Counties ..	25	14 16	21	20½	24⅝	24⅛	14 16 0	23¼	22¾	24¾	24
Edinb. and Glasgow	50	50 0	—	71	74	74	50 0 0	75	74½	76	—
Great Western	100	85 0	144	143	155	152	85 0 0	—	140½	147	143¼
Hull and Selby	50	50 0	100	100	101½	101½	50 0 0	103	102½	104	103½
London & N. Westn.	Stock.		219	217	228	227	Stock.	228	223	229	224
London and York..	£50	£ 2 10	1¾	0¾	2½	2¼	2 10 0	2¼	1¼	2½	1½
Manchester & Leeds	100	82 0	116	116	132	130	82 0 0	—	116	124	118½
Midland Counties..	Stock.		144½	143	157	155	Stock.	149¼	147	150	149
North British	£25	£20 0	24	23¼	28½	27¾	22 10 0	29¾	29	30¼	29¾
North Kent........	50	2 10	1¼	1⅛	1⅝	1½	2 10 0	1⅜	1⅛	1½	1½
South Eastern	Av. £33 : 2 : 4		34¾ ex.d	34	39½	38¼	Av. 33 : 2 : 4	39¾	38¾	40¾	40½
Do. Western	Av. £41 : 6 : 10		76½	75	82½	81¼	Av. 41 : 6 : 10	79½	77	80	77½
York & N. Midland	£50	£50	96	96	98	—	50 0 0	98¼	98	99	98
Boulogne & Amiens	20	12	12⅛	11¾	12⅜	12¼	12 0 0	11½	10⅞	13¼	13
Dutch Rhenish....	20	5	5¾	5½	7	6¾	6 0 0	7⅞	7½	8	7½
Northern of France	20	5	15½	14½	15¾	15½	5 0 0	14¼	12½	14⅞	14
Orleans & Bordeaux	20	6	12⅛	10⅛	12	11	6 0 0	10	9⅛	10⅛	9½
Paris and Rouen ..	20	20	41	40	41	—	20 0 0	—	38½	39½	—
Sambre and Meuse .	20	6	3½	2¾	5½	5½	8 0 0	5	4	5¼	4⅝

As far as the intent of the Government measure was concerned it could not be said to be altogether unproductive of benefit. It was some time, however, before its action was admitted to be satisfactory. Under its process attempts were made by directors and others, whose management would not bear investigation, to over-ride the decisions of scrip-holders by a forced system of voting arising from the use of unappropriated shares. Another class of speculators, scrip-holders, who had purchased at very depreciated prices, also exercised their right or presence purely with the intent of breaking up companies whose remnant of deposits, it was calculated, would yield a larger distribution than the market value of the shares. Thus it will be perceived, that throughout the several phases of the mania, the distinctive features of fraud and chicanery were prominently presented, and that in the grand drama, each change of scene was accompanied by incidents as remarkable as any which had already preceded them.

Distressing as was the havoc, made manifest from the course of liquidation pursued under legislative authority, and highly culpable as were the proceedings of the greater number of the companies, whose affairs stripped from all concealment, were exposed to public notice, yet there was some slight gratification experienced when, in the midst of all this alarm and confusion, it was discovered that the Act as it came steadily into operation, furnished the means of escape, though unfortunately at a great sacrifice. But the sacrifice was not caused by the operation of that measure, which, despite the opinion expressed by its adversaries, unquestionably was, in the long run, productive of much relief. The extravagance of engineers and solicitors, and the large costs incurred for surveys, parliamentary proceedings, and compliance with other requisite formalities, and losses on the Stock-exchange, occasioned by "running prices to a premium," were, when taken together, fairly chargeable with the absorption of the funds which were subscribed.

The great executive staff of projected undertakings, hydra-headed as they were, swallowed without compunction, the chief of the deposits when paid. Payments to promoters of £10,000 and £20,000 each; engineering charges varying from £30,000 to £100,000; parliamentary and law expenses for amounts in proportion to the nature and magnitude of the scheme, most of which disbursements were arranged in anticipation of receipts, besides other incidental items, all swelling the grand total, constituted the catalogue of claims dischargeable from that source. Under such circumstances, was it to be supposed that in case of dissolution, the return to the subscriber would bear any comparison to the original sum entrusted to the custody of a managing committee?

Unveiling, as Lord Dalhousie's Act did, the most nefarious transactions in companies where deposits in full, or nearly so, had been freely placed at the disposal of such irresponsible bodies, the worst results were to be expected; but as the mischief was done, and what was more, the money had disappeared, the dilemma could not well be avoided, since the alternative of attacking the most influential directors, left but a sorry prospect of success, they having either beggared themselves, or cast aside the mask of respectability,* and thus placed it out of the power of dissentients to make them amenable for their acts.

The month of July it will be ascertained from the examination of the following figures established in comparison with the

---

* In the early part of 1846, when the great dispersion of committee-men and directors took place, an anecdote was circulated to the effect that a civic functionary, who in consequence of his continued residence abroad, has since thought fit to resign his gown, was served with upwards of 400 writs by creditors of the companies with which he was associated. Another story was told of a noble Lord, who finding himself subjected to annoyances of a similar description sought the advice of his lawyer and asked him for what amount he could relieve him from the embarrassment. "Give me £15,000" said the professional gentleman, "and I will undertake to settle all your affairs in connexion with railways." His Lordship with much coolness declined the proffered assistance, adding, that "as his yacht was at Cowes, he should try the efficacy of a trip up the Mediterranean before parting with any of the proceeds of his sales of scrip." As a final sample of the recklessness displayed by parties who had engaged in the speculation we quote the following case from the *Railway Record*, of April, 1846:—"A WHOLESALE DIRECTOR.—In the Sheriffs' Court last week, Mr. ———, an assistant surgeon, sought to recover £9 4s. 6d., the balance of salary due to him by Mr. ———, of Parliament-street. The defence was, that

three previous months, a favorable market for railway shares. The funds were not so good. After that date, notwithstanding the Bank, in August, reduced its rate of discount to 3 per cent., the stock of bullion in its coffers having then increased to £16,000,000, the value of shares again gave way, and went on declining, owing to the commencement of "calls," until they stood at the point quoted in September.

GOVERNMENT SECURITIES.

	JULY, 1846.				SEPTEMBER, 1846.			
	Price on the 1st.	Lowest Price.	Highest Price.	Price on the 31st.	Price on the 1st.	Lowest Price.	Highest Price.	Price on the 30th.
Consols, Money	Shut	95¼	96⅛	95⅞	96	95⅛	96¼	95⅜
Do. Account....	95½ ex. d.	95¼	96⅜	96⅛	96¼	95¼	96½	95⅝
Exchequer Bills, 1½d.	11/ pm.	9/ pm.	17/ pm.	11/pm.	19/pm.	8/pm.	21/pm.	16/pm.

RAILWAY SECURITIES.

	JULY, 1846.						SEPTEMBER, 1846.						
	Amount per Share.	Amount paid.	Price on the 1st.	Low-est Price	High-est Price	Price on the 31st.	Amount Paid.			Price on the 1st.	Low-est Price	High-est Price	Price on the 30th.
	£	£					£	s.	d.				
Brighton	50	50	65⅝	64⅝	66¼	66	50	0	0	63½	58¼	62½	59¼
Caledonian	50	15	9½	8¼	14⅛	13½	25	0	0	16¼	15¾	21¼	21
Chester & Holyhead	50	£22 : 10	20¾	20½	27½	26¾	27	10	0	26¾	23¾	27	24
Croydon	Av. £13 : 15 : 9		22¾	22¼	23¾	23⅝	Av. 13	15	9	23¼	21¼	23⅛	21⅝
Direct Northern ..	50	£2 : 10	1¼	0¾	1¼	1⅝	2	10	0	1¾	1⅜	1⅞	1½
Eastern Counties ..	25	£14 : 16	24⅛	23⅞	24⅞	24	14	16	0	23	21⅛	23	21¾
Edinb. and Glasgow	50	50	—	72½	74	74	50	0	0	72	70	72½	72
Great Western	100	85	147½	147½	153½	152	85	0	0	148	136	148½	137
Hull and Selby	50	50	—	105	109	106	50	0	0	103	103	105¾	105½
London & N. Westn.	Stock.		223	222	233	232	Stock			207	198	206	200
London and York ..	50	2 10	1⅜	0¾	1⅞	1¾	2	10	0	2¼	1¾	2¼	1⅞
Manchester & Leeds	100	82	119½	115	120	116	82	0	0	116	106	116	—
Midland	Stock.		149½	145	152	147	Stock			139	135	141	136
North British	25	£22 : 10	29⅜	29⅜	38½	37½	25	0	0	38¾	32½	38¾	34
Do. Kent	50	£2 : 10	1⅜	1⅜	2	1¾	2	10	0	1⅝	1⅝	1⅝	—
South Eastern	Av. £33 : 2 : 4		40⅝	40½	46	45¾	Av. 33	2	4	43¾	38⅝	43¾	39¼
Do. Western . ..	Av. £41 : 6 : 10		77½	76½	79½	76¾	Av. 41	6	10	71¾	69½	73	70
York & N. Midland	£50	£50	98½	98½	102	—	50	0	0	98	94	98	—
Boulogne & Amiens	20	14	12¾	11¾	12⅞	12½	14	0	0	13⅜	13⅛	15⅛	14¾
Dutch Rhenish	20	6	7⅝	5¾	7¾	6	6	0	0	6	4¼	6⅛	4¾
Northern of France	20	5	14	12⅛	14½	13	5	0	0	13⅛	13⅛	14⅛	14
Orleans & Bordeaux	20	6	9½	6¾	10	7¾	6	0	0	8¾	8⅛	8⅞	8¼
Paris and Rouen ..	20	20	—	38	40	38¼	20	0	0	37⅜	36½	37½	—
Sambre & Meuse ..	20	8	4⅝	3⅝	4¾	3¾	8	0	0	4⅛	3	4¼	3¼

Mr. ——— had procured for complainant an allotment of shares in the Madrid and Valentia Railway, of which Mr. ——— was a director, and supplied the means of paying the deposit.

Mr. ———, assistant to Mr. ———, said he knew the plaintiff, and recollected

Towards the close of the year a sudden change was noticeable in the aspect of affairs generally. The future condition of the Money-market was viewed with some uneasiness, and various causes were regarded as indicating the probability of a pressure. The grain and potatoe crops at home and abroad were extremely deficient; high prices were ruling in Mark-lane; railway calls visibly increased each month; and the evils attending the speculation, now the grand movement of "dissolution and distribution" was nearly terminated, more forcibly than ever developed themselves. Few political elements of discord existed—they were mostly commercial. The virtual abolition of the Corn-laws had already been some time settled; the campaign of the Sutlej had concluded most favourably for British interests; and the apprehended collision with America had been set aside by the adjustment of the Oregon question.

In the midst of the doubt and suspense resulting from the state of the railway markets, and the certainty of a bad harvest, mercantile credit encountered a severe blow from the failure of Messrs. Harman & Co.,* Russian merchants and agents to the Imperial Court at St. Petersburg. The event created universal surprise, as it was considered the resources of the establishment, even excluding the private wealth of its individual members,

---

his having an allotment of shares in the Madrid and Valentia Railway. The plaintiff told him that Mr. ——— had given him the money to pay for them, and he hoped they would soon be at a premium.

Mr. Parry.—Was Mr. ——— provisional director of more than one railway? Witness—I believe he was a director of a great number of railways.

Mr. Parry.—There was a great deal of business done in the railway line at the defendant's surgery, I believe? Witness—There was.

Mr. Parry—Did not plaintiff sit up until three o'clock in the morning conducting Mr. ———'s railway business? Witness—Sometimes.

Mr. Parry—How many railways was Mr. ——— a director of? Witness—I don't know.

Mr. Parry—You can guess. Was he a director of ten? Witness—More.

Mr. Parry—Twenty? Witness—More than twenty.

Mr. Parry—Have you not written letters for Mr. ———? Witness—I have.

Mr. Parry—Then you have been 'stagging it?' Witness—A little.

Verdict for the plaintiff."——The names were published in the report.—Ed.

* *Vide* Statement of affairs. Appendix, page i.

were of a character to have placed it beyond all suspicion. The truth, however, soon came out. The firm had been utterly insolvent for nearly a quarter of a century; its debts and liabilities were enormous, and the assets barely capable of paying a respectable dividend.*

---

* Messrs. Harman & Co. stopped payment in the month of October. Mr. Jeremiah Harman, the head of the firm, having died in February, 1844, the two surviving partners were Mr. Edward Harman and Mr. Henry Harman. The debts and liabilities of the house amounted to £540,000, and the assets to £100,000, or about 3s. 3d. in the pound. The claim of the Russian Government allowed against the estate was upwards of £410,000. An examination of the books effected under the direction of inspectors, proved that the house was solvent in 1817, the period of the decease of the partners' father, Mr. John Harman. Between that date and 1825, its difficulties gradually increased; in the latter year its affairs stood in this position.

"Statement of affairs in December, 1825."

The account of Jeremiah Harman was overdrawn in the private ledger, to the extent of	£35,207	4	5			
Against which he had a credit balance in the trade ledger of	23,333	6	8			
Leaving a debit balance of				£11,873	17	9
The account of Edward Harman was overdrawn in the private ledger to the extent of	£92,951	1	6			
Against which he had a credit balance in the trade ledger of	22,333	6	8			
Leaving a debit balance of				£70,617	14	10
The deficiency in the cash and bills balance at this date was ..				107,029	11	2
The bad debts which ought to have been written off at this time, amounted to				96,353	8	6
				£285,874	12	3
Against which—						
The account of Henry Harman in the private ledger had a credit balance of	£68,212	8	0			
Ditto ditto, in the trade ledger..........	20,333	6	8			
	£88,545	14	8			
Profit and loss account at this period had a credit balance of	47,908	2	8	136,453	17	4
Deficiency of the joint estate at December, 1825				£149,420	14	11

So painful were the revelations, when an investigation of the estate was entered into, that the greatest efforts were made to keep a knowledge of their real circumstances from the public mind. These efforts succeeded for awhile, but eventually they were surmounted, and the proceedings of the partners, when they transpired, were considered to have constituted " an act of great commercial delinquency."

The only remaining distinguishing feature of the year was the demand for cotton that sprung up in the month of December on the report of short American supplies. The activity, however, was not of lengthened duration. Strong symptoms of an increased demand for money in the mean time were apparent, and the state of the foreign exchanges, together with the possibility of large shipments of gold to the United States in payment of grain were pointedly alluded to by all banking and monetary authorities as circumstances which ought to engender caution.

Comparing the prices of October and December, it will be observed that the value of Government as well as railway secu-

---

Deficiency—brought over				£149,420	14	11
Assuming the separate estates at this period to be as follows :—						
Jeremiah Harman	£65,000	0	0			
Edward Harman	55,000	0	0			
Henry Harman	8,000	0	0			
				128,000	0	0
Still at this rate the estate was insolvent to the extent of				£21,420	14	11

In a sheet appended to the accounts termed the " Analysis of Losses," the ill-success of the speculations of the firm during their trading, from the year 1818 to the year 1845, is thus established.

	£	s.	d.
Sugar	5,415	14	1
Tobacco	1,460	9	3
Coffee	11,126	8	9
Sundries, Lead, &c.	10,334	17	1
Consignments	6,292	2	11
Oil	1,353	11	8
Tallow	2,383	8	6
Quicksilver	233	14	8
Wool, Cotton, &c.	10,976	19	8
Cochineal and Indigo	35,512	14	1
Rum, Brandy, &c.	1,882	1	9
	£86,972	2	5

rities were undergoing decline, the causes already mentioned operating in that direction. The position of most of the Continental Share-markets was now rapidly assimilating to that of our own; in Paris, Hamburg, Frankfort, and Amsterdam, sales were effected at a great depreciation, failures of bankers and brokers, who had too deeply adventured in them, followed; and cash was scarce and in request at advancing rates. The final close of 1846 was therefore far from cheering, and although many refused to recognize the indications presented, nothing satisfactory could be elicited to alter the conviction at which sound thinking and observant individuals had arrived.

GOVERNMENT SECURITIES.

	OCTOBER, 1846.				DECEMBER, 1846.			
	Price on the 1st.	Lowest Price.	Highest Price.	Price on the 31st.	Price on the 1st.	Lowest Price.	Highest Price.	Price on the 31st.
Consols, Money	95¼	94⅛	95½	94½	95⅛	93¼	95⅝	93⅝
Do. Account	95½	94½	95½	94⅝	95¼	93⅜	95⅝	93¾
Exchequer Bills, 1½d.	16/pm.	8/pm.	19/pm.	10/pm.	8/pm.	6/pm.	14/pm.	9/pm.

RAILWAY SECURITIES.

	OCTOBER, 1846.						DECEMBER, 1846.				
	Amount per Share.	Amount Paid.	Price on the 1st.	Lowest Price	Highest Price	Price on the 31st.	Amount Paid.	Price on the 1st.	Lowest Price	Highest Price	Price on the 31st.
	£	£					£. s. d.				
Brighton	50	50	59¼	58	60½	59¼	50 0 0	59	58¼	59½	59
Caledonian	50	25	21	20¾	24	23⅝	30 0 0	23⅞	23¼	30⅛	—
Chester & Holyhead	50	27 : 10	24	22½	24	—	27 10 0	25½	25	25¾	25⅝
Direct Northern ..	50	2 : 10	1½	1⅛	1⅝	1⅝	2 10 0	2	2	3¾	2¾
Eastern Counties ..	25	14 : 16	21¾	20⅞	22⅝	22⅜	14 16 0	23	22⅝	23¼	23
Edinb. & Glasgow..	50	50	72	68	76	76	50 0 0	—	74	78	77½
Great Western	100	85	137	135	140	—	85 0 0	129	126	134	132
Hull and Selby	50	50	105½	105½	108½	108¼	50 0 0	108¼	106	108½	106½
London & N. Westn.	Stock.		200	192	200	199¼	Stock.	194	193	196	195½
London and York ..	50	2 : 10	1⅞	1½	2⅛	2	2 10 0	2¼	2¼	3⅛	3
Manchester & Leeds	100	82	—	101	106	105¼	82 0 0	104	104	112¼	111
Midland	Stock.		136	130	138	133	Stock.	124	123	131	130½
North British......	25	25	34	31¾	37¾	36¾	25 0 0	36¾	35½	38	36⅛
South Eastern	Av. £33 : 2 : 4		39¼	36⅞	39½	38¼	Av. 33 : 2 : 4	37⅛	36¾	41	40½
Do. Western	Av. £41 : 6 : 10		70	67	72	67¾	Av. 41 : 6 : 10	63	61	64	63¾
York & N. Midland	£50	£50	—	94	97	—	50 0 0	92¼	91½	95	94
Boulogne & Amiens	20	16	14¾	14⅛	14⅞	14½	16 0 0	13⅝	13⅜	15⅝	15½
Dutch Rhenish	20	6	4¾	4⅜	5½	5¼	6 0 0	5	4¾	5¼	—
Northern of France	20	5	14	11½	14	11⅝	5 0 0	10⅛	9⅞	13¾	13¾
Orleans & Bordeaux	20	6	8¼	7⅛	8⅜	7½	6 0 0	7½	7⅝	8¾	8½
Paris and Rouen ..	20	20	—	36	36	—	20 0 0	34¼	34¼	36	36
Sambre and Meuse .	20	8	3¼	3⅛	5⅛	4⅝	10 0 0	—	4	4¾	4¾

And now at the termination of this eventful period, embracing within little more than two years the general circumstances identified with the progress of the railway mania, it is perhaps fitting to glance rapidly at what may be properly conceived its prominent characteristics and consequences.

No one will, it is thought, attempt to controvert the assertion that an almost unexampled abundance of money, combined with the profits derived from this class of investment encouraged in the first instance the extension of the railway system, and that subsequently the mania itself was fostered by the daring spirit of speculation, which at all times distinguishes a nation like the English in the cherished pursuit of commercial adventure.

Again it must have been almost universally perceived long before the mania subsided, that its altered aspect could not fail to bring with it results, which if less dangerous than those following "the panic period of 1825," must nevertheless be productive of much inconvenience and distress; and yet in the face of the experience afforded by the history of similar "financial delusions," so great was the madness of all classes, that from the peer to the peasant, few ultimately escaped unscathed.

How bankruptcy and ruin was spread far and near through the explosion of the bubble; and how the public suffered through the depreciation of every kind of railway security, may be in some degree estimated from the substance of the narrative already furnished; but enormous as were the losses and sacrifices made to withstand what was then regarded as "the crowning blow of destruction," they bear trivial relation to the disasters which hereafter require to be detailed.

EPOCH THE SECOND.

THE FOOD AND MONEY PANIC.

SEVERE as had been the crisis growing out of the prodigal patronage bestowed upon railway enterprise, its effects, in its first stage, were limited, contrasted with the baneful influence it subsequently exercised, in conjunction with other powerfully operating causes, upon the trade and credit of the country at large.

The rough outline of the mania given in the preceding pages brings down "the strange eventful history" to the date when the community were relieved from the burden of the majority of incohate schemes; and when Lord Dalhousie's Bill may be said to have nearly exhausted its power. So far, therefore, as abortive projects were concerned, not much additional mischief was to be apprehended.

But if in this respect all present danger was supposed to have passed, the subsequent remarkable increase in the amount of railway calls, the payments which it was anticipated would have to be made for imports of foreign corn, and the continuous decline in the exchanges, were circumstances which tended to create apprehensions as to the course of events in 1847.*

* "There has been a general concurrence of opinion amongst the witnesses examined before your Committee, that the primary cause of the distress was the deficient harvest, especially of the potatoe crop, in the year 1846, and the necessity of

And these apprehensions were somewhat encouraged by the want of active interference on the part of the Bank authorities, whose facilities for advances and discounts were stated to be in undue proportion to the progressive and legitimate demand for capital.

As early as November, 1846, The *Times*, in its city article, calling attention to the prospective position of affairs, remarked, "It is well understood that under the last Bank Charter Act the condition of the foreign exchanges must afford an infallible index of the circulation, and it is therefore desirable to point out to those who neglect the warning, and who now appear to entertain a belief that the possibility of a contraction of the currency need in no way induce them to limit their engagements—that they will have no right, if they eventually find themselves inconveniently pressed upon, to complain of the action of a measure the timely indication of which they have deemed it expedient to disregard." Notwithstanding sound advice from this and other quarters, no counteractive steps were adopted, and the year commenced with appearances of distrust, though little disposition was exhibited to regard the premonitory symptoms with the attention which they strictly deserved.

The calls payable on railways in January represented £6,150,000, of which £4,500,000 arose from the demands of English companies. The remainder was on behalf of foreign lines, a great number of whose shares were held in this country. At this period the Bank of France was found to be in difficulties from the absence of an adequate supply of silver to meet

---

providing the means of payment in the year 1847, for the unprecedented importations of various descriptions of food which took place in that year. Among other causes, the deficient supply of cotton, the diversion of capital from its ordinary employment in commercial transactions to the construction of railroads, the undue extension of credit, especially in our transactions with the East, and exaggerated expectations of an enlarged trade, have been stated, by some of the witnesses, as having contributed to the same result. Your committee see no reason to doubt that these causes have in different degrees, in different parts of the country, produced the effect thus ascribed to them."—*First Report (Commons' Committee) on Commercial Distress.*

their current demands; to obviate the difficulty Messrs. Baring, Brothers, stepped in, and arrangements were effected for assisting the establishment to the extent of about £1,000,000, the Bank of England agreeing to facilitate as far as possible the purchases of bullion required. As money was now advancing in value, and as the demand on the Continent experienced no abatement, these adverse circumstances with the attendant consequences of a depressed exchange and a continuous drain of capital shortly aroused notice, and the Bank directors on the 14th of January, raised the rate of interest to 3½ per cent., and again on the 21st to 4 per cent.

These advances in the rate of accommodation by the Bank, although they exerted some influence upon the Money-market, did not operate altogether disadvantageously, until it was ascertained that besides the prospect of large shipments of gold abroad, particularly to America, and the absorption of capital by railway calls, the necessities of Ireland, through the failure of the potatoe crop, would have to be satisfied from the national treasury. The loss estimated to have been sustained by that calamity being set down at £13,000,000, and the subscriptions started, although unprecedently large, not reaching near that amount, the difference was so considerable as to render the negociation of a loan a matter of extreme probability.

Notwithstanding the discouraging circumstances, viz., the gradual decline in the produce markets, which exemplified the progress of business during January and February, aggravated by distress in Ireland, and food riots in Scotland, confidence, although in some degree failing, was far from being paralyzed. Yet the cause for alarm was great, since, combined with railway calls, calculated at £1,400,000 for the latter month, the price of grain was rising uninterruptedly, not alone in the markets of the United Kingdom, but also throughout the Continent of Europe.

Continuous gloom on the subject of famine, with the increase of corn speculation, created at the end of February further distrust; money was getting dearer; the Government had intimated a desire to contract a loan, bút the Bank directors had not then made any fresh alteration in the rate of interest.*

On the first of March the Irish loan of £8,000,000 was taken by Messrs. Rothschild and Messrs. Baring, Brothers, conjointly, at the rate of £89 10s. for every £100 Three per Cent. Stock, a price considered at the time low, but which subsequent events proved was quite an equivalent value, and the scrip came out at 1½ to 2 premium. It did not however long maintain this quotation, and gradually sunk to a discount, capital fetching higher rates of interest by employment in the general Money-market.† Between the first week in January, and the first week in March, the Bank's stock of bullion had without the least check descended from £14,950,000 to £11,590,000, the outflow of gold being Continental and American; and the railway calls for March, English and Foreign, amounted in gross to £3,508,000. At the end of March, the stock of bullion dropped to £11,000,000.

The table of prices here inserted, accurately illustrates the decline in all kinds of public securities, the rally in Consols, which occurred when the fact transpired that the Russian government had arranged for the purchase of 50,000,000 3 per cent. Rentes (£2,000,000 sterling) belonging to the Bank of France,—not having been sustained. This financial operation for the moment placed our French neighbours in a better position, and was not without some temporary effect here, as it provided funds for the payment of advances made by English capitalists. The

* "Was the raising of the rate of interest postponed by the Bank during that time, with a view of facilitating any operation by the Government; I allude to the apparent necessity of Government raising money?—I think there was a discussion at the period at which the loan was being negociated in the Money-market; and some members of the Court thought that, in the face of the negociation of a loan by the Government, it would be desirable, not immediately to raise the rate of interest. —*Evidence of Mr. Morris, Governor of the Bank, before the Commons' Committee on Commercial Distress.*

† Between April and May Consol scrip fluctuated considerably, and had been quoted as low as 3¼ discount. In June the price recovered and supported a premium. Once more there was a reaction, and in October, when the last instalment was paid it was marked 6 discount.

fall in railway shares, not excepting the best securities, commenced in earnest, the three months' contrast marking in most cases a severe depreciation.

GOVERNMENT SECURITIES.

	JANUARY, 1847.				MARCH, 1847.			
	Price on the 1st.	Lowest Price.	Highest Price.	Price on the 30th.	Price on the 1st.	Lowest Price.	Highest Price.	Price on the 31st.
Consols, Money	Shut	90¼	93⅞	91½	90⅝	87⅞	91¼	88½
Do. Account....	93⅞	90½	94	91½ ex.d.	91	88¼	91¼	88½
Exchequer Bills, 1½d.	8/ pm.	2/ pm.	15/ pm.	7/ pm.	*5/ pm.	1/ dis.	8/ pm.	par.

RAILWAY SECURITIES.

	JANUARY, 1847.						MARCH, 1847.						
	Amount per Share.	Amount paid.	Price on the 1st.	Lowest Price	Highest Price	Price on the 30th.	Amount Paid.			Price on the 1st.	Lowest Price	Highest Price	Price on the 31st.
	£	£					£	s.	d.				
Brighton	Stock.	50	59	54	59¼	55¾	50	0	0	55¾	52	56	52¼
Caledonian	50	30	29¾	24⅞	30½	26½	30	0	0	27½	25¾	28¾	26⅛
Eastern Counties ..	25	£14 : 16	23¼	20⅝	23¼	22¼	20	0	0	21⅜	19	21⅝	19¼
Edinb. and Glasgow	50	50	77½	72	79	75	50	0	0	78¾	70	80	71
Great Western	100	85	131½	121	139	126	85	0	0	120¾	110	121	116
Hull and Selby	50	50	106½	106½	108	—	50	0	0	104½	102	105	102½
London & N. Westn.	Stock.		195½	190	202	193	Stock			186½	175	188	176
Manchester & Leeds	100	82	111	105	114	109½	82	0	0	—	104	110	—
Midland	Stock.		130½	118	132	126½	Stock			122¼	114	123	115¼
South Eastern	Av. £33 : 2 : 4		40½	36	41	37½	Av. 33	2	4	39	36¾	39½	36¾
Do. Western . ..	Av. £41 : 6 : 10		63¾	60½	66	64½	Av. 41	6	10	64	60½	65	64
York & N. Midland	£50	£50	94	90	95	91	50	0	0	86½	83½	87½	84
Boulogne & Amiens	20	18	15½	13⅞	15¾	14½	18	0	0	14½	13½	16¾	16¾
Northern of France	20	8	13¾	10⅛	13⅞	12	8	0	0	13	12½	13½	12⅞
Orleans & Bordeaux	20	6	8½	6¾	8¾	7	6	0	0	—	6½	7¾	6½
Paris and Rouen ..	20	20	36	35	36¼	—	20	0	0	34¾	33¾	35	—

The state of business at the close of March most forcibly denoted the approach of pressure. The weekly accounts of the Bank of England had for some weeks been regarded with extreme anxiety. It was seen that the export of bullion abroad was operating adversely, and the conduct of the Bank directors was animadverted upon, for not adopting measures sufficiently vigorous to counteract the evil consequences, which, it was predicted, must result from the drain.† From January up to this

* Exchequer-bills now carried 2d. interest per *diem*.

† Mr. S. J. Loyd in his evidence before the Commons' Committee on Commercial

time repeated admonitions had been given to the public, not to trust the Bank's rate of interest as indicative of the real value of money, but to look to the state of its accounts, and so prepare for difficulties, the advent of which was at hand.

The principal demand was for gold to send to America, in payment for corn and cotton. Besides this source of abstraction, the instalments on the loan were becoming due, and the railway calls for April amounted to £4,314,000, of which not more than £100,000 were for foreign lines. The Funds, already fluctuating, further declined; Exchequer Bills, although raised to 2d. per day interest, from par went to a discount; and the shares of the most favourite undertakings suffered severely from forced sales. The *Times* and The *Economist* were again loud in their warnings, and emphatic in their denunciation of the feeble course of action followed by the Bank.

The *Economist*, on the 3d of April, said—" It is impossible to look at the Bank accounts, from week to week, to observe a uniform and rapid current in one direction, to see the bullion, and with it the reserve of notes, rapidly sinking, while an eager demand exists for discounts and advances, as is best shown by the weekly increase of securities, and to observe the value of the public funds, and of stocks of all kinds rapidly falling, with-

---

Distress, says—" It seems to me to be a matter of the clearest inference, that but for the positive provisions of the Act, the course pursued by the Bank from January to April would have been continued until the bullion was all but exhausted.—The fact is this, that from the beginning of the year 1847 up to April they went on this system, viz., of continually increasing the amount of their securities and paying for them by a continual drain on the Bank reserve, which led to a continual export of the same amount of gold, and they pursued that course till they had reduced the reserve to that point at which it became the subject of general remark and alarm. The Bank then suddenly paused; declared that it could do no more for the public, but must now take care of itself; and it was that understanding pervading the public mind that produced the temporary panic of April."

In answer to the question " Did they not take steps for the purpose of checking the reduction of bullion, by raising the rate of interest, twice in January and once in the beginning of April?" Mr. Loyd says—" They did take a step in the right direction, but the feebleness of that step was quite puerile, as compared with the magnitude of the evil which they had to deal with."

out feeling an increasing apprehension that a period of considerable pressure is not far distant: of this, however, we should be much less apprehensive, did we only see the Bank of England pursuing that only course which, while it could not avert a difficulty, would at least materially modify it when it arrived. We must confess the policy of the Bank is entirely beyond our comprehension, to permit so rapid a decline in its means, without using any measures to check it, or avert the threatening difficulties. It was on the 21st of January that the rise took place in the rate of discounts to 4 per cent. Since that time, up to the present week no steps, except the sale of about £767,247 of securities, seems to have been taken by the directors for their own safety. Let us compare the changes which, during that period, have taken place in those items of the Bank account, which most particularly indicate its condition, viz.; the private deposits, the securities, the bullion, and the reserve. The comparison of the accounts published on the 22d January and those of the present week is as follows:—

	January 22.	This week.	Increase.	Decrease.
Private deposits..........	£10,339,726	£9,403,132	———	£936,594
Government securities in Banking department ..	12,757,326	11,990,079	———	767,247
Other securities on Bills of Exchange, &c.	14,450,711	17,824,355	£3,373,644	———
Bullion	13,948,681	11,015,583	———	2,933,098
Reserve	6,545,965	4,876,015	———	1,669,950

"It would be difficult to point to any period of the same length, when such decided changes took place in the situation of the Bank, without some greater effort being used to check them; for beyond the sales of £767,247 of Government securities, literally no effort had been used whatever. Yet during that period, while the private deposits have fallen £936,594—while the bullion has diminished £2,933,098—while the reserved has sunk £1,669,950—the amount of bills under discount has increased by no less than £3,373,644—nor is this all; the shipments of bullion during the present week, by the Sarah Sands, and Cambria alone, will not be less than £800,000, which will in the next week's accounts, reduce the bullion to little above £10,200,000, and the reserve to £4,000,000; and the payments of dividends next week will act further upon the bullion, but more particularly upon the reserve of notes in the hands of the Bank, and in a two-fold way—first, by increasing the notes in circulation, and secondly, by decreasing the amount of bullion, if any is withdrawn from the issue department for that purpose. * * * * * The great facility afforded in discounting bills at so low a rate as 4 per cent, in the present state of the market, has added to the facility of exporting gold; for especially that which has been sent to the United States, has been shipped chiefly as a speculation for a profit in a return exchange, but for which bills were first discounted, and the rate at which that operation could be done, must ever form one of the elements of the calculation of profit. We cannot but feel that it would have been wise had the Bank raised the rate of discount to 5 per cent, for some weeks since. And we trust, for the sake of the permanent interests of the community, and to prevent a severe crisis, that immediate steps will be taken to check the present downward course of the Bank, by raising the rate of discounts, and by a further sale of securities."

The opinion entertained of the temporizing nature of the measures pursued by the court, who instead of at once meeting the emergency by an advance in the rate of discount, created increased excitement and distrust, by refusing to negociate more than a limited amount of paper—particularly in cases where it was suspected that such paper was connected with corn speculations or shipments of specie to America, at length induced a change in the feeling of the majority of the directors and constrained by increasing apprehension, as the period for the payment of the dividends was near, notice was on the 15th of April given, that the Bank's rate would, after that date, be 5 per cent. Nor was this the full extent of the advance. That quotation it was found, when paper was presented, merely applied to such as had about a week or so to run. For bills, the period of maturity for which was further advanced, higher terms were exacted; and accommodation was also curtailed by a peremptory demand for the repayment of the general quarterly advances, the Bank at the same time declining to renew facilities of the kind.

Under the operation of this restrictive policy, which although it occasioned much distress was perfectly justified by the current of circumstances, the Bank's accounts exhibited considerable change; and the item of Government securities, was, "by the united action of the repayment of loans, and the reduction of discounts, reduced in one week nearly £3,000,000." Energetic, however, as had been the endeavours of the Bank administration to retrieve their position, the reserve in the banking department in the meanwhile touched the low margin of £2,558,000, and this fact being noticed through the weekly publication of the Bank accounts, it exerted an unfavourable influence in commercial circles, and aggravated in a considerable degree public alarm.

"The effect of this severe contraction of accommodation," says an acknowledged writer,* "was to paralyze nearly all transactions on credit throughout the country. No merchant, or manufacturer, however well stocked his portfolio might be with the most solid bills, could be sure of their being available to meet his immediate engagements, unless at most exhorbitant rates of discounts. To apply the term "panic" to the state of things as it existed during the last three weeks of April, and the first four days of May, would convey a very inadequate idea of the suffering of that period, seeing how indiscriminately that expression, as also the term crisis has been applied to comparatively slight cases of pressure.†"

---

* Tooke's History of Prices, 1839 to 1847.

† A diversity of opinion appears to prevail on the question whether the state of affairs in April, when the Bank's restrictive measures were in full force, could really be called "a panic." The evidence before the Committee on Commercial Distress does not altogether support the assertion. Mr. Morris, the Governor of the Bank distinctly described the state of affairs in April as "a pressure" and not as "a panic." Mr. S. J. Loyd considered that "the panic feeling was exaggerated." Mr. Samuel Gurney did not clearly describe the pressure of April as a period of panic. Mr. Charles Turner, of Liverpool, said "there was a pressure in April, but by no means a panic." Other witnesses expressed somewhat similar views. Mr. Joshua Bates, in his evidence, says:—"The panic of April, I conceive, was brought on by the Bank being

At the close of April, the policy adopted by the Bank Court brought about a beneficial alteration. Such, however, had been the alarm, from the posture of credit *ad interim*, that the working of the Bank Act was made a case of special appeal to the ministry, and a deputation waited on them representing the state of distress requesting an increased issue of notes on securities other than specie, while the Bank itself was besieged with applications from mercantile houses for assistance, with which for the instant, it was utterly impossible the directors could comply. It had also been found impracticable to obtain discounts for long dated paper, unless the most exhorbitant charges were sanctioned, notwithstanding the securities offered were unquestionable and emanated from the best firms.

Between the 25th and 28th of April confidence in a slight degree revived. The Bank was then discounting more freely; and the important news was announced that the Emperor of Russia had issued a Ukase "ordering an investment of about four millions and a half sterling in home and foreign securities." Under the impression that a large amount of the money would find employment in Consols, as ultimately was the case, this circumstance, coupled with the greater disposition of the Bank to grant facilities for accommodation, tended to abate the pressure;* and as the month of May progressed there was a sensible amelioration,

---

called upon to advance heavily on deficiency bills; the Bank authorities could have done this without producing a panic, but for the necessity of publication, which would have shown the reserve of notes to be almost nothing; that is my view of it. I cannot say that I am correct; but it is believed that their loans would have come in, in the course of two or three days; and after all, the advances to the Government do not go out of the Bank, at least not immediately; all would have gone right but for the necessity of publication; the Bank was thus compelled to borrow on the Stock-exchange, and stop suddenly its advances on securities; this gave the first general intimation to the commercial community of the altered power of the Bank, and the panic ensued."

* Mr. A. Hodgson, of Liverpool, in his evidence before the Commons' Committee on Commercial Distress, bore high testimony to the conduct of the Bank directors relative to the relaxation they made when they received the deputation from that town in April.

the Bank's weekly accounts presenting a more encouraging prospect with a steadily augmenting reserve. The directors, however, maintained or rather inclined towards an advance in discounts. Very little paper, whatever its character, was done at 5 per cent. First class bills falling due in May and June were negociated at 5½ per cent.; and similar bills falling due in the early part of July were charged at the rate of 6 per cent. Subsequently terms were altogether regulated in this manner, just as it suited the interest of the Court to deal with their customers.

In the course of May the exportation of bullion to America sensibly declined, and the Continental exchanges took a more favourable turn. Railway calls, however, continued heavy, and although not so large as in January, March, or April, the sum demanded this month was £3,400,000, the proportion due to foreign companies not exceeding £400,000.

It was announced this month by the Chancellor of the Exchequer, that the issues from that department would bear interest at the increased rate of 3d. per diem, and on this understanding the Bank consented to make advances on them. Shortly before this the Bank of Ireland raised their rate of discount to 7 per cent. Notwithstanding more general easiness prevailed in the Money-market, great difficulty was still experienced in the negociation of long dated paper. The current rate in the Discount-market was slightly in advance of the Bank price, and stood at 6 per cent, for bills having but a few weeks to run. The East India Company, also, increased the interest on their bonds from 3½ to 4½ per cent. per annum.

May was the month in which the Corn-market reached its highest price, sales having been effected in Mark-lane at 115s. per quarter.* The close of the month brought a fall, promoted by the fineness of the weather, and the expectation of a good harvest.

---

* At two or three country markets a more advanced quotation was given. At Romford 120s. and 121s. per quarter was paid. Mr. Tooke says a transaction took place at Uxbridge, in which 124s. was returned as the price.

Contrasting the prices of public securities in April and May, the fluctuations appear to have been adverse in the earlier month. Then Consols and Shares experienced a general decline. May, however, brought a decided change. The pressure, crisis, or panic, whichever term may seem most suited to the state of things at that period, having abated, the reaction in Government securities was considerable, and railway shares also supported a better and readier market.

GOVERNMENT SECURITIES.

	APRIL, 1847.				MAY, 1847.			
	Price on the 1st.	Lowest Price.	Highest Price.	Price on the 31st.	Price on the 1st.	Lowest Price.	Highest Price.	Price on the 31st.
Consols, Money	88¼	85⅝	88⅜	87	87⅝	86	88¾	88⅝
Do. Account....	88¼	86	88⅝	87¼	87¾	86½	99⅛	89⅛
Exchequer Bills, 2d..	par.	10/dis.	4/pm.	5/dis.	5/dis.	11/dis.	6/pm.	3/pm.

RAILWAY SECURITIES.

	APRIL, 1847.						MAY, 1847.				
	Amount per Share.	Amount Paid.	Price on the 1st.	Lowest Price	Highest Price	Price on the 31st.	Amount Paid.	Price on the 1st.	Lowest Price	Highest Price	Price on the 31st.
	£.	£.					£. s. d.				
Brighton	Stock	£50.	52¼	50	52½	51¼	50 0 0	51	50½	50¼	53¾
Caledonian	50	30	26⅛	21	26¼	24	30 0 0	24¼	23¼	29¾	29½
Eastern Counties ..	20	20	19¼	17¾	19¾	18¾	20 0 0	19	18½	20⅛	19¾
Edinb. and Glasgow	50	50	71	69	72	69½	50 0 0	69½	67	70	68½
Great Western	100	85	116	112	117	113¼	85 0 0	113¾	107	118	116
Hull and Selby	50	50	102½	102	103½	102¾	50 0 0	102¾	102	103½	103½
London & N. Westn.	Stock.		176	169	177	171¾	Stock.	173	168	180	178
Manchester & Leeds	100	82	—	99	104½	101	82 0 0	100¼	98	106	104
Midland Counties..	Stock.		115¼	112	116	114½	Stock.	115¾	112½	121	119½
South Eastern	Av. £33 : 2 : 4		36¾	34½	37	36½	Av. 33 : 2 : 4	36½	35	37¼	37
Do. Western	Av. £41 : 6 : 10		64	61½	65	62¾	Av. 41 : 6 : 10	62¾	59½	68	66½
York & N. Midland	£50	£50	84	80¼	84	82¼	50 0 0	82¼	81½	85	84½
Boulogne & Amiens	20	20	16¾	16½	17	16½	20 0 0	16½	15¾	16½	16¼
Northern of France	20	8	12⅞	12¼	13⅜	12½	8 0 0	12½	10¾	12⅞	12
Orleans & Bordeaux	20	6	6½	5⅞	6⅝	6½	6 0 0	6½	5¾	6½	6¼
Paris and Rouen ..	20	20	—	35	37	36¼	20 0 0	36¼	35	37	37

In June the railway calls amounted to nearly the same sum as in the previous month, being £3,200,000 of which £750,000 was requested in aid of foreign lines. The shipment of gold to America had, however, at this period almost entirely ceased.* The prices of grain were now rapidly receding, the reaction being facilitated by the prospect of abundant supplies from America, together with a continuance of good harvest weather at home; the Bank accounts were also steadily improving, the reserve at the end of the month having reached £5,600,000, and the stock of bullion being upwards of £10,000,000.

The Money-market remaining for the moment in a comparatively easy condition, and payments on the Irish loan, under the terms of discount eventually sanctioned by Government, having come in freely, there was less apprehension observable among merchants, the Chancellor of the Exchequer himself speaking favourably of the future.

With July commenced another drain of specie to America. There were also the railway calls (£4,300,000 English, and £1,000,000 foreign) in gross, £5,300,000; and another instalment on the Irish loan. These demands, with the repayment of advances to the Bank, granted as usual during the six weeks prior to the discharge of the dividends, again created a scarcity of money, and a sensible increase of difficulty was felt. Between the 26th of June and the 31st of July, such had been the change in the appearance of affairs, that the stock of bullion in the Bank

* Statement of the quantity of Gold exported to the United States, between the 30th April and 31st October, 1847, from the Port of Liverpool.

STEAMER.	£	s.	d.
4 May	148,998	16	4
19 ,,	186,646	12	8
4 June	20,368	17	0
19 ,,	16,814	9	6
4 July	55,852	17	4
20 ,,	18,446	8	6
4 August	71,366	17	11
19 ,,	41,109	15	0
4 September	15,302	13	10
19 ,,	6,761	0	0
5 October	4,438	0	0
19 ,,	6,827	0	0
Total	£592,933	8	1

By sailing packets and other vessels the shipments had almost ceased prior to the 30th April; the whole amount they took in the same period being under £20,000.—*Mr. J. Bates' evidence before Commons' Committee on Commercial Distress.*

had declined to £9,200,000, and the reserve to £3,700,000. Grain suffered a further considerable fall this month; and the Irish and Liverpool markets were between the 28th and 31st in a state of panic. The speculation in Indian corn had exploded, and prices were rapidly descending.

Before proceeding to the consideration of the events in August, when the first series of corn failures occurred in London, it may be as well to state that in the previous seven months few stoppages, either metropolitan or provincial, were announced. The only suspensions worth mentioning were the North of England Joint Stock Banking Company (March); Cattley and Stephenson, Russia merchants, London, (June); Sewell & Co., sugar trade, London, (June); Messrs. Claytons, bankers, Preston, (July); R. Mutrie & Co., London and Glasgow, merchants, (July.)

Looking at the figures furnished in the annexed table, the hopeful prospect held out by the Chancellor of the Exchequer of the future condition of the Money-market, but which unfortunately was never realized, seems to have encouraged, towards the end of June and the beginning of July, a stimulus to business in shares.* As the grounds on which it was presumed that brighter days were in store did not prove tenable the market was not long maintained, and hence at the close of July prices once more exhibited a confirmed depreciation.

GOVERNMENT SECURITIES.

	JUNE, 1847.				JULY, 1847.			
	Price on the 1st.	Lowest Price.	Highest Price.	Price on the 30th.	Price on the 1st.	Lowest Price.	Highest Price.	Price on the 31st.
Consols, Money	88⅛	87½	88¾	Shut.	Shut.	88 ex. d.	89¼	88⅝
Do. Account	88⅝	87½	89⅜	89¼	89⅛ ex.d.	88	89½	89
Exchequer Bills, 2d..	3/pm.	1/pm.	12/pm.	10/pm.	†10/pm.	6/pm.	15/pm.	9/pm.

† In July Exchequer Bills ranked at 3d. *per diem.*

* "It will be remembered, that when, in May last, the attention of the Chancellor of the Exchequer was called to the then impending crisis, he said, "I believe the panic has arisen more from groundless fear and distrust than any other cause; for trade, generally, was never in a sounder or more healthy state, whilst the capital of the country, instead of, as in 1825 and 1837, being sunk in foreign countries, and in profitless speculations, is being wisely and usefully employed at home in the construction of railways; the which cannot but be regarded, as a most gratifying and

RAILWAY SECURITIES.

	JUNE, 1847.						JULY, 1847.				
	Amount per Share.	Amount Paid.	Price on the 1st.	Lowest Price	Highest Price	Price on the 30th.	Amount Paid.	Price on the 1st.	Lowest Price	Highest Price	Price on the 31st.
	£	£					£. s. d.				
Brighton	Stock.	50	53¾	52¾	56⅝	56	50 0 0	56	53¾	56½	54¼
Caledonian	50	35	29½	29	30⅝	29¾	35 0 0	29⅞	28⅝	34	13¾
Eastern Counties ..	20	20	19¾	19⅜	21¼	21⅛	20 0 0	21⅛	19⅝	21¼	19¾
Edinb. & Glasgow..	50	50	68½	68	69½	68¾	50 0 0	68¾	67½	69	—
Great Western	100	85	115	112½	123	122	85 0 0	122	112	123	114
Hull and Selby	50	50	103½	103	106	106	50 0 0	106	104¼	106	—
London & N. Westn.	Stock.		178	173½	186	183½	Stock.	183½	174	185	175
Manchester & Leeds	100	82	104	101	106	103¾	82 0 0	103¾	100	104¼	100
Midland	Stock.		119½	117	132	131	Stock.	131	123½	132	125½
South Eastern	Av. £33 : 2 : 4		37	36	38	37¾	Av. 33 : 2 : 4	37¾	35½	38	35⅝
Do. Western	Av. £41 : 6 : 10		66½	64½	68	67½	Av. 41 : 6 : 10	67½	66½	70	67
York & N. Midland	£50	£50	84½	84	88¾	88¼	50 0 0	88¼	84	90	85
Boulogne & Amiens	20	20	16¼	15⅞	16½	16½	20 0 0	16⅛	13⅝	16⅛	14¼
Northern of France	20	8	12⅛	10⅜	12¼	10¾	8 0 0	10⅝	10⅜	12⅞	12⅛
Orleans & Bordeaux	20	6	6¼	6	6⅜	6¼	6 0 0	6¼	5	6¼	—
Paris and Rouen ..	20	20	37	37	38½	—	20 0 0	—	37¾	38½	37¾

The great decline occurring in the prices of Corn, and which had now been continuous since May, produced a feeling of considerable distrust for the position of those engaged in the trade, especially for many who were known to have operated more with the view to speculative than legitimate profit. In May, the highest point of the average price of wheat was 105s. 2d.; and in August it had descended to as low as 64s.* At this latter date, the provincial markets were altogether paralyzed.

The Governor and Deputy-Governor of the Bank, on Monday the 2d of August, without waiting for the sanction of the Court, again raised the rate of interest to 5 per cent. on one month's bills, 5½ per cent. on two months' bills, and 6 per cent. on bills above that date. Between this interval and Thursday the 5th, when the alteration was confirmed, the panic commenced, and corn failures were announced.†

encouraging fact, and one which strengthens my conviction that the groundless panic now prevailing will be of short duration;—in fact," said he, "I believe the worst is now past."—*Banker's Magazine.*

* *Vide* Tables of prices—Wheat.

† The panic began by the failures in the corn trade. Large arrivals of grain from the continent of Europe and from America, coupled with the prospect of an early

The first important suspension was that of Sampson, Langdale, & Co., of Stockton-on-Tees. The downfall of this firm at once compromised parties in London, and Charles Douglas and Son, were reported to be incapable of meeting their engagements. Their failure was made public on the 6th. Other provincial stoppages were mentioned. Between the 6th and 9th of the month no London firms suspended. The respite however was but a short one, for then successively followed, Lesley Alexander & Co.;* Coventry and Sheppard; King, Melvil, & Co.; and Giles, Son, & Co.,† all engaged in the Corn trade, and all figuring for large amounts. The failure of Lesley Alexander & Co. was the subject of earnest discussion.‡ Their fate was regarded as most distinctly evincing the consequences of ill-advised and precipitate speculation, during a period when character ought to have restrained the partners from entering into such objectionable transactions.

The next large London corn-house that failed was Messrs. W. R. Robinson & Co., and occupying, as the principal member of the firm did, the important post of Governor of the Bank of England, the surprise expressed was scarcely more than commensurate with the event.§ The accounts of the firm presenting a surplus, and being found fully equal to 20s. in the pound,

---

and abundant harvest, caused a sudden fall in price to about 60s., with a corresponding decline in Indian corn. The failure of most of the corn speculators followed this great reduction in price, and their failure caused the stoppage of an eminent discount broker, having a large country connexion.—*Mr. Morris's Evidence before the Committee on Commercial Distress.*

* *Vide* Statement of affairs, Appendix, page lxxii.

† *Vide* Statement of affairs, Appendix, page lxxv.

‡ *Vide* Statement of affairs, Appendix, page lxxii. The immediate granting of the bankrupts' certificate by Mr. Commissioner Goulburn, has been severely commented on as a piece of judicial leniency seldom witnessed in that Commissioner's Court.

§ Mr. W. R. Robinson retired from the Bank Court immediately his failure became public. He was then succeeded, on an election, by Mr. Morris, and Mr. Prescott was appointed to fill the Deputy Chair previously occupied by Mr. Morris. It was noticed as a curious fact, that no less than six parties during the last eighteen years, who have gone through the rotation of this office have failed.

a discovery so agreeable,* exerted some influence upon the creditors. As far however as public feeling was concerned, no mitigation of the evil was effected, and consternation became more than ever widely spread.

Following this unfortunate catastrophe, came the difficulties of Messrs. Castellain, Sons, & Co., merchants, and their prospects were hardly ascertained,† before Messrs. W. & J. Woodley, corn-factors, were announced to have suspended.‡ After these were reported, Fraser, Neilson, & Co., in the West India trade, and a small house in the Mauritius trade. Several other provincial failures were declared, which it is only necessary to enumerate in the month's list here appended.

August.	C. Douglas and Son,	London,	Corn Trade.
,,	Lesley Alexander & Co.,	London,	Corn Trade.
,,	Coventry and Sheppard,	London,	Corn Trade.
,,	King, Melvil, & Co.,	London,	Corn Trade.
,,	W. R. Robinson & Co.,	London,	Corn Trade.
,,	Castellain, Sons, & Co.,	London,	Merchants.
,,	W. & J. Woodley,	London,	Corn Trade.
,,	E. Robinson (deceased),	London,	Mauritius Trade.
,,	Fraser, Neilson, & Co.,	London,	West India Trade.
,,	Giles, Son, & Co.,	London,	Corn Trade.
,,	Nevins and Allen,	London,	Corn Trade.
,,	H. & G. Gregg,	Liverpool,	Corn Trade.
,,	Lyon and Finney,	Liverpool,	General Merchants.
,,	S. & J. O'Neal,	Liverpool,	Corn Trade.
,,	Perrin and Sons,	Liverpool,	Corn Trade.
,,	W. Rowett & Co.,	Liverpool,	Merchants.
,,	Sampson, Langdale, & Co.,	Stockton-on-Tees,	Corn Trade.
,,	A. Dickson & Co.,	Belfast,	Corn Trade.
	The principal foreign failures were :—		
,,	Fraser & Co.,	Antwerp,	Merchants.
,,	Cropp and Marchand,	Hamburg,	Merchants.

The state of excitement occasioned by these disasters may be easily imagined. Railway calls were lighter, amounting barely to £2,280,000—£2,220,000 being for English, the remainder for foreign lines. Money nevertheless was in full demand. Out of doors, two and three months' paper could not be negociated under 7 and 8 per cent., according to the character of the names upon it.

---

* *Vide* Statement of affairs, Appendix, page lxxiv.

† *Vide* Statement of affairs, Appendix, page lvi.

‡ *Vide* Statement of affairs, Appendix, page lxxvi.

Already it will be noticed, eight London corn-houses had failed, whose aggregate liabilities were reckoned as exceeding £1,500,000 sterling.

The month of August 1847, passed, and September commenced, but in the course of its career not the least diminution of pressure was experienced. On the contrary it increased, and the apprehensions entertained that the Bank would be compelled to pursue restrictive measures were so soon realized, that distrust and alarm spread through all circles; and houses, whose fair fame had never before encountered suspicion, did not long escape "the withering tongue of rumour."

The failures that had hitherto occurred, with the exception of Messrs. Castellain & Co., were principally identified with the corn trade. These had extended their ramifications through all the great cities and towns of the United Kingdom; foreign suspensions had also been reported, swelling the gross amount of liabilities, yet Lesley Alexander & Co. were still ranked as the largest and most prominently important of the failed firms.

The first great mercantile house that succumbed was Messrs. Gower, Nephews, & Co.* That event was regarded with intense anxiety. Although the perfect stability of the firm had, to persons thoroughly acquainted with the internal movement of the metropolitan Money-market, been a matter of doubt for some short time, still its affairs were not presumed to have been in such a deplorable condition as to have rendered its existence uncertain. The gains too, which the partners were known to have acquired by successful promotion of railway projects, had tended in a measure to reassure their credit even in quarters where it had been in reality questioned. But now the stern truth was disclosed; they were hopelessly insolvent. Facts extremely discouraging having transpired relative to their actual position, the public mind was more than ever excited, particularly since one of the prophecies of rumour and the Stock-exchange was said to have been fulfilled. The circumstance of Mr. A. L. Gower

* *Vide* Statement of affairs, Appendix, page xxvii.

having held a seat in the Bank direction, besides other high commercial appointments, was also found to create more than usual comment when the actual state of his affairs became known.

The Company of Copper Miners in England, in which he held the office of Governor, was immediately mentioned as being in difficulties. This for the moment was contradicted as "an unfounded assertion." Its stoppage of payment was not however long delayed, and subsequent disclosures have shown, that from a lengthened course of mismanagement an involvement in loss to an enormous extent will accrue to those who have unfortunately made it a medium of investment.

But if the failure of Messrs. Gower & Co. caused surprise, what was the consternation promoted by the suspension of Messrs. Sanderson & Co.,* bill-brokers? It is true that the announcement of the ability of the firm to pay in full, mitigated the alarm first exhibited, but then the extent of country connexion liable to be crippled by the temporary stoppage, through the curtailment of accommodation, was not without its influence, and in that way the catastrophe was productive of much mischief.

In the early part of the month the Corn trade again suffered; Booker, Sons, & Co.; Usborne and Son;† Hastie and Hutchison;‡ three London firms, were severally notified as incompetent to meet their engagements. But the Corn trade was not alone destined to be interfered with.

Rumour, in the mean time, had insiduously pointed her finger at several houses which, she avouched, would be unable to resist the strong current of the crisis now so inevitably apparent. The Stock-exchange speculators singularly enough gave credence to these shadowy predictions, and prices fluctuated in accordance with the seeming probability of their verification. Three days only elapsed from the failure of Sanderson & Co.,

---

* *Vide* Statement of affairs, Appendix, page lviii.

† *Vide* Statement of affairs, Appendix, page lxxvi.

‡ *Vide* Statement of affairs, Appendix, page lxxvii.

when Messrs. Reid, Irving, & Co.* were openly reported as a failed firm. The importance of this establishment, the high position of the partners,† and their extensive operations, created more uneasiness than ever for the state of credit.

Money was now rapidly advancing in value; general difficulty was experienced in obtaining what were previously looked upon as ordinary facilities of accomodation; and the Bank directors, who on the 2d of the month made loans at 5 per cent. until the payment of the dividends in October, were considered to have again injudiciously tampered with the market value of cash, in a period that presented such a combination of perilous circumstances.

While all this excitement was going forward in the metropolis, the chief provincial towns were also the scene of great commotion. In Scotland several heavy failures took place, Gemmell, Brothers, & Co., East India trade, and Denny & Co., Corn-trade, Glasgow, being among the number; Liverpool and Manchester sent up distressing accounts of the failures in those towns, and from most points the intelligence was of a truly desponding character.

On the 23d of the month the Bank of England made a further alteration in its rate of discount. The *minimum* was now advanced to 5½ per cent. on two months' paper and 6 per cent. on that of three months' date, the most rigid scrutiny being exercised in the selection of bills negociated. Reports continued to be circulated of failures which in the majority of cases ultimately turned out to be correct.

The next great metropolitan firm that suspended was that of Messrs. Cockerell, Larpent, & Co., engaged extensively in the East India trade.‡ This announcement was no less potential in its influence than that of the stoppage of Messrs. Reid, Irving, & Co.

---

* *Vide* Statement of affairs, Appendix, page xxi.

† Sir John Rae Reid was Governor of the Bank of England in 1839 and one of the senior Directors at the time of suspension.

‡ *Vide* Statement of affairs, Appendix, page v.

The two houses had been looked upon as extremely substantial, but now they were prostrate, it was feared, notwithstanding the most vaunted boastings of ultimately realizing twenty shillings in the pound, that creditors would have to submit to considerable losses. Sir George Larpent, one of the leading members of Cockerell, Larpent, & Co., if he had not occupied the post of Governor of the Bank, had, after representing an English borough, aspired to sit in Parliament as one of the members for the city of London, and hence his position was regarded as accompanied by very distressing circumstances.* Quickly following these suspensions, came Messrs. Bensusan & Co.,† Mogador trade; Messrs. Perkins, Schlusser, & Mullens, East India and Baltic trade;‡ Messrs. Lyall, Brothers, & Co.,§ and Messrs. Samuel Phillips & Co., both in the East India trade; ‖ each London firms of note in the various branches, and Messrs. Fry, Griffiths, & Co., Colonial brokers.¶

---

* "The inscrutable and omnipotent decree which had gone forth struck one of the Queen's kingdoms with famine, and the great efforts obliged to be made by the merchants of this country in consequence of that tremendous visitation led, in addition, no doubt, to other causes, to a commercial crisis, perhaps, of unprecedented severity. There were uprootings of commercial dynasties in England not less striking than the fall of those political houses of which we have lately heard so much. Day after day, gentlemen whom we had lived with in this house, and whom we respected and regarded, merchants of the highest European reputation, were during that crisis rudely torn, I may say, from these benches, if not with disgrace and dishonour, yet with circumstances of pitiable vicissitude seldom equalled. When Parliament met there was this commercial distress of unprecedented severity—private credit was paralyzed, trade was more than dull, it was almost dead—and there scarcely was a private individual in this kingdom, from the richest and noblest in the land down to the most humble among the middle classes, who was not smarting under the circumstances of that commercial distress, which was of a nature so severe and striking that it was one of the main causes alleged for calling the Parliament together in November.—*Mr. Disraeli's celebrated Speech delivered in the House of Commons, August 30th*, 1848.

† *Vide* Statement of affairs, Appendix, page lxxx.

‡ *Vide* Statement of affairs, Appendix, page xxxiv.

§ *Vide* Statement of affairs, Appendix, page xxix.

‖ *Vide* Statement of affairs, Appendix, page xxxv.

¶ *Vide* Statement of affairs, Appendix, page lxvi.

At the close of September, the list of failures, including some few foreign firms, presented a formidable appearance, and as accurately as they can be ascertained may be thus classified.

September.	Booker, Sons, & Co.,	London,	Corn Trade.
,,	T. Usborne and Son,	London,	Corn Trade.
,,	Hastie and Hutchison,	London,	Corn Trade.
,,	A. A. Gower, Nephews, & Co.,	London,	Mauritius Trade.
,,	Alison, Cumberlege, & Co.,	London,	South American Trade.
,,	Sanderson & Co.,	London,	Bill Brokers.
,,	Reid, Irving, & Co.,	London,	Mauritius Trade.
,,	Cockerell, Larpent, & Co.,	London,	East India Trade.
,,	Cockburn & Co.,	London,	Bankers & Army Agents.
,,	Cockburn & Co.,	London,	Wine Merchants.
,,	M. L. Bensusan & Co.,	London,	Mogador Merchants.
,,	Perkins, Schlusser, & Mullens,	London,	E. India & Baltic Trade.
,,	Fry, Griffiths, & Co.,	London,	Colonial Brokers.
,,	Lyall, Brothers, & Co.,	London,	East India Trade.
,,	Samuel Phillips & Co.,	London,	East India Trade.
,,	W. Tulloch Fraser,	London,	East India Trade.
,,	Burnell & Co.,	London,	Coal Trade.
,,	A. M'Donald & Co.,	London,	South American Trade.
,,	Shewell and Sons,	London,	Stock Exchange.
,,	W. Atherton,	Liverpool,	Merchant.
,,	Kirkpatrick & Co.,	Liverpool,	Provision Trade.
,,	Watson, Brothers, & Co.,	Liverpool,	Merchants.
,,	Wilson, Nash, & Co.,	Liverpool,	Merchants.
,,	J. A. Armstrong,	Manchester,	Merchants.
,,	Burts, Watson, & Co.,	Manchester,	Merchants.
,,	E. M. Cooper & Co.,	Manchester,	Manufacturers.
,,	F. H. Glover,	Manchester,	Merchant.
,,	Y. Guest,	Manchester,	Spinner.
,,	Stocks and Tait,	Manchester,	Bleachers.
,,	Westlake & Co.,	Southampton,	Corn Trade.
,,	D. and A. Denny,	Glasgow,	Corn Trade.
,,	Gemmel Brothers,	Glasgow,	East India Trade.
,,	Watson, M'Knight, & Co.,	Glasgow,	Merchants.
,,	M. Perston,	Glasgow,	Merchant.
,,	Gray and Roxburgh,	Greenock,	Merchants.
,,	Neilson & Co.,	Kirkland,	Spinners.
,,	Dennison & Co.,	Limerick,	Provision Trade.

The principal foreign failures were—

,,	Forbin, Janson, & Co.,	Marseilles,	Sugar Refiners.
,,	J. A. Barthlingth,	St. Petersburg,	Merchant.
,,	Custe & Co.,	Genoa,	Merchants.
,,	Excels & Co.,	Venice,	Corn Trade.
,,	Oczle & Co.,	Venice,	Mill Proprietors.
,,	A. Roux & Co.,	Paris,	Merchants.
,,	Prime, Ward, & Co.,	New York,	Merchants.

But if the month of September had been prolific in failures, the course of events in October threatened more disturbing consequences, which, although clearly prophesied at the time, were not believed to be possible, until their destructive effects were realized throughout the country.

During September twenty firms of rank had been brought to the ground, and the aggregate of their liabilities was reckoned as approaching between £9,000,000 and £10,000,000 sterling. The suspensions, however, that subsequently took place were so varied in their character, that to attempt anything like a calculation of their gross amount, would in truth be futile.

At the end of September, it was manifest that the crisis was increasing in its intensity; that the measures adopted by the Bank, instead of alleviating the pressure, further augmented it; and that such was the spreading distrust consequent upon the failures which had already occurred, that no hope of relief was apparent; besides, railway calls continued to press heavily upon the public; for September they had amounted to £4,160,000, and now in October, they were £3,760,000, the proportion for foreign lines out of this gross sum of £7,920,000 being merely £1,220,000.

The annexed tables of prices shew the course of fluctuation in Government and railway securities in August and September. Comparing the highest and lowest prices of Consols, it appears that the extreme difference was about 4½ per cent. Exchequer Bills had also violently alternated, the increased rate of interest —3d. per diem—not even maintaining them in a good position. As would have been anticipated, railway shares were exceedingly depressed, especially in the latter month.

GOVERNMENT SECURITIES.

	AUGUST, 1847.				SEPTEMBER, 1847.			
	Price on the 2d.	Lowest Price.	Highest Price.	Price on the 31st.	Price on the 1st.	Lowest Price.	Highest Price.	Price on the 30th.
Consols, Money	88¾	86¼	88⅞	87½	87¼	85¼	87⅞	85¼
Do. Account....	89	86½	89⅛	88⅛	87⅞	85½	88⅜	85⅞
Exchequer Bills, 3d..	9/pm.	5/dis.	10/pm.	5/pm.	3/pm.	par.	10/pm.	2/pm.

RAILWAY SECURITIES.

	AUGUST, 1847.						SEPTEMBER, 1847.				
	Amount per Share.	Amount Paid.	Price on the 2d.	Lowest Price	Highest Price	Price on the 31st.	Amount Paid.	Price on the 1st.	Lowest Price	Highest Price	Price on the 30th.
	£.	£.					£. s. d.				
Brighton	Stock	£50.	54¼	47¾	54¾	48¾	50 0 0	49	41¾	49¼	43¼
Caledonian	50	40	33¾	31¾	34	32¼	40 0 0	32¼	29	39	37½
Eastern Counties ..	20	20	19¾	18	20	18¼	20 0 0	18¼	16⅜	18¼	16¾
Edinb. and Glasgow	50	50	—	63	67	63	50 0 0	61	51	61	—
Great Western	100	85	114	107	116	110½	85 0 0	109¼	98	110	100
Hull and Selby	50	50	—	101	104	—	50 0 0	102½	99	102½	99
London & N. Westn.	Stock.		175	162	176	165	Stock.	166	155	167	158
Manchester & Leeds	100	85	100	92	100	95½	—	—	—	—	—
Midland Counties..	Stock.		125½	114	127	118	Stock.	118½	108½	119½	112¾
South Eastern	Av. £33 : 2 : 4		35⅝	33¾	35½	35	Av. 33 : 2 : 4	35	30½	35¼	30¾
Do. Western	Av. £41 : 6 : 10		67	59½	67½	61¼	Av. 41 : 6 : 10	61½	56¾	62	58¼
York & N. Midland	£50	£50	85	76	86	76½	50 0 0	76½	72	78	73½
Boulogne & Amiens	20	20	14¼	13¾	14¼	13⅞	20 0 0	13⅞	12⅞	14	13¼
Northern of France	20	10	12⅛	10¾	12⅜	11¼	10 0 0	10⅞	9½	11⅜	10
Orleans & Bordeaux	20	6	—	4¾	5	—	6 0 0	—	3	4¼	3⅞
Paris and Rouen ..	20	20	37¾	36	37¾	36⅞	20 0 0	36¾	33¾	37	33¾

On the 1st of October the Bank Court gave notice that the *minimum* rate of discount would be 5½ per cent. on all bills becoming due before the 14th of that month; and also intimated that no advances whatever would for the present be made upon public securities. This total revision in the terms of money accommodation granted by the great national establishment, forthwith gave birth to universal panic; the cry that railways with their calls were breaking down mercantile credit, was again raised, and with more success than previously, since it was soon seen that the companies, who could not collect sufficient funds to carry on their works, came into the market for loans without delay, almost regardless of the rate of interest so long as they secured the required aid.

In the midst of all the excitement, the weekly accounts of the Bank were consulted with the most anxious feeling. Between September the 4th and October the 2d, the reserve sank from £4,189,000 to £3,409,000. The stock of bullion, though slightly in decrease, had not suffered material alteration, having only fluctuated between £8,850,000, and £8,564,000.

Hitherto the failures had been confined to mercantile establishments. Now a more important class of institutions felt the extreme severity of the crisis. Joint-stock banks and private bankers could no longer withstand the pressure, and several were stated to be in difficulties. The Royal Bank of Liverpool, although it had received aid from the Bank of England,* the Liverpool Banking Co., the North and South Wales Bank, and the Newcastle Union Joint-stock Bank, were severally compelled to succumb in the course of a few days. Cotemporaneously with, or closely following the suspension of these four Joint-stock Banks, numerous small country bankers were declared insolvent, Mr. Knapp, of the Abingdon and Wantage Bank; Messrs. Scholes & Co., of the Oldham Bank; Messrs. Brodie & Co.; and Messrs. Brodie and King, of Salisbury and Shaftesbury, comprising the most important of them.

And whilst so disastrously affecting banking establishments in the provinces, the metropolis did not escape the ravages of the panic. In London, however, fortunately not one bank suspended its payments. The weakness of two establishments was recklessly spoken of, when the storm, which threatened for the moment to

---

* "You stated that you lent £300,000 to one Bank in Consols?"—"Yes, £300,000 to one Bank, and £100,000 to another."

"In what way did that operation take place?"—"We transferred the Consols in September or October, and in January they re-transferred them to us; we received no remuneration except the dividend which accrued upon them."

"Did they ask you for Consols, or did you offer them Consols?"—"We refused to discount bills; upon which they were anxious to have some other means of meeting their engagements, and I forget whether we offered them Consols or whether they asked for them; I think the proposal came from ourselves."

"You refused discounting, not from any doubt of their own solvency or the value of the bills which they offered?"—"They stated that they required a certain amount of assistance, and, in answer, we told them that they might have Consols to the amount of £300,000, upon the distinct understanding that it was to carry them through; I do not think they proposed taking Consols."—(Mr. Prescott.)—"The Royal Bank of Liverpool, to which the question refers, applied to us for an advance of money to meet the claims made upon them; we said that they had already had a large amount of discount, and that we were not in a condition to make a further advance of money, but that as they were hard pressed we were willing to make an advance of stock, which they might realize in the market; it was the same thing as if the Bank itself had realized the stock in order to render them assistance."—(Mr. Morris.) "It suited us better to give them Consols than Bank-notes."—*Commons' Report on Commercial Distress.*

overthrow the whole of the structure of commercial credit, was raging in all its fury, but the report was immediately contradicted, and proved in the completest sense a fabrication. But if banks did not stop, there was no arrest to mercantile suspensions. Messrs. Rougemont Brothers, Continental merchants and banking agents;* Messrs. John Thomas, Son, & Lefevre, Russia trade;† Messrs. Rickards, Little, & Co., East India trade;‡ Messrs. Barclay, Brothers, & Co., Mauritius trade;§ Messrs. Lawrence Phillips, & Sons, East India trade;‖ Messrs. Scott, Bell, & Co., East India trade;¶ and Messrs. Boyds and Thomas, East India trade,** one after another, found themselves so embarrassed as to be unable to proceed.

Allusion has before been made to the Company of Copper Miners in England. If the directors, after the resignation of their governor, Mr. A. L. Gower, in September, had anticipated that they would have been in a position to carry on their works, there was little prospect of it afterwards. Assisted readily as they had been by the Bank directors,†† Messrs. Bruce, Buxton,

---

* *Vide* Statement of affairs, Appendix, page lxxi.

† *Vide* Statement of affairs, Appendix, page lv.

‡ *Vide* Statement of affairs, Appendix, page xxxiii.

§ *Vide* Statement of affairs, Appendix, page xxv.

‖ *Vide* Statement of affairs, Appendix, page xxxvi.

¶ *Vide* Statement of affairs, Appendix, page xlv.

** *Vide* Statement of affairs, Appendix, page lv.

†† Mr. Morris, the Governor of the Bank, in his evidence before the Commons' Committee on Commercial Distress, giving a statement of the "extraordinary aid" afforded by the Bank of England to different establishments, between the 15th of September and 15th of November, 1847, for the purpose of preventing their stopping payment, thus alludes to the Copper Mining Company. "1. The Bank of England being applied to by a very large firm in London, who had at that time liabilities to the extent of several millions sterling, advanced £150,000 on the security of debentures to that amount of the Governor and Company of Copper Miners in England, and thereby prevented them from stopping payment; it was distinctly understood that the operation was for that purpose. 2. The Bank advanced £50,000 to a country banker on the security of real property. 3. On the urgent representations of several parties of the first importance in the City of London, the Bank advanced £120,000 to the Governor and Company of the Copper Miners, on the guarantee of approved names, taking at the same time a mortgage on the Company's property for £270,000 to cover this sum, and the amount of £150,000 debentures before advanced upon; it

& Co., bill-brokers, supporting and negociating the advances, they perhaps possessed confidence, and thought doubtlessly that they could stem the torrent, strong as it was; but when Messrs. Bruce, Buxton, & Co., themselves were surrounded by difficulties, which could no longer be staved off, then all confidence vanished, and the company, as well as their agents, ranked in the category of failed firms. No positive public announcement of these " suspensions" was made at the time, though from circumstances which have since transpired, the fact is placed beyond all dispute.

One element of concern that presented itself to many minds when the estates of the suspended houses underwent examination, was their extreme indebtedness and the generally disheartening spectacle exhibited by their assets. If not really exaggerated,

---

was stated that the stoppage of this company would have thrown 10,000 people out of employment. 4. The Bank advanced £300,000 to the Royal Bank of Liverpool, on the security of bills of exchange, over and above their usual discounts to this bank; this advance unfortunately proved inadequate, and the Royal Bank, having no more security to offer, stopped payment. 5. The Bank assisted another joint-stock bank in the country with £100,000, on the security of bills of exchange, over and above usual discounts. 6. The Bank advanced £130,000 on real property to a large mercantile house in London. 7. The Bank advanced £50,000 to another mercantile house on the guarantee of approved names. 8. The Bank advanced £50,000 to a joint-stock issuing bank on bills of exchange, and agreed to open a discount account with the said bank, on condition that it should withdraw its issues, but the joint-stock bank stopped payment before the arrangement could be completed. 9. The Bank advanced £15,000 on real property to a large establishment in London. 10. The Bank assisted, and prevented from failing, a large establishment in London, by forbearing to enforce payment of upwards of £100,000 of their acceptances, and engaging to give further aid if required. 11. The Bank assisted a very lage joint-stock bank in the country with advances on loans on bills of exchange to the extent of about £800,000 over and above usual discounts. 12. The Bank advanced £100,000 to a country banker on real property. 13. The Bank advanced a joint-stock bank in the country £200,000 on the security of local bills, besides discounting £60,000 of London bills. 14. The Bank assisted another joint-stock bank in the country with an advance of £100,000 on local and London bills. 15. The Bank advanced £100,000 to a large mercantile house in London, on approved personal security. 16. The Bank assisted a large house at Manchester to resume payment by an advance of £40,000 on approved personal security. 17. The Bank advanced £30,000 to a country bank on real property. 18. The Bank assisted many other houses both in town and country, by advances of smaller sums on securities, not admitted by the Bank under

the balance sheets which were laid before the meetings of creditors, were at least so constructed as to give the best possible appearance to affairs, and as it was endeavoured to be shewn that by patient care and watchfulness many of the firms would satisfy claims in full, the process of inspectorship was with extraordinary unanimity resolved upon as the most advantageous and inexpensive mode of liquidation. But although these sanguine expectations were held out, it was then in several instances perceived that they could never be realized, since the course of trading pursued by the most eminent of the East India houses had so entangled them through locking up their capital by ad-

---

ordinary circumstances; nor did the Bank, during the period in question, reject at their London establishment any one bill offered for discount, except on the ground of insufficient security." As fully illustrating the amount of such assistance, Mr. Morris presented the annexed statement:—

From 15th September to 25th October, 1847, the Bank advanced—

		£
(1.)	At 5, 5½, 6, 6¼, 6½, 7, 7½, 8, and 8½ per cent.	890,000
	And on their account,	
(2.)	On mortgage at 5 per cent.	90,000
(3.)	On the security of real property at 5 % (part of £50,000)	15,000
(4.)	A loan of Consols	300,000
(5.)	A loan of Consols	100,000
(6.)	At 5 per cent. on real property	100,000
(7.)	" " "	50,000
(8.)	At 8 per cent.	50,000
(9.)	At 5 per cent. on security of real property	15,000
(10.)	At 9 per cent.	100,000
(11.)	At 6, 6½, 7, 7½, 8, 8½, and 9 %	545,000
		£2,255,000

From the 26th October to 16th November, 1847, the Bank made further advances—

		£
(1.)	At 8 and 8½ per cent.	92,000
(3.)	At 5 %, on mortgage	30,000
(2.)	At 5 %, on mortgage	15,000
(6.)	At 5 %, on real property	30,000
(11.)	At 8½ and 9 per cent.	223,000
(12.)	At 8 %	100,000
(13.)	At 8½ and 9 per cent.	260,000
(14.)	At 1½ per cent.	100,000
(15.)	At 8½ per cent.	30,000
(16.)	At 9 %	46,000
(17.)	At 5 %, on mortgage	30,000
		£950,000

First Period	£2,255,000
Second ditto	950,000
Total	£3,205,000

vances on Sugar, Indigo, and other estates, and in credit accommodation with agents, branch houses, &c., as to have incurred liabilities beyond all prudent bounds, and from which they could not hope to relieve themselves without a general insolvency on the part of all concerned. Nor was the evil alone confined to the system of credit pursued between the principal firms and their agents, but it also extended to the facilities with which it enabled them to raise funds to keep their paper afloat, and so long as money continued easy at low rates of interest, there was not much difficulty experienced in maintaining the deception.*

---

* The Chancellor of the Exchequer, alluding to the course of the East India trade, said, in his speech of 30th November, 1847,—" He had ascertained the system on which the trade of India had been carried on. It appeared to be carried on less with a view to profit and loss than as a mode of raising money, by the creation of bills. Persons were drawn upon at nine or ten months, and the bills sent home to be discounted by the produce-broker and then by the bankers, and these practices, though not new, had been carried on to a great extent, and to them no small portion of the discredit attached to that trade was owing. He admitted that trade must be carried on partly by capital and partly on credit, but there must be a due proportion of capital to support the superstructure of credit which was built upon it. And when persons overstepped those proper limits, he was afraid they must pay the penalty of their own acts, nor did he believe that any issue of notes—of paper which was not capital—could prevent or avert such consequences. * * * * * * He would only say, that not only had he (the Chancellor of the Exchequer) been appalled by circumstances which had been brought under his knowledge in the last six months, but so also had persons who had been long accustomed to trade when they witnessed the reckless character of that system. It would be improper in him to do more than allude to this in general words, and he hoped the house would believe that he did not state it without a knowledge which justified him in doing so."

Sir Robert Peel also said, on the 3d December, 1847,—" It is, no doubt, painful to refer to individual houses; but I have the less reluctance in doing it, when I have seen published, on the highest authority, comparisons of their liabilities with their assets. And I hesitate not to say, that if the commerce of the country is conducted on such principles, in vain may you look to any legislative regulations, or any regulation but discretion, to prevent the evils which must flow from such a reckless course of conducting commercial affairs. Sir, when I see amongst the mass of houses (I will not mention names, though they have been published in the public papers,) when I see one whose liabilities are to the extent of £50,000, and its assets to the extent of £3,000.* I say, if that is the practice of your commerce, don't complain of the

* Sir Robert here doubtless alluded to Messrs. Bensusan & Co.—*Vide* Balance-sheet filed in the Court of Bankruptcy, October 24th, 1848. Appendix, page lxxx.

That imprudent speculations, as well as a vicious mode of business, had crippled many of the largest firms previous to the operation of the Bank Act, at whose door all the mischief was laid, was a matter very generally believed, and this was clearly established when statements were probed, and no further opportunity was left for concealment.*

Act of 1844. Is it not monstrous that the standard of this country should be endangered, in order to cover or facilitate such transactions as these? What security can I give to a bank that has £600,000 of paid-up capital, and lends £500,000 of that capital to one house?† What is it to me that the shareholders repose discretion and confidence in their directors? Why do they not take an active part in the conduct of their own affairs? They fail; and then, like this gentleman whose liabilities are to the extent of £50,000, and his assets £3,000, they exclaim—'This infernal Act of 1844, this detestable restriction Act of Peel's, is the cause of all our difficulties.' (Cheers and laughter.) 'We want money, and the Act of 1844 prevents our getting it.' To such persons I would say—thank the Act of 1844 that your difficulties are not aggravated. Just consider what would have been the state of affairs if 'Northern and Central Banks,' and 'Manchester Banks,' and 'Norfolk and Norwich Banks,' had been entitled to foster all these speculations by an unlimited issue of paper."

* Mr. C. Turner, of Liverpool, in his evidence before the Commons' Committee on Commercial Distress, says:—"As regards the over-trading, there has, no doubt, been a vast deal of over-trading; a matter which has tended still further to embarrass matters. Of course we are all aware of the events which have taken place as regards the Mauritius trade, and other trades of that kind. The brokers have been in the habit, we all know now pretty well, not only of advancing upon goods after their arrival, to meet the bills drawn against those goods, which is perfectly legitimate, and upon the bills of lading, which, to a certain extent might also be done; but beyond that, they have done what is perfectly illegitimate; they have advanced upon the produce before it was shipped, in some cases before it was manufactured. Now, to speak of my own individual case: I had bought bills in Calcutta to the extent of six or seven thousand pounds in one particular instance; the proceeds of the bills went down to the Mauritius, to help in the growth of sugar; those bills came to England, and above half of them were protested; for when the shipments of sugar came forward, instead of being held to pay those bills, it had been mortgaged to third parties to pay previous engagements before it was shipped, in fact, almost before it was boiled. Now, nothing can be more unsound and worse than such a state of things, and which has gone on to a considerable extent." Again, the same witness says in answer to the question—"You do not attribute the failures of the commercial houses that have taken place this year to the recent speculations of those houses?—"Most of them have their origin at a much older date than that, and some of them I believe

† The amount of the Royal Bank of Liverpool's advances to Barton, Irlam, and Higginson.

When these disclosures were therefore made, and the complete incapacity of the mercantile interest to struggle through their difficulties was rendered apparent "confusion became worse confounded" and no hope and no assistance being looked for from the Bank, utter despair prevailed in all quarters.

The "week of terror"* previous to the issue of the Government letter will long linger in the remembrance of those who witnessed its career. Deputations from Liverpool and most of the manufacturing districts waited on Lord John Russell and Sir C. Wood as the heads of the Ministry. The Liverpool memorialists said they "did not require any permanent measure of assistance. All they asked was a temporary measure of relief to enable them to meet what they hoped and believed to be only a temporary peril." Sympathy was expressed at the severity of the distress under which the commercial classes laboured, but not the least prospect was held out "that the Government could interefere in such a way as to allay the public apprehension and relieve individuals from pressure."

Calculated as the extent of the pressure was to excite universal alarm, and the Stock markets having become wholly prostrate from the large sales of Consols and Exchequer Bills effected to supply means for urgent necessities, the most unfounded statements were circulated respecting the position of houses of undoubted wealth. Consols falling to 78¾, and Exchequer Bills scarcely finding takers at 37s. discount, while commanding interest at the rate of 3d. per diem, and failures continuing throughout the United Kingdom were causes sufficiently co-operative, without the aid of exaggeration to lead the public into the depths of despondency, and to regard their condition as one which seemed removed beyond all remedy or palliation.

---

to have been insolvent for a long period. The largest houses that have failed may have been insolvent the last year or two, but not longer; one or two of them may have been insolvent for the last three or four years.

* *Vide* Speech of Mr. Alderman Salomons, at the March (1848) meeting of the London and Westminster Bank, when he announced a loss of £20,000 on securities sold by that establishment during the panic period.

The intensity of the alarm; the measures which London and Country bankers resorted to in order to strengthen their own resources;* and the tremendous decline which was daily quoted in all kinds of produce† marked in rugged, but intelligible lines, the fearful precipitancy of the retrograde movement. There was no relief, and no prospect of it, and hence terribly wild rang the panic cry. Previous commercial revulsions were considered by many not at all analogous to the course of ruin in operation, and though this opinion, freely expressed at the time, may have since received some qualification, the vicissitudes experienced will in after ages, when calmly considered, afford data for comparison free from prejudices, which at present surround them.‡

---

* Mr. Samuel Gurney says, in his evidence before the Parliamentary enquiry into Commercial Distress, " The failures began to take place in August. The number of failures in each week was increased, and was at last followed by a considerable panic. The effect of that panic was to cause very general distrust, and a gradual running down of the reserved fund of the Bank as well as of the bullion. After a little time people began to think, under the influence of this panic, how are we to get circulating medium? And the wealthy and more powerful took care very largely to over-provide themselves, and drew upon the reserves of the Bank infinitely beyond the real necessities of the case. The consequence was, that the amount of notes in the hands of the public amounted to nearly £21,000,000; and I have not the slightest doubt that at that period at least from four to five millions sterling of the notes issued were locked up and inoperative, in consequence of the alarm and of a fear of not being able to get Bank notes at all.

† *Vide Table of Prices*—Sugar, Coffee, &c.

‡ In the evidence before the Parliamentary Committee on Commercial Distress various opinions on this point are given. All those here quoted are to be regarded as banking authorities.

Mr. S. Gurney thought, as far as he knew, " that the catastrophes of last autumn were beyond all parallel in our monetary history."

Mr. George Norman considered that in 1837 and 1839 the causes of pressure were much less extreme than in the year 1847. In the latter period " every one seemed afraid of his neighbour."

Mr. Morris, the Governor, and Mr. Prescott, the Deputy-Governor, thus allude to the question.

" You said that you thought that the Act of 1844 had worked extremely well to secure the convertibility of the notes; do you apprehend that there would have been any danger of the notes of the Bank of England not being convertible if it had not

At length a final resolve was made by the London bankers, that they would seek an interview with the Government, and

---

passed?"—"I think they would have been in danger. On one or two previous occasions I think they were in danger,—in 1825 and 1839.

"And you think that they would have been in danger now but for this Act?"—"They might have been."

Mr. Prescott—"I agree with the Governor. I think that the pressure was not so great in 1839 as it was in 1847, and therefore that the danger in 1847 would have been greater but for this Act."

"Was not the pressure this year greater than you have ever witnessed?"—"My own experience scarcely carries me back to 1825, but I should conceive that the pressure in one or two weeks in 1825 was greater than in 1847.

Mr. Morris—"I believe that the pressure probably has been greater in London and in Lancashire, and probably in other places, but I doubt whether the pressure generally throughout the country has been so great as it was at the former periods."

* * * * * * * * * * *

"Without assuming at the present moment that we have actually recovered from it, but looking at the course of affairs since October, should you say that there has been less severe distress consequent upon the panic than there has been upon previous occasions"—"I think that the re-action has taken place sooner than it otherwise would have done.

"The question is, not as to what would have happened if the Act of 1844 had not passed, but merely as to the matter of fact, whether the distress and the sacrifice of capital, and the general damage, both to the commercial character as well as the credit of this country, has not exceeded in the last year anything that in your experience you ever witnessed?"—"I think in the failure of large houses it has exceeded, but whether it has as far as the whole country is concerned, I am not prepared to say. My impression is, that the damage to the country from the panic of 1825 was greater and more general then, than any which has taken place in 1847."

Mr. Prescott.—"I think as many as sixty or seventy banks failed in the end of 1825, and now there has not been a dozen."

Mr. W. Cotton considered the distress to have been "greatly exaggerated and nothing equal to what existed in 1825 and 1837."

Mr. Jones Lloyd expressed his opinion thus:—"I believe that the disturbance of credit was greater and more widely spread in 1825 than it was in 1847."

"Do you suppose that any evil can occur to a great commercial city, greater than that which happened during the year 1847 in the City of London, or that there ever were instances in which so complete a sacrifice of property, and so complete an impoverishment of commercial capital, has taken place in any country?"—"I have no doubt that there existed much greater pressure, and that the evils alluded to in the question, occurred in a severer form in this country in 1783, in 1793, and in 1825;" quoting M'Pherson, Chalmers, Tooke, and Lord Ashburton, as his comparative authorities.

accordingly on Saturday the 23d of October, Mr. Masterman, Mr. Abel Smith, Mr. Glyn, Mr. Bevan, Mr. Barnett and others, proceeded to Downing-street, to ask " relief" by a suspension of the Bank Charter Act. Already it was seen that the Bank was placed in an extremely critical situation, by the progressive declension of the reserve, and so great a dearth of the circulating medium existed, that it was found utterly impossible under any terms to procure a supply to meet ordinary trading engagements.* As the fate of commerce depended upon an affirmative answer to this last appeal, the decision of the Government was awaited with feverish impatience. On the return of the deputation, the feeling that the subject was likely to be favourably considered, though the answer was delayed until the Monday, created speculative business on the Stock Exchange, and as prices rose in consequence, sanguine anticipations were entertained that some " relaxation" would be authorized.

The panic continued on Monday the 25th, and great difficulty was experienced to procure any accommodation whatever. Shortly after mid-day, however, the annexed communication was made from the Bank, which immediately changed the entire aspect of business.†

Mr. G. C. Glyn, M.P., said—" In the last week of October, before the issue of the Government letter, the symptoms of want of confidence which presented themselves were very much like those which occurred at the end of 1825."

Mr. Tooke stated that it appeared to him in October, that the time was approaching " when nobody would pay anybody."

* *Vide* The Lords' report on Commercial Distress.

† The effect of the Government letter is described in the evidence of Mr. Glyn thus :—

" It produced the same effect as if the Bank of England had made an issue; because it brought out the hoards of notes, and they went into circulation. It thereby added to the circulation of the country, and it removed the cause of the panic, which is stated to have arisen from the Act of 1844."

Mr. Samuel Gurney illustrated this statement by his own case. He observes :—

" We required about £200,000, and had it at 9 per cent. On the Monday morning we had again a very heavy demand upon us; and we applied to the Governor, and said that, to supply Lombard-street with what was wanted, we should require £200,000 more. It was a case of difficulty for the Bank under its reduced reserve, and under

"Downing-street, Oct. 25, 1847.

"Gentlemen—Her Majesty's Government have seen with the deepest regret the pressure which has existed for some weeks upon the commercial interests of the country, and that this pressure has been aggravated by a want of that confidence which is necessary for carrying on the ordinary dealings of trade.

"They have been in hopes that the check given to transactions of a speculative character, the transfer of capital from other countries, the influx of bullion, and the feeling which a knowledge of these circumstances might have been expected to produce, would have removed the prevailing distrust.

They were encouraged in this expectation by the speedy cessation of a similar state of feeling in the month of April last.

"These hopes have, however, been disappointed, and her Majesty's Government have come to the conclusion that the time has arrived when they ought to attempt, by some extraordinary and temporary measure, to restore confidence to the mercantile and manufacturing community.

"For this purpose, they recommend to the Directors of the Bank of England, in the present emergency, to enlarge the amount of their discounts and advances upon approved security, but that, in order to retain this operation within reasonable limits, a high rate of interest should be charged.

"In present circumstances, they would suggest that the rate of interest should not be less than 8 per cent.

"If this course should lead to any infringement of the existing law, her Majesty's Government will be prepared to propose to Parliament, on its meeting, a Bill of Indemnity. They will rely upon the discretion of the directors to reduce as soon as possible the amount of their notes, if any extraordinary issue should take place, within the limits prescribed by law.

"Her Majesty's Government are of opinion that any extra profit derived from this measure should be carried to the account of the public, but the precise mode of doing so must be left to future arrangement.

"Her Majesty's Government are not insensible of the evil of any departure from the law which has placed the currency of this country upon a sound basis; but they feel confident that, in the present circumstances, the measure which they have proposed may be safely adopted, and at the same time the main provisions of that law, and the vital principle of preserving the convertibility of the Bank-note, may be firmly maintained.

"We have the honour to be, Gentlemen,

"Your obedient humble servants,

(Signed) "J. RUSSELL,

"CHARLES WOOD.

"The Governor and the Deputy-Governor of the Bank of England."

To this communication the Bank returned the following reply:—

---

the limitations of the Act. The Governor postponed a decision on our application till two o'clock. At one o'clock, however, the letter from the Government authorising relaxation was announced. The effect was immediate. Those who had sent notice for their money in the morning sent us word that they did not want it—that they only ordered payment by way of precaution. And after the notice we only required about £100,000 instead of £200,000. From that day we had a market of comparative ease."—*Extract from Lords' Report.*

The same document referring to the position of the Bank's accounts of this period remarks—

"Bank of England, Oct. 25, 1847.

Gentlemen—We have the honour to acknowledge your letter of this day's date which we have submitted to the Court of Directors, and we inclose a copy of the resolutions thereon, and

"We have the honor to be, Sirs, your most obedient servants,

(Signed) JAMES MORRIS, Governor.
H. J. PRESCOTT, Deputy-Governor.

"To the First Lord of the Treasury and the Chancellor of the Exchequer.

"Resolved—That this Court do accede to the recommendation contained in the letter from the First Lord of the Treasury and the Chancellor of the Exchequer, dated this day, and addressed to the Governor and Deputy-Governor of the Bank of England, which had just been read.

"That the minimum rate of discount on bills not having more than 95 days to run be 8 per cent.

"That advances be made on bills of exchange, on stock, on Exchequer-bills and other approved securities, in sums of not less than £2,000, and for periods to be fixed by the Governors, at the rate of 8 per cent. per annum."

"The state of the Bank reserve on the 23d of October is shewn to have been as follows:—

Reserve.		London.		Country.	
	£		£		£
Notes	1,547,276	Notes	981,615	Notes..........	565,655
Coin	447,240	Gold coin	209,844	Gold coin	78,399
	£1,994,516	Silver coin	104,045	Silver coin......	54,958
			1,295,504		£699,012
		Country	699,012		
			£1,994,516		

But on the 23d of October it had been intimated that the Government letter was to be issued on the 25th, and it was understood that the Bank was to act on the 23d according to the spirit of that Government letter. The accommodation given in consequence, on the 23d of October, was on that understanding, and the reserve was necessarily to some extent diminished. On the 30th of October the accounts stood as follows:—

Reserve.		London.		Country.	
	£		£		£
Notes........	1,176,740	Notes	568,470	Notes..........	608,270
Coin	429,384	Gold coin	151,053	Gold coin	119,554
	£1,606,124	Silver coin	105,787	Silver coin......	52,990
			825,310		£780,814
		Country	780,814		
			£1,606,124		

Thus, the reserve of notes, which had been £2,630,000 on the 16th of October, had fallen on the 23d to £1,547,000, and to £1,176,000 on the 30th of October, having decreased nearly £1,500,000 within the short space of fourteen days. At this

Immediately this correspondence was made public, a steady advance in Government securities took place, much of the

---

last period, of the total reserve of notes, amounting to £1,176,740, no more than £568,470 was held in London, making with the gold coin in the banking department, £719,523. At the same time the private deposits for which the Bank was responsible amounted to £8,580,000, independently of upwards of £4,766,000 of Government deposits. The total deposits on the 30th of October were £14,500,000; the deposits of the London Bankers being more than £2,000,000 at the same time. In reference to this state of things, the following important evidence was given by the Governor and Deputy-Governor of the Bank of England:—

" You had only £1,600,000 in the banking department for the payment of your liabilities ?—Yes.

" If any body had called upon you for anything beyond that million and a-half, you must have stopped payment,—Yes, we must.

" At that time, if there had been no separation between the two departments, and the Bank of England had been conducted on its old principle, instead of being within one million and a-half of stopping, there would have been very nearly £8,500,000 of treasures in your vaults ?—We should have had £8,500,000 in our vaults.

It is, however, right to add that the same witnesses state that they could not admit that the Bank was in any danger of suspending its payments. " We should not have been able to give the same extent of accommodation that parties were requiring of us. We might have put into account a considerable sum by selling Consols. We had going off weekly bills to the extent of £1,500,000; so that, by discounting even at the rate of £100,000 a day to give the public some accommodation, our reserve would still have increased at the rate of £900,000 a week. It is certain that in a very short period we should have had as large a reserve as would be necessary for our purposes, and therefore the Bank was never at any period in jeopardy."

The correctness of this conclusion, however, depends on the practicability of the remedial measures recommended—namely, first, the sale of stock; and secondly, the limitation of discounts. A further question also remains, assuming these measures to have been practicable and successful, for the security of the Bank, in the first instance, whether their consequences would not have been ruinous both to public and private credit, and ultimately fatal to the Bank of England itself. On the point of the difficulty of making such extensive sales of stock on Exchequer Bills, Mr. Glyn in his evidence to the question,

" Are you aware that it was the opinion of the Bank broker that a very large sum might have been sold without materially affecting the price of stocks ? replies,—I was not aware that the Bank broker had stated that. I should say, from what I saw at the time, that a sale of a million or two millions, which were the figures talked of, would have been almost impossible without knocking down the funds to such a price as would have created a further panic."

Mr. Browne, M.P., did not think such sales could have been effected, unless at a great sacrifice; adding, " that if the panic had been equal to what we might suppose

pervading gloom was dissipated, and from that date henceforward, a gradual but progressive return to confidence was manifested. The relaxation, considered as a "triumph of the banking principle," was duly heralded by the advocates of the measure, as it was declared to be, a "virtual repeal of the Act of 1844."

From the variations in Consols, Exchequer Bills, and railway securities, it will be at once noticed what was the condition of business during the memorable month of October, 1847.

GOVERNMENT SECURITIES.

OCTOBER, 1847.

	Price on the 1st.	Lowest Price.	Highest Price.	Price on the 30th.
Consols, Money	84¾	78¾	85⅜	80¾
Do. Account	85	79½	85½	81
Exchequer Bills, 3d.	1/ pm.	37/dis.	3/ pm.	17/dis.

RAILWAY SECURITIES.

OCTOBER, 1847.

	Amount per Share.	Amount Paid.	Price on the 1st.	Lowest Price.	Highest Price.	Price on the 30th.
	£	£				
Brighton	Stock.	50	43¼	36¾	44¾	39¼
Caledonian	50	50	37½	33	39	35
Eastern Counties	20	20	16¾	15⅛	17	15¾
Edinburgh & Glasgow	50	50	—	47	51	47¾
Great Western	100	85	100	85	102	93
Hull and Selby	50	50	99	96	99	98½
London & North Western	Stock.		158	138½	161	148½
Midland	Stock.		112¾	100	116	106¼
South Eastern	Av. £33 : 2 : 4		30¾	24	31¼	27¼
Do. Western	Av. £41 : 6 : 10		58¼	52½	59	54¾
York & North Midland	£50	£50	73½	66½	75	70
Boulogne & Amiens	20	20	13¼	13	14	13¾
Northern of France	20	10	10	9⅝	11⅜	10⅞
Orleans & Bordeaux	20	6	3⅞	3¼	4¼	4⅛
Paris and Rouen	20	20	33¾	33	34½	—

it might have been, under such circumstances, I doubt whether they could have been sold at all."

Mr. Tooke expressed an adverse opinion to the facility of such sales.

Mr. Horsley Palmer also believed sales of the kind almost impracticable.

Mr. Cotton did not go so far as Mr. Palmer on such sales, he thought there would of course have been a fall in prices.

The failures that took place in October may be thus classified. Although several important metropolitan firms are included in the list, bank suspensions will be found to present with numerous provincial disasters, the chief interest. The foreign failures had also assumed in some respects an important character.

October.	Company of Copper Miners in England,	London,	Miners, &c.
,,	Bruce, Buxton, & Co.,	London,	Bill Brokers.
,,	Rougemont, Brothers,	London,	Continental Merchants.
,,	John Thomas, Son, and Lefevre,	London,	Russia Trade.
,,	F. J. Van Zeller,	London,	Portuguese Trade.
,,	Rickards, Little, & Co.,	London,	East India Trade.
,,	E. Bernoulli,	London,	Levant Trade.
,,	M. J. Soares,	London,	Portuguese Trade.
,,	J. and W. Morley,*	London,	Warehousemen.
,,	W. Nash,	London,	Warehouseman.
,,	Barclay, Brothers, & Co.,	London,	Mauritius Trade.
,,	Lawrence Phillips and Sons,	London,	East India Trade.
,,	F. Barnes & Co.,	London,	Hardwaremen.
,,	Scott, Bell, & Co.,	London,	East India Trade.
,,	Howard & Co.,	London,	Colonial Brokers.
,,	W. T. Clagget,	London,	American Trade.
,,	W. S. Hadlow,	London,	Stock Exchange.
,,	R. Oakley,	London,	Stock Exchange.
,,	J. P. Cruickshank & Co.,†	London,	East and West India Trade.
,,	C. Sutherland & Co.,	London,	Colonial Brokers.
,,	Boyds and Thomas,	London,	East India Trade.
,,	Brown, Todd, & Co.,	Liverpool,	Provision Trade.
,,	Dalgleish & Co.,	Liverpool and Glasgow,	Merchants.
,,	V. Higgins and Sons,	Liverpool,	Iron Trade.
,,	Lake, Calrow, & Co.,	Liverpool,	East India Trade.
,,	T. and H. Murray,	Liverpool,	East India Trade.
,,	W. Maury,	Liverpool,	American Trade.
,,	Mocatta and Son,	Liverpool,	Spanish American Trade.
,,	W. Pearce & Co.,	Liverpool,	Merchants.
,,	Platt, Hammill, & Co.,	Liverpool,	East India Trade.
,,	W. Steele and Son,	Liverpool,	Soap Boilers.
,,	M. S. Synnot,	Liverpool,	Ship-owner.
,,	W. and T. Tomlinson,	Liverpool,	Corn Trade.
,,	Brooke and Wilson,	Liverpool,	Ship-owners.
,,	Gazebrooke & Co.,	Liverpool,	Iron Trade.
,,	W. Jones & Co.,	Liverpool,	Merchants.
,,	Livingstone & Co.,	Liverpool,	East India Trade.
,,	J. Logan & Co.,	Liverpool,	Canadian Merchants.
,,	M'Tear, Hadfield, & Co.,	Liverpool,	Ship Brokers.
,,	Molyneux and Hulbert,	Liverpool,	Tea Brokers.
,,	R. Taylor,	Liverpool,	Soap Boiler.
,,	Wotherspoon, Stewart, & Co.,	Liverpool,	Share Brokers.
,,	Warden & Co.,	Liverpool,	Merchants.
,,	Berey, Young, & Co.,	Liverpool,	Cotton Brokers.

* *Vide* Statement of affairs, Appendix, page lxxxv.
† *Vide* Statement of affairs, Appendix, page lii.

,,	Royal Bank of Liverpool,	Liverpool,	Bankers.
,,	Liverpool Banking Company,	Liverpool,	Bankers.
,,	North and South Wales Bank,	Liverpool,	Bankers.
,,	Barton, Irlam, and Higginson,	Liverpool,	East and West India Trade.
,,	Cornthwaite & Co.,	Liverpool,	Tea Dealers.
,,	De Jersey & Co.,	Manchester,	Merchants & Manufacturers.
,,	Watson, Elder, & Co.,	Manchester,	Manufacturers.
,,	Scholes & Co.,	Manchester,	Bankers.
,,	Wilson & Eber,	Manchester,	Merchants & Spinners.
,,	R. and S. Farbridge,	Manchester,	East India & Russia Trade.
,,	R. Gardner,	Manchester,	Spinner.
,,	Gael & Co.,	Manchester,	Spinners.
,,	Martin and Hartwright,	Manchester,	Yarn Merchants.
,,	James, Nephew, & Co.,	Manchester,	Merchants.
,,	E. Potter & Co.,	Manchester,	Agents.
,,	Render and Milner,	Manchester,	Agents.
,,	Abingdon and Wantage Banking Company, (H. Knapp)	Abingdon,	Bankers.
,,	Newcastle Joint Stock Bank,	Newcastle,	Bankers.
,,	The Oldham Banking Company,	Oldham,	Bankers.
,,	Gibson and Sturt,	St. Alban's,	Bankers.
,,	W. B. Brodie & Co.,	Salisbury,	Bankers.
,,	Brodie and King,	Shaftesbury,	Bankers.
,,	Adams, Warren, & Co.	Shrewsbury and Market Drayton	Bankers.
,,	Flood & Co., Old Bank,	Honiton,	Bankers.
,,	Grundy & Co., Bridport Bank,	Bridport,	Bankers,
,,	Ridehalgh & Co.,	Halifax,	Worsted Spinners.
,,	Rogers and Brierley,	Blackburn,	Cotton Spinners.
,,	Southam & Co.,	Ashton,	Cotton Spinners.
,,	Gellows & Co.,	Preston,	Spinners.
,,	M'Gregor, Brownrigg, & Co.,	Glasgow,	Merchants.
,,	Reid, Robinson, & Co.,	Glasgow,	Merchants.
,,	A. and J. Wingate,	Glasgow,	Calico Printers.
,,	Cowan, Smith, & Co.,	Glasgow,	Corn Agents.
,,	Kilgour and Leath,	Glasgow,	West India Trade.
,,	Pearson, Wilson, & Co.,	Glasgow,	Merchants.
,,	Molley and Mergin,	Dublin,	Cattle Dealers.
,,	T. Murphy,	Waterford,	Provision Trade.
,,	White & Co.,	Waterford,	Corn Trade.

The principal foreign failures in the month of October included

,,	Legrelle & Co.,	Brussels,	Bankers.
,,	Pehmoller and Tollens,	Hamburg,	Merchants.
,,	L. W. A. Jacobs,	Hamburg,	Merchant.
,,	Rosing & Co.,	Bremen,	Merchants.
,,	Wittenstein & Co.,	Elberfeld,	Spinners.
,,	E. Alessio & Co.,	Genoa,	Corn Merchants.
,,	G. Calcagne,	Genoa,	Money Broker.
,,	L. Arbid & Co.,	Leghorn,	Merchants.
,,	Morfeurgo and Tedeshchi,	Leghorn,	Merchants.
,,	De Pegra Guttiers, & Co.,	Leghorn,	Merchants.
,,	J. L. Valentin & Co.,	Leghorn,	Merchants.
,,	N. Bertrand & Co.,	Courtray,	Merchants.
,,	Vernein and Giells,	Courtray,	Manufacturers.
,,	C. Riva & Co.,	St. Petersburg,	Merchants.
,,	Vermechren & Co.,	St. Petersburg,	Merchants.
,,	J. Van Zeller and Sons,	Lisbon,	Merchants.
,,	M. Ventura & Co.,	Venice,	Merchants.

As a description of the panic of October, and the reasons which induced Government interference, the speech of Sir C. Wood on the 30th November in the House of Commons may be usefully consulted.

Sir C. Wood in his capacity of Chancellor of the Exchequer said, " When he came to town in October he found the City in a state of panic. He saw persons of all classes and description, from the time he was up until he went to bed, and he never passed so painful a week. The interest of money rose to an exorbitant rate, and 60 per cent. per annum was charged for what were called " continuations" for one day. It was thought impossible that the loans could be repaid, and if reliance for the payment of the dividends was placed on the return of those loans, that there would be a disappointment, and that it would be impossible for the public creditors to be paid. The next week came, and the dividends being due the loans were repaid. The Governor and Deputy-Governor of the Bank acted with extreme prudence and discretion, and received the payments of the loans, and on the whole they were punctually paid. The notes which were paid in were issued in payment of the dividends, and the result was that in this extraordinary period of demand for notes there was taken out of the Bank in the four days for payment but £300,000 more than in the corresponding days of last year. When the parties had a right to demand £7,000,000 extra, they only drew £300,000 more than in 1846. The gloomy anticipations of the week before the payment of the dividends were not realized, and in spite of the failure of the Royal Bank of Liverpool on the Monday following, there was in London a better feeling in the early part of the week, and one of the papers, in its money article, stated that matters were steadier although they had been affected by the failure of the Newcastle Joint Stock Bank. There was a decided change in the accounts on Thursday, Friday, and Saturday. The payments of the dividends did not indicate any improved feeling. By this time, too, accounts were received of the state of the country, and from various parts they were very alarming.

"On Monday the Royal Bank of Liverpool failed—a failure which was only caused by gross neglect, for, with a paid-up capital of only £600,000, £500,000 had been advanced to one house. At the same time apprehensions were entertained with regard to a broker whose name he had mentioned.* He applied to the Bank for assistance, and they gave it. Another bank stopped at Liverpool, and apprehensions were entertained for the safety of other country banks, especially in the commercial districts, for in the agricultural parts of the country they had been comparatively at ease. There was an alarm as to the banks in the west of England, one of which had since failed, and was reported to be likely to pay a very small dividend. News came of the stoppage of the Newcastle Union Bank on Thursday, and later in the day there were accounts of severe runs on several district banks. Allusion had been made to the assistance given to that bank. The fact was that Mr. Richardson, the manager, came to London to get assistance from the Bank of England, and left without still obtaining it. So far was it from being true that there was any recommendation from the Government on the subject. It was true that that bank was saved by the interference of the branch bank of the Bank of England, and Mr. Grote took on himself a fearful responsibility, for seeing the danger that would arise, even to the peace of the country, unless that bank was saved, he furnished it with the means of standing the run which was made on it on Friday and half of Saturday; and parties who had withdrawn gold and notes in the morning tendered them as re-deposits in the evening. It did not appear that there was a run for Bank-notes, but a steady run for deposits on the banks of Liverpool and Manchester in the course of the few days preceding the Thursday and Friday.

"Then came a fearful aggravation of the supposed danger. It was a matter of notoriety now that applications for assistance had

* Messrs. Littledale, of Liverpool, brokers, who, when the Royal Bank of Liverpool failed, sought facilities for discount at the Bank of England and readily obtained them.

been made by the banks of Scotland. It was generally considered that those banks were on so safe a footing that they were able to take care of themselves, and that they would not find it necessary to apply to the Bank of England; but applications were made, and occasioned much alarm. For when it was considered how enormous the deposits were in the Scotch banks which might be readily withdrawn, and most of which were made on security which, though solid, was not easily realized, there was just cause for alarm. The demands on the Bank of England for assistance, and on the London banks, to assist these correspondents, were extensive. Two bill-brokers had stopped,* and others were paralysed, and the whole discount business was thrown on the Bank of England, and they refused to discount no bills which came within their rules, but a large mass of paper, which was usually done by bill-brokers, was refused.

"This was the state of things which was represented to the Government from all parts of the country, and a feeling arose in commercial quarters, the least likely to be biassed, who came to them, and whose opinions they took, that matters were growing serious unless some measure was adopted by the Government to restore confidence. He did not deny that the statements which had been laid before him were alarming. He took pains to examine their accuracy, and he could not deny that most unwillingly and most reluctantly he came to the conclusion that it was necessary to interfere, and having come to that conclusion, he should have thought himself unworthy of the place he held if he had hesitated, owing to any former opinions of his own, to do what he thought his duty. Not only did he think the exercise of this discretion was required by other circumstances, but it was evident that notes had been hoarded to a great extent and a circulation which, under other circumstances, would have been adequate to its purposes, and when the pressure or panic was removed, would have proved abundant for its objects, was prevented by this hoarding from performing its functions. As a proof

* Messrs. Sanderson & Co. and Messrs. Bruce, Buxton, & Co.

of this, tens of thousands of notes which had been hoarded in the boxes had been brought into circulation ; and when the House remembered that under £400,000 was the amount of notes taken out of the Bank of England after the 25th of October, it furnished a proof that there was an adequate amount of circulation in the hands of the public, but from fear and alarm it had been hoarded up, and thereby rendered incapable of being brought into use.

"His noble friend (Lord J. Russell) and himself had seen parties of all descriptions, and the universal application which had been made to his noble friend and himself was to this effect: —They said, 'We do not want notes—what we desire is that you should give us confidence, it is only for you to say you will stand by us, and nothing in the world else will give us confidence. We do not want notes, but only to know where we can get them.' They added, 'Charge any rate of interest you please, ask what you like.' ('No, no,' from Mr. Spooner.) The hon. gentleman said 'No, no,' but he (the Chancellor of the Exchequer) must be permitted to know what had been stated to him, and he would say distinctly such was the constant tenor of the applications which had been made. He repeated, that they said 'Charge 10 or 12 per cent. interest if you like—we do not mean to take notes, but let us know that at some rate of interest we can get them, and that will amply suffice.' An honorable member had asked the other day what had been the change of circumstances which had induced the Government to act on Saturday in a manner different from the course they had declined but a short time before? In reply to that question, he could now state that the accounts received on the Thursday, Friday, and Saturday had been of a totally different description from those which had preceded them, and they then had believed that according to the passage he had quoted from Mr. Huskisson, they had come to this—that a stagnant circulation wanted life—it every day became more embarrassed, whilst these new calamities contributed to increase the general apprehension of the country. It was because on that Saturday, and not before that, he and his noble friend thought it right and proper to act, because then they were in possession of information which afforded them a justification for the violation of the statute.

" Having determined to act in the emergency, of course the next question which had arisen was the mode in which it should be done. He and his noble friend had long before considered the matter, and had made up their minds as to the best mode of action in case action should become necessary, and he should have been glad if there had been any mode of action that would have been effectual, other than that which they had taken. It had been suggested that they ought to have advanced Exchequer-bills on goods and produce ; but he was not quite clear whether at the time goods and produce were just as saleable as Exchequer-bills, and, therefore, that mode of action would have failed. Others invited an advance of Consols, and a third suggestion was, that the issue of some description of Government note would have answered the purpose. Now, in his judgment, it would clearly have been absurd and foolish to act at all, unless in a way which they were pretty sure would be effectual ; and therefore having determined to act, they had acted in that manner which, approved by practised and practical authorities, they believed would be certain to ensure its purpose.

" He must also state that to nine-tenths of the parties who had applied to the Government to sanction the issue of notes in this way, it was stated it would be essentially necessary that some limit should be put upon it, and the first suggestion was that a limited amount of notes should be issued, with an increasing rate of interest. To this plan there was, he thought, a decided and fatal objection,—namely, that there would have been a scramble for the first and second million, and that as soon as that was over the same state of things would have occurred again. But if they were not to limit the amount of notes, the other, and he thought, the wiser, suggestion was, that a limit should pe put on the rate of interest. That course had been adopted, and in the recommendation made to the Bank of England was a high rate of interest, because if a high rate of interest had not been adopted they would have done that which would have been most mischievous—namely, to check the importation of capital and bullion into this country. At the same time, he (the Chancellor of the Exchequer) had been as anxious as any body not to impose a rate of interest higher than was necessary, and therefore instead of adopting a minimum rate of 10 per cent., they had adopted 8 per cent., the lowest amount suggested to the Government by the applicants being 7 per cent. The rate of 7 per cent. clearly would not have answered the object which was in view, for when the rate had been fixed by the Bank of England on the direction of the Government at 8 per cent., what was the rate of interest out of doors? At that time the rate of interest at Hamburgh was 7 per cent. He held in his hand a letter from the consul at Hamburgh, dated the 22d of October, which stated that then the discounts there were at the rate of 6 and 7 per cent. per annum, and it was not less in any part of Europe. At New York, on the 30th of October, before the intelligence of what had happened here had reached that country, money was in active demand there at the rate of 7 per cent, and in some cases higher rates had been paid.

" Again, though the Bank of England had discounted a small amount of bills at 5½ per cent., yet at the time the letter of his noble friend and himself had been addressed to the Bank, the average rate charged by the Bank was 7½ per cent., so that the real extent to which that letter raised the rate was not more than half per cent. upon the rate then charged at the Bank of England, and 1 per cent. upon the rates on the Continent and in America. It was desirable that capital and bullion should be attracted to this country, and it was only by the attraction of a high rate of interest that this desideratum could be accomplished. He conceived, therefore, that the mode in which the Government had acted was the one best calculated to attain the end they had in view—namely, the influx of capital and the importation of bullion, and thereby the removal of the panic.

" But it had been said that the Government ought to have left it to the Bank of England to fix the rate of interest; but he thought it was much fairer, both to the public and to the Bank that, they (the Government) should take that responsibility from which neither he nor his noble friend were disposed to shrink. It had also been remarked that the Government ought to have made the increased rate to apply only to such portions of the advances as were made by the Bank in consequence of the letter. He, however, contended that it would have been utterly impossible for the Bank to have acted in a different spirit after the receipt of that letter, and to have drawn a distinction between the advances made in consequence of the Government letter and those which, without the letter, would have been made.

" Again, an exception had been taken to that paragraph in the letter which referred to the extra profit being carried to the account of the public, but that was inserted for the purpose of protecting the Bank, in conformity with the 6th clause of the Act of 1844—a clause inserted at the instance of the Bank itself. He thought that the purpose for which the letter had been issued—not to create capital—not to support credit, which had no security to offer, but to release the circulation which had been closed by fear and alarm, had been answered, and he believed that those engaged in the commerce and trade of the country would admit that the effect intended had been completely realized."

With the commencement of November the Bank accounts shewed an improved appearance; the funds continued to advance; and the state of the exchanges which had throughout the severest period of the panic been in favour of this country, attracted increased supplies of bullion not only from the Continent and Russia, but also from America. Railway calls were proportionately lighter, amounting this month to £2,040,000, of which £146,500 was on behalf of foreign companies. Still, however, the inconvenience of these contributions was felt, no effective stoppage of railway works having taken place, notwithstanding the most strenuous remonstrances made in that respect. But despite the improving tendency existing in the aspect of public affairs, the high *minimum* of 8 per cent. was not without its influence, and already crippled, through diminished resources, numbers of houses in London and the country, found themselves compelled to submit to the painful ordeal of suspension.

The attempts vigorously made to remodel the various Country Joint Stock Banks and enable them to resume business on a fresh basis, and which were shortly consummated, assisted to reassure the public and allayed much of the feeling previously so destructive to credit. Inasmuch as the anticipated resumption of business by these establishments was attended by a revival of confidence, a great general good was effected, and although their original management suffered in almost all instances strong condemnation, the arrangements subsequently devised would, it was thought, hereafter check if not entirely remove all future ground of complaint.

Restoration to a healthy position could not suddenly be effected. Confidence borne down and laid completely prostrate by a series of such lamentable disasters, could not momentarily rouse itself and recover lost ground. Difficulties, augmented on all sides, had worked their way to the heart of trade, and these difficulties, which had been for the most part the growth of years, could not be removed in a day, a week, or a month. To seem conscious that an approach to recovery was being made, and, that progress in that direction was certain, was the most that could under the circumstances be looked for.

Symptoms of this description were not long wanting to buoy up hopes. If failures had not entirely ceased; if large houses were still reported to be struggling with losses, encountered from the suspension of their intimate connexions, the Money-market was relatively speaking in a much easier condition, Messrs. Overend, Gurney, & Co., having reduced their rate to 5 per cent. for money on call. The Scotch banks had also been relieved by the intervention of the Bank of England, and, regarded in most points of view, appearances were decidedly for the better. But the blow once struck, the effects could not be avoided. The East India trade, doomed as it were to temporary annihilation, was the scene of fresh embarrassment, and Messrs. Thurburn & Co.;* Messrs. Johnson, Cole, & Co.;† Messrs. Lackersteen & Co.,‡ increased the catalogue of suspended firms in that branch of business.

About this time occurred the stoppage of Messrs. Trueman and Cook, Colonial brokers. The event was not altogether unanticipated. Their system of advances to the great East India, West India, and Mauritius houses, to whom through the extent of their wealth and credit they had, in order to secure the sales of their produce, acted in the capacity of bankers and discounters, rendered it almost impossible that they could sustain themselves against a course of events so paralyzing in their nature as those which had been witnessed. It was not therefore surprising that a broker's firm, who had assisted in this manner, Messrs. Cockerell, Larpent, & Co.; Messrs. Reid, Irving, & Co.; Messrs. Gower & Co.; Messrs. Barclay, Brothers, & Co.; and other establishments of less note and pretensions, should discover that their involvements were of a character to compel them to suspend. This mode of granting advances, (or, as it was termed by many, "relief bills,") especially in connexion with forthcoming crops, met severe censure from the commercial community; but some satisfaction was expressed when it was ascertained, contrary to rumour, that the accounts of the house would admit of a liquidation in full.§

Another firm of some consideration that failed this month, as produce brokers, were Messrs. Sargant, Gordon, & Co.|| Among other metropolitan suspensions which created gossip for the time, were Judah Cohen and Sons, West India trade; J. & H. Reay,

---

* *Vide* Statement of affairs, Appendix, page xl.

† *Vide* Statement of affairs, Appendix, page xli.

‡ *Vide* Statement of affairs, Appendix, page xxxix.

§ *Vide* Statement of affairs, Appendix, page lix. Since the above was written Messrs. Trueman & Cook have notified their inability to pay the third instalment on the date named. They however promise to meet their engagements at the earliest possible period.—*Vide* Supplemental Statement in Appendix, page lxiv.

|| *Vide* Statement of affairs, Appendix, page lxx.

wine trade;* Coates and Hillard, American trade; Leaf, Barnett, Scotson, & Co., warehousemen; † and Tanner and Ward, leather factors. ‡ Messrs. Job Wright & Co., in the Russia trade, also stopped, but arrangements were speedily made for the payment of 20s. in the pound.

The frequenters of the Stock-exchange through the fluctuations occasioned by the Government letter, received the unpleasant intimation that several of their members would be unable to meet their differences, and nine defaulters were declared.

Circumstances, however, in the meantime, favoured a rectification of the Bank accounts, and by the 20th, the reserve had increased to £4,228,000, and the stock of bullion to £10,000,000. Hence, so far was a steady progress towards confidence believed to have been achieved, that on the morning of the opening of Parliament, when the Royal Speech alluded to an amelioration in the existing state of commercial distress, the withdrawal of the Government letter was effected by the publication of the following correspondence.

"Downing-street, Nov. 23, 1847.

Gentlemen,—Her Majesty's Government have watched with the deepest interest the gradual revival of confidence in the commercial classes of the country.

"They have the satisfaction of believing that the course adopted by the Bank of England on their recommendation has contributed to produce this result, whilst it has led to no infringement of the law.

"It appears from the accounts which you have transmitted to us, that the reserve of the Bank of England has been for some time steadily increasing, and now amounts to £5,000,000. This increase has in great measure arisen from the return of notes and coin from the country.

"The bullion exceeds £10,000,000, and the state of the exchanges promise a further influx of the precious metals.

"The knowledge of these facts by the public is calculated to inspire still further confidence.

"In these circumstances it appears to her Majesty's Government that the purposes which they had in view in the letter which we addressed to you on the 25th of October has been fully answered, and that it is unnecessary to continue that letter any longer in force.

"We have the honour to be, Gentlemen,
"Your obedient humble servants,
(Signed) J. Russell.
"The Governor and Deputy-Governor of the Bank of England." Charles Wood,

---

* *Vide* Statement of affairs, Appendix, page lxxix.

† *Vide* Statement of affairs, Appendix, page lxxxiii.

‡ *Vide* Statement of affairs, Appendix, page lxxxvi.

Bank of England, Nov. 23, 1847.

"Gentlemen,—We have the honour to acknowledge the receipt of your letter of this day's date, in which you communicate to us that, in consequence of the gradual revival of confidence in the commercial classes of the country, it appears to Her Majesty's Government that the object they had in view in the letter they addressed to us on the 25th October had been fully answered, and that it is unnecessary to continue that letter any longer in force.

"We have the honour to be, Gentlemen,
"Your most obedient servants,

(Signed) James Morris, Governor.
H. J. Prescott, Deputy-Governor.

"To the first Lord of the Treasury and the Chancellor of the Exchequer."

The Bank directors the day before reduced their *minimum* rate of discount to 7 per cent. At the end of November confidence decidedly increased, but still the country was suffering greatly from the exhausting course of the panic. The failures this month in the provinces, were not of a light or unimportant character, and foreign stoppages were more than previously numerous, including among them the Union Bank of Madrid.

November.	Coates and Hillard,	London,	American Trade.
,,	L. S. Curtis,	London,	Hide Factor.
,,	Judah Cohen & Sons,	London,	West India Trade.
,,	Thurburn & Co.,	London,	East India Trade.
,,	Johnson, Cole, & Co.,	London,	East India Trade.
,,	Ryder, Weinholt, & Co.,	London,	East India Trade.
,,	Abbott, Nottingham, & Co.,	London,	Warehousemen.
,,	Trueman and Cook,	London,	Colonial Brokers.
,,	R. Farrand,	London,	Corn Factor.
,,	J. & H. Reay,	London,	Wine Merchants.
,,	A. A. Lackersteen,	London,	East India Trade.
,,	Lackersteen and Crake,	London,	East India Trade.
,,	Tanner & Ward,	London,	Leather Factors.
,,	Sargant, Gordon, & Co.,	London,	Produce Brokers,
,,	Leaf, Barnett, Scotson, & Co.,	London,	Warehousemen.
,,	W. Abbott,	London,	Stock Exchange.
,,	A. Arkill,	London,	Stock Exchange.
,,	W. Eykin,	London,	Stock Exchange.
,,	J. H. Hawkins,	London,	Stock Exchange.
,,	Secretan and Capper,	London,	Stock Exchange.
,,	T. Turner,	London,	Stock Exchange.
,,	H. Whitmore,	London,	Stock Exchange.
,,	J. Williams, Jun.,	London,	Stock Exchange.
,,	C. B. Young,	London,	Stock Exchange.
,,	Job Wright & Co.,	London,	Russian Merchants.
,,	J. B. Branckner and Son,	Liverpool,	Brokers.
,,	Carter and Baines,	Liverpool,	Merchants.
,,	Coleman and Todd,	Liverpool,	Share Brokers.
,,	Hargreaves & Co.,	Liverpool,	Merchants.
,,	T. Ashburner,	Liverpool,	Leather Factor.
,,	G. & J. Blake,	Liverpool,	Soap Boilers.
,,	J. Brownrigg & Co.,	Liverpool,	East India Trade.
,,	A. E. Byrne,	Liverpool,	Merchant.

November.	J. Edwards & Co.,	Liverpool,	Wool Brokers.
,,	Ricardo and Harding,	Liverpool,	Merchants.
,,	D. Ainsworth,	Manchester,	Warehouseman.
,,	Coates, Hillard, & Co.,	Manchester,	Warehousemen.
,,	P. Cowrill,	Manchester,	Calico Printer.
,,	Ewing, Anderson, & Co.,	Manchester,	East India Trade.
,,	Z. Just,	Manchester,	Manufacturer.
,,	Kershaw, Hillard, & Co.	Manchester,	Manufacturers.
,,	Marsland, Veltman, & Co.,	Manchester,	Manufacturers.
,,	J. T. H. Pindleton,	Manchester,	Manufacturer.
,,	J. P. Clarke,	Leicester.	Merchant.
,,	W. H. Kaye,	Huddersfield,	Merchant.
,,	Farthing, Son, & Co.,	Hull,	Merchants.
,,	Norrison Levett,	Hull,	Manufacturer.
,,	J. Gales,	Sunderland,	Ship Builder.
,,	R. Imreay,	Newcastle,	AlkaliManufacturer.
,,	M. Walker,	Leeds,	Flax Spinner.
,,	Campbell and Batty,	Glasgow,	Agents.
,,	D. M'Kenzie, jun.,	Glasgow,	East India Trade.
,,	Ogilvie, Clarke, & Co.,	Glasgow,	Agents.
,,	Pattison and McGibbon,	Glasgow,	Calico Printers.
,,	G. Young & Co.,	Glasgow,	Calico Printers.
,,	R. Buchan,	Glasgow,	Broker.
,,	A. & J. Downie,	Glasgow,	Wool Trade.
,,	A. Rankin,	Glasgow,	West India Trade.
,,	D. Napier,	Glasgow,	Iron Founder.

The foreign failures were—

,,	Kantzow and Biel,	Stockholm,	Merchants.
,,	N. Breebart,	Amsterdam,	Merchant.
,,	Roothan & Co.,	Amsterdam,	Bankers.
,,	J. H. Rupe and Son,	Amsterdam,	Sugar Refiners.
,,	Bonaffè & Co.,	Havre,	Merchants.
,,	Defosse and Noete,	Antwerp,	Bankers.
,,	Grosjean, Nephews,	Brussels,	Bankers.
,,	Hennekinne Briard,	Mons,	Banker.
,,	Salvador Pacifico,	Trieste,	Merchant.
,,	Patengat & Co.	Bayonne,	Corn Trade.
,,	Riewit and Langevelt,	Rotterdam,	Merchants.
,,	B. Rouffaer & Sons,	Rotterdam,	Merchants.
,,	Union Bank,	Madrid,	Bankers.
,,	Muir, Taylor, & Co.,	New York,	Merchants.

December was comparatively a quiet month.* Although suspensions occasionally were announced, they did not assume in any respect a serious character. The most considerable firm that then became embarrassed was Messrs. Cotesworth, Powell, and Pryor, engaged in the Brazilian and Spanish American trade. Their stoppage was reported on the last day of the year. An examination of their accounts happily showed that they were

* Messrs. Fletcher, Alexander, & Co., in the East India trade, received assistance from the Bank directors about this date, to the extent, it was asserted, of £300,000.

in a solvent position;* and this served in a measure to allay the apprehension which would, in all probability, have otherwise resulted from the publication of their difficulties.

The explosion of the General Maritime Association † was an event deserving notice, and following in the midst of these catastrophes, assisted to keep alive the prevailing excitement. The affairs of the company, when investigated, afforded an additional instance to those already on record of the mismanagement of public bodies, and from the responsibilities connected with which, two of the directors sought relief in bankruptcy, while others were compelled to contribute large sums to compromise outstanding liabilities. Its career had been one continuous series of losses, contracted on a scale which would have ruined a more wealthy proprietary than the one identified with its existence.

Among the foreign houses, the news of whose failures were received at the close of December, were those of the Frankfort and Carlsruhe bankers and manufacturers, Von Haber; Von Haber and Sons; Gontard and Sons; and L. H. Flersheim. To render them assistance their Government interfered, as it was considered essential that their factories should not suspend, owing to the quantity of labour employed. The first of the Calcutta suspensions was mentioned this month, viz., Messrs. Saunders, May, Fordyce, & Co.

December.	General Maritime Association,	London,	Assurance Brokers.
,,	W. Pemberton,	London,	Canada Trade.
,,	Charles Trueman & Co.,	London,	Silk Merchants.

---

* The house has since made arrangements for a liquidation in full, and, with a modification of partnership, continues business.

† As a curious fact, illustrative of the origin and decline of Companies, it may be recorded, that the Colombian, the New Granada, and the Anglo-Mexican Mining Companies, all of which received birth in, or shortly after the great mania of 1825, have struggled on and combated with increasing difficulties, until the present panic; and it has now been determined that each of these shall be wound up with every possible expedition. That favourite speculation of all speculations, the Real del Monte Mining Association—so universally known for its once brilliant but unrealized prospects, and the enormous premium of its shares, is also to undergo a course of liquidation, and the property, and plant if possible, is to be disposed of for the benefit of those who are now interested in the Company.

December.	Gates, Coates, Bartlett, & Co.,	London,	Warehousemen.
,,	W. Thorne,	London,	Canada Trade.
,,	Lysaght, Smithett, & Co.,	London,	East India Trade.
,, ,,	Cotesworth, Powell, and Pryor,	London,	{ Brazilian & Spanish American Trade.
,,	Blain & Son,	Liverpool,	Corn Dealers.
,,	Froske & Co.,	Liverpool,	Ship Owners.
,,	G. Hargreaves,	Liverpool,	East India Trade.
,,	T. and J. Sands,	Liverpool,	Merchants.
,,	Oak Farm Company,	Kingswinford,	Iron Trade.
,,	Oakes and Jones,	Kingswinford,	Iron Trade.
,,	J. Marsland,	Manchester,	Cotton Spinner.
,,	B. Bartley & Co.,	Halifax,	Manufacturers.
,,	Baillie, Honeyman, & Co.,	Glasgow,	Merchants.
,,	Campbell, Harvey, & Co.,	Glasgow,	Silk Merchants.
,,	Fergusson, Watson, & Co.	Glasgow,	Silk Merchants.
,,	Mitchell & Co.,	Glasgow,	Canada Trade.
,,	R. Forrester,	Glasgow,	Warehouseman.
,,	Rankine & Co.,	Glasgow,	Warehousemen.
,,	Ayrshire Iron Company,	Glasgow,	Iron Trade.
,,	W. S. Hamilton & Co.,	Dublin,	West India Trade.
,,	Henrys & Co.,	Dublin,	Calico Printers.
,,	Deaves, Brothers,	Cork,	Russia Trade.
,,	Saunders, May, Fordyce, & Co.,	Calcutta.	East India Trade.

The principal foreign failures were—

,,	C. Bruyn and Sons,	Amsterdam,	Sugar Refiners.
,,	Dervieu, Sen. & Co.,	Algeria,	Corn Trade.
,,	Parangue and Sons,	Marseilles,	Bankers.
,,	Richer & Co.,	Prague,	Manufacturers.
,,	Tercelin Sigart,	Mons,	Banker.
,,	Baron de J. Von Haber,	Carlsruhe,	Banker & Manufact.
,,	S. F. Gontard and Sons,	Frankfort,	Bankers.
,,	L. H. Flersheim,	Frankfort,	Banker.
,,	S. Von Haber and Sons,	Frankfort,	Bankers.
,,	J. B. Spengel,	Hamburg,	Merchant.

The contrast of the state of the Stock markets in November and December, denote that notwithstanding excessive fluctuations, the prices of Government securities were on the whole steadily improving. Railway shares, on the other hand, were for a time almost stationary, but weakness was generally considered their prominent characteristic.

GOVERNMENT SECURITIES.

	NOVEMBER, 1847.				DECEMBER, 1847.			
	Price on the 1st.	Lowest Price.	Highest Price.	Price on the 30th.	Price on the 1st.	Lowest Price.	Highest Price.	Price on the 31st.
Consols, Money	81¾	81¼	86⅛	85⅛	85⅝	85	86	Shut
Do. Account....	81⅞	81⅜	86⅝	85⅝	86	84⅞	86½	85¼ ex.d.
Exchequer Bills, 3d..	16/ dis.	20/dis.	2/ pm.	1/ dis.	1/ pm.	par.	12/pm.	10/pm.

RAILWAY SECURITIES.

	NOVEMBER, 1847.						DECEMBER, 1847.				
	Amount per Share.	Amount Paid.	Price on the 1st.	Lowest Price	Highest Price	Price on the 30th.	Amount Paid.	Price on the 1st.	Lowest Price	Highest Price	Price on the 31st.
	£.	£.					£. s. d.				
Brighton	Stock	£50.	39¼	38	44¾	42⅞	50 0 0	43¾	40½	44½	42½
Caledonian	50	50	35	34	36¾	35½	50 0 0	36½	35	37½	36¼
Eastern Counties ..	20	20	15¾	15⅜	16⅝	16¼	20 0 0	16⅜	15	16⅝	15⅝
Edinb. and Glasgow	50	50	47¾	43	49	46½	50 0 0	47½	43	48	43
Great Western	100	85	93	89½	103	100¾	85 0 0	101	92	102	93⅝
Hull and Selby	50	50	98½	98	99½	99½	50 0 0	99¼	98½	99½	99
London & N. Westn.	Stock.		148½	147	157	154	Stock.	155¾	145	157	149¼
Midland	Stock.		106¼	105	111	107¾	Stock.	110½	105	112	108½
South Eastern	Av. £33 : 2 : 4		27¼	26½	30¾	30⅛	Av. 33 : 2 : 4	31	28¾	31½	30
Do. Western	Av. £41 : 6 : 10		54¾	54	56	54¾	Av. 41 : 6 : 10	55	47	55½	51¼
York & N. Midland	£50	£50	70	69	76	75½	50 0 0	75¾	72	76½	72½
Boulogne & Amiens	20	20	13¾	13½	15⅜	15	20 0 0	15¼	14¼	15½	14¼
Northern of France	20	10	10⅞	10¾	13⅛	12½	10 0 0	12¾	11⅜	13	11⅞
Orleans & Bordeaux	20	6	4⅛	4⅛	6	5½	6 0 0	—	5⅛	5¾	5¼
Paris and Rouen ..	20	20	—	34¼	35⅞	35½	20 0 0	—	34¼	35¼	—

If December 1847 may not be considered to have brought to a complete termination the effects of the crisis and panic changes of April, August, and October, it must be admitted that the heighth of their severity had been mitigated by the measures adopted by the Government in co-operation with the Bank directors.

The measure of distress, if not equal to that which prevailed in 1825, or remoter periods, was great and appalling, and accompanied as it had been by varied shocks upon the monetary system, the Bank administration, in the mean while raising their rates of discount from 3½ to 8 per cent. and again reducing them from 8 to 5 per cent, (*minimum* in all cases,) acted in conjunction with our inflated state of business so rigourously, as to affect all classes of merchants, traders, &c., whose affairs were in the least concerned.

Concluding as 1847 did with a train of mercantile disasters that involved losses which could not be brought within the bounds of reasonable calculation,* the faint hopes entertained of a revival in trade did not encourage sanguine feelings for the future, and therefore it was only in respect of what might be

* *Vide* Mr. J. Bates' evidence before the Committee on Commercial Distress.

considered a course of amendment that opinions were with any freedom expressed.

A cursory glance at the lists of failures, will show that in London, Liverpool, Manchester, and Glasgow, the career of ruin was extensively felt; the Corn trade, and the East India and Mauritius trade, being the particular victims of this excited and unhealthy condition of affairs, which occurring in close contact with the engagements of the nation to an unprecedented amount for public works, wholly maintained by private enterprise,* so shattered credit, as to render it completely unavailing in any channel of commerce whatever.

Under such circumstances, the year closed gloomily and heavily, for, notwithstanding it had been calculated that several of the most important of the failed houses would liquidate in full, assurances were wanting to prove the truth of so desirable a consummation.† It was also clearly manifest, whatever the stage of progress for the better, and however satisfactory the symptoms, that a length of time must elapse before a sufficient advance could be made to restore a state of order in commercial circles, which should promise firmness and durability.

---

* The gross amount of railway calls in 1847 was £42,071,893, £36,281,393 being for English lines, and £5,790,500, for foreign lines.

† Mr. Morris, the Governor of the Bank, said before the Commons' Committee on Commercial Distress,—" There are about thirty-three houses, comparatively speaking, large houses, which have failed in London; they failed to the amount of £8,129,000. The first seven are expected to pay in full; of the other houses there is one expected to pay 5s. 6d., another 5s. 6d., another 6s. 6d., another 9s., another 12s., another 8s., another 3s., another 5s., &c. The result is, that with respect to a large majority of those houses no assistance would have been sufficient to carry them through those difficulties."

" Is the average above 12s.?—With the exception of the first seven, which are expected to pay in full, it is believed that the average will not be more than 6s. 8d. in the pound." Since this statement was made, two or three of the firms reported to pay 20s. shew on a revision of accounts, a most serious deficiency. Those who have already, or will in all probability, liquidate in full, include Messrs. Sanderson & Co., bill brokers; Messrs. Scott, Bell, & Co., East India trade; Messrs. Trueman and Cook, Colonial brokers; Messrs. John Thomas, Son, and Lefevre, Russia trade; and Messrs. Job Wright & Co., Russia trade.

EPOCH THE THIRD.

THE FRENCH REVOLUTION.

It would be difficult, perhaps, to conceive, after the excitement occasioned by the prostration of trade, and the failure of mercantile houses, a greater or more sudden change in the aspect of relations, social and political, than that which was brought about by the immediate success of the ultra reform movement in Paris at the beginning of 1848.

The English public, scarcely rccovering from the depression which had so seriously afflicted their mercantile position, (for difficulties were not altogether removed, and fresh suspensions continued to be mentioned) were called upon to witness a revulsion in political sentiments abroad, as astounding as it was wide spread and devastating, and which, placed in juxta-position with their own casualities, promised to produce results equally serious throughout the Continent of Europe.

Notwithstanding Louis Phillippe and his administration were known to be encompassed with difficulties, arising from the menacing position of their opponents, it was not anticipated that their rule would have so abruptly closed, and hence, in January, there was no general disposition to view their perplexing condition as one threatening imminent danger, beyond what might have been assuaged by calling in other statesmen to reinvigorate the Government's fast declining supremacy. Apart from this consideration, there were favourable circumstances attending the symptoms of reaction which, though gradual, were every day becoming more apparent in our own country; and the Bank of England having felt themselves justified in relaxing their terms for discounts to a *minimum* of 4 per cent., the long desired approach of a restoration to healthiness in trading affairs, was regarded as a subject of more direct interest than French ministerial embarrassments.

February, however, had not far advanced before certain discouraging indications tended to arouse attention. The budget disclosures proving far from satisfactory, and a proposal for an additional income tax exciting popular indignation, there was evident cause for alarm at home. At the same time the critical position of the ministry of M. Guizot produced an unfavourable effect on our funds, and when the intelligence of the dethronement of the King arrived, the decline was considerable.

With the object of exhibiting concisely the range of fluctuation in English securities on the occasion, the state of business during the last week in February is here detailed.

On the 24th news was received of the forced resignation of M. Guizot. The funds then only declined in a slight degree, the speculators presuming that the dismissal of the minister would appease the populace.

The next day the market, on opening, showed no symptoms of excessive fluctuation. Ranging between 88½ and 88. Consols were, towards the close of business, quoted at the latter price. But as soon as it was notified that Louis Phillipps had abdicated, the quotation rapidly descended, and after the regular hour of dealing, settled down at 85½. Even this figure was an uncertain one, for so great was the excitement, that the coffee-houses were thronged by all classes of operators, eager sellers at any price the jobbers chose to make.

As there was a partial blank in the accounts of the 26th, though the fact of a provisional government having been constituted was fully accredited, the market was less subject to alteration. The majority of the dealers continued sellers, but in the absence of specific intelligence, much difficulty was experienced in finding " takers of stock."

No regular communication had yet been opened between Paris and Boulogne, owing to the breaking up of the rails on the Great Northern Railway, but the letters received left no doubt respecting the career of the revolutionists. A regency was said to have been established—this was speedily contradicted, and the republic, with *Libertè*, *Egalitè*, and *Fraternitè* for its motto, was pronounced to have been proclaimed. Opening at about 84, Consols receded to 83, whence they rose to 85⅜. This point was not long sustained, and sales at the close of the market brought them to 84. Business being, however, prolonged till late in the evening, 83½ was the nearest average quotation finally current among the " outside" fraternity.*

The *Times*, describing the state of business on the 28th, said, " It may safely be affirmed, that since the fall of Napoleon, the City has never been in a state of greater excitement than that which has prevailed to day. As compared with the closing prices of Saturday (the 26th,) the English funds have gone down nearly 4 per cent. The first quotation of Consols was 81½ to 82½. From this they receded to 81, and upon the appearance of a few buyers they rallied to 83. A continued succession of sales then took place, and the price went to 80½, the

* A comparative statement of fluctuations published in the city article of The *Times* at this date, exhibited the influence exerted upon the value of our national securities by the revolutions of July 1830 and February 1848. The three days of July produced a fall of about 3 per cent. in Consols, the highest price on the 27th being 92¾, and the lowest price on the 31st 89⅞. The effect of the February revolution was much greater, the decline amounting to 6 per cent., the difference between 89½, the price on the 22d, and 83½, the price on the 27th. But Consols in 1830 did not touch their lowest quotation at the period of the French revolution. It was also shown that the lowest price was marked on the 8th November, when the visit of William IV. to the city was postponed, their quotation then descending to 78, being little less than 12 per cent. under the worst price of July; the market having from September suffered through the alarm occasioned by agricultural incendiarism, and the general uneasiness which preceded the assembling of the new Parliament after the demise of George IV. By the end of the year Consols recovered to 82½.

market ultimately closing at 80⅝ to ⅞ for money, and 81 to ¼ for the account. Immediately after this, however, a *third edition* of The *Times* came, and a panic ensued, during which bargains were done at 79¾. At six o'clock the quotations were 80 for money and 80¼ for the account."*

Notwithstanding Consols continued to oscillate, the market on the 29th was generally considered to have assumed a somewhat steadier aspect. Belgium, reported to have declared for a republic, was then known to remain staunch to her king, and prices having fluctuated between 83 and 81½, a reaction followed, and about 82¾ was the latest quotation.

In January and February, the failures notified were principally connected with England and her dependencies. The worst fears entertained for the Calcutta houses in correspondence with the London suspended establishments were realized, and in these months the intelligence came that as many as sixteen of them had fallen. The Union Bank at Calcutta, and the West India Bank at Barbadoes, were also discovered to be in a lamentable condition of insolvency, thus setting at rest all questions respecting the expediency of the course adopted by their London agents refusing in November to accept their drafts. The suspension of Messrs. Cargill, Headlam, & Co., of Newcastle-upon-Tyne, in the East India trade, was the great provincial failure in January. In February the only London house reported, deserving notice, with the exception of the Stock-exchange failures, resulting from the heavy decline in all foreign securities, was Messrs. John Kingston & Co., in the West India trade, whose assets exhibited a considerable surplus.

January.	Durand and McKenzie,	London,	American Trade.
,,	Hoilbut, Rubens, & Co.,	London,	American Trade.
,,	J. Brightman & Co.,	London,	East India Trade.
,,	J. Anderson & Co.,	Glasgow,	S. American Trade.
,,	W. and A. Taylor,	Glasgow,	Manufacturers.
,,	McPhails & Co.,	Glasgow,	Spinners.

* Another calculation in this journal stated the capital of the French funded debt, including the loan of 1847, to be about £209,000,000. The capital invested in French railways is set down at £44,000,000, of which £30,686,000, it appears, has been called up.

January.	Gilmour and Kerr,	Glasgow,	Spinners.
,,	J. Lacey,	Glasgow,	West India Trade.
,,	Anderson, M'Gregor, & Co.,	Glasgow,	West India Trade.
,,	Cargill, Headlam, & Co.,	Newcastle-upon-Tyne,	East India Trade.
,,	Bertram and Parkinson,	Newcastle-upon-Tyne,	General Merchants.
,,	West India Bank,	Barbadoes,	Bankers.
,,	Cockerell & Co.,	Calcutta,	East India Trade.
,,	Lyall, Matheson, & Co.	Calcutta,	East India Trade.
,,	Church, Lake, & Co.,	Calcutta,	East India Trade.
,,	Shearman, Mullens, & Co.,	Calcutta,	East India Trade.
,,	Livingstone & Co.,	Calcutta,	East India Trade.
,,	Smith, Cowell, & Co.	Calcutta,	East India Trade.
,,	Hughesdon, Brothers,	Calcutta,	East India Trade.
,,	Ewing, Aird, & Co.	Calcutta,	East India Trade.
,,	Lake, Hammel, & Co.,	Calcutta,	East India Trade.
,,	Colville, Gilmore, & Co.,	Calcutta,	East India Trade.
,,	B. T. Ford & Co.	Calcutta,	East India Trade.
	The foreign failures were—		
,,	Julius Cohen,	Paris,	Banker.
,,	J. C. Plitt,	St. Petersburg,	Merchant.
,,	Crozet, Nephew, & Co.,	Marseilles,	Merchants.
,,	Kramer and Son,	Amsterdam,	Merchants.
,,	A. Baert,	Frankfort,	Merchant.
,,	M. Bass,	Paris,	Banker.
,,	M. Cochetaux & Co.,	Lille,	Manufacturers.
February.	John Kingston & Co.,	London,	West India Trade.
,,	William Clay & Co.,	London,	Warehousemen.
,,	J. C. M'Mullen,	London,	Stock Exchange.
,,	Hanbury and Wright,	London,	Stock Exchange.
,,	R. M. Preece,	London,	Stock Exchange.
,,	J. Duffell,	London,	Stock Exchange.
,,	S. Ridge,	London,	Stock Exchange.
,,	Jevons, Sons, & Co.,	Liverpool,	Iron Trade.
,,	J. G. Campbell & Co.,	Liverpool,	West India and Mexican Trade.
,,	Hemmingway & Co.,	Liverpool,	African Trade.
,,	Union Bank,	Calcutta,	Bankers.
,,	Owen, Allhusen, & Co.,	Calcutta,	East India Trade.
,,	H. and A. Crooke,	Calcutta,	East India Trade.
,,	John Weinholt & Co.,	Calcutta,	East India Trade.
,,	Lackersteen, Brothers,	Calcutta,	East India Trade.
,,	Vinay, Cardoza, & Co.,	Madras,	East India Trade.
,,	H. Adam & Co.,	Mauritius,	Merchants.
,,	H. Barlow & Co.,	Mauritius,	Merchants.
	The chief foreign failures in this month were—		
,,	M. L. Luuyt & Co.,	Paris,	Bankers.
,,	Dubois & Co.,	Havre,	The Havre Commercial Bank.
,,	Jaques Reinach & Co.,	Mentz,	Bankers.

With regard to the variations in public securities in these two months, the subjoined table clearly indicates a considerable fall, Government and railway stocks alike suffering from the state of business produced by the revolution, French shares declined to a low point, and were scarcely marketable at any depreciation.

In January prices had rapidly advanced, and in the early part of February Consols stood at 90. Towards the close of the month, however, they were quoted in the official list at 80½. The Bank accounts were improving, and the bullion had reached £14,759,000.

The railway calls in January amounted to £4,800,000, including £220,000 for foreign companies, and in February to £2,200,000, the calls for foreign companies then being £132,000.

GOVERNMENT SECURITIES.

	JANUARY, 1848.				FEBRUARY, 1848.			
	Price on the 1st.	Lowest Price.	Highest Price.	Price on the 31st.	Price on the 1st.	Lowest Price.	Highest Price.	Price on the 29th.
Consols, Money	Shut	85½ ex.d.	89¾	89⅜	89½	80½	90	82¼
Do. Account....	85⅛ ex.d.	85½ ex.d.	89¾	89⅜	89½	80⅝	90	82¼
Exchequer Bills, 3d..	11/ pm.	9/ pm.	39/ pm.	36/ pm.	37/ pm.	4/ pm.	41/ pm.	8/ pm.

RAILWAY SECURITIES.

	JANUARY, 1848.						FEBRUARY, 1848.				
	Amount per Share.	Amount Paid.	Price on the 1st.	Lowest Price	Highest Price	Price on the 31st.	Amount Paid.	Price on the 1st.	Lowest Price	Highest Price	Price on the 29th.
	£	£					£. s.				
Brighton	Stock.	50	42⅝	42	44½	42¾	50 0	42¾	28¾	43¼	30¾
Caledonian	50	50	36⅝	35¼	36½	36½	50 0	36½	29	35½	32
Eastern Counties ..	Stock.	20	15	15⅜	16¼	16	20 0	16	13¼	16½	14 ex. d.
Edinb. and Glasgow	Stock.	50	43½	43½	45¼	44	50 0	44	37¼	44¼	37½
Great Western	100	85	93	92	105½	103¾	90 0	103¾	94	104½	97 ex. d.
Hull and Selby	50	50	—	100	102½	—	50 0	—	98	104	98½
London & N. Westn.	Stock.		148½	148	155	153	Stock.	153	130	154	135 ex. d.
Midland	Stock.		109¼	109	116½	115¼	Stock.	115¼	98	116½	104 ex. d.
South Eastern	Av. £33:2:4		30¼	29¾	31½	31⅜	Av. £33:2:4	31⅜	24	31¾	27
Do. Western . ..	Av. £41:6:10		51	50½	56	54⅝	Av. £41:6:10	54⅝	47½	55	49½ ex. d.
York & N. Midland	Stock.	50	73	72½	78	77¾	£50 0	77¾	66	79	66½ ex. d.
Boulogne & Amiens	20	20	14	13⅜	14¼	13¾	20 0	13¾	7¾	13⅞	9¼
Northern of France	20	10	12	10⅝	12	11¼	10 0	11¼	5	11½	6⅝
Orleans & Bordeaux	20	6	5⅜	4⅞	5½	5	6 0	5	2¾	5¼	2⅞
Paris and Rouen ..	20	20	—	34¾	35½	35¼	20 0	35¼	24	35¼	26½

The declaration of presumed popular ideas through the French provisional government, soon brought conviction that the irresponsible character of the parties of which it was composed would at least peril the safety of trade; and every one, while concurring in the desire expressed by Lamartine to preserve universal peace, only too plainly saw that the visionary schemes enunciated with his sanction, and the free and unrestrained license given to the populace in accordance with their assumed rights as recognized by the advocates of Communism, must, sooner or later, destroy the small share of confidence remaining between the upper and lower classes. The pressing necessities of the state, with a failing treasury and the extreme delapidation of resources, were shortly productive of serious consequences to the Bank of France, and while in this instance the precautionary measure of a suspension of specie payments was forthwith adopted and carried out, the greater number of other banks in Paris declared their inability to meet their engagements, and all were said to be making arrangements for a contraction of business and final liquidation. From Paris, Havre, and Marseilles, lengthy catalogues of failures were received, and the only prospect of assistance held out to the mercantile community was through the organization of discount banks supported by Government security.

Following the example so promptly set, the Belgian Government decreed that the notes of the Bank of Belgium and the Sociètè Générale should be a legal tender, and also adopted measures for raising a forced loan by increased taxation on real and personal property, and state salaries. Projects of law, sanctioning these schemes, were passed with great celerity in the Chambers, so that with official notices respecting financial aid, relief, and employment for the working classes, the ministry of Brussels were nearly as actively engaged in legislative formulæ as their Parisian neighbours.

It was quite impossible at this period to watch the current of affairs on the Continent without being painfully impressed with the certainty of the vast amount of commercial ruin occasioned by the progress of the French revolution. With the exception of Vienna, where there was an unprecedented degree of confidence among a populace in a state of open revolt, the advices from all parts of Europe contained particulars of distressing mercantile disasters; and panic reigned throughout Belgium, Germany, and Holland.

The stoppage of banks and bankers had now become a matter of such every day occurrence, that any fresh intimation of the kind almost failed to create a sensation. The general disarrangement of credit not only acted prejudicially on Paris establishments, but also penetrated the most distant Bourses, and to the astonishment of most people, so outrageously assaulted the solidity of Amsterdam, that no fewer than fifteen or twenty money changers and stock dealers were at once reduced to a state of insolvency.

To have disturbed the tranquillity of Belgium, to have created a run upon the banks at Antwerp and Brussels, or, to have caused, as was the case, all similar establishments in the cities of the departments to suspend specie payments, was a consequence not unexpected; but to find that prices among the Hamburg brokers should have so soon receded from 5 to 15 per cent. on the most stable securities, and about 20 per cent. on railway shares, and that such a series of disasters should have attended their doughty Dutch compeers, were eventualities not for a moment calculated. Unfortunately, however, such was the case, and without stopping to inquire whether fortuitous circumstances wholly conspired to produce this result, or whether it was facilitated by their own imprudent course of locking up capital in dangerous and inconvertible securities, the fact was chronicled as part and parcel of the current news of the hour. Ranging in its course, the panic equally paralyzed the funds at Vienna and at Frankfort, and so alarming were the accounts received from most quarters, that few persons who possessed connexions with monetary concerns within the scope of its influence, dared to hope an escape from loss.

The extraordinary enthusiasm pervading the European States, and the almost universal rising consequent throughout them, when the French Republican Government appeared to have been firmly established, were in a minor degree reflected in this kingdom and in Ireland by the impotent efforts of Chartist leaders and Repeal confederates. No pressing danger from these sources of agitation being feared, desperate as were the measures it was alleged their originators would resort to, opportunity was given to watch more narrowly the course of proceedings elsewhere.

The preservation of peace between England and France, consolidated by mutual assurances of dependence upon each other's assistance to maintain in strict integrity the rights of the family of nations, removed suspicions prematurely entertained of the imminent risk of a collision, and under the tranquilizing influence of this declaration, the Schleswig-Holstein dispute, the war between Austria and Sardinia, the severence of Sicily from Naples, and other surrounding disturbances, failed to shadow forth in their various phases any immediate cause for apprehension.

Between March and May the funds and railway stocks continued to fluctuate; sometimes up and sometimes down; on the average, however, the tendency was towards improvement. The interest on Exchequer Bills, it will be noticed, had been reduced. Even

GOVERNMENT SECURITIES.

	MARCH, 1848.				MAY, 1848.			
	Price on the 1st.	Lowest Price.	Highest Price.	Price on the 31st.	Price on the 2d.	Lowest Price.	Highest Price.	Price on the 31st.
Consols, Money......	82⅞	80½	83¾	81¼	83⅛	82⅞	84⅝	84
Do. Account....	82⅞	80½	83⅞	81⅜	83¼	82⅞	84⅝	83⅞
Exchequer Bills .... 2½d. & 3d.	11/pm.	7/pm.	35/pm.	33/pm.	41/pm.	30/pm.	47/pm.	32/pm.

RAILWAY SECURITIES.

	MARCH, 1848.						MAY, 1848.						
	Amount per Share.	Amount paid.	Price on the 1st.	Lowest Price	Highest Price	Price on the 31st.	Amount Paid.			Price on the 2d.	Lowest Price	Highest Price	Price on the 31st.
	£	£					£	s.	d.				
Brighton	Stock.	50	31¾	29⅛	32¼	29½	50	0	0	31½	30¼	34½	31⅝
Caledonian	50	50	30¼	26	31	26¾	50	0	0	30¼	29	33¼	31⅜
Eastern Counties ..	Stock.	20	13¾	13	14⅛	13⅜	20	0	0	13⅜	13¼	15⅞	14¼
Edinb. and Glasgow	Stock.	50	—	35	40	38	50	0	0	41¾	41	48	44½
Great Western	100	90	94	88½	97	89¾	90	0	0	90¾	90	97½	92¾
Hull and Selby	50	50	98½	96½	99½	—	50	0	0	98	98	100	—
London & N. Westn.	Stock.		135	124	137	126½	Stock			129¼	127	137	128
Midland	Stock.		103½	95½	106	97½	Stock			99½	97½	107½	102½
South Eastern	Av. £33 : 2 : 4		26¾	23	28	23½	Av. 33	2	4	22⅛	22¼	25½	24½
Do. Western	Stock.	£50	49½	43½	50	44½	50	0	0	44¾	44	49½	48
York & N. Midland	Stock.	50	66	60	69	62¾	50	0	0	66	65	73	69½
Boulogne & Amiens	£20	20	9	5	9½	5¾	20	0	0	6⅜	5¾	6¾	6⅜
Northern of France	20	10	5½	2	7	2½	10	0	0	3⅞	3	4¼	4⅛
Orleans & Bordeaux	20	6	3	1⅝	3½	—	6	0	0	1¾	1½	1⅞	—
Paris & Rouen	20	20	23	13	24	13¾	20	0	0	15	15	15½	—

railway shares were in some degree better. The markets at this period were in a measure acted upon by the influx of foreign capital for investment. The Bank accounts continued improving. Railway calls for March were £3,100,000—English, £1,800,000; Foreign, £1,300,000: for April £2,750,000—English, £2,200,000; Foreign, £550,000: for May, £3,240,000—English, £2,200,000; Foreign, £40,000.

The list of failures for March, April, and May, chiefly comprised the foreign houses that then suspended. The London and provincial stoppages were few. Messrs. Kewney and King, bankers at Grantham, failed in March. The Merchant-Traders' Ship-Loan and Insurance Association also wound up in London. In April Messrs. Birley, Corrie, & Co., East India Trade, Manchester, suspended, and in May, Messrs. Gouger and Stewart, East India trade, and Messrs. Roberts, Mitchell, & Co., East India trade, London; Messrs. Leys, Masson, & Co., spinners, and Messrs. A. Hadden & Sons, spinners, of London and Aberdeen; and Messrs. Eccles, Burnley, & Co., West India trade, Glasgow, all firms of consideration were severally announced. There were also Indian failures, Messrs. Carr, Tagore, and Co., and others.

March.	De Mattos and De Leon,	London,	General Merchants.
,,	T. H. Evans,	London,	Stock Exchange.
,,	Merchant Traders' Ship Loan and Insurance Association,	London,	Insurance Brokers.
,,	Kewney and King,	Grantham,	Bankers.
,,	Danger & Co.,	Paris,	Bankers.
,,	Gouin & Co.,	Paris,	Bankers.
,,	Lafitte, Blount, & Co.,	Paris,	Bankers.
,,	C. Pagny,	Paris,	Banker & MoneyDealer.
,,	Philip Fourchon,	Paris,	Banker & MoneyDealer.
,,	Baudon & Co.,	Paris,	Bankers.
,,	P. J. Chedaux & Co.,	Paris,	Bankers.
,,	E. Bechet & Co.,	Paris,	Bankers.
,,	E. De la Chaume & Co.,	Paris,	Bankers.
,,	Ganneron's Joint Stock Bank,	Paris,	Bankers.
,,	D. S. Königswater,	Paris,	Merchant and Money Dealer.
,,	De la Hante & Co.,	Paris,	Bankers.
,,	A. Bourget & Co.,	Paris,	Discount Bankers.
,,	D'Eichthal and Son,	Paris,	Bankers.
,,	Quertier and Godefroy,	Havre,	Merchants.
,,	L. P. Devot & Co.,	Havre,	Merchants.
,,	Widow Melum & Co.,	Havre,	Merchants.
,,	E. de Pierre,	Havre,	Merchant.
,,	Courant & Co.,	Havre,	Merchants.
,,	R. Aubin,	Marseilles,	Banker.

March.	Chataud, Sons, and Desages,	Marseilles,	Merchants.
,,	Boutaux, De la Hante, & Co.,	Lyons,	Bankers.
,,	M. G. Serret & Co.,	Valenciennes,	Bankers.
,,	F. Perret and Sons,	Neufchatel,	Bankers.
,,	M. Fonvent & Co.,	Namur,	Bankers.
,,	Commercial Bank of Antwerp,	Antwerp,	Bankers.
,,	F. de Kinder Theunissens,	Antwerp,	Bankers.
,,	Beyfus Brothers,	Frankfort,	Bankers.
,,	Mendes De Costa,	Amsterdam,	Money Dealer.
,,	Mendes De Leon, & Co.,	Amsterdam,	Money Dealers.
,,	Bleecker and Toosting,	Amsterdam,	Money Dealers.
,,	De Haan & Co.,	Amsterdam,	Money Dealers.
,,	La Maison, Bouwer, & Co.,	Amsterdam,	Money Dealers.
,,	Westerndorp & Co.,	Amsterdam,	Money Dealers.
,,	Rutgers and Rosenberg,	Amsterdam,	Money Dealers.
,,	M. Beeldsnyder,	Amsterdam,	Money Dealer.
,,	J. Boissevain,	Amsterdam,	Money Dealer.
,,	T. D. Ruys,	Amsterdam,	Money Dealer.
,,	Pieterse & Co.,	Amsterdam,	Money Dealers.
,,	M. Roseboom,	Amsterdam,	Money Dealer.
,,	Carp & Co.,	Amsterdam,	Money Dealers.
,,	A. L. Van Harpen & Co.,	Amsterdam,	Money Dealers.
,,	Firmin Kirchheim,	Berlin,	Banker.
,,	Hirschfeld and Wolff,	Berlin,	Bankers.
,,	M. Heyman,	Berlin,	Banker.
,,	J. F. De Courts & Co.,	Dordt,	Merchants.
April.	Day, Binns, & Co.,	London,	Provision Trade.
,,	Birley, Corrie, & Co.,	Manchester,	East India Trade.
,,	Caird & Co.,	Greenock,	Steam Ship Builders.
,,	Hickey, Bailey, & Co.,	Calcutta,	East India Trade.
,,	Collomb and Iselin.	New York,	Merchants.
,,	B. Paccard, Dufour, & Co.,	Paris,	Bankers.
,,	M. Thurneyssen & Co.,	Paris,	Bankers.
,,	W. Iselin,	Havre,	American Trade.
,,	D. Labilè,	Havre,	Merchant.
,,	B. Oxnard and Choix,	Marseilles,	Merchant.
,,	Cucurney, Uncle, & Co.,	Marseilles,	General Merchants.
,,	Naegley and Escher,	Marseilles,	Merchants.
,,	Lantelme, Senior, & Co.,	Marseilles,	Bankers.
,,	L. Benet & Co.,	Marseilles,	Engineers.
,,	Guerro & Co.,	Marseilles,	Spanish Trade.
,,	M. Badetti,	Marseilles,	Greek Trade.
,,	Henry Brothers,	Marseilles,	Merchants.
,,	Chancel Brothers,	Marseilles,	Dry Salters.
,,	Mantricher & Co.,	Marseilles,	American Merchants.
,,	D'Andouard & Co ,	Marseilles,	Seed Crushers.
,,	Lavison, Novach, & Co.,	Marseilles,	American Trade.
,,	Laubon & Co.,	Marseilles,	Bankers.
,,	A. Schaafhausen,	Cologne,	Banker.
,,	Oeder & Co.,	Aix la Chapelle,	Bankers.
,,	Riley and Reussner,	Magdeburg,	Bankers.
,,	W. Delvaux & Co.,	Mons,	Bankers.
,,	J. C. Van der Beek,	Elberfeldt,	Manufacturer.
,,	W. T. Jaeger,	Frankfort,	Banker.
,,	E. Warburg,	Hamburg,	Banker and Bill Broker.
,,	J. Heine and Sons,	Hamburg,	Stock Brokers.
,,	Heuss and Mencke,	Hamburg,	Merchants.
,,	F. Braasch & Co.,	Hamburg,	Merchants.

April.	Samson, Brothers & Co.,	Hamburg,	Dealer in Manufactured Goods.
,,	W. Elliot & Co.,	Hamburg,	Merchants.
,,	Ewald & Co.,	Hamburg,	Commission Merchants.
,,	Pluym and Bakker,	Amsterdam,	Bankers.
,,	Goldschmidtson & Co.,	Amsterdam,	Bankers.
,,	J. Seligmann & Co.,	Amsterdam,	Merchants.
,,	Jacob Sigrist,	Amsterdam,	Banker.
,,	Viet, Brothers, & Co.,	Berlin,	Bankers.
,,	A. Busse & Co.	Berlin,	Bankers.
,,	Poppe & Co.,	Berlin,	Bankers.
,,	L. B. Cohn,	Berlin,	Banker.
,,	Schrieber and Sons,	Breslau,	Bankers.
,,	Klecks & Co.,	Breslau,	Bankers.
,,	F. A. Conte,	Cadiz,	Banker.
May.	Gabain & Co.,	London,	German Trade.
,,	Leys, Masson, & Co.,	London & Aberdeen,	Flax Spinners.
,,	A. Hadden and Sons,	London & Aberdeen,	Worsted Spinners.
,,	Shaw and Caffray,	London,	Merchants.
,,	Weber & Co.,	London,	East India Trade.
,,	H. W. Schwartz,	London,	Merchant.
,,	Gouger and Stewart,	London,	East India Trade.
,,	Roberts, Mitchell, & Co.,	London,	East India Trade.
,,	Eccles, Burnley, & Co.,	Glasgow,	West India Trade.
,,	Carr, Tagore, & Co.,	Calcutta.	East India Trade.
,,	Hawarth, Hardman, & Co.,	Calcutta,	East India Trade.
,,	Continental Flax Company,	Boulogne,	Manufacturers.
,,	H. F. Fetschow and Son,	Berlin,	Bankers.
,,	G. R. Enet & Co.,	Hamburg,	General Merchants.
,,	H. C. Schmidt,	Hamburg,	Belgian Trade.
,,	W. J. C. Schultza,	Hamburg,	Sugar Refiner.
,,	Windmuller, Brothers, & Co.,	Hamburg,	Merchants.
,,	M. Van der Bogaerts,	Antwerp,	Merchant.
,,	Fox and Livingstone,	New York,	Merchants.
,,	Barnwell & Co.,	New York,	Merchants.
,,	E. D. Hurlbut & Co.,	New York,	Merchants.
,,	J. Thompson, Jun.	New York,	Merchant.
,,	G. F. Darby & Co.,	New York,	Merchants.
,,	Hays, La Fontaine, & Co.	Constantinople,	Merchants.
,,	J. Van Sennep & Co.,	Smyrna,	Merchants.

Within the space of the next three months fierce struggles occurred among the population of the various European states, for rights and privileges deemed requisite to the advancement of liberty and the cause of social order. The distrust experienced here from the puerile attempts of the republican government in France to carry out the projects propounded by the more violent classes of its supporters, did not apparently check the growing influence of the movement; and Lamartine and his friends having temporarily suppressed the disaffection exhibited in May, their success was regarded as affording fresh encouragement to those who desired to organize similar administrations, and hence renewed attempts were made throughout Germany and Austria to overthrow existing institutions.

But the rule of Lamartine was not long triumphant—the elections over, and the National Assembly in debate, opinion ran counter to the views expressed by the more moderate republican party. The Clubs thundered their denunciations against them, Socialists and Communists re-echoed the cry, and then followed the insurrection of June, which terminated in the elevation of General Cavaignac to absolute power, and the proclamation of martial law in Paris.

Amidst the conflicts resulting from these disturbances abroad, attention was at length called to the re-organization of rebellion in Ireland, which, aided by Smith O'Brien, and other active members of the Repeal movement, threatened to involve the country in a civil war. It was not until prompt measures were adopted from this side, accompanied by the suspension of the Habeas Corpus Act and the military occupation of the island, that the alarm of the public was alleviated. The fate of the chief delinquents is already known; the capture of some, and the surrender of others, with their trials and sentences, will be handed down to posterity in history.

The events which subsequently occurred throughout Europe, more or less affected our markets for public securities, though they do not demand extended notice. The victories of Austria in Italy, the maintainance of peace by France, and the attempted arrangement of the Schleswig-Holstein question, were, in their several stages, productive of changes; but not of so violent a character as those which immediately succeeded the revolution of February.

The prices of public securities in June and August here subjoined, will trace the course of fluctuation in those months. In June the Bank reduced the rate of interest from 4 to 3½ per cent.; the stock of bullion in its coffers having, between the 3d and the 24th, increased from £13,597,000 to £14,307,000. After July 8th, when the amount stood at £14,350,000, there was a gradual decrease, and on the 26th of August it represented £13,503,000.

GOVERNMENT SECURITIES.

	JUNE, 1848.				AUGUST, 1848.			
	Price on the 1st.	Lowest Price.	Highest Price.	Price on the 30th.	Price on the 1st.	Lowest Price.	Highest Price.	Price on the 31st.
Consols, Money	83⅞	83¾	84¾	Shut.	87¼	85⅝	87½	86¼
Do. Account....	83⅞	82¼	84⅞	84 ex. d.	87⅜	85¾	87½	86⅜
Exchequer Bills...... 2d. & 2½d.	33/pm.	30/pm.	42/pm.	38/pm.	36/pm.	21/pm.	45/pm.	26/pm.

RAILWAY SECURITIES.

	JUNE, 1848.						AUGUST, 1848.				
	Amount per Share.	Amount Paid.	Price on the 1st.	Lowest Price	Highest Price	Price on the 30th.	Amount Paid.	Price on the 1st.	Lowest Price	Highest Price	Price on the 31st.
	£	£.					£. s.				
Brighton	Stock.	50	31⅝	28⅞	31¾	30¾	50 0	31¾	27⅞	32	28⅜ ex. d.
Caledonian	50	50	31⅜	28¾	31½	29¾	50 0	26¾	22½	26¾	22¾
Eastern Counties ..	Stock.	20	14¼	13½	14⅜	14	20 0	14¾	13⅝	14⅞	13⅞ ex. d.
Edinb. and Glasgow	Stock.	50	44½	43	44½	44½	50 0	—	37	42	41¾
Great Western	100	90	92¾	82	93½	85½	90 0	85½	81	88	82½ ex. d.
Hull and Selby	50	50	—	97½	99½	—	50 0	—	98	101	99¼
London & N. Westn.	Stock.		128	115	129	120	Stock.	126¾	113	128	115½ ex. d.
Midland Counties..	Stock.		102½	96	104	100¼	Stock.	102½	87½	103¾	90½ ex. d.
South Eastern	Av. £33 : 2 : 4		24½	23	24½	23¾	Av. £33:2:4	23¾	23⅜	26½	25⅝ ex. d.
Do. Western	Stock.	£50	48	45	48¼	45½	50 0	48	38	48	39½ ex. d.
York & N. Midland	Stock.	50	69½	65½	70	66¼	50 0	67½	59½	67½	60½ ex. d.
Boulogne & Amiens	£20	20	6⅜	5⅞	6½	6⅛	20 0	6½	5¾	6¾	6
Northern of France	20	10	4⅛	3⅞	4½	4¼	10 0	5½	5¼	7⅝	7
Orleans & Bordeaux	20	6	—	1⅝	1⅞	—	6 0	2	1⅛	2	1⅜
Paris and Rouen ..	20	20	—	14¾	16	16	20 0	—	16½	17	17

Throughout this period the unfavourable state of the weather for the harvest, together with the appearance of disease in the potatoe, and a deficient revenue,* created, as far as local interests were concerned, temporary depression. Another alteration had been made in the rate of interest payable on Exchequer Bills. Railway calls were as follows:—June, £2,277,000; or English, £2,159,000, and Foreign, £118,000.—July, £4,077,000; or English, £3,900,000, and Foreign, £177,000.—and August, £3,122,000; or English, £3,023,000, and Foreign, £99,000.

* The Chancellor of the Exchequer, in his new financial statement, stated the deficiency at about £2,000,000, to supply which, he took power to sell stock whenever he might require the funds.

Referring to the quotations of railway shares, it will be perceived, that after recovering a little a fresh decline took place, which continued up to the close of August, when the reaction became most severe.

Failures had now nearly altogether ceased; and with the exception of Kelsalls & Co., announced in June, and Mr. G. T. Braine* in July, both engaged in the East India trade, none in London were regarded as of more than ordinary interest. The refusal of the Bank of England to render Mr. Braine assistance, notwithstanding his estate presented a large surplus, was a topic of much conversation, and the decision of the Court in that respect incurred almost universal condemnation.

June.	Kelsalls & Co.,	London & Manchester,	East India trade.
,,	Speir & Co.,	London,	East India trade.
,,	Ackland, Boyd, & Co.,	Ceylon,	Merchants.
,,	Schroeder & Co.,	Porto Rico,	West India trade.
,,	Durand, Delapanche, & Co.,	Rouen.	Bankers.
,,	A. J. Adan,	Brussels,	Bankers.
,,	Jacob Post,	Amsterdam,	Merchant.
,,	G. W. Arnemann and Son,	Altona,	Bankers.
,,	M. Robinow and Sons,	Hamburg,	Bankers.
,,	Dirks, Brothers,	Hamburg,	Commission agents.
July.	G. T. Braine,	London,	East India trade.
,,	Green & Co.,	Ceylon,	Merchants.
,,	Losh, Spiers, & Co.,	Trinidad,	West India trade.
,,	De Castro & Co.,	Porto Rico,	West India trade.
,,	G. H. Sontag & Co.,	Hamburg,	African and West India trade.
August.	Alston, Bevan, & Co.,	London,	Mediterranean trade
,,	Rowand and Dunlop,	Liverpool & Glasgow,	Australian trade.
,,	Gibson, Read, Davidson, & Co.,	Ceylon,	Mill Proprietors and Merchants.

The month of September was remarkable for ushering in a new species of agitation with respect to railway investments. The mania having produced its results, and the amount of calls having afterwards exercised great influence upon prices, another change now came, working effects as discouraging as any that had preceded them. Throughout 1847 the continuous decline in shares was fully apparent, but the last few months in 1848

* *Vide* Statement of affairs, Appendix, page xxx.

marked more strongly than ever the extent of depreciation to which they are liable.

The general reduction of dividends in the last half of the former year,* aggravated by the pressure of calls, few of the companies manifesting a disposition to restrict expenditure, although professing to do so, engendered much distrust in the public mind, and no active measures being adopted for the suspension of works, but on the contrary, strenuous endeavours being made to raise capital by the issue of preference shares, at rates of interest varying from 6 to 7 per cent., alarm gradually increased until the market was almost absolutely abandoned by investors.

The returns for the first half-year of 1848† again presenting diminished profits, and the complexity of railway accounts, exciting suspicion, particularly on the point of existing liabilities‡ and ultimate resources, these circumstances created large speculative sales, which, whether justified or not by the real position of affairs, ended in so violent a declension of quotations, that the brokers were perfectly paralyzed, and, in October, a complete suspension of business was predicted.

---

* The following tabular statement, published in the "London Weekly Share List," exhibits the rates of dividend paid during the last four half-years, by the undermentioned companies:—

	Dividends per cent. per annum.			
	1846.	1847.		1848.
	2d Half.	1st Half.	2d Half.	1st Half.
Eastern Counties	$6\frac{3}{4}$	5	4	4
Great Western	8	8	7	7
Glasgow and Ayr	7	7	6	4
London and North Western	10	9	8	7
London and South Western	$9\frac{3}{4}$	9	8	6
Brighton	7	4	4	$2\frac{1}{2}$
Midland	7	7	7	6
South Eastern	6 . 34	6 . 34	6 . 34	6 . 34
York and North Midland	10	10	10	8
York, Newcastle, and Berwick	9	9	9	8

† See Note above.

‡ The "Bankers' Magazine," in October, 1848, stated that a return issued by the Commissioners of Railways set forth the amount of authorized capital to be raised, up to the 12th of April, 1848, as £334,280,000, while the amount of share capital actually paid up on the 1st December, 1847, was £121,640,000, and the total debts of the Companies at the same date, £39,510,000.

It was not until the London and North Western and other companies issued elaborate statements respecting present and future proceedings, that any reaction followed, or the market became restored to comparative firmness; and as the contents of these documents premised the abandonment of numerous subsidiary undertakings,* the revision of expenditure, and were believed to render a tolerably accurate exposition of their financial condition, the current of dealing was turned, and a considerable advance temporarily maintained. This reaction occurring almost simultaneously with a reduction of the rate of discount by the Bank to a *minimum* of 3 per cent., (notified to the public on the 2d of November,) naturally co-operated to stimulate business, and support the improvement.

Without attempting to enter into, or descant upon the actual and prospective position of railway property,—questions which

---

* The annexed statement of railway calls shows the rate of expenditure on these undertakings during the years 1847 and 1848:—

	FOREIGN.	ENGLISH, &c.	TOTAL.
Due in January, 1847	£1,612,000	£4,545,863	£6,157,865
,, February ,,	nil	1,393,026	1,393,025
,, March ,,	466,000	3,042,065	3,508,065
,, April ,,	100,000	4,214,955	4,314,931
,, May ,,	402,000	3,083,675	3,440,676
,, June ,,	750,000	2,463,481	3,213,485
,, July ,,	1,032,000	4,334,155	5,366,155
,, August ,,	62,000	2,224,859	2,280,854
,, September ,,	800,000	3,361,934	4,161,939
,, October ,,	420,000	3,342,342	3,762,320
,, November ,,	146,500	1,896,218	2,042,718
,, December ,,	nil	2,423,820	2,423,824
Total calls for 1847	£5,790,500	£36,281,393	£42,071,893
Due in January, 1848	£221,590	£4,638,630	£4,860,220
,, February ,,	132,000	2,140,541	2,272,541
,, March ,,	1,287,000	1,848,922	3,135,922
,, April ,,	550,000	2,209,795	2,759,795
,, May ,,	38,500	3,208,348	3,246,848
,, June ,,	118,309	2,159,365	2,277,674
,, July ,,	176,750	3,900,496	4,077,246
,, August ,,	99,422	3,023,351	3,122,773
,, September ,,	66,000	2,559,936	2,625,936
,, October ,,	412,500	1,281,155	1,693,655
,, November ,,	nil	1,691,629	1,691,629
,, December ,,	nil	1,496,010	1,496,010
Total calls for 1848	£3,102,071	£30,158,178	£33,260,249

time alone can solve,—a comparison of the prices of the leading shares in August 1845, the period when the mania reached its climax, with those in October 1848, the period when the lowest prices ever yet quoted were recorded, significantly intimates the enormous depression to which these securities have, in the space of little more than three years, been subjected.

RAILWAY SECURITIES.

	AUGUST, 1845.						OCTOBER, 1848.				
	Amount per Share.	Amount Paid.	Price on the 1st.	Lowest Price	Highest Price	Price on the 30th.	Amount Paid.	Price on the 1st.	Lowest Price	Highest Price	Price on the 31st.
	£	£					£. s.				
Brighton	50	50	80	76	80½	78¼	50 0	26¾	25	29	28½
Caledonian	50	5	10⅝	10	12⅝	12½	50 0	20	16¼	20⅜	19
Eastern Counties ..	25	£14:16	21¼	19	21½	20½ ex. d.	20 0	12⅞	11¾	13⅝	13¼
Great Western	100	80	224	175	236	176 ex. new	90 0	77	65½	80	78
London & N. Westn.	Stock.		245	214	254	223 {ex. d. & ex. new}	Stock.	109¼	99	121	117
Midland	Stock.		181	170	183	175 ex. d.	Stock.	83	64	86	83
South Eastern	Av.£33 : 2 : 4		45⅝	44¾	48½	48	Av.£33:2:4	23¼	20	24¼	23½
Do. Western	Av.£41 : 6 : 10		81½	77	84	78¼	Stock.	38½	35½	42	40
York & N. Midland	50	50	—	106	112	108½	Stock.	54	41	54	51
Boulogne & Amiens	20	6	10¾	10⅜	11⅛	11¼	£20 0	5¾	5⅜	6¼	6¼
Northern of France	20	4	6	5¾	7⅜	7	12 0	6⅜	5⅞	6⅜	6⅛
Paris and Lyons ..	20	2	3	1⅞	4⅛	3¼	11 0	5⅞	4⅝	5⅞	5

As the close of 1848 approached, the railway excitement, growing out of the sudden fall in prices and their subsequent partial recovery, having in a great degree disappeared, a feeling of increased confidence sprung up, domestic and foreign politics presenting an ameliorated aspect. True it was that as concerned the latter, Austria and Prussia exhibited in connexion with internal arrangements scenes of disorder and disaffection, but the course of policy pursued both by England and France was so unmistakeably pacific, even on the elevation of Louis Napoleon Bonaparte to the Presidentship of the Republic, that little apprehension was displayed of affairs in the North of Europe involving the general powers in those dissensions.

Trade here was in the meanwhile steadily progressing and disasters in the mercantile world being with the exception of ordinary events of the kind almost wholly unknown, the public at last seemed inclined to believe, more particularly when the auriferous resources of California were fully confirmed,* that the stream had once more reached a favourable point, and that prosperous times were not far distant.

The failures in September, October, November, and December, the majority of them of minor importance are annexed. The only London firm which suspended in that period it will be perceived was Messrs. G. Capper and Nephew, engaged in the Irish trade.

September,	Kelsall & Co.,	Calcutta,	East India Trade.
,,	Planters Bank,	Jamaica,	Bankers.
,,	Dancott, Adams, & Co.,	Trinidad,	Merchants.
October.	Jacob Reese & Sons,	Philadelphia,	Merchants.
,,	Wilcox, Maris, & Co.,	Philadelphia,	Merchants.
,,	Wells, Brothers, & Co.,	New York,	Merchants.
,,	Christo Martyrt,	Vienna,	Merchant.
November,	F. Xavier Albert,	Madrid,	Banker.
,,	Henshaw, Ward, & Co.,	Boston,	Drug Trade.
,,	Ballard, Vale, & Co.,	Boston,	Dry Goods Trade.
,,	Fales and Dana,	Boston,	Dry Goods Trade.
,,	M. P. Wilder,	Boston,	Wholesale Grocery Trade.
,,	E. Bogart,	New York,	Commission Merchant.
,,	Emanuel & Van Clief,	New York,	Produce Dealers.
,,	Dale & Co.,	New York,	Produce Dealers.
December,	George Capper & Nephew	London,	Irish Trade.
,,	Story & Co.,	St. Albans,	Bankers.
,,	R. M. M'Clelland	North of Ireland,	Linen Trade.
,,	H. L. Layard & Co.,	Ceylon,	Merchants.

Coupling the condition of the Bank's accounts in December, which showing a stock of bullion of about £14,700,000 fully justified the directors in reducing the rate of discount to 3 per cent. and contrasting these results with the markets for public securities in that month and the previous September, the advance in prices will be found to have been steady and progressive, and sufficient to induce a hope that 1849 would be entered upon under encouraging auspices.

GOVERNMENT SECURITIES.

	September, 1848.				December, 1848.			
	Price on the 1st.	Lowest Price.	Highest Price.	Price on the 30th.	Price on the 1st.	Lowest Price.	Highest Price.	Price on the 30th.
Consols, Money......	86	$85\frac{5}{8}$	$86\frac{1}{4}$	86	$87\frac{1}{2}$	$87\frac{3}{8}$ ex.d.	$88\frac{1}{4}$ ex d.	Shut.
Do. Account	86	$85\frac{5}{8}$	$86\frac{1}{2}$	$86\frac{1}{4}$	$87\frac{5}{8}$	$87\frac{1}{4}$ ex.d.	89 ex. d.	$88\frac{1}{2}$ ex.d.
Exchequer Bills .... 2d. & 2½d.	25/ pm.	22/ pm.	34/ pm.	29/ pm.	43/ pm.	37/ pm.	46/ pm.	40/ pm.

* The first intelligence of the discovery of gold in California reached England in September and October, but it was not thoroughly authenticated until December.

RAILWAY SECURITIES.

	SEPTEMBER, 1848.						DECEMBER, 1848.				
	Amount per Share.	Amount Paid.	Price on the 1st.	Lowest Price	Highest Price	Price on the 30th.	Amount Paid.	Price on the 1st.	Lowest Price	Highest Price	Price on the 1st.
	£	£					£				
Brighton	Stock	50	28½ ex. d.	25⅛	28⅞	26¾	50	28	27¾	31¾	31½
Caledonian	50	50	22¾	18¾	22⅞	20	50	18¾	18⅜	22¼	21¾
Eastern Counties ..	Stock	20	13¾ ex. d.	12⅝	14⅛	12⅞	20	11¼	11¼	12⅜	12
Edinb. & Glasgow ..	Stock	50	41¾	37½	42½	—	50	38½	37½	39	39
Great Western	100	90	82½ ex. d.	72	84	76½	90	74½	73	82	79¼
Hull & Selby	50	50	99¼ ex. d.	97	100½	97	50	96	95	99	—
London & N. Westn.	Stock		115½ ex. d.	106	116	109½	Stock	117¼	116	125	124
Midland Counties ..	Stock		90 ex. d.	81	92½	82½	Stock	77¼	76½	85	84¼
South Eastern	Av. £33 : 2 : 4		25½ ex. d.	23	26	23¼	Av. £33:2:4	22½	22	24¾	23¾
Do. Western	Stock	£50	39½ ex. d.	35½	40½	38¾	£50	38	37¾	40½	40½
York & N. Midland	Stock	50	60½ ex. d.	53	60½	54¼	50	48¼	48	54½	54½
Boulogne & Amiens	£20	20	6	5¾	6	—	20	5¾	5⅝	9½	8½
Northern of France	20	12	7¼ ex. int.	6½	7⅝	6½	12	5¾	5¾	9	8⅛
Orleans & Bordeaux	20	6	1½ ex. int.	¾	1⅝	⅞	7	—	1⅝	3½	2⅝
Paris & Rouen	20	20	17 ex. d.	15½	17	16	20	—	15⅛	20¼	18¾

Before entirely dismissing the subject of the " Commercial Crisis, 1847-48," occasion may be taken to revert to some of the prominent circumstances which have distinguished its career; and these, when considered in their true character, have, it may be distinctly asserted, embraced events which are scarcely likely to occur again concurrently for ages.

Within the period comprised in these pages, the railway share market has experienced a succession of violent revulsions, each notable in itself; the first following the mania in October 1845, the second, associated with the ravages made by commercial distress in October 1847, and the third, connected with the fearful development of railway liabilities in October 1848.

The progress of commercial distress, the shock credit received in April 1847, its subsequent complete prostration in the autumn of the same year, and its train of attendant circumstances, including the impeachment of the Bank Charter Act of 1844, and the measures taken by Government to give relief to the mercantile community, cannot fail to carry with them disagreeable remembrances; and while this is the case on one hand, the number of failures enumerated will, on the other, be hereafter regarded as furnishing, in the absence of more authentic records, a painful memorial of what then were the effects of the prevailing Crisis.

The French revolution has pourtrayed in strong colours the influence of political excitement upon surrounding nations. Rendering trade perfectly stagnant, and making a severe irruption upon the stability of European credit, it has been productive of much mercantile calamity among these several states; and, exclusive of the damage sustained by commerce in general from such disturbing causes, unequivocal testimony is afforded of the severity of the blow wherever it has fallen, by the occurrences of February, March, April, and May.

BANK OF ENGLAND RETURNS FOR 1845.

1845.	ISSUE DEPARTMENT.		BANKING DEPARTMENT.	
	Notes Issued.	Gold and Silver Bullion.	Notes in Reserve.	Gold and Silver Coin.
	£	£	£	£
JANUARY 4	28,087,000	14,087,000	8,418,000	714,000
,, ...11	28,163,000	14,163,000	7,772,000	612,000
,, ...18	28,133,000	14,133,000	7,588,000	654,000
,, ...25	28,128,000	14,128,000	7,418,000	691,000
FEBRUARY 1	28,232,000	14,232,000	7,642,000	666,000
,, ... 8	28,447,000	14,447,000	8,128,000	700,000
,, ...15	28,537,000	14,537,000	8,395,000	700,000
,, ...22	28,679,000	14,679,000	8,889,000	773,000
MARCH 1	28,952,000	14,952,000	8,952,000	777,000
,, ... 8	29,040,000	15,040,000	9,340,000	836,000
,, ...15	29,148,000	15,148,000	9,454,000	796,000
,, ...22	29,213,000	15,213,000	9,673,000	786,000
,, ...29	29,471,000	15,471,000	9,747,000	732,000
APRIL 5	29,352,000	15,352,000	9,252,000	722,000
,, ...12	29,216,000	15,216,000	8,001,000	675,000
,, ...19	29,184,000	15,184,000	7,791,000	658,000
,, ...26	29,253,000	15,253,000	8,101,000	631,000
MAY 3	29,167,000	15,167,000	7,827,000	641,000
,, ...10	29,222,000	15,222,000	8,140,000	638,000
,, ...17	29,340,000	15,340,000	8,734,000	658,000
,, ...24	29,412,000	15,412,000	9,014,000	860,000
,, ...31	29,635,000	15,635,000	9,182,000	776,000
JUNE 7	29,732,000	15,732,000	9,382,000	779,000
,, ...14	29,917,000	15,917,000	9,854,000	696,000
,, ...21	30,051,000	16,051,000	9,837,000	587,000
,, ...28	30,047,000	16,047,000	9,717,000	554,000
JULY 5	29,891,000	15,891,000	9,279,000	526,000
,, ...12	29,682,000	15,682,000	8,068,000	513,000
,, ...19	29,393,000	15,393,000	7,890,000	485,000
,, ... 26	29,243,000	15,243,000	7,942,000	549,000
AUGUST 2	29,196,000	15,196,000	7,849,000	503,000
,, ... 9	29,141,000	15,141,000	7,682,000	528,000
,, ...16*	29,075,000	15,075,000	7,494,000	603,000
,, ...23	29,022,000	15,022,000	7,832,000	580,000
,, ...30	29,009,000	15,009,000	7,959,000	583,000
SEPTEMBER .. 6	28,953,000	14,953,000	8,255,000	473,000
,, ...13	28,790,000	14,790,000	8,430,000	593,000
,, ...20	28,798,000	14,798,000	8,237,000	549,000
,, ...27	28,557,000	14,557,000	7,946,000	602,000
OCTOBER 4	28,355,000	14,355,000	7,095,000	509,000
,, ...11	28,068,000	14,068,000	7,037,000	511,000
,, ...18	27,778,000	13,778,000	5,525,000	411,000
,, ...25†	27,415,000	13,415,000	5,389,000	585,000
NOVEMBER 1	27,267,000	13,267,000	5,219,000	617,000
,, ... 8	27,202,000	13,202,000	5,437,000	520,000
,, ...15	26,974,000	12,974,000	5,483,000	595,000
,, ...22	27,036,000	13,036,000	6,076,000	522,000
,, ...29	26,733,000	12,733,000	5,932,000	503,000
DECEMBER 6	26,540,000	12,540,000	5,945,000	526,000
,, ...13	26,626,000	12,626,000	6,506,000	642,000
,, ...20	26,819,000	12,819,000	6,768,000	558,000
,, ...27	26,771,000	127,71,000	6,914,000	554,000

* Height of the Railway Mania.
† Commencement of the Railway Panic.

BANK OF ENGLAND RETURNS FOR 1846.

1846.	ISSUE DEPARTMENT. Notes Issued.	ISSUE DEPARTMENT. Gold and Silver Bullion.	BANKING DEPARTMENT. Notes in Reserve.	BANKING DEPARTMENT. Gold and Silver Coin.
	£	£	£	£
JANUARY 3	26,675,000	12,675,000	6,418,000	605,000
,, ...10	26,541,000	12,541,000	5,672,000	652,000
,, ...17	26,573,000	12,573,000	5,393,000	565,000
,, ...24	26,525,000	12,525,000	5,416,000	677,000
,, ...31	26,587,000	12,587,000	5,113,000	700,000
FEBRUARY.... 7	26,698,000	12,698,000	5,363,000	637,000
,, ...14	26,800,000	12,800,000	6,674,000	667,000
,, ...21	26,973,000	12,973,000	6,887,000	678,000
,, ...28	27,015,000	13,015,000	6,994,000	760,000
MARCH........ 7	27,079,000	13,079,000	7,576,000	707,000
,, ...14	27,177,000	13,177,000	7,712,000	717,000
,, ...21	27,264,000	13,264,000	8,033,000	700,000
,, ...28	27,269,000	13,269,000	7,683,000	718,000
APRIL 4	27,181,000	13,181,000	7,316,000	643,000
,, ...11	27,030,000	13,030,000	6,728,000	541,000
,, ...18	27,031,000	13,031,000	6,515,000	595,000
,, ...25	27,049,000	13,049,000	6,488,000	656,000
MAY 2	27,072,000	13,072,000	6,408,000	661,000
,, ... 9	27,244,000	13,244,000	6,836,000	635,000
,, ...16	27,520,000	13,520,000	7,497,000	664,000
,, ...23	27,706,000	13,706,000	7,774,000	706,000
,, ...30	27,993,000	13,993,000	8,043,000	704,000
JUNE.......... 6	28,325,000	14,325,000	8,468,000	686,000
,, ...13	28,603,000	14,603,000	9,011,000	736,000
,, ...20	29,005,000	15,005,000	9,631,000	683,000
,, ...27	29,273,000	15,273,000	9,664,000	742,000
JULY.......... 4	29,322,000	15,322,000	9,303,000	625,000
,, ...11	29,266,000	15,266,000	8,425,000	596,000
,, ...18	29,139,000	15,139,000	8,139,000	630,000
,, ...25	29,312,000	15,312,000	8,562,000	636,000
AUGUST 1	29,292,000	15,292,000	8,796,000	510,000
,, ... 8	29,386,000	15,386,000	9,075,000	558,000
,, ...15	29,456,000	15,456,000	8,601,000	588,000
,, ...22	29,653,000	15,653,000	9,506,000	522,000
,, ...29	29,875,000	15,875,000	9,449,000	490,000
SEPTEMBER .. 5	29,760,000	15,760,000	9,231,000	512,000
,, ...12	29,864,000	15,864,000	9,846,000	488,000
,, ...19	29,758,000	15,758,000	9,817,000	550,000
,, ...26	29,665,000	15,665,000	9,788,000	568,000
OCTOBER...... 3	29,359,000	15,359,000	8,809,000	456,000
,, ...10	29,078,000	15,078,000	8,305,000	504,000
,, ...17	28,741,000	14,741,000	7,409,000	401,000
,, ...24	28,437,000	14,437,000	7,157,600	456,000
,, ...31	28,309,000	14,309,000	6,934,000	498,000
NOVEMBER .. 7	28,235,000	14,235,000	7,264,000	524,000
,, ...14	28,246,000	14,246,000	7,836,000	602,000
,, ...21	28,317,000	14,317,000	8,109,000	605,000
,, ...28	28,313,000	14,313,000	8,325,000	694,000
DECEMBER.... 5	28,269,000	14,269,000	8,402,000	733,000
,, ...12	28,410,000	14,410,000	8,623,000	742,000
,, ...19	28,413,000	14,413,000	8,864,000	749,000
,, ...26	28,442,000	14,442,000	8,813,000	624,000

BANK OF ENGLAND RETURNS FOR 1847.

1847.	ISSUE DEPARTMENT.		BANKING DEPARTMENT.	
	Notes Issued.	Gold and Silver Bullion.	Notes in Reserve.	Gold and Silver Coin.
	£	£	£	£
JANUARY 2	28,258,000	14,258,000	8,227,000	693,000
,, ... 9	27,552,000	13,552,000	6,715,000	755,000
,, ...16	27,225,000	13,225,000	6,545,000	723,000
,, ...23	26,766,000	12,766,000	6,167,000	676,000
,, ...30	26,172,000	12,172,000	5,703,000	728,000
FEBRUARY.... 6	25,504,000	11,504,000	5,890,000	783,000
,, ...13	25,471,000	11,471,000	5,747,000	827,000
,, ...20	25,458,000	11,458,000	5,976,000	756,000
,, ...27	25,349,000	11,349,000	6,016,000	695,000
MARCH........ 6	24,993,000	10,993,000	5,714,000	601,000
,, ...13	24,786,000	10,786,000	5,554,000	663,000
,, ...20	24,487,000	10,487,000	5,418,000	743,000
,, ...27	24,320,000	10,320,000	4,876,000	695,000
APRIL 3*	23,554,000	9,554,000	3,699,000	691,000
,, ...10	23,236,000	9,236,000	2,832,000	630,000
,, ...17	22,801,000	8,801,000	2,558,000	528,000
,, ...24	22,549,000	8,549,000	2,718,000	664,000
MAY 1	22,506,000	8,506,000	2,741,000	831,000
,, ... 8	22,788,000	8,788,000	3,196,000	799,000
,, ...15	22,967,000	8,967,000	3,793,000	902,000
,, ...22	23,200,000	9,200,000	4,420,000	747,000
,, ...29	23,290,000	9,290,000	4,628,000	879,000
JUNE.......... 5	23,434,000	9,434,000	5,088,000	802,000
,, ...12	23,592,000	9,592,000	5,375,000	765,000
,, ...19	23,632,000	9,632,000	5,664,000	879,000
,, ...26	23,676,000	9,676,000	5,652,000	849,000
JULY.......... 3	23,562,000	9,562,000	5,158,000	834,000
,, ...10	23,304,000	9,304,000	4,331,000	781,000
,, ...17	23,232,000	9,232,000	4,068,000	685,000
,, ...24	23,119,000	9,119,000	4,216,000	651,000
,, ...31	22,666,000	8,666,000	3,774,000	664,000
AUGUST ...... 7†	22,634,000	8,634,000	3,946,000	618,000
,, ...14	22,648,000	8,648,000	3,992,000	638,000
,, ...21	22,614,000	8,614,000	4,488,000	624,000
,, ...28	22,565,000	8,565,000	4,330,000	573,000
SEPTEMBER .. 4	22,396,000	8,396,000	4,189,000	562,000
,, ...11	22,307,000	8,307,000	4,466,000	607,000
,, ...18	22,205,000	8,205,000	4,272,000	675,000
,, ...25	22,190,000	8,190,000	4,112,000	591,000
OCTOBER...... 2	22,121,000	8,121,000	3,409,000	443,000
,, ... 9	21,961,000	7,961,000	3,321,000	447,000
,, ...16	21,989,000	7,989,000	2,630,000	441,000
,, ...23‡	21,865,000	7,865,000	1,547,000	447,000
,, ...30	22,009,000	8,009,000	1,176,000	429,000
NOVEMBER .. 6	22,426,000	8,426,000	2,030,000	303,000
,, ...13	22,848,000	8,848,000	2,797,000	410,000
,, ...20	23,525,000	9,525,000	4,228,000	491,000
,, ...27§	23,956,000	9,956,000	4,986,000	576,000
DECEMBER.... 4	24,366,000	10,366,000	5,583,000	666,000
,, ...11	24,769,000	10,769,000	6,448,000	656,000
,, ...18	25,309,000	11,309,000	7,551,000	681,000
,, ...24	25,609,000	11,609,000	7,786,000	627,000

* First period of Commercial pressure.

† Commencement of Corn failures and second period of Commercial distress.

‡ On the 25th the Government Letter was issued fixing the Bank's minimum rate of discount at 8 per cent.

§ The Government Letter was withdrawn on the 23d and the Bank reduced its rate of discount.

BANK OF ENGLAND RETURNS FOR 1848.

1848.	ISSUE DEPARTMENT. Notes Issued.	ISSUE DEPARTMENT. Gold and Silver Bullion.	BANKING DEPARTMENT. Notes in Reserve.	BANKING DEPARTMENT. Gold and Silver Coin.
	£	£	£	£
JANUARY 1	25,790,000	11,790,000	7,865,000	613,000
" 8	25,876,000	11,876,000	7,315,000	701,000
" 15	26,247,000	12,247,000	7,152,000	576,000
" 22	26,559,000	12,559,000	7,447,000	617,000
" 29	26,782,000	12,782,000	7,640,000	608,000
FEBRUARY.... 5	27,210,000	12,210,000	8,074,000	610,000
" 12	27,582,000	13,582,000	9,064,000	621,000
" 19	27,890,000	13,890,000	9,806,000	678,000
" 26	28,101,000	14,101,000	9,922,000	658,000
MARCH........ 4	28,205,000	14,205,000	9,830,000	668,000
" 11	28,235,000	14,235,000	10,544,000	711,000
" 18	28,414,000	14,414,000	10,967,000	708,000
" 25	28,556,000	14,556,000	10,953,000	760,000
APRIL 1	28,542,000	14,542,000	10,874,000	668,000
" 8	28,008,000	14,008,000	9,767,000	594,000
" 15	27,165,000	13,165,000	8,568,000	598,000
" 22	26,621,000	12,621,000	7,860,000	606,000
" 29	26,261,000	12,261,000	7,658,000	616,000
MAY 6	26,176,000	12,176,000	7,554,000	649,000
" 13	26,364,000	12,364,000	8,036,000	725,000
" 20	26,661,000	12,661,000	8,566,000	717,000
" 27	26,743,000	12,743,000	8,931,000	771,000
JUNE.......... 3	26,860,000	12,860,000	9,080,000	737,000
" 10	27,132,000	13,132,000	9,505,000	707,000
" 17	27,352,000	13,352,000	9,975,000	816,000
" 24	27,536,000	13,536,000	10,007,000	771,000
JULY.......... 1	27,646,000	13,646,000	10,064,000	772,000
" 8	27,673,000	13,673,000	9,312,000	684,000
" 15	27,593,000	13,593,000	8,488,000	669,000
" 22	27,451,000	13,451,000	8,410,000	657,000
" 29	27,063,000	13,063,000	8,118,000	646,000
AUGUST 5	26,690,000	12,690,000	7,998,000	706,000
" 12	26,693,000	12,693,000	8,528,000	671,000
" 19	26,763,000	12,763,000	8,450,000	607,000
" 26	26,853,000	12,853,000	8,734,000	650,000
SEPTEMBER .. 2	26,883,000	12,883,000	8,784,000	626,000
" 9	26,958,000	12,958,000	9,114,000	707,000
" 16	27,198,000	13,198,000	9,511,000	623,000
" 23	27,237,000	13,237,000	9,926,000	627,000
" 30	27,120,000	13,120,000	9,571,000	557,000
OCTOBER...... 7*	26,823,000	12,823,000	9,348,000	593,000
" 14	26,739,000	12,739,000	8,405,000	520,000
" 21	26,592,000	12,592,000	8,032,000	570,000
" 28	26,608,000	12,608,000	8,018,000	664,000
NOVEMBER .. 4	26,796,000	12,796,000	8,242,000	610,000
" 11	26,961,000	12,961,000	8,894,000	717,000
" 18	27,198,000	13,198,000	9,355,000	721,000
" 25	27,386,000	13,386,000	9,986,000	753,000
DECEMBER ... 2	27,415,000	13,415,000	10,088,000	851,000
" 9	27,733,000	13,733,000	10,771,000	789,000
" 16	27,982,000	13,982,000	11,246,000	807,000
" 23	28,184,000	14,184,000	11,309,000	815,000
" 30	28,226,000	14,226,000	11,095,000	728,000

* Commencement of the third Railway Panic.

TABLES

Shewing the various changes in the leading articles of produce Commercial Crisis. Arranged in the subjoined order it is business through-

WHEAT.—*Average price per quarter*

	1845.	1846.
Jan.	48s. to 49s.4d.—Market steady.	61s.5d. to 63s.4d.—A quiet market, the trade waiting the intention of ministers, with respect to the repeal of the Corn Laws.
Feb.	47s.4d. to 48s.11d.—Moderate trade, and lower prices.	58s.2d. to 60s.4d.—Moderate business at lower prices.
Mar.	47s.8d. to 49s.—Trade dull; condition of samples bad at market.	58s.3d. to 61s.3d.—Dull market, and little doing.
April.	48s.4d. to 49s.6d.—Steady market.	58s.2d. to 61s.10d.—The unsettled state of the Corn Laws still check business.
May.	47s.11d. to 49s.7d.—Steady demand at full rates.	54s.6d. to 62s.2d.—Market quiet; little doing.
June.	49s.9d. to 52s.—Weather favourable for crops; dull market, but an average demand.	54s.1d. to 60s.3d.—A good demand; fine weather for crops.
July.	51s.8d. to 56s.2d.—Unsettled weather; firmer market, and more doing.	50s.4d. to 56s.1d.—Corn Laws passed 3d July, which caused a larger trade at lower prices.
Aug.	58s.9d. to 61s.5d.—Ditto at commencement of month, but weather improved towards the close; and prices declined.	49s.2d. to 54s.3d.—The unsettled state of the weather caused a better demand at firmer rates.
Sept.	56s.1d. to 60s.—A brisk demand, and all kinds dearer, owing to the unfavourable state of the potatoe crop at the end of the month.	50s. to 58s.6d.—A good business at full prices.
Oct.	61s.6d. to 65s.4d.—A good demand, but prices falling.	61s.4d. to 68s.5d.—More doing for export and home use at better prices.
Nov.	62s.11d. to 65s.10d.—Little doing, on account of the expected alteration in the Corn Laws.	63s.9d. to 66s.10d.—Business brisk at lower prices.
Dec.	58s.8d. to 66s.—Supplies small; the demand improving as well as prices.	63s. 3d. to 69s.1d.—Market steady with a fair average business; prospect of further advance.

OF PRICES.

during the four years comprised in the narrative of the presumed they will be found lucidly to explain the state of out that period.

for the years 1845, 1846, 1847, 1848.

	1847.	1848.
Jan.	70s.2d. to 76s.6d.—Short supplies; a good demand for Ireland.	54s.8d. to 56s.10d.—Large supplies; market steady.
Feb.	71s.7d. to 76s.4d.—Market opened dull and lower, supplies large, but recovered towards the end of the month.	50s.11d. to 54s.4d.—Small business and lower.
Mar.	74s.2d. to 78s.7d.—Sales for France.	51s.6d. to 54s.2d.—Do. do.
April.	77s.1d. to 77s.11d.—Business quiet, but large sales for the Continent caused a brisk demand at the latter part of the month.	52s.9d. to 54s.2d.—Do. do.
May.	84s.4d. to 105s.2d.—Short supplies caused prices to run up considerably, but receded towards the close; market dull.	50s.4d. to 56s.6d.—Fine weather for crop, market dull.
June.	93s.5d. to 102s.2d.—Reports of the potatoe disease, improved prices, but large supplies checked the advance.	48s.3d. to 51s.7d.—Wet weather; market firmer.
July.	76s. to 96s.1d.—Fine weather; prices decline; supplies large.	50s.11d. to 52s.9d.—Unsettled weather, report of potatoe disease; market firmer.
Aug.	64s. to 78s.10d.—New crop at market of fine quality; commencement of failures; supplies larger; prices going down.	52s.9d. to 55s.—Do. do., with a quiet market.
Sept.	51s. to 60s.6d.—Several failures and parcels pressed on the market; prices rather recovered towards the close of the month.	52s.4d. to 56s.10d.—Favourable weather caused a dull market and lower prices.
Oct.	54s.8d. to 59s.1d.—Prices giving way; a small trade.	51s. to 52s.5d.—Market flat and prices going down.
Nov.	54s. to 57s.2d.—Millers buy sparingly; prices lower.	51s.2d. to 52s.2d.—Moderate demand, but trade dull towards the close, at lower prices.
Dec.	53s.2d. to 54s.10d.—Do. do.	47s. to 50s.3d.—Steady demand and price.

COTTON.—*Surat, low to good, per lb.*

	1845.	1846.
Jan.	$2\frac{3}{8}$d. to 4d.—A firm market, but little business done.	$2\frac{1}{2}$d. to 4d.—A good business done on speculation, in anticipation of the alteration in the Corn Laws.
Feb.	$2\frac{1}{2}$d. to 4d.—A large business done by speculators and exporters, at better prices, as the accounts from the manufacturing districts were satisfactory.	$2\frac{1}{4}$d. to $3\frac{3}{4}$d.—Market rather dull and lower; less doing on the part of speculation.
Mar.	$2\frac{1}{2}$d. to 4d.—Speculators and exporters large buyers at commencement of month, but business dull at end, and prices not so firm.	$2\frac{1}{4}$d. to $3\frac{3}{4}$d.—More doing, owing to the unfavourable advices from America, respecting the Oregon question.
April.	$2\frac{5}{8}$d. to 4d.—A quiet market at early part of the month, but got firmer, owing to the decided measures taken by Government, respecting the Oregon question.	$2\frac{1}{4}$d. to $3\frac{3}{4}$d.—Steady prices, but more doing.
May.	$2\frac{1}{2}$d. to 4d.—Fair business at commencement, but flat towards the close, owing to the pressure of large sales.	$2\frac{1}{2}$d. to 4d.—Firmer market with a good business.
June.	$2\frac{3}{8}$d. to 4d.—Dull market, and prices rather lower.	$2\frac{3}{4}$d. to 4d.—Market firm with less on offer.
July.	$2\frac{1}{2}$d. to $3\frac{7}{8}$d.—Speculators and others bought more freely at the low prices, and the market became firm at the end of the month.	$2\frac{5}{8}$d. to 4d.—A good trade; prices fully up.
Aug.	$2\frac{5}{8}$d. to $4\frac{1}{4}$d.—Large purchases at higher prices, but market dull at at the end of the month, owing to the unsettled weather for the grain crops.	$2\frac{5}{8}$d. to 4d.—Market rather quiet at previous terms.
Sept.	$2\frac{5}{8}$d. to $4\frac{1}{4}$d.—A steady demand at commencement of the month, but dull at latter end, owing to weather for the harvest.	$2\frac{7}{8}$d. to $4\frac{1}{4}$d.—A large business done for export and speculation at higher prices, owing to the unfavourable accounts of the American crop.
Oct.	$2\frac{5}{8}$d. to $4\frac{1}{4}$d.—Steady, but quiet market.	3d. to $5\frac{1}{4}$d.—Speculation large; the crop in America proved less than expected, and prices advanced.
Nov.	$2\frac{5}{8}$d. to $4\frac{1}{4}$d.—A better feeling on the part of merchants, but little done.	$3\frac{3}{8}$d. to $5\frac{1}{4}$d.—Less doing, but prices firm.
Dec.	$2\frac{1}{2}$d. to 4d.—Quiet market, with steady demand.	$3\frac{3}{8}$d. to $5\frac{1}{2}$d.—A more active demand at better rates, but towards the close of the month markets became dull.

WOOL.—*English Sheep, per lb.*

	1845.	1846.
Jan.	6d. to 1s.4d.—A fair trade, and prices firm.	9d. to 1s.$5\frac{1}{2}$d.—Steady business at full prices.
Feb.	6d. to 1s.4d.—Steady market.	7d. to 1s.5d.—Business more active at lower terms.
Mar.	6d. to 1s.4d.—Ditto; but prices rather in favour of the buyers.	7d. to 1s.5d.—Market steady, but not active.
April.	7d. to 1s.$4\frac{1}{2}$d.—Small stock; market dull.	7d. to 1s.5d.—Little doing; prices steady.

COTTON.—*continued.*

	1847.	1848.
Jan.	4d. to $5\frac{1}{2}$d.—Exporters bought freely, but at the close of the month business was checked, owing to a slight advance in the rate of interest.	$2\frac{7}{8}$d to $4\frac{1}{2}$d.—Good steady business at these rates.
Feb	$3\frac{3}{4}$d. to $5\frac{3}{8}$d. — Little done; market steady.	$2\frac{3}{4}$d. to $4\frac{1}{2}$d.—Do. do., by exporters.
Mar.	$3\frac{1}{2}$d. to 5d.—High prices of provisions caused few sales, and rates gradually gave way.	$2\frac{3}{4}$d. to $4\frac{1}{4}$d.—Revolution on the Continent stopped trade; dull market.
April.	$3\frac{5}{8}$d. to $5\frac{1}{4}$d.—Money easier and more doing; accounts from America unfavourable for the crop.	$2\frac{3}{4}$d. to 4d.—Do. do.
May.	$3\frac{7}{8}$d. to $5\frac{1}{4}$d.—Very little business, as money is getting scarce; prices up; bread high.	$2\frac{3}{4}$d. to $3\frac{7}{8}$d.—Dull market, ditto.
June.	$3\frac{7}{8}$d. to $5\frac{1}{4}$d.—Rather more doing at steady prices.	$2\frac{1}{4}$d. to $3\frac{7}{8}$d.—Forced sales, but a good business.
July.	4d. to $5\frac{1}{2}$d.—Prices falling for corn; trade better at improving prices.	$2\frac{3}{8}$d. to $3\frac{3}{4}$d.—More doing and prices firmer.
Aug.	$4\frac{1}{8}$d. to $5\frac{1}{2}$d.—Steady demand, but higher rates of discount checked trade.	$2\frac{1}{2}$d. to 4d.—Steady, but not active.
Sept.	4d. to $5\frac{1}{2}$d. — Market quiet through the extensive failures; still a steady business at rather lower prices.	$2\frac{1}{2}$d. to $3\frac{7}{8}$d.—Inactive market early in the month; but improved as the Continent was more quiet.
Oct.	$3\frac{1}{2}$d. to $5\frac{1}{4}$d.—Market dull; high rates of discount; large failures and pressure of sales.	$2\frac{1}{2}$d. to $3\frac{7}{8}$d.—Large sales offered, but bought in; market dull.
Nov.	3d. to $4\frac{3}{4}$d.—Prices lower, owing to forced sales for cash.	$2\frac{5}{8}$d. to $3\frac{7}{8}$d.—A good business for export.
Dec.	3d. to $4\frac{1}{2}$d.—Market quiet, at low rates, owing to the general stagnation of trade.	$2\frac{3}{4}$d. to 4d.—Market firmer; more doing at higher prices.

WOOL.—*continued.*

	1847.	1848.
Jan.	8d. to 1s.4d.—A fair business; stock small; market firm.	5d. to 1s.$0\frac{1}{2}$d.—More doing at lower prices, and the market rather firmer.
Feb.	8d. to 1s.$3\frac{3}{4}$d.—The rise in money has checked business.	5d. to 1s.1d.—Firmer and more doing.
Mar.	8d. to 1s.$3\frac{3}{4}$d.—Moderate trade; stock still small.	6d. to 1s.1d. — Disturbed state of France and market dull.
April.	8d. to 1s.$3\frac{3}{4}$d.—Do. do.	$6\frac{1}{2}$d. to 1s.$0\frac{1}{2}$d.—Dull.

WOOL.—*continued.*

	1845.	1846.
May.	7d. to 1s.4½d.—Rather a better demand; manufacturers getting higher prices.	7d. to 1s.5d.—Flat market, owing to the public sales of Colonial going off 2d. to 3d. per lb. lower.
June.	7d. to 1s.4½d.—More business, and better prices than could have been previously obtained.	7d. to 1s.5d.—Demand good; manufacturers complaining of the low prices of their goods not being equal to those paid for the raw material.
July.	7d. to 1s.4½d.—A good business at full prices.	7d. to 1s.5d.—Market dull and rather easier.
Aug.	8d. to 1s.5½d.—A large trade and stock reduced; prices firmer.	8d. to 1s.4½d.—Market dull, but more doing.
Sept.	9d. to 1s.5½d.—Do. do.	8d. to 1s.4½d.—More doing at firm prices.
Oct.	9d. to 1s.5½d—Fine kinds full up and a good trade, but inferior dull and almost unsaleable.	8d. to 1s.4½d.—Business steady at full rates.
Nov.	9d. to 1s.5½d.—Very quiet, owing to the large demand for money for railway purposes.	8d. to 1s.4½d.—Business quiet; little doing.
Dec.	9d. to 1s.5d.—Little doing, and prices lower.	8d. to 1s.4d.—Rather more doing and the market firmer.

SILK.—*Bengal Novi, per lb.*

	1845.	1846.
Jan.	8s.6d. to 20s—Little doing and prices steady.	9s. to 19s.—Improving market at full prices.
Feb.	8s.6d. to 19s.—Quiet market at lower prices.	9s. to 19s.—Government measures respecting the duties on various articles quieted the market.
Mar.	8s.6d. to 19s.—Heavy market and little done.	8s.6d. to 19s.—Market dull; prices rather lower.
April.	8s. to 18s.—More doing; prices lower.	8s. to 18s.—Good business at easier terms.
May.	8s. to 18s.—Heavy market, but a much better trade at the end of the month.	8s. to 18s.6d.—Market steady.
June.	8s. to 18s.—More doing and rather firmer.	8s. to 18s.6d.—A fair trade at steady terms.
July.	8s. to 19s.6d.—Do. and higher rates.	8s. to 18s.6d.—The public sales went off better than expected, but the market quiet.
Aug.	9s. to 19s.6d.—Good trade and a firm market.	8s. to 18s.6d.—Business generally flat, but full prices obtained for the parcels sold.
Sept	9s. to 19s.6d.—Market steady.	8s. to 18s.6d.—Rather more doing at steady rates.
Oct.	9s. to 19s.6d.—Do., at full prices.	8s. to 18s.6d.—Market rather firmer and more doing.
Nov.	9s. to 19s.6d.—Do.	8s. to 18s.—A dull market at commencement of the month, but improved at the close.
Dec.	9s. to 19s.6d.—Do.	8s. to 18s.—Market quiet at former prices.

WOOL.—*continued.*

	1847.	1848.
May.	8d. to 1s.3¾d.—Market dull.	6½d. to 1s.0½d.—Dull.
June.	8d. to 1s.3¾d.—Do. do.	6½d. to 1s.0½d.—Do.
July.	7½d. to 1s.3½d.—Do. do.	6½d. to 1s.0½d.—More willing sellers at lower prices; but little done.
Aug.	7d. to 1s.3d.—The state of the money market checked demand; prices dull and little doing.	6½d. to 1s.3½d.—Quiet, but firmer.
Sept.	7d. to 1s.3d.—Market dull.	6½d. to 1s.0½d.—A good business; market firm.
Oct.	7d. to 1s.3d.—Failures and money matters worse; dull market.	6½d. to 1s.0½d.—Stocks small, and a good trade at full prices.
Nov.	7d. to 1s.3d.—Light stocks held by growers; prices steady.	6d. to 1s.—Steady business.
Dec.	5d. to 1s.2d.—Several failures in this trade; prices going down although stock small.	6d. to 1s.—More doing, and stocks getting low.

SILK.—*continued.*

	1847.	1848.
Jan.	8s. to 18s.—Market firmer.	7s. to 15s.—Quiet, but firmer, as several parcels were withdrawn from the market.
Feb.	8s. to 18s.—Do.	7s. to 15s.—Steady.
Mar.	8s. to 18s.—Market quiet; supplies exceed the wants of manufacturers.	7s. to 15s.—Do.
April.	8s. to 18s.—Do. do.	8s.6d. to 15s.—Rather more doing.
May.	7s.6d. to 18s.—More doing at rather lower prices.	8s.6d. to 15s.—Do.
June.	7s.6d. to 18s.—Steady trade.	8s. to 15s.—Dull and lower.
July.	8s. to 16s.—Business brisker; at rather lower prices, owing to the fall in corn.	8s. to 15s.—Do. do.
Aug.	8s. to 16s.—Steady demand.	8s. to 13s.—Very dull.
Sept.	8s. to 16s.—Do.	8s. to 12s.6d.—China, accounts of damage done to crops; firmer market.
Oct.	8s. to 16s.—Do.	8s. to 13s.—Advices confirmed; dearer and a better market.
Nov.	7s. to 15s.—General stagnation in trade; large public sales; depressed prices and money tight.	8s. to 13s.—Good business at higher prices.
Dec.	7s. to 15s.—Quiet.	8s. to 13s.—Firm market.

INDIGO.—*Low to fine purple, per lb.*

	1845.	1846.
Jan.	2s.6d. to 5s.10d. — Steady demand, prices rather lower.	2s.4d. to 6s.8d.—Trade dull; buyers waiting the public sales, which went off heavily and lower.
Feb.	3s. to 5s.10d.—More doing; better prices for the lower sorts.	2s.4d. to 6s.3d.—Rather more doing at reduced rates.
Mar.	3s. to 5s.10d.—A good demand at former terms.	2s.4d. to 6s.3d.—Trade steady at full prices.
April.	3s. to 6s.—Steady but firm market.	2s.4d. to 6s.3d.—Market dull, and prices barely supported.
May.	3s.6d. to 6s.—Business quiet at firm prices.	2s.3d. to 6s.3d.—More business doing, and a firmer market.
June.	3s.6d. to 6s.—Less doing, but firm.	2s.3d. to 6s.3d.—A fair trade done at steady prices.
July.	2s.9d. to 5s.9d.—Large sales; but a good business at low prices.	2s.3d. to 6s.3d.—Market steady.
Aug.	2s.9d. to 5s.9d.—More doing in the lower kinds at full prices.	2s.3d. to 6s.3d.—Business quiet, but full prices paid.
Sept.	2s.9d. to 5s.9d. — Quiet and steady rates.	2s.3d. to 6s.3d.—Do. do.
Oct.	2s.9d. to 6s.8d.—A large business done at the sales at firmer prices.	2s.6d. to 6s.7d. — More doing, and prices firm.
Nov.	2s.9d. to 6s.8d.—Market dull at previous terms.	2s.6d. to 6s.7d —Market firm; fair business done at good prices.
Dec.	2s.9d. to 6s.8d.—Do. do.	2s.6d. to 6s.7d. — Steady trade, and the market firm.

SUGAR.—*Jamaica, low Brown to fine Yellow, per cwt.*

	1845.	1846.
Jan.	51s. to 68s.6d.—A steady trade, at declining prices.	46s. to 56s.—The proposed reduction of 3s.6d. on free Foreign, caused the market to be firm, and a good business was done during the month at full prices.
Feb.	51s.6d. to 69s.—Sir R. Peel's plan for altering the duties on all kinds of B. P. sugar caused a large business, and better prices.	44s.6d. to 56s. — Steady market at commencement of the month, but owing to money getting scarce, it closed dull and lower.
Mar.	42s. to 68s.—Unsettled state of duties; very little trade; on the 15th March new duties came into operation, which caused an immense business, at stiffer rates.	44s.6d to 57s.—A moderate trade at full prices.
April.	38s. to 58s.—A very large demand, and prices firm.	45s. to 57s. — Short supply; market generally dull.
May.	39s.6d. to 59s.—Do., and improving prices.	47s. to 57s.—Good trade, and a firm market.
June.	42s.6d. to 59s.6d.—Extensive sales, and better prices.	46s.6d. to 56s.—Larger supplies; a good demand at lower prices, the question of duties being postponed until 5th August.

INDIGO.—*continued.*

	1847.	1848.
Jan.	2s.7d. to 6s.7d.—Trade moderate.	2s. to 5s.10d.—Market very quiet, but prices rather firmer.
Feb.	2s.7d. to 6s.7d —More doing, and better spirit in the biddings at the sales.	2s. to 5s.10d. —More doing; money market easier, increased trade.
Mar.	2s.9d. to 6s.7d.—Steady market.	2s.4d. to 5s.10d.—Quiet market, no orders for export, continental excitement.
April.	2s.9d. to 6s.7d.—Do. do.	2s. tc 5s.10d.—Do. do.
May.	2s.6d. to 6s.7d.—Money market flattened business, and only a moderate demand.	2s. to 5s.4d.—Do. do.
June.	2s.6d. to 6s.2d.—Steady market, and prices firm.	2s. to 5s.4d.—Do. do.
July.	2s.6d. to 6s.2d.—Do. do.	2s. to 5s.6d.—Do. do., but rather firmer towards close.
Aug.	2s.6d. to 6s.2d.—Do. do.	2s. to 5s.6d.—More doing, at rather firmer prices.
Sept.	2s.6d. to 6s.2d.—Market dull, owing to failures.	1s.6d. to 5s.6d.—Good market, stiff prices.
Oct.	2s. to 6s.2d.—General stagnation in trade, and the monetary crisis. Sales forced with parcels belonging to many of the suspended firms.	1s.6d. to 5s.6d.—Quarterly sales; irregular prices, except for fine kinds, which went dearer.
Nov.	2s. to 5s.10d.—Market very quiet.	1s.6d. to 5s.5d.—Dull market, owing to favourable account of crop.
Dec.	2s. to 5s.10d.—Do. do., but prices rather firmer.	1s.6d. to 5s.5d.—Market quiet and easier.

SUGAR.—*continued.*

	1847.	1848.
Jan.	44s.6d. to 59s.—Short supply, with a good demand.	35s. to 46s.6d.—Gradual improvement in trade, and a good business.
Feb.	48s.6d. to 57s.—Unsettled market till the middle of the month, when the new law came into operation for allowing brewers and distillers to work from sugar.	35s. to 46s.6d.—Chancellor of Exchequer stating no change in duties; dull market.
Mar.	48s.6d. to 57s.—Less doing; small stock checking business; prices nominal.	34s.6d. to 45s —More doing; steady market.
April.	40s. to 54s. —Large supplies; dull market.	34s.6d. to 45s.—Do. do.
May.	40s.6d. to 52s.6d.—Steady business, but stock increasing.	35s. to 46s.—Expected change in duties; more doing.
June.	38s. to 51s. — More desire to sell; prices lower; stock large.	36s. to 44s.6d.—Proposed change in navigation laws dull market & lower prices, but subsequently improved in expectation of alteration in duties.

SUGAR.—*continued.*

	1845.	1846.
July.	42s.6d. to 56s.—A large business, and easier rates.	44s. to 54s.—Trade not inclined to buy until the question of duty is finally settled; prices gradually giving way about the middle of the month, new duties on all foreign Muscovado brought forward.
Aug.	43s.6d. to 58s.—Extensive business at higher rates, all for home trade.	43s.6d. to 53s.—New duties received at the Customs (19th); market dull, through the admission of slave grown sugar.
Sept.	45s. to 57s.6d.—Increased trade, with firm prices.	44s. to 55s.—A moderate business at lower terms.
Oct.	46s. to 57s.—Do. do.	43s.6d. to 56s.6d.—Steady market at commencement of the month, but an expectation that sugar would be allowed to be used in the distilleries, caused a firmer market, and at better prices.
Nov.	48s. to 59s.—Trade large at the commencement of the month, owing to a report that sugar would be allowed in the distilleries, but less doing towards the end, and market flat.	44s. to 56s.—Market good, owing to the bad accounts from Havannah, but buyers not inclined to take more than their wants require.
Dec.	46s.6d. to 57s.—A good business, but at lower prices.	43s. to 57s.—A better demand at full prices.

SUGAR.—*Mauritius Low Brown to Fine Yellow, per cwt.*

	1845.	1846.
Jan.	39s. to 66s.—Large sales and firm market.	35s.6d. to 54s.—Business good, but large arrivals force prices down, owing to the proposed reduction on foreign free labour sugar.
Feb.	41s. to 66s.6d.—More doing, owing to the expected alteration in duty, and better prices.	35s.6d. to 54s.—Steady market, but prices barely supported.
Mar.	32s.6d.to64s.6d.—Business good; new duties came into operation; full prices.	35s.6d. to 54s.—Large parcels brought forward, but a steady market.
April.	33s. to 59s.—Large sales, and firm prices.	37s.6d. to 57s.—More doing, and prices advancing.
May.	32s. to 57s.—Do.; terms lower.	38s.6d. to 57s.—A good business doing, but large sales prevent prices advancing.
June.	32s. to 57s.—Extensive sales at former rates.	38s. to 57s.—The postponement of the Sugar Bill to the 5th Aug. caused a firmer market, and a good business done.
July.	35s.6d. to 56s.—Good trade at easier rates.	38s. to 56s.—The trade not inclined to buy until the final settlement of the sugar duties.
Aug.	36s.6d. to 58s.—Extensive purchases at higher rates.	37s. to 52s.6d.—A quiet market at commencement of month, but a more general demand when the new duties (19th Aug.) came into operation sent prices down.

SUGAR.—*continued.*

	1847.	1848.
July.	37s. to 51s.—More desire to sell; prices lower; stock large.	35s. to 43s.6d.—New duties in operation 10th of this month; pressure of sales; dull market in consequence of a large quantity of foreign sugar paid duty under the act of 1846, at 18s.6d. for Muscovado, and the admission of Dutch crushed; prices lower.
Aug.	36s.3d. to 50s.6d.—Do. do., but partly recovered towards the end of the month.	35s.6d. to 43s.6d.—Alteration in Dutch crushed; market steady; and large trade done.
Sept.	37s. to 50s.6d.—Steady market; supply more moderate than of late.	34s. to 42s.—Large business owing to low prices.
Oct.	34s. to 49s.—Anxiety to sell, owing to the pressure in the money market, and the failures.	34s. to 41s.6d.—Trade purchased freely at end of month, but lower prices taken; stocks still very large.
Nov.	34s. to 46s.6d.—Market rather firmer, and more doing.	34s. to 41s.6d.—Quiet market opening of the month, but improved towards the end; prices steady.
Dec.	35s. to 46s.6d.—Large stock, and dull market.	34s. to 41s.—A fair good business, and prices somewhat improving.

SUGAR.—*continued.*

	1847.	1848.
Jan.	36s. to 59s.—Short supplies, and a large trade.	26s. to 47s.6d.—More firmness, and a large trade, chiefly by refiners, at improving prices.
Feb.	38s. to 61s.—More doing, but the market unsettled till the brewers and distillers were allowed to work from sugar.	28s. to 47s.6d.—Do. do.
Mar.	37s. to 58s.—Lower prices, with more doing.	28s. to 47s.—Good business; market steady.
April.	36s. to 55s.—Do. do.	28s. to 44s.—Do. do.
May.	36s. to 53s.—Steady market.	28s. to 44s.—More doing; expected change in duties.
June.	35s. to 51s —Lower prices; trade brisk.	28s. to 44s.—Proposed alteration in Navigation laws caused a dull market, but the proposed change caused more firmness, and greater activity.
July.	33s. to 50s.—Flat and lower.	28s. to 44s.—New duties in operation 10th of this month; more doing, at lower prices.
Aug.	31s. to 51s.—Large supplies; prices gradually giving way.	28s. to 43s.6d.—Larger trade, prices steady.

SUGAR.—*continued.*

	1845.	1846.
Sept.	35s. to 57s.—Good business at full prices.	34s. to 58s.—A better demand at steady prices.
Oct.	35s. to 56s.6d.—Less doing, and prices not so firm.	32s. to 58s.—The market firmer, as little was brought to public sale.
Nov.	35s. to 57s.—Steady demand at former rates.	35s. to 58s.—Demand good, at rather lower prices; merchants meeting the views of buyers.
Dec.	38s.6d. to 57s.—Do. do.	34s. to 55s.—Prices going down, and but little business doing.

SUGAR.—*Bengal, low to fine white and brown, per cwt.*

	1845.	1846.
Jan.	38s. 6d. to 70s.—A good business at gradually lower prices.	35s.6d. to 60s.—Large sales brought forward caused prices to recede, but trade good.
Feb.	39s.6d. to 70s.—Large sales in anticipation of reduced duties.	35s.6d. to 58s.—Prices still falling, owing to large parcels being brought forward, but a good business.
Mar.	32s. to 68s.—A good business, but at lower prices.	35s.6d. to 57s.—Trade good, at steady prices.
April.	27s. to 59s.—Do. do.	37s.6d. to 57s.6d.—Moderate demand; rates firm.
May.	26s.6d. to 58s.—Large sales at steady prices.	38s.6d. to 57s.6d.—Large sales brought forward, but a good business done at full prices.
June.	32s. to 58s.—Extensive business at full prices.	35s.6d. to 57s.6d.—The duty question being postponed, caused a brisk trade at steady terms.
July.	35s. to 59s.—Sales large, but prices not so firm at close of the month.	35s. to 57s.6d.—Unsettled state of duties; buyers less anxious to make sales; quiet market.
Aug.	35s. to 59s.6d.—Large trade; prices firmer.	35s. to 57s.6d.—New duties (19th) caused a steady demand
Sept.	36s to 60s.—Do. do.	35s. to 56s.—A steady market at rather lower prices.
Oct.	36s. to 64s.—Large sales, and for the finer sorts, dearer rates.	35s. to 57s.6d.—More business doing; prices rather firmer.
Nov.	36s. to 61s.—A good business at full prices.	35s. to 57s.6d —A good business done at full rates.
Dec.	37s. to 61s.—Less doing; market not so firm.	35s. to 56s.—Lower prices caused the trade to buy more freely.

SUGAR.—*continued.*

	1847.	1848.
Sept.	31s. to 51s.—Steady business.	27s.6d. to 42s.—Steady demand, and better prices.
Oct.	28s. to 50s.6d.—Parcels belonging to fallen houses pressed for sale; flat market.	27s. to 42s.—Dull at commencement of month, but improved and closed steady.
Nov.	26s. to 47s.6d.—At lower prices; the market more active.	27s. to 41s.—A good demand at full prices.
Dec.	26s. to 47s.6d.—Large stock, and dull market.	27s. to 40s.6d.—Market opened quiet, but improved towards the close.

SUGAR.—*continued.*

	1847.	1848.
Jan.	40s. to 58s.—A large business done on speculation in brown, owing to the expectation of sugar being allowed in the breweries and distilleries; prices advancing, and firm market.	28s. to 40s.—Gradual improvement and a good business.
Feb.	38s. to 57s.—Steady trade.	28s. to 50s.—Do. do.
Mar.	36s. to 55s.6d.—Lower prices, and a pressure of sales, but a good business.	28s. to 48s.—Moderate business.
April.	35s. to 54s.—Do. do.	28s. to 44s.6d.—Do. do.
May.	35s. to 53s.—Do. do.	28s. to 45s.6d.—More doing; expectation of alteration in duty.
June.	34s. to 53s.—Do. do.	28s. to 45s.6d.—Proposed alteration in the Navigation laws; quiet market at the commencement of the month, but more doing towards the end, owing to the proposed change in duty.
July.	33s. to 53s.—Corn falling, brewers and distillers less inclined to buy; a steady business done by the trade.	28s.6d. to 45s.—New duties in force, and lower prices; less doing.
Aug.	32s. to 52s.—Supply moderate; trade steady at lower prices.	28s.6d. to 45s.—Moderate business; and prices steady.
Sept.	32s. to 52s.—Steady market.	27s. to 45s.6d.—Full average business, at better prices.
Oct.	28s. to 52s.—Pressure of sales of parcels belonging to the suspended firms; lower prices; business good.	27s.6d. to 44s.—Lower rates, but good trade.
Nov.	28s. to 50s.—More doing; steady prices.	28s. to 44s.—More doing, with little change in price.
Dec.	28s. to 49s.—Steady trade, but heavy stock.	27s. to 43s.—A moderate business at easy rates, but afterwards improved.

SUGAR.—*Refined standard lumps, per cwt.*

	1845.	1846.
Jan.	72s.6d. to 74s.—A good business, at full prices.	64s. to 65s.6d.—A moderate business at steady prices.
Feb.	70s. to 72s.6d.—Expectation of refined being admitted from the Colonies, caused a dull market, and lower prices.	62s.6d. to 64s.—Market flat, and prices receding.
Mar.	65s.6d. to 70s.—Unsettled state of duties; further decline in price, but a good trade.	63s.6d. to 65s.6d.—The trade bought more freely; better prices paid.
April.	65s.6d. to 70s. — A good demand; terms steady.	63s.6d. to 64s.—Market rather dull, and prices not so firm.
May.	67s. to 72s.—Brisk business, at improving rates.	66s. to 68s.6d.—Supply being small better prices paid; a good trade done.
June.	71s.6d. to 74s. 6d.—Goods scarce, and a brisk demand, at higher prices.	67s.6d. to 70s.—Refiners working less freely, waiting the settlement of the duties on raw sugar; market very firm, and prices higher.
July.	67s.6d. to 72s.6d.—Lower prices, but good business for consumption.	65s.6d. to 69s.6d.—Less doing on the part of the trade, and prices not so firm.
Aug.	67s. to 69s.—Large trade; full prices.	63s.6d. to 64s.6d.—Supplies larger; demand good, as the refiners have taken lower prices.
Sept.	67s. to 68s.—Trade good at steady rates.	62s. to 65s.—Quiet market, at commencement of the month, at lower prices, but towards the close, a good business, at better prices.
Oct.	65s. to 67s.—Less doing, and prices going down.	63s. to 66s.—Supplies less abundant; a good demand at firmer rates.
Nov.	66s. to 67s.6d.—Small business, but steady prices.	63s.6d. to 66s.—A good business done early in the month, but declined towards the end, and prices gave way.
Dec.	64s. to 66s.—A dull market at lower prices.	62s.6d. to 64s.6d.—Business steady at full prices.

RUM.—*Proof Leewards, average price per gallon.*

	1845.	1846.
Jan.	2s.2½d. to 2s.3½d.—Little business transacted throughout the month, and market quiet.	2s. to 2s.1d.—The market dull; very little doing, and prices going down.
Feb.	1s.11d. to 2s. 2d.—Prices going down, but little doing.	1s.10d. to 2s.—A flat market at commencement of the month, but more doing towards the close, and prices dearer.
Mar.	1s.10d. to 2s.—Small sales only, at lower prices.	1s.9d. to 1s.10½d.—Stocks on the increase, and very little doing, at lower prices.
April.	1s.9d. to 1s.11d.—Do. do.	1s.9½d. to 1s.11½d.—More business done, and prices rather better, with a firmer market.
May.	1s.7d. to 1s.9d.—More doing, owing to the low prices accepted, but market not brisk.	2s. to 2s.2d.—A large trade done, and at better rates; supplies still large, but good deliveries.

SUGAR.—*continued.*

	1847.	1848.
Jan.	65s. to 71s.—Short supply; good demand.	54s. to 55s.6d.—Business good.
Feb.	64s.6d. to 68s.—Good demand, at lower prices.	54s. to 55s.6d.—Steady, but dull.
Mar.	64s. to 65s.6d.—More doing at better prices.	53s.6d. to 55s.—More doing.
April.	63s.6d. to 65s.—Do.; supply larger; prices lower.	54s. to 56s.—Moderate trade.
May.	63s. to 64s.—Steady trade.	56s.6d. to 57s.—Good business.
June.	60s. to 63s.—Fair business at receding prices.	54s.6d. to 56s.—Lower, but more doing.
July.	57s. to 59s.—Large supply; trade good at lower prices.	53s.6d. to 56s.—Admission of Dutch crushed loaves; market dull, and lower.
Aug.	55s. to 57s.—Trade dull.	53s. to 55s.—Quiet market, and lower prices.
Sept.	55s. to 55s.6d.—Do., and a good supply.	49s.6d. to 52s.—Market steady, with a fair business.
Oct.	52s.6d. to 55s.—Dull and lower.	48s.6d. to 52s.—Good business at lower prices.
Nov.	53s. to 54s.6d.—More doing, and prices steady.	48s. to 51s.—Large business, but fell off at the end of the month.
Dec.	52s.6d to 53s.6d.—Fair trade.	47s. to 48s.—Moderate trade

RUM.—*continued.*

	1847.	1848.
Jan.	2s.8d. to 4s.—A brisk demand, owing to distillers advancing the price of corn spirits; stock small.	1s.7d. to 1s.8d.—More doing at rather lower prices.
Feb.	3s. 9d. to 4s.—Stock small; trade steady.	1s.8d. to 1s.10d.—Expectation of the change in duties; more doing at early part of the month, but less doing at end, and prices giving way; stock large.
Mar.	3s.8d. to 3s.9d.—Dull market.	1s.9½d. to 2s.—More doing; speculators operating for lower duties.
April.	3s.1d. to 3s.7d.—Supply getting large; market dull.	1s.9d. to 1s.10d.—Market dull and lower; heavy stock.
May.	3s.1d. to 3s.5d.—Reduction in the duty of 3d. per gallon; market firmer; steady demand.	1s.8d. to 1s.10d. Steady trade.

RUM.—*continued.*

	1845.	1846.
June.	1s.7½d. to 1s.9½d.—Market firmer, and a good trade done at better prices.	2s.2d. to 2s.3d.—Little business done but a firm market.
July.	1s.8½d. to 1s.10d.—A good demand, and a firmer market at higher rates.	2s.2d. to 2s.6d.—The proposed reduction in duty caused a large business, and at much higher prices.
Aug.	1s.9d. to 1s.10½d.—Market firm, and more doing.	2s.5½d. to 2s.6d.—Duties on Rum settled 6d. per gallon less, caused the market to be less excited, and very little done.
Sept.	1s.9d. to 1s.11d.—Prices gradually rising,& more doing; market firmer.	2s.3d. to 2s.5½d.—Less doing, and prices declining, with a dull market.
Oct.	1s.10½d. to 2s.1d.—A steady demand at commencement of the month; but subsequently increased. Prices dearer towards the close, with less disposition to sell.	2s.3d. to 2s.5d.—A dull market at commencement of month, but a good demand towards the close, and at higher prices.
Nov.	2s.1d. to 2s.3d.—Market firmer, with a full average business.	2s.6d. to 2s.8d.—A steady demand throughout the month, although buyers slackened at the end.
Dec.	2s. to 2s.2½d.—A dull market, and prices flat, with more pressing for sale.	2s.6d. to 2s.8d.—Quiet market, and prices not so well supported.

COFFEE.—*Ceylon, native good ordinary, per cwt.*

	1845.	1846.
Jan.	51s. to 53s.6d.—A good business doing; prices gradually lower.	48s. to 50s.—A steady demand, at full prices.
Feb.	46s. to 51s.6d.—Do. do.	47s. to 49s.—Supplies larger; prices lower, but a good business done.
Mar.	46s. to 47s.—A steady market, at full prices.	46s. to 47s.6d.—Little doing, and prices gradually falling.
April.	43s.6d. to 46s.6d.—More doing, and towards the close of the month, better prices.	45s.6d. to 46s.6d.—A quiet market, at lower rates.
May.	44s. to 46s.6d.—A good business, at full rates.	43s.to 45s.6d.—Lower prices caused rather large sales; mkt. slightly firmer.
June.	47s. to 50s.—Large sales, and prices advancing.	41s. to 44s.6d.—Large supplies brought forward and pressed for sale; lower prices, but a good business done.
July.	46s. to 48s.—Prices not so firm, and less demand.	41s. to 43s.—A better demand, at steady rates.
Aug.	44s. to 48s.—Less doing, and not so much pressing on the market; prices rather higher at end of the month.	40s. to 42s.—A pressure of sales made prices decline, still good business done.
Sept.	47s. to 48s.6d.— good trade at firmer rates.	39s. to 41s.—Do. do.
Oct.	44s.6d. to 48s.6d.—Steady demand at commencement of the month, but dull at the close, and prices lower.	37s.6d. to 40s.6d.—Merchants continuing to press sales, further reduced rates accepted; a good business done.
Nov.	47s. to 49s.6d.—A large business on speculation owing to the bad accounts from Ceylon, and higher prices paid.	37s. to 39s.6d.—Trade steady, but at lower rates.
Dec.	48s. to 49s.—Steady demand, at full prices.	36s. to 38s.—Market quiet; rates lower; merchants bringing forward larger parcels than the wants of the trade.

RUM.—*continued.*

	1847.	1848.
June.	2s.11d. to 3s.1d.—A fall in the price of grain, with a dull market.	1s.8½d. to 1s.9d.—Expected change in duties; little doing.
July.	2s.6½d. to 2s.11d.—Dull sale, and free sellers.	1s.7d. to 1s.8½d.—New duties, large stocks, and dull market.
Aug.	2s.5d. to 2s.7d.—More doing early in the month, but dull towards the close, and lower prices.	1s.7d. to 1s.9d.—Moderate business at lower prices.
Sept.	2s.2d to 2s.5d.—Lower rates, with a dull sale; supplies large.	1s.6½d. to 1s.8d.—Quiet and dull market.
Oct.	1s.8d. to 2s.2d.—Pressure of sales of parcels belonging to fallen houses.	1s.5d. to 1s.6d.—Very dull, and prices almost nominal.
Nov.	1s.8d. to 1s.9d.—More doing; steady market.	1s.3d. to 1s.6d.—Dull market at lower prices.
Dec.	1s.7d. to 1s.9d.—Little done, and prices going down.	1s.4d. to 1s.5d.—Better trade at firmer rates.

COFFEE.—*continued.*

	1847.	1848.
Jan.	39s.6d. to 42s.6d.—Demand good, with a small supply.	32s.6d. to 33s.—Good business at steady rates.
Feb.	41s. to 43s.—Do. do.	33s. to 35s. 6d.—Speculation; trade good, but drooped towards the close of the month.
Mar.	40s. to 45s.—Good trade early in the month, but large supplies caused the market to go flat and lower.	31s. to 34s.—Dull and lower; pressure of sales.
April.	38s. to 42s.6d.—Money getting scarce caused a pressure of sales, with lower prices.	30s. to 31s.6d.—Do. do.
May.	36s. to 39s.—Dull market; high prices of provisions; supplies large.	29s. to 31s.—More doing, at easier prices.
June.	37s. to 39s.—Steady market.	28s. to 31s.—Dull and lower; pressure of sales, stocks large.
July.	37s. to 38s.—Do. do.	28s. to 30s.—Steady market.
Aug.	37s. to 38s. 6d.—Do. do.	28s.6d. to 30s.6d.—Dull, with increasing stocks.
Sept.	34s. to 37s. 6d.—Market steady at commencement of the month, but by a pressure of sales declined.	26s.6d. to 28s.6d.—Large supplies brought forward; prices lower; dull market.
Oct.	32s. to 35s.6d.—Bankrupts' parcels being pressed, prices gave way, but a good business.	26s.6d. to 28s.—Shippers bought largely owing to the low prices.
Nov.	32s. to 34s.—Steady business, at full prices.	26s. to 28s.—Do. do.
Dec.	33s.6d. to 35s.—More doing at stiffer rates.	27s. to 30s.6d.—Large business by the trade at higher prices.

RICE.—*Bengal, low to fine white, per cwt.*

	1845.	1846.
Jan.	10s. to 12s.6d.—Market quiet at lower prices.	14s.6d. to 17s.6d.—A steady market at full prices.
Feb.	10s. to 12s.6d.—A steady trade at full prices.	14s.6d. to 17s.6d.—Business restricted owing to the scarcity of money and prices going down.
Mar.	10s.6d. to 13s.—More doing and firmer market.	13s. to 17s.6d.—A steady demand at full prices.
April.	10s. to 13s.—A good demand; rates steady.	12s. to 15s.—Market dull; holders pressing sales; lower prices.
May.	10s.6d. to 13s.—Several speculators purchased owing to the unfavorable weather for the crops; prices firmer.	10s.6d. to 14s.—More business done for export owing to the low prices accepted.
June.	10s.6d. to 13s.6d.—Large sales at full prices.	11s. to 13s.6d.—A steady demand for export and home use at full prices.
July.	10s.6d. to 13s.6d.—Less doing and prices giving way.	11s. 6d. to 16s.—Less doing at commencement of the month, owing to the fine weather for harvest, but many orders for the Continent and the West Indies arriving, more business was done towards the close, and prices firmer.
Aug.	11s.9d. to 19s.6d.—Unfavourable weather for crops, and report of potatoe disease, with large orders from Holland, caused an extensive business at considerably higher prices.	13s.6d. to 19s.6d.—The accounts more favourable for the potatoe crop, but a good demand for Ireland, owing to the reports on the crops being less satisfactory.
Sept.	16s. to 24s.—A large demand for the Continent; prices higher.	16s.6d. to 20s.—The rise in the Corn-market and the unfavourable reports respecting the potatoe crop, caused a large business partly on speculation at higher prices.
Oct.	17s.6d. to 22s.—Lower prices and less doing, owing to more satisfactory accounts from the Continent.	15s. to 20s.—A dull market; prices going down.
Nov.	17s.6d. to 22s.—Less doing; market dull.	15s. to 19s.—Rather more doing for home use and speculation, but the market became dull towards the end of the month.
Dec.	14s.6d. to 20s.—Prices going down and a dull market.	15s.6d. to 20s.—Dull and lower at commencement of month, but brisk towards the middle; large sales for Ireland and the Continent at higher prices.

RICE.—*continued.*

	1847.	1848.
Jan.	19s.6d. to 26s.6d.—Large business for Ireland and other outports.	9s.6d. to 15s.—Large stock and fair business.
Feb.	22s. to 24s.6d.—Market opened dull, but further sales for Ireland caused prices to recover slightly.	9s.6d. to 14s.6d.—Quiet; stocks increasing.
Mar.	19s.6d. to 24s.—Market quiet, with lower prices.	9s. to 14s.6d.—Dull market and lower prices.
April.	16s. to 23s. — Speculative demand; prices advanced towards the close.	9s. to 12s.6d.—Small trade; dull market.
May.	20s. to 25s.—Large orders and a rise in the Corn-market, speculative and home buyers bought largely, but later in the month prices receded, owing to a fall in the Corn-market.	7s.6d. to 12s.—Fine weather for crops, dull market and lower prices.
June.	17s. to 21s.6d.—Prices of corn falling, rice followed; market dull.	7s.6d. to 12s.—Do. do.
July.	15s. to 19s.6d.—Lower prices at the early part of the month, but large orders for Holland, and the reports respecting the potatoe blight caused a firmer market.	7s.6d. to 12s.6d.—Dull at commencement of month; reports respecting the potatoe blight, however, created an Irish speculative demand.
Aug.	14s.6d. to 18s.6d.—Fine weather for harvest; market dull.	11s. to 14s.—Large business; weather unsettled.
Sept.	13s.6d. to 18s.6d.—A decline in the grain market; large buyers of rice for Holland.	9s. to 16s.—Good business early, but fine weather and better accounts of potatoe crop; market dull.
Oct.	10s.6d. to 17s.6d.—Dull market and prices lower.	9s. to 13s.6d.—Dull market, and prices going down.
Nov.	10s.6d. to 16s.6d.—Small business at former prices.	9s.6d. to 14s.—Steady trade, but dull towards the close of the month.
Dec.	10s. to 17s.—Large stocks; small business.	9s. to 13s.—Free sellers, but few buyers, prices lower.

COCHINEAL.—*Low to fine, per lb.*

	1845.	1846.
Jan.	4s.5d. to 5s.11d.—Prices firm, and a fair business.	5s.1d. to 7s.6d.—A good business at steady prices.
Feb.	4s.8d. to 6s.3d.—Steady market, with better rates.	5s.1d. to 7s.4d.—The market steady at firm rates.
Mar.	4s.8d. to 6s.3d—Do. at full prices.	5s 2d. to 7s.4d.—Do. do.
April.	4s.8d. to 6s.3d.—Firm market, with a fair business doing.	5s.2d. to 7s.4d.—More business doing for all purposes, and prices firm.
May.	4s.8d. to 6s.5d.—More doing at improved prices.	5s.2d. to 7s.4d.—Prices steady, with a firm market.
June.	4s.11d. to 6s.5d.—Firmer market; trade good.	5s.6d. to 7s.4d.—Market firmer and dearer, owing to the rupture between America and Mexico.
July.	4s.10d. to 6s.5d.—Less doing, but firm prices.	5s. to 7s.—Large supplies and a pressure of sales caused prices to fall; trade good.
Aug.	4s.10d.to 6s.8d.—Market very firm,and but little offering; fair sales for export.	5s.3d. to 6s.7d.—Market quiet at lower prices.
Sept.	4s.11d. to 6s.10d.—A good business at better rates both for home use and export.	4s.8d. to 6s.9d.—A much better demand owing to the low prices accepted.
Oct.	5s.5d. to 7s.3d.—Finer sorts dearer; market on the whole quiet.	4s.4d. to 6s.7d.—Lower prices; business small.
Nov.	5s.3d. to 7s.3d.—Less active; prices rather lower.	4s.4d. to 6s.6d.—A steady sale at full terms.
Dec.	5s.1d. to 7s.2d.—Market dull; business slack.	4s.7d. to 6s.9d.—Market firmer, but not much doing.

IRON.—*Scotch Pig, per ton, cash.*

	1845.	1846.
Jan.	60s. to 65s.—The market very firm, and a large trade.	75s. to 85s.—Business large for home use and speculation; prices advancing.
Feb.	65s. to 100s.—Extensive business to complete contracts for home use and export for railway purposes.	77s.6d. to 82s.6d.—The scarcity of money stopped trade in a great measure, and prices were not so firm.
Mar.	105s. to 120s.—Increasing demand for speculation; large contracts for railway purposes, but market became dull, and declined towards the close of the month.	70s. to 77s.6d.—The unsettled state of political affairs and money slackened business; prices lower.
Apr.	90s. to 115s.—Speculators pressing sales; a dull and heavy market with lower prices, but a good business done.	67s. to 70s.—Prices going down and little doing.
May.	70s. to 80s.—Speculators still pressing sales; market flat, and much lower, but a very large business done.	67s.6d. to 72s.6d.—A better business and a firmer market.
June.	60s. to 77s.6d.—Do. at commencement of the month, but improved towards the middle, at higher prices, but again went flat and lower.	67s. to 70s.—Business large, owing to lower prices.

COCHINEAL.—*continued.*

	1847.	1848.
Jan.	6s.1d. to 6s.—Good demand for export and home use.	4s.6d. to 6s.4d.—Good trade; better prices.
Feb.	5s.4d. to 6s.2d.—Do. do.	4s.7d. to 5s.4d.—Quiet and steady; stock increasing.
Mar.	5s.6d. to 6s.5d.—More doing, and prices higher.	4s. to 5s.4d.—Revolution on the Continent stopped business; market dull.
April.	5s.5d. to 6s.2d.—Larger supply, but lower rates; a good trade.	3s.11d. to 5s.10d.—Do. do.
May.	4s.7d. to 5s.7d.—Dull market and more sellers.	3s.6d. to 5s.9d. — More doing and prices firmer.
June.	4s.8d. to 5s.9d.—Less offering, with a steady demand for export and home use.	3s.4d. to 5s.10d.—Dull market; pressure of sales; stock large.
July.	4s.9d. to 5s.9d.—Steady.	3s.4d. to 6s.—Do. do.
Aug.	4s.8d. to 5s.7d.—Market quiet; sales small.	3s.3d. to 5s.10d.—Dull market.
Sept.	4s.8d. to 5s.9d.—Steady.	3s.4d. to 5s.10d.—Good business at better prices.
Oct.	3s.10d. to 5s.9d.—Depressed state of trade caused prices to fall considerably, with more offering; money tight.	3s.4d. to 6s.—Pressure of sales, but a good business at lower prices towards end of the month.
Nov.	3s.11d. to 5s.—More doing; prices steady.	3s.4d. to 6s.—Very quiet market, and easier.
Dec.	4s.1d. to 5s.2d.—Do.; prices rather looking up.	3s.5d. to 6s.—A good business at better prices.

IRON.—*continued.*

	1847.	1848.
Jan.	71s. to 77s.6d.—Good trade doing in the early part of the month, but through the advance of interest for money, the market became dull and lower.	45s. to 51s.—Good business at improving prices.
Feb.	72s. to 77s.6d.—More doing for export, and prices recovering.	49s. to 52s.—Speculators purchased, and prices dearer; good trade.
Mar.	70s. to 76s.6d.—Money market tight; lower prices, and only a small trade.	42s. to 51s.—Revolution in France; flat market, and lower prices.
April.	67s. to 74s.—A good business done early in the month, but cash getting scarce, prices fell.	40s. to 43s.6d.—Full market and lower.
May.	63s. to 67s.6d.—Large business done on speculation, but prices gradually gave way.	42s. to 44s.—More doing; the article getting scarce.
June.	63s.6d. to 67s.6d.—Moderate trade at steady prices.	41s. to 44s.—Moderate sales.

IRON.—*continued.*

	1845.	1846.
July.	60s. to 67s.6d.—A steady market, and but little done.	67s. to 75s.—Speculators have again bought freely; a large business done at higher rates.
Aug.	60s. to 70s.—More doing, and market firmer.	74s. to 76s.—A good business at full prices.
Sept.	77s.6d. to 87s.6d.—A large business on speculation and for home use; prices much higher.	74s. to 77s.6d.—Large sales; prices rose at the end of the month.
Oct.	82s.6d. to 97s.6d.—Brisk demand with higher prices, but gave way towards the close; market dull.	69s. to 77s.6d.—A pressure of sales for money caused prices to fall; a good business done.
Nov.	70s. to 85s.—Less doing, and prices giving way.	70s. to 72s.6d.—Good demand at free rates.
Dec.	70s. to 80s.—A steady demand, and towards the close, improved in price.	73s. to 75s.—A large speculative business; prices higher.

IRON.—*continued.*

	1847.	1848.
July.	63s.6d. to 72s.6d.—Speculators purchased freely, and prices improved.	43s.6d. to 46s.6d.—Firmer and more doing, but at the end of the month dull.
Aug.	67s. to 72s. — Good business, but money scarce; at the end of the month prices fell.	44s. to 45s.6d.—Quiet market.
Sept.	66s.6d. to 68s.—Little doing; prices going down.	45s. to 46s.—More doing towards the end of the month, and better prices.
Oct.	57s. to 66s.—Money market very tight, and extensive failures; prices fell considerably.	42s.6d. to 45s.6d.—Dull market and lower; free sellers.
Nov.	48s. to 54s.—Large business done for export; full consumption at lower prices.	42s. to 43s.—A moderate business at steady rates.
Dec.	45s. to 50s.—Flat market.	40s. to 42s.6d.—Market firmer at end of month, and more doing.

APPENDIX.

The Balance Sheets and other documents here inserted, exhibit in detail the condition of the greater number of the most important houses which suspended in London during the late crisis, and in themselves furnish much valuable matter for future reference.

MESSRS. HARMAN & CO.,

RUSSIA TRADE.

At a meeting of creditors, held in the month of October, 1846, it was agreed to wind up this estate under the process of Inspection.

Annexed are EXTRACTS FROM THE INTRODUCTORY REPORT made on this estate, to the Inspectors, by Mr. J. E. COLEMAN, 23d November, 1846, and forwarded to the Russian Government.

"I commenced my enquiry at the time of the decease of Mr. John Harman, which was in July, 1817, and find that he died possessed of property to the extent of about £233,000, consisting of Consols, Bank and other stock, which realized about £102,000; a bond debt of £7,500; land and estates £24,600; mine and other shares £25,600; and two balances in his favor of money left in the business with Messrs. Jeremiah, Edward, and Henry Harman, amounting to £73,467 7s. 1d. Mr. John Harman bequeathed by his will certain legacies and investments to the extent of nearly £200,000, including a legacy to the Messrs. Harman of £5,000 each, and in addition to which they were left residuary legatees, and by which they benefited to the extent of nearly £20,000, as shown in detail in a further part of this Report. It is here necessary to observe, that Mr. John Harman had retired from business so far back as June 1810.

"The proportions of the business carried on by Messrs. Jeremiah, Edward, and Henry Harman, were as follows:—Jeremiah, nine 24ths; Edward, eight 24ths; and Henry, seven 24ths.

"On looking at the balance statement of the year 1817, and comparing the same with the books at that period, I find that the following sums stand to the credit of the partners—Jeremiah, in the general ledger, £23,333 6s. 8d., and in the private ledger, £23,336 7s. 8d., together £46,669 14s. 4d.; Edward, in the general ledger, £22,333 6s. 8d., and in the private ledger, £5,234 5s. 3d., together £27,567 11s. 11d.; Henry, in the general ledger, £20,333 6s. 8d., in the private ledger, £70,057 7s. 8d., together £90,390 14s. 4d. At this time it appears a very minute investigation of the whole accounts both due to and from the firm was drawn out, as will be shewn by a document made at that time, and which will be laid before you at the meeting this day.

"The profit and loss account, as made up at this time, is as follows:—

DEBTOR.	£	s.	d.	CREDITOR.	£	s.	d.
1817.				1816.			
Feb. To cash put on private ticket*	120,000	0	0	Dec. By Old balance	144,820	11	3
To Charges in trade	2,031	9	1	By gross amount of interest charged	14,894	0	3
,, Sundry small losses	310	17	2	,, Profit on Government securities	45,206	0	2
,, Interest allowed	12,253	17	6	,, Several sums due to parties, not claimed since 1793	325	4	5
,, Bad debts written off	32,404	19	5				
,, Balance carried to credit of 1818	38,244	12	11				
	£205,245	16	1		£205,245	16	1

"On the statement of 1817 before referred to, I find that several debts due to the Messrs. Harman, amounting together to £71,404 15s. 7d., were taken as "debts partly to be recovered," and on tracing these through the books, I find the loss on them amounted to £55,936 19s. 2d., in addition to this there was an entry of a sum of £40,779 19s. 1d. as cash balance taken credit for in the private ledger, which was but a fiction, as no such fund existed, but the amount was the balance due to the cash book of the firm, and arose from entries passed to the debit of the three several partners, and other like accounts in the private ledger, and which entries were not made in the general cash book; the following are

"The Balances of the Private Ledger at December, 1817.

DEBTOR.	£	s.	d.	CREDITOR.	£	s	d.
Estate of John Harman	33,245	6	5	By Jeremiah Harman	23,366	7	8
Elizabeth Harman	96	1	9	,, Edward Harman	5,234	5	3
Masterman & Co.	22,888	0	11	,, Henry Harman	70,057	7	8
Cash in the desk	304	18	3	,, Sundry small debts	1,463	18	8
Bank of England	157	17	10				
Fletcher, J.	24	0	0				
Estate of J. Harford, dec.	1,600	0	0				
Bills	1,025	15	0				
Balance of cash	40,779	19	1				
	£100,121	19	3		£100,121	19	3

"Therefore, taking the two amounts of £55,936 19s. 1d. and £40,779 19s. 1d. added together, and passed to the debits of the three accounts of Messrs. Jeremiah, Edward, and Henry, in their respective proportions, their real balances at that period, viz. 1817, would be as follows:—Jeremiah would have a credit balance of £10,400 17s. 5d., Edward would be a debtor to the extent of £4,671 7s. 7d., and Henry would have a credit of £62,181 12s. 6d. I do not think any doubt can be entertained of the solvency of the house at this time, the two balances of Jeremiah and Henry giving a sum (after deducting Edward's debit balance) of £67,911 2s. 4d., added to which there was the private property of all three partners.

"I find that the business transactions of the house have gradually declined, and the profits have diminished, leaving a debit to the profit and loss account to December, 1845, of £134,556 15s. 8d., to which must be added the amount of debts now to be written off, and which is specified hereafter.

"The drawing accounts, with the interest added, of the two are as follows:—Jeremiah Harman to December, 1843, (as he died in February, 1844,) £161,366 16s. 8d., Edward to October 22d, 1846, £260,427 0s. 6d., and Henry has a credit of £22,553 13s. 2d., being the difference between the amount that he drew out and the amount that was paid to his credit, by sums of interest allowed, and monies paid in at various times.

"In addition to this there will be a sum of about £130,000 to be passed to their respective debits, according to their proportions, being the amount that will have to be written off on bad debts, interest, &c., to the present time.

* The explanation to the above is as follows:—The Private Tickets mean the Private Ledger, in which in February, 1817 £45,000 was passed to the credit of Jeremiah's account; £40,000 in like manner to the credit of Edward's account; and £35,000 in like manner to the credit of Henry's account.

"The monies they each received from their father's estate was, in September, 1817, £4,950; in January, 1822, £2,104 2s. 11d.; in December, 1823, £1,500; in January, 1824, £2,000; in April, 1824, £500; and in May, 1825, £500, making a total of £11,554 2s. 11d. to each; these sums, together with others which are specified afterwards, would therefore be the amounts for which each partner would have to render an account of the manner in which such sums have been expended.

" But on liquidation of the same, there is to be deducted as follows:

	Jeremiah Harman.			Edward Harman.			Henry Harman.		
	£.	s.	d.	£.	s.	d.	£.	s.	d.
Amount passed to the debit as part of purchase of the premises in Adam's-court in 1820	2,625	0	0	2,333	6	8	2,041	13	4
(Making a sum of £7,000 which was passed to the credit of Jeremiah Harman's account, being the amount of purchase by the firm from him.)									
There are also various sums of gratuities to clerks, &c., passed to their separate accounts, which should properly have gone to charges	1,413	15	0	1,256	13	4	1,199	11	8
In 1845 the accumulation of dividends that had been paid on stock which had not been invested was £11,162 10s., and was passed in like manner to the debit of the private account	4,185	18	9	3,720	16	8	3,255	14	7
In 1841 the interest and discount paid to Masterman & Co. was passed in like manner	1,594	18	0	1,417	13	9	1,240	9	6
They amount to	£9,819	11	9	8,728	10	5	7,737	9	1

" There may be some other small sums to come to the credit of the three accounts in like manner, but I have not had sufficient time to go more minutely into these details.

	£	s.	d.
" Thus, taking the drawing account of Jeremiah Harman from December, 1817, to December, 1843, amounting to	£144,901	1	10
Less paid in	1,790	7	2
	143,110	14	8
To which add—Property left by John Harman	11,544	2	11
In October 1823, he received a legacy, left him by Baron Dopft, of	4,500	0	0
	159,164	17	7
From which must be deducted, as detailed above	9,819	11	9
Leaving this amount to be accounted for, independent of any receipts from any private source	£149,345	5	10

	£	s.	d.
" Taking the drawing account of Edward Harman from December, 1817, to October, 1846, which is	£166,113	0	5
To which add property left by John Harman	11,554	2	11
	177,667	3	4
From which may be deducted, as above	8,728	10	5
Leaving this amount to be accounted for by Edward Harman, independent of receipts from any private resources	£168,938	12	11

" The drawing account of Henry Harman is considerably in his favour.

" Assuming that the amount of £120,000 ought to have been written off to the debit of profit and loss at the time of Mr. Jeremiah Harman's death, the respective balances in round numbers at that time would have been as follows:—

Jeremiah Harman was a debtor to the amount of £180,000
Edward Harman was a debtor to the amount of 285,000
and Henry Harman had a credit balance of about £65,000.

" The balances that will appear against the two surviving partners will, I apprehend, be increased by about £30,000 from 1843 to October 1846; thus making in round numbers a balance to the debit of Edward Harman of £300,000, and a balance to the credit of Henry Harman of £50,000.

" The explanation of the two items mentioned in the detailed particulars of accounts, is as follows:—

" In the year 1823, from information which Messrs. Harman had obtained, an old balance of £6,758 14s. 1d., due to them from Boyd, Kerr, & Co., (and which had been previously carried to the debit of profit and loss) was re-credited in the full amount; but in 1824 they passed a debit for £3,025 6s. 7d., being the difference of the above amount so credited and what they actually received. In the same year 1823, Mr. Miles Mc Donnell induced Messrs. Harman to make an extensive speculation in barilla, by which they made a profit of £14,596 1s. 11d., which amount was passed to the credit of profit and loss, but in the year following a settlement took place, and they gave to Mr. Mc Donnell £6,619 10s. as his proportion.

" I have thus, as far as time has allowed me, touched upon the various points upon which I was instructed, as well as such others that presented themselves to notice in my investigation; and I beg to observe, that no doubt whatever can exist of the accuracy of the books; although I must say that the state of the affairs of the house was at all times visible; in fact, the private books, as kept by Mr. Edward Harman, are in that state that the accounts were balanced monthly, but the private drawings were never carried to the debit of profit and loss; nor do I think that any regard whatever has been paid either as to the exigencies or capabilities of the house in the drawings that were made by the several partners. * * * * *

" As regards the present liabilities and assets of the estate, I find that the statement submitted to you showed creditors £553,743, and assets £108,748, and so far as I have at present been enabled to trace the same, I do not think any material alteration will arise." * * * * * * * * * * * *

From a Second REPORT on the Estate of Harman & Co., made by Mr. Coleman on the 16th of December, 1846, the following is extracted:—

" In the amount of £414,429 14s. 5d., for which the Russian Government stands as creditor, is included a sum for interest to the extent of £152,830 0s. 11d. The liabilities on the estate are decreased, and the amount of same now is £541,439 14s. 2d., whilst on the other hand the assets are increased, and shew a total of £110,193 16s. 8d., and will, in my opinion, yield that amount. With reference to the position of Jeremiah Harman's estate, it will be observed, that the balance now due from him is £10,410 16s. 9d. less than at the time of his decease, this arises from the surplus of proceeds of sales of his separate estate, and of which the firm have received the benefit.

STATEMENT OF AFFAIRS.

	£	s.	d.		£	s.	d.
To sundry creditors	541,439	14	2	By Sundry assets	12,978	3	5
				,, Good debts	21,325	13	3
				,, Estimated produce of doubtful debts	6,000	0	0
				,, Estimated surplus from the separate estate of the late Jeremiah Harman	20,940	0	0
				,, Estimated surplus from the separate estate of Edward Harman	41,400	0	0
				,, Estimated surplus of the separate estate of Henry Harman	7,550	0	0
				,, Balance deficiency ..	431,245	17	6
	£541,439	14	2		£541,439	14	2"

The estate of Messrs. Harman & Co. has realized the expectations entertained of its assets, which will pay about 3s. 3d. in the pound, dividends to the amount of 3s. having been already declared.

Messrs. COCKERELL, LARPENT, & Co.

East India Trade.

A meeting was held on the 18th October, 1847, of the creditors of Messrs. Cockerell, Larpent, & Co. at which the chair was taken by Mr. Samuel Gregson, M.P.

The chairman stated that the object of the meeting was to take into consideration the affairs of the house, and to adopt such course of liquidation as, under the circumstances, should be thought most beneficial for the creditors generally.—The chairman then referring to a balance-sheet of the books of the house, made up to the 27th of September, 1847, the day of its suspension of payments, and to other documents laid on the table, submitted to the meeting the following statement:—

DEBTS.

	£	£	£
That the debts of the house, in open accounts, amount to	..	..	154,761
That the house is under acceptances for	..	606,585	
Part of these acceptances are secured by bills of lading from India, to the amount of..........	57,677		
Further part of these bills will be retired by the third parties, to the amount of	84,276	141,953	464,632
			£619,393

That the assets of the house, consisting of cash, goods, debts, and other property, amounted, as they appeared upon the balance-sheet of the books to ....

And stand in the following order:

ASSETS.

Balance at the banker's	..	2,317
Bills of exchange and goods	..	15,600
Various balances due to the house in the course of realization	..	40,000
Amount in the hands of Cockerell & Co., of Calcutta, due to the present house of Cockerell, Larpent, & Co., of London, and which is in course of remittance..................	..	339,118
Amount due by Messrs. Cockerell & Co., of Calcutta, to Cockerell & Co., of London	..	435,000
Mauritius estates (cost upwards of £200,000.)		
Say present value	100,000	
Less mortgage	50,000	
		50,000
Various miscellaneous property	..	10,000
Amount of various claims secured	335,380	
Amount of property given in security	352,099	
	Surplus	16,719
		909,254
The London house holds a security for £129,500, part of the £435,500; but £100,000, part of this £129,000, has been transferred by the London house in security: it is therefore deducted from assets	..	100,000
		£809,254

In regard to the amount of the before-mentioned sum of £339,118, that amount arises from goods shipped by the London house during the past and present year, for bills drawn by the Calcutta house, to be covered by consignment of goods and bills to the London house, and for similar transactions, all of which are in the regular course of business to be remitted for during the present season. In regard to the old balance of £435,500, the London house also holds securities on indigo factories and other properties for the balance, subject to a prior mortgage of £100,000, the surplus being estimated at £90,000. There is a balance-sheet of the Calcutta house up to the end of April, 1846, in London, which has been carefully examined by Mr. Martin, formerly a partner in the Calcutta house, and intimately acquainted with the numerous properties, and by others long conversant with the commerce of India, and their very confident opinion is, that the house in Calcutta is fully competent to meet all its liabilities, and that nothing but a most unwarrantable sacrifice of property by panic and forced sales, or by the operation of the Insolvent Court, where very heavy expenses, and much waste and destruction of property necessarily take place, can defeat the house's capacity, ultimately, to liquidate all its liabilities. The opinion of the partners and of the gentlemen who have given their assistance in looking into the concern is, that by the 1st day of January there ought to be realized a sufficient sum to make assignment to the creditors of twenty per cent. on all the debts of the house.

The chairman further stated, that Mr. Martin, who had retired from the house in Calcutta, in April, 1845, was prepared to proceed to Calcutta by the packet of the 20th instant. And it was also contemplated, with the sanction of the inspectors to be now appointed, to make arrangements for some other competent person wholly unconnected with either house, to proceed to Calcutta, with the view to protect the interest of the creditors generally, and that of the London house also. The chairman further stated, that although there was no balance-sheet of the Calcutta-house of a date later than the 30th of April, 1846, the end of the commercial year; yet, from the opinion of Mr. Martin, confirmed also by that of the partners in the London house, the debts of the Calcutta house would be but comparitively of small amount beyond the bills drawn and now in the hands of the creditors, and the two sums already stated as being due to the London house. The chairnan further stated, that powers of attorney had been sent out by the last packet in favour of Mr. Mackenzie, of the house of Mackillop, Stewart, & Co., and of Mr. Martin, to protect the interest of all parties until the creditors in England had the opportunity of coming to a resolution on the course which they might deem it most expedient to have pursued in the liquidation.

It was then moved by Mr. Kirkman Hodgson, and seconded by Mr. Charles Dashwood Bruce, and unanimously resolved:—" That the interest of the creditors would be best consulted by the partners devoting their services to the realization of the property and to the liquidation of the affairs of the house under the direction of inspectors."

It was moved by Mr. Alex. Colvin, and seconded by Mr. Edmund Buxton, and resolved:—" That in the event of the house in Calcutta not meeting its engagements it is the opinion of this meeting that it would be greatly to the advantage of the creditors that the concerns of the house in Calcutta should be liquidated by the partners, under the inspection of two or three gentlemen of standing and character in Calcutta, and that reasonable time and facility should be afforded for the liquidation and realization of the property, by avoiding sacrifices and forced sales; and that the heavy expenses and official forms of the Insolvent Court ought to be avoided; and that all bill-holders be strongly recommended to send out their protests, but for the present to retain their bills and to give a discretion to their correspondents in Calcutta to concur with other parties who have an equal interest with themselves in carrying the substance of this resolution into effect so as to promote the interest of all parties and avoid the sacrifice of property."

It was then moved by Mr. James Heron, seconded by Mr. Charles Riley, and resolved:—" That the following gentlemen be named inspectors: Mr. Samuel Gregson, Mr. Edward Mills, Mr. John Horsley Palmer, and Mr. John Deans Campbell."

It was then moved by Mr. Frederick Hodgson, seconded by Mr. William Pigott, and resolved:—" That a dividend be paid as funds can be realized, and that a deed be in the mean time prepared with such clauses as are usual and necessary. Such deed to be settled and approved by the inspectors on behalf of the creditors, and signed by the creditors on receiving the dividend."

It was moved by Mr. George Arbuthnot, seconded by Mr. John H. Palmer:—" That a sum not exceeding £5,000 be applied in discharge of small claims, in the discretion of the partners and sanctioned by the inspectors."

" The accounts," remarked the *Times*, " show a nominal surplus of £190,000, and, from what transpired during the discussion, which took place, the prospects of the creditors, supposing no very serious difficulties to arise in Calcutta consequent upon the disasters on this side, may, on the whole, be considered favourable. In the formidable item of £435,500, which appears to be due from the Calcutta house, we have a sufficient explanation of the cause of the stoppage, and also the indication as to the principal contingency upon which the character of the liquidation will depend. It appears that securities are held against a portion of the amount in the shape of Indigo factories and other property, which have hitherto estimated at £200,000, although, of course, it must be expected that they will not produce that sum when a realization shall be attempted. The item of £339,000, 'which is in course of remittance,' arises, it was stated by the chairman, from goods shipped by the London house during the past and present year, all of which are, in the regular course of business, to be remitted for during the present season."

In the beginning of the month of February, 1848, the Overland Mail brought accounts respecting the position of the greater number of the Calcutta houses; and the exhibit made by the Calcutta firm of Cockerell & Co. was as subjoined, the proceedings being extracted from the *Bengal Hurkaru* of the 17th of December.

"On the motion of Mr. C. J. Richards, Mr. Adam Freer Smith was called to the chair, and read the advertisement calling the meeting, also a statement of the liabilities and assets of the firm, when

"It was proposed by Mr. J. C. Richards, and seconded by Mr. R. H. Hunter :— 'That it is expedient for the interests of the creditors that the estate be put into the hands of the Insolvent Court-'—Carried unanimously.

"It was then proposed by Mr. C. B. Skinner, and seconded by Mr. M. Gladstone, —'That Messrs. William Martin and Henry Cowie be recommended to the court as co-assignees to the estate.'—Carried by a majority.

LIABILITIES.		Rs.
Balances due on open accounts		8,68,873
Bills payable		28,32,097
Cockerell & Co., and Cockerell, Larpent, & Co., of London, including their acceptances and bills drawn under credit *		65,94,101
Deceased and retired partners' balances		15,01,994
Bills drawn on London which had not been accepted, Rs. 72,029		7,29,290
Ditto drawn from premiums, payable to the Atlas Insurance Office, not due up to the failure of the London firm, £2,578		37,780
Office rent and pay of the establishment		18,876
		Rs. 125,83,011

Besides their claim for bills remitted on our own account current, which are most likely to be paid, £25,740.

ASSETS.		
Cash balance in the Bank of Bengal		Rs. 29,873
Ditto in the hands of the Banian		5,496
Balances in open accounts		8,56,106
Ditto due by planters and others, secured by blocks of factories, and other property		74,19,871
Ditto due by indigo and sugar factories the property of the firm		13,99,447
Outlay of cultivation of the above, Season 1847-48	Rs.11,31,461	
Season 1847-48	1,62,108	
		12,93,569
Natmoo estate		10,74,808
Government paper, banks, insurance, and other shares		7,91,875
Glasgow purchase amount		1,39,000
Bills receivable		36,153
		Rs. 130,46,198

Of the above liabilities Rs. 41,24,000 are understood to be covered by securities standing in the credit side in this statement at Rs. 62,00,000; and by indigo, the produce of the season, valued at Rs. 6,30,000—together Rs. 68,30,000.

ASSETS EARLY REALIZABLE.		Rs.
Cash balance, 18th November		35,000
Bills receivable		17,000
Proceeds of piece goods, and twist sold*		96,500
Estimated value of ditto unsold		42,500
Shell lac and lac dye, godown		41,000
Indigo produce of season, less lien on it		2,06,000
Sugar and saltpetre in transit to Calcutta		23,500
Bank of Bengal shares (3) with dividend		20,000
Union Bank shares (14) balance recoverable from Natmoo		2,67,100
Timber, elephants, and outstandings not included		...
Balance due by Kishnaghur Rajah for talook		10,000
Advances for indigo and sugar cultivation produce not included above		2,31,000
Personal balances early realizable, less included on bills receivable		1,44,100
Balance of Mr. Larpent's personal estate after paying all private liabilities		15,000
Ditto, ditto, Mr. Beckwith's ditto		15,000
Bu Dukaobadee talook, yielding 2,300 Rs. per annum		25,000
Shares in insurance offices		47,900
Balance of produce with Pelletreau and Evans and Co.		50,000
Five Bengal Indigo Company shares of Mr. Forlong		25,000
Old copper, per Emma Colvin*		3,700
Government paper on hand		2,600
Proceeds of teak timber, per Sir Robert Seppings, estimated at	6,000	
Less Captain Trail's share, after deducting his share of the balance of debit of ship	1,500	
		4,500
Government paper deposited at indigo and other factories:—		
Balacole, in 1844-45	1,000	
Ditto, 1846-47	2,000	
Cooleadah ,,	2,000	
Ameerpore rum and sugar works in 1844-45	5,000	
		10,000
		Rs. 13,32,400

On full investigation, however, this statement did not prove correct, and as the fearful loss which it was estimated would have to be submitted to in the winding up of the Calcutta house, together with other reductions occasioned by further failures, made a vast alteration in the prospects of assets, a fresh report was prepared, which shewed that instead of 20s. in the pound being the amount which the creditors might reasonably hope to receive, the outside dividend would scarcely exceed 4s. 4d. This report, containing much interesting matter, is given *in extenso.*

REPORT, 1st MAY, 1848, founded on the investigation of Mr. J. E. COLEMAN, the accountant employed.

" On the 18th October, 1847, at a general meeting of the creditors of COCKERELL, LARPENT, & Co., a statement of the affairs of the house was laid before them, and certain resolutions adopted thereon.

" Six months having elapsed, it becomes imperative to see what is the present position of these affairs, and to examine item by item the component parts of this statement, in relation to the information intermediately obtained.

" The statement of October was formed upon an abstract of the balance-sheet of the *books* of the house, made up to the 27th September, 1847.

* The Banian claims a lien on part of these goods.

1st, The debts upon open accounts were taken at £154,761

2nd, The outstanding acceptances were taken at........ 464,632

Together £619,393

On the 26th February, 1848, they prove to be 196,594

(The difference arising from interest on deposits to 27th September, and from bills under acceptance since taken up by the drawers, which had been previously deducted from their cash-balance)

They are reduced to 402,765

£599,360

But to this account must be added the liabilities arising from bills receivable which were not taken into account.

They have now been gone over, and may be briefly stated as follows :—

1st. Bills discounted, outstanding in October, 1847	£367,352	
Of these have run off	205,790	
Leaving outstanding .	161,562	
A large portion of which are on houses that have since suspended payment, but of the amount above it is expected that a portion will be duly honoured to the extent of...............	73,332	
	£88,230	
2nd. Bills drawn by Cockerell, Larpent, & Co., on Calcutta, accepted by Cockerell & Co., but not paid	30,126	
3rd. Bills accepted by the Union Bank of Calcutta, and endorsed by Cockerell, Larpent, & Co.	38,946	
		157,302
		£756,662

It appears by the preceding, therefore, that the debts—

per statement of October, 1847, were £619,393

per statement of 26th February, 1848, were.................. £756,662

The assets taken in Oct., 1847, were as follows :—

1st. Cash at bankers	2,317
Bills of exchange and goods	15,600
	17,917

Of which goods to the extent of £2,100 have been delivered to the consignors or their order under legal advice.

1st. The cash and bill receipts on general account have been 13,106

And the balance in cash and bills is now 12,974

In the bills per contra were included—

Bills on Lyall, Brothers, & Co...	.£5,000	these 2 houses have since suspended payments.
,, Barclay & Co...	5,000	
	£10,000	

Brought over	£17,917	Brought over		£12,974
		And payment has been made to Mr. Martin, for outfit, &c. to India	900	
		Ditto to Partners	816	
		Ditto to Establishment now broken up	1,915	
		And the bankers have written off the balance in their hands ...	2,317	
2nd. Balances in course of realization	40,000	2nd. These are now taken as per schedule at............		46,860
Per statement of October, 1847	57,917	Per statement of 26th February, 1848		£59,834
3rd. Balances in the hands of Cockerell & Co., of Calcutta, in course of remittance	£339,118	This item was supposed to be in course of remittance from Calcutta upon the following grounds:— 1st. The whole being composed either of liabilities incurred here for property actually held in Calcutta, or for cash received there for bills drawn on the firm of Cockerell, Larpent, & Co., of London, in pursuance of the new house; and 2nd. On account of the repeated assurances of the Calcutta firm.		

The property held in Calcutta, and the cash received, was as follows:—

Manchester and Glasgow goods, for which returns had not been made, (shipped in 1846 and 1847)	£78,000
Bills drawn on "Produce Account"	45,000
Bills drawn on "London Account"	60,000
Bills drawn on "General Account"	153,000
	£336,000

Of assurances in their letters, there were amongst others, the following:—

In their No. 203, 5th December, 1846, they state their intention to open an account to be called "Produce Account, 1847," against which they would draw from time to time, as their expenditure for indigo, sugar, and timber, might render necessary, which drafts were to be provided for from the returns of the several articles, either in the shape of consignments, or, if circumstances rendered sales on the spot desirable, in bills.

In their letter No. 17, Private Series, 7th January, 1847, they advise having specifically drawn for cultivation purposes.

In No. 20, Private Series, 4th February, 1847, they state that they may fairly calculate upon the bulk of the sugar and timber shipments arriving in London in time to be available for the early engagements in this account.

In No. 23, Private Series, 20th March, 1847, they repeat that every draft drawn in produce account will be literally provided for by the returns from produce which will have been realized or shipped.

No. 27, Private Series, 1st May, 1847.

"We are happy to be able to speak most favourably of our prospects for this year. "In no preceding year do we remember to have received such universally favo-"rable accounts from our factories, for we may say, with the sole exception of "Midnapore, where matters are not so promising, our factories in every district "promise full crops, and we have every reason to expect a return fully equal to "the maximum figure given in our detailed statement of our indigo produce."

"Our accounts from our sugar factories are also very satisfactory, and matters at "Natmoo are progressing."

No. 34, Private Series, 7th August, 1847.

" To this moment we have been unable to obtain advances upon any of our indigo, " of which we have a large quantity actually housed at the factories, the ship- " ping documents of piece goods held by us have also been unavailable, our " prospects of indigo continue reasonably satisfactory, although the very large " returns we at one time expected, cannot now be realized.

4th. Amount due by the Statement of October, to Cockerell & Co., London, by Cockerell & Co., Calcutta ...... £435,500.

This large item was the estimated amount of the debt due to the old firm of Cockerell & Co., which closed 31st December, 1846, and it is necessary to explain the circumstances that led the London house to suppose that it was fairly estimated and covered by property ultimately available in India for its liquidation.

In 1839, the capital of the Calcutta firm amounted to £385,390, and the debt due to the London house was only 416,905, C.R., or £41,690.

Balance-sheets from 1839 to 1846 has been annually transmitted by the Calcutta firm, and although in consequence principally of the large payments made by the London house on behalf of the Calcutta firm, to the Messrs. Spiers on their retirement, and to Mr. Howe Cockerell's executors, on his death, the debt of the London firm had greatly increased; there was no reason to suppose that the capital of the Calcutta firm would not be amply sufficient to cover the increased debt created by such retirement, independently of security, which had been taken on factories and other property amounting together to £180,000.

The nett profits of the Calcutta house from 1st May, 1839, to 30th April, 1846, amounted to Rs. 33,73,420, but in the years 1843, 1844, and 1845, various amounts were written off, amounting to Rs. 10,62,990, leaving the amount of profits actually passed to credit of the several partners Rs. 22,10,430, say £231,400, averaging £33,000 per annum for seven years.

From the perusal of the correspondence and inspection of accounts between the two houses during the above period, it appears that the whole of the former throughout, carry perfect confidence in their stability, and of their power to meet in every manner their various engagements, which the accounts that accompanied the same, fully corroborated, and such accounts (down to the balance-sheet of 30th April, 1846,) as they were received periodically, were strictly examined, classified, and estimated by the London house, under the direct inspection of Mr. Martin, he being the last partner who retired from Calcutta, and was most intimately acquainted with the details and values of all the properties in which the Calcutta house was interested; and the best proof of his belief in the accuracy of his estimate, is, the fact of his having left the whole of his balance in the house, and which still remains.

Throughout the whole of this period up to the time of failure, Messrs. Cockerell, Larpent, & Co., had every reason to suppose, that the local engagements of the firm were comparatively of no considerable amount, and by the letter which had accompanied the last balance-sheet of the 30th April, 1846, and which letter was dated the 7th January, 1847, Messrs. Cockerell & Co. had expressed themselves as follows :—

" Our operation in indigo, sugar, and timber, shew a large estimated surplus on " returns over outlay, and in addition to our profits from other sources, ought " to make our reducing, annually, the permanent amount against us, without " infringing in any way upon the new firm's operations."

" We hope to be enabled by the exercise of the strictest economy in all depart- " ments of our business, and losing no opportunity of realizing " locks up," to " liquidate the amount of the rate of £50,000 per annum; in naming this sum " we have had considerable hesitation, and can assure you, it is the utmost we " can expect to do under ordinary circumstances."

It should be remarked, that this letter is in reply to one from Cockerell & Co., of London, dated 2d October, 1846, informing the Calcutta house of the intended new partnership of Cockerell, Larpent, & Co., and requesting from them some terms of liquidation for the balance due to the old firm of Cockerell & Co., thereby shewing that the house in Calcutta at this period, felt confident of being able to meet all their engagements.

After the suspension of the London house on 27th September, 1847, and with a view to the statement afterwards submitted to the creditors, Mr. Martin was requested to go over all his statements, and the following is the result of his investigations as primarily founded on the last balance-sheet, and which formed the basis of the estimate in the statement of October, 1847.

That the LIABILITIES of the Calcutta house are therein taken as follows:—

Balances to sundries		Rs. 7,61,183
Balances to London house (without security,) except the surplus on the mortgages to the estate of R. H. Cockerell		30,60,000
Balances to London house (with security)		12,95,000
Balance to R. H. Cockerell's estate (with security)		9,00,000
Balance to Mr. Martin		6,00,000
Aggregate		Rs. 66,16,183
Or say		£661,600
To these liabilities Mr. Martin added the acceptances of the London house		345,000
		£1,006,600

That the ASSETS of the Calcutta house are taken as follows:—

Balances, civil and military (good)		Rs. 1,26,000
Indigo and sugar factories		27,30,199
Planters' balances		25,98,178
Pelletreau and Even (Mirzapore advances)		15,25,835
Advances on indigo outstanding at that date		2,00,000
Natmoo estate, Moulmein		7,50,000
Shares in the Bengal Indigo Company		3,00,000
Miscellaneous accounts		5,88,472
Shares in Companies		2,85,130
Ships sold	Rs. 1,60,000	
Timber at Natmoo	2,80,000	
		4,40,000
Indigo season, 1847, 11,411 maunds at Rs. 100		15,40,000
Sugar, 2,500 maunds at Rs. 8		2,00,000
Goods and produce in godowns, 15,000 maunds, sugars, and sundries		2,05,000
Glasgow goods		7,89,430
Ships building at Natmoo, 1820 tons, at £15 per ton		2,73,000
Freight by the same between Moulmein and Calcutta		1,00,000
Total		Rs. 1,26,51,244
Or say		£1,265,100

From these Mr. Martin took miscellaneous balances.		
Bad	£12,000	
Loss on shares	7,840	
Loss on Pelletreau and Even's balance	70,000	
Loss on factories	100,000	
Loss on planters' balances	180,000	
		369,800
		£895,300
Balance, being deficiency		111,300
		£1,006,600

It was upon these data that the London house believed not only that there would be provision for the liabilities outstanding, say £339,118 on account of Cockerell, Larpent, & Co., but ultimate provision for the debt of the old firm of Cockerell & Co.

Mr. Martin proceeded to Calcutta shortly after the suspension of the London house, with a power of attorney to himself and Mr. McKenzie, to act on their behalf.

The following Memorandum has been sent home by Mr. Martin.

"Memorandum by Mr. Martin, 16th December, 1847."

"On my arrival in Calcutta, I was surprised to find the assets of the Calcutta "house so much below what, from the information in possession of the London "house, and from the balance-sheet to 30th April, 1846, (which was the latest "in possession of the London house) I and others had supposed they would "turn out to be, and I have given as much of my time as possible to look into "accounts for the information of the creditors of the London house."

"The following will shew the difference between the estimates in London, and the "real results in Calcutta."

"1st. The heavy loss in the indigo season, 1845-46, "amounting to			Rs. 7,61,000
"It was supposed that there was a loss upon a portion of the "factories, and a memorandum was down in the London "house's statement to that effect, but nothing more was "known in London."			
"2nd. The London estimate of the present "season's indigo crop was made up in the "latest letters from Calcutta, it gave	Mds. 11,411		
"Whereas so great a change has taken place, "that the quantity is now supposed to be	7,600		
Difference	3,811 at 140 Rs. Per Maund	....	5,52,000
"3rd. I find a mortgage of old date on "sundry factories still remaining with the "Union Bank, it formed part of several, "all the rest having been paid off	Rs. 6,00,000		
"New Loan	5,00,000		
	Rs. 11,00,000		
"of which a large portion was remitted to "the London house, for which have been "assigned 5,138 Mds. indigo, valued at "140 Rupees	7,19,000		
"Indigo factories of the value of 6 Lacs	6,00,000		
			13,19,000
	Carried forward	....	Rs. 26,32,000
"4th. Shares deposited with sundry parties:—			
"60 shares Bengal Indigo Company	Rs. 2,40,000		
"155 bonded warehouse shares	38,750		
"30 Union Bank shares	24,000		
			3,02,750
			Rs. 29,34,750

"There are several other accounts where differences are shewn, but it has been im-"possible to estimate them all. Then there are heavy charges for interest, &c., "the state of the Money-market here and in London, during the last two "years, and the constantly recurring panics, and the extreme depression of "prices for all produce, and the succession of unfavorable indigo seasons, and "the high rates of interest and charges paid, have altogether been the cause of "the heavy losses the Calcutta house has sustained."

The above mentioned causes would thus increase the deficiency which was estimated in October, 1847, at		£111,300
And increase as above Rs. 29,34,750		293,500
Total deficiency		£404,800
Or say reducing the assets of		895,300
By losses on indigo	76,100	
and	55,100	
Carried over	131,200	895,300

Brought over	£131,200	£895,300
Pledges of shares	30,270	
Ditto of indigo, &c., to Union Bank	132,000	
		293,500
		£601,800 to pay

Liabilities of £1,006,600	
Of which the claims of Cockerell, Larpent, & Co., are	£345,000
And Cockerell & Co., old account	435,000
	£780,000

To what extent the special securities will cover the special liabilities charged thereon is uncertain. The charge of 9 Lacs, say £90,000 on mortgages to the estate of R. H. Cockerell, is supposed to be fully covered by the Natmoo property alone, taking therefore from the given liabilities say £1,006,600
that claim say 90,000

It reduces the amount of liabilities to £916,600 and from the assets of	£601,800	
The valuation of that property therein, say	90,000	
It reduces the amount of assets to		£511,800

Whether the factories held by Cockerell, Larpent, & Co., under special mortgages will give them advantage over the general creditors, it is impossible to say; nor can any judgment be formed upon the imperfect information hitherto obtained of the value of those factories, or of the planters' balances; but the last advices dated March 8th, 1848, from Calcutta (from Mr. Martin and Mr. Mackenzie), report more favorably on these two items than general circumstances would have allowed us to expect, and they look forward to some considerable assets from them at the end of the year: and a question exists as to the ranking between the two firms in respect of the outstanding acceptances. More recent and specific information is looked for from Calcutta, and in the meantime no estimate of what may be forthcoming from thence can be relied on. The assets immediately available for division are calculated by Mr. Beckwith, and by Messrs. Martin and Mackenzie, at Rs. 13,32,300, or £133,000; and it is stated loosely that the estate of Cockerell & Co., of Calcutta, may pay 16 to 20 per cent. after allowing for specialties.

The Natmoo estate, which yields a vast quantity of teak and other timber, is to be carried on by the assignees, and nearly all the several indigo factories are also to continue working during the current season, in order that the proceeds of the crop may be made available for the benefit of the estate.

One of the great causes of the difference between the estimate in October last, of the estate of Cockerell & Co., of Calcutta, compared with that now laid before the creditors, arises from the balance due to the Union Bank and the securities pledged to that establishment.

The only items in the balance-sheet of Cockerell & Co., of Calcutta, 30th April, 1846, which can be traced as apparently connected with the Union Bank, are as follows:—

Cutchoa and Burragang Bank advance	Rs. 93,930
Union Bank	69,407
Union Bank cash credit account	4,597
	Rs. 1,67,934

No intimation either direct or indirect, except the above, is given in any of the accounts or correspondence of any debt to the Union Bank. In the statement received since the failure, and purporting to be the unfinished balance-sheet, 30th April, 1847, the Union Bank appears Dr. .... Rs. 11,757
And creditor post bill account 7,60,000

And in a paper annexed to the list of liabilities of the Calcutta firm, which has also been recently sent over, the Union Bank stands thus:—

Cash credit account		Rs. 10,90,000
Discounts on securities		6,48,138
Ditto on acceptances	Rs. 2,23,000	
Ditto on indorsers	93,500	
		3,16,500
Interest		50,000
		Rs. 21,04,638

And against this balance the bank is stated to hold mortgages on Indigo factories—

Of 6 Lacs; now valued at		Rs. 4,50,000
5,138 maunds indigo, at 130 Rupees per maund		6,67,940
60 shares in the Bengal Indigo Company		3,00,000
		Rs. 14,17,940
Claim on Cockerell, Larpent, & Co., for their credits	Rs. 3,50,000	
And bills discounted to be taken up by others	2,35,000	
		5,85,000
		Rs. 20,02,940

N.B. These claims on Cockerell, Larpent, & Co., are for letters of credit, which were sent to Cockerell & Co., of Calcutta, sanctioning their drafts for produce and other operations, and which were lodged with the Union Bank by the Calcutta firm.

It is quite impossible to reconcile the foregoing statements, and application has been made to the parties in Calcutta, to furnish an account of all the transactions between the Calcutta house and the Union Bank, from 1st May, 1845, to the latest period, stating likewise, the dates of the several securities pledged, and the particulars thereof.

During the period from 1839 to the stoppage, it becomes not unimportant to report the respective positions of the members of the firm.

In January, 1839, the firm of Cockerell & Co., London, consisted of Mr. I. S. Brownrigg, Mr. John Cockerell, and Sir George Larpent, and their united capital was £203,351 16s. 9d., the firm continued without alteration until December, 1846, when Mr. Brownrigg retired, and Mr. John Noble, (who had been for some time a salaried partner) with Mr. I. S. Stopford, and Mr. C. E. Newcomen, were admitted partners.

It was arranged that Mr. Stopford and Mr. Newcomen should each bring in a capital of £20,000, and that they should also place a like amount in the hands of the house, to be as a loan, and for which they were to receive interest; Mr. Newcomen did not bring in any capital whatever, but Mr. Stopford had up to the time of the suspension, paid £20,000.

From January, 1839, to the date of suspension, the amount of profits of the house, was £219,182 15s. 8d., which was passed in equal proportions to credit of the several partners, except in the years 1845 and 1846, when Mr. Brownrigg had a sum of £3,000 for each of those years, and the remaining amount of profit was equally divided between Mr. Cockerell and Sir George Larpent.

In the last year, viz. 1847, the profits were divided in the following proportions, Mr. John Cockerell, two-eighths; Sir George Larpent, two-eighths; Mr. I. Noble, one-eighth; Mr. I. S. Stopford, one-eighth; and Mr. C. E. Newcomen, one-eighth; and the remaining one-eighth was passed to the credit of an account opened as a reserved fund.

The drawings of the several partners during the period in question were as follows:

	£	s.	d.
Mr. I. S. Brownrigg	£53,849	12	10
Mr. John Cockerell	42,030	7	10
Sir George Larpent	36,339	6	2
Mr. John Noble	392	19	5
Mr. I. S. Stopford	886	14	5
Mr. C. E. Newcomen	1,623	8	10
	£135,122	9	6

Thus shewing a surplus balance between profits and drawings, amounting to £84,060 6s. 2d., at present represented in their several credit balances, which stands as follows:—

	£	s.	d.
Mr. John Cockerell	£130,379	9	0
Sir George Larpent	59,992	0	2
Mr. John Noble	6,659	14	5
Mr. C. E. Newcomen	2,588	13	6
Mr. I. Stopford	21,745	2	11
	£221,365	0	0
To the above must be added the amount standing at Mr. Brownrigg's credit, and which amount was under agreement to remain until the balance due from Cockerell & Co. of Calcutta, to Cockerell & Co. of London, was reduced to £100,000, say	33,727	17	4
	£255,092	17	4

Thus the capital standing at the date of suspension 27th September, 1847, in all was £255,092 17s. 4d., shewing an excess of capital since 1839, of £51,741 0s. 7d.

The 5th item in the statement of October last, is the Mauritius estates, taken at £50,000.

These estates consist of 3,787 acres of land, of which 1,500 are under cultivation, the value was taken in 1844-45 by the manager, at dols. 490,000, reduced in 1846, by dols. 50,000, say dols. 440,000 or £90,000. The last year's produce was about 1,000 to 1,100 tons, and the expectation of the manager makes the future produce 1,500 tons. The position of the Sugar-market is a matter of notoriety, and it is impossible, under existing circumstances, to state any value to these properties. They are legally (it is understood) the property of Mr. Cockerell and Sir George Larpent, and are mortgaged primarily to pay a bond given by them and Mr. Brownrigg to the late Lord Metcalfe. If the sale of the estates, or the profit on the produce, should give a surplus, after paying the prior charge, that surplus would be applicable to the debt to the house of Cockerell, Larpent, & Co., amounting to £117,655, which now stands at the debit of the said estates. The losses on these properties written off, amount to £95,000. Of the produce of the season just past, part has been retained in the island in consequence of bills having been returned, and part, which had been secured to the bankers, has been delivered to them under their security.

The 6th item in the statement of October last.—Miscellaneous property taken at £10,000, now taken at £4,000.

The 7th item in the statement of October last.—Amount of various claims secured	£335,380
Amount of property given in security	352,099
Leaving as an available asset a surplus of	£16,719

It now appears that the above claims of £335,380 have been reduced to

		£249,764	partly secured,
		And 25,110	wholly secured.
		£274,874	
And the securities taken at	£352,099		
And now worth	178,044	178,044	
	£174,055	96,830	difference in claim.

{ £174,055 Deficiency in security, which is to be accounted for by the loss on the shares in the Bengal Indigo Company, say £60,000 now considered all but valueless, (though having cost that sum,) and by the various bills lodged with bill-holders and the Bank of England, on houses which have since failed.

The result, as it at present stands, is therefore nearly as follows:—

LIABILITIES.

On open accounts	£196,594	
Acceptances	402,765	
Bills discounted; bills drawn on Calcutta; and Union Bank acceptances	157,303	
Excess of liabilities to parties holding securities, the portion thereof, in shares, &c. being considered valueless	96,830	
		£853,492

The assets are all comprised under five denominations, viz:—

1st. Estimated dividend of 3s. 3d. on claim of Cockerell & Co. of Calcutta, would produce	£102,881 11 1		
2nd. Surplus on sale of estates beyond the claims of the representatives of Mr. R. H. Cockerell, who hold the first mortgage on same	25,000 0 0		
		127,881 11 1	
3rd. Balance due to the firm of Cockerell, Larpent, & Co., now in course of collection, estimated to produce		40,000 0 0	
4th. Sundry suspense accounts, dividends on old estates, &c., also in course of settlement		4,000 0 0	
5th. Bills and cash		12,974 19 2	
			£184,856 10 3

In regard to the first and second items, Mr. Martin and Mr. Mackenzie, who are acting under the power of attorney of Cockerell, Larpent, & Co., have taken all necessary preparatory measures for enforcing all their rights, and are also urging the liquidation of the estate of Cockerell & Co., of Calcutta, with as much speed as circumstances and prudence as to forced sales, will allow. Some of the estates have been sold, others are under offer, and some will be carried on as before-mentioned, (under the authorities of the Insolvent Court of Calcutta and the assignees appointed to act with them,) to give the estate the benefit of the next forthcoming indigo crop.

Negociations were also in treaty for the sale of some of the mortgaged estates, and should they be carried out, the item of £25,000 will be shortly forthcoming.

In regard to the third item, viz. the book-debts, the greater portion of them are due from correspondents in various parts of the globe, and in ordinary times, goods or remittances would be coming forward for a great portion of them, without much delay, and it is anticipated the usual course will be adopted.

The fourth item will necessarily be delayed some time, depending upon the realization of some sales which cannot be made until the year 1849.

The fifth and last item is in the hands of the bankers, and will become cash as the bills mature.

Under all the circumstances connected with this matter, and after a full investigation of the accounts by their accountant, the inspectors have come to the conclusion, that this estate being now rendered a mere matter of receipt and distribution, it must remain with the creditors to decide whether they will avail themselves of the services of some of the partners to realize the assets under the deed, which is already signed to a considerable extent, or to adopt such other course as they may deem more conducive to their interests.

The whole of the establishment, with the exception of one or two clerks, has been broken up, and it is intended so soon as an occupant can be found for the extensive premises in Austin Friars, to remove the books and necessary documents to some convenient and less expensive office.

Austin Friars,
London, 1*st May*, 1848.

In forwarding the within report prepared by order of the inspectors under whom we have acted in the management of our affairs since our suspension in September last, we have to express our regret that the ultimate result will be far less favorable than, from the representations made to us, we had reason to expect, and that it does not hold out better prospects of immediate realization. This is partly to be attributed to the unfortunate state of all mercantile affairs in Bengal, and to the absorption of the available funds of Messrs. Cockerell & Co., of Calcutta, our principal debtors, by their assignees having applied them in carrying through the present season the cultivation of the indigo and sugar factories, and in supporting the valuable property at Natmoo.

We are informed by our attornies in Calcutta that "these arrangements are considered by every person possessing the slightest acquaintance with such concerns as "very advantageous to all parties, and that they have been adopted to recover the "large advances already made for the season 1847-48, and to prevent these properties becoming valueless."

We trust that this opinion will be confirmed by enabling the assignees to declare a much larger dividend at the close of the season than could otherwise have been realized, and that our estate will thereby receive a corresponding benefit.

We beg respectfully to call your attention to the concluding paragraph of the report, and to assure you that should you adopt the suggestion therein made, two members of our late firm, Sir George Larpent and Mr. Noble, will willingly devote themselves to the winding up of our affairs, under the conviction that by so doing, not only will considerable expense be saved to the estate, but from their knowledge of its complicated concerns, and the nature and value of the assets, they may be rendered more productive than by any other course of management.

To carry this suggestion into effect, it will be necessary for you to signify your consent by returning the accompanying paper with your signature, which will not be binding upon you, unless adopted by the general body of creditors.

We venture further to state that, irrespective of the balance due to us, by the Calcutta house, we confidently rely on realizations from other sources of more than sufficient for an early dividend of 5 per cent. on the total amount of every possible liability as stated in the report.

We remain,

Your very obedient servants,

COCKERELL, LARPENT & CO.

In liquidation.

Since the progress of Inspection, two of the junior members of Cockerell, Larpent, & Co. have passed through the ordeal of bankruptcy; viz., Mr. James Sidney Stopford, and Mr. C. E. Newcomen. In each case the bankrupts obtained their certificates.

BALANCE-SHEET OF JAMES SIDNEY STOPFORD, passed in the Court of Bankruptcy, 30th May, 1848.

DEBTOR.	£	s.	d.	CREDITOR.	£	s.	d.
To Sundry creditors	8,218	12	6	By Debtors	481	10	0
,, Creditors holding securities	14,330	0	0	,, Property	6,061	12	4
,, Capital	31,342	2	0	,, Do. held by creditors, per contra..........	14,330	0	0
,, Profits	5,356	15	1	,, Do. under settlement .	3,062	0	0
				,, Loss by depreciation in value of estates, &c. .	10,165	17	8
				,, Expenses...........	1,877	14	4
				,, Expenses of house....	1,523	12	4
				,, Balance at my credit in the books of the firm of Cockerell, Larpent, & Co...............	21,745	2	11
	£59,247	9	7		£59,247	9	7

COURT OF BANKRUPTCY, BASINGHALL STREET, December 20th.

The Bankrupt, CHARLES EDWARD NEWCOMEN, was a member of the firm of Cockerell, Larpent, & Co., of Austinfriars, East India Merchants. He became a bankrupt on his own petition. The fiat is dated September 1, 1848. This was the certificate meeting.

Mr. James opposed, and Mr. Reyroux supported, the application.

The BALANCE-SHEET was as follows:—

DEBTOR.	£	s.	d.	CREDITOR.	£.	s.	d.
To Creditor	88	7	6	By Amount due from the firm of Cockerell & Co., of Calcutta	36,400	0	0
,, Capital	1,062	8	4	,, Shares in the East India Railway, (on hand) cost	9	10	0
,, Agreed amount due to me by Cockerell & Co. of Calcutta, at the time that I retired from the firm	36,400	0	0	,, Expenses of house-rent, rates, taxes, &c.	2,322	3	6
,, To profits	4,004	11	2	,, Loss by balance standing to the credit of my account with Cockerell, Larpent, & Co., at the date of the dissolution of partnership on the 22d March, 1848, and which balance is absorbed by the proportion of losses that have arisen	2,823	13	6
	£41,555	7	0		£41,555	7	0

Mr. James said he attended on behalf of the Union Bank of Calcutta, to oppose the granting of the certificate. It appeared that the bankrupt had for some years been a member of the firm of Cockerell & Co., of Calcutta, the East India correspondents of Cockerell, Larpent, & Co. He became a member of the latter firm in January, 1847. The Union Bank of Calcutta is a joint-stock company, established at Calcutta in June, 1839, and carried on its business under a deed of partnership, duly authorized by the Indian Legislature, until its recent suspension. A considerable portion of its funds and of money raised upon the credit of the bank was allocated to the use of firms now insolvent, which had partners in the direction of the bank, and two firms alone received £600,000, one of which was Cockerell, & Co., of Calcutta. On December 31st, 1847, the firm of Cockerell & Co. stood in the bank books as debtors to the amount of £230,000, nearly £130,000 of which was unsecured. It was also alleged that the bank had a further claim for £122,700 upon bills discounted. At the last examination meeting, two claims, amounting together to £352,000, were sought to be established against the bankrupt's estate by the bank, but they were not substantiated. The ground of opposition to the certificate arose in this way:—The Union Bank has for several years been in the habit of issuing paper known in the Calcutta money-market as bank post-bills. In the month of June, 1847, Mr. W. P. Grant, then Master in Equity of the Supreme Court of Judicature at Calcutta, and a director of the finance committee of the Union Bank, in order to assist the bank with ready money, made the following arrangement with Cockerell & Co., of Calcutta, and the secretary of the bank—that Mr Grant should draw upon Cockerell, Larpent, & Co., for the sum of £40,000 in the whole; that the drafts for this amount should be sold in the Calcutta money-market, collaterally secured by Union Bank post-bills, and that the purchase money should be received by the bank; that the bank should undertake to put Messrs. Cockerell, Larpent, & Co. in funds by satisfactory remittances to provide for Mr. Grant's drafts upon them before maturity, and that as a collateral security for the performance of the last engagement, the bank's secretary should hand to Mr. Grant, and he should forward to Messrs. Larpent & Co., another set of bank post-bills for £45,000. This arrangement having been concluded, Mr. Grant, on the 25th June, 1847, drew upon Messrs. Cockerell, Larpent, & Co. five bills at ten months' date, amounting together to £30,000, which were (collaterally secured by bank post-bills) sold to Messrs. Jardine & Co., of Calcutta, and the purchase money was paid to the Union Bank, whose secretary thereupon gave Mr. Grant the promised engagement to provide for his drafts before maturity, and handed him another set of bank post-bills for 340,000 Company's rupees in the whole. Mr. Grant on the 25th June, 1847, wrote to Messrs. Cockerell, Larpent, & Co., informing them that he had drawn upon them for drafts (enumerated) to the extent of £30,000, and adding, " as security for your acceptance of the above bills, I beg to hand you herewith post-bills of the Union Bank of Calcutta for 340,000 rupees, being the equivalent of the same, 1s. 10d. exchange; and I also enclose a copy of a letter from the secretary of the Union Bank undertaking on behalf of the bank that remittances shall be sent to you in due course, so as to prevent the possibility of your coming under cash advance on this account." The engagement referred to was enclosed. Messrs. Larpent and Cockerell, of London, wrote to Messrs. Cockerell, of Calcutta, undertaking the engagement, and stating that they had accepted the drafts in reliance that the Calcutta Bank would furnish them in due time with the necessary funds. In further persuance of this arrangement Mr. Grant, in July, 1847, drew upon Messrs. Cockerell, Larpent, & Co., of London, eight bills at six months' sight for £10,000 in the whole, which were sold (collaterally secured by bank post-bills) to Messrs. Kelsall, of Calcutta, and the purchase-money was paid to the Union Bank, whose secretary gave Mr. Grant an engagement similar to the former, and handed him another set of bank post-bills for 110,000 rupees. Mr. Grant again wrote to Messrs. Cockerell & Larpent as before, drawing upon them to the extent of £10,000, and enclosing as security Union Bank post-bills to the amount of 110,000 rupees. The learned counsel having recapitulated those transactions, charged the bankrupt, as a member of the firm of Cockerell, Larpent, & Co., with having negociated the largest portion of the bank post-bills forwarded to them by Mr. Grant as collateral security for his drafts, and stated that it had been ascertained that all such bills were negociated in September, 1847, the very month in which they stopped payment. The effect of of such negociation was to make the Union Bank of Calcutta liable both to the holders of Cockerell, Larpent, & Co's acceptances (in respect of their being collaterally secured to the purchasers, Messrs. Jardine and Messrs. Kelsall, by post-bills,) and to the English holders of the post-bills sent home to Cockerell, Larpent, & Co. The bank having received consideration only for the post-bills issued in Calcutta, the effect of the negociation by Messrs. Cockerell, Larpent, & Co., was a loss to the bank of £45,000. The learned gentleman complained that the bankrupt firm of which Mr. Newcomen was a member had appropriated the proceeds of those bills to their own purposes, instead of meeting the acceptances to which they were applicable, and that they had done so in violation of Mr. Grant's instructions, which stated that " when the transaction is closed by your receipt of satisfactory remittances from this, I should feel obliged by your returning the bills to me." Messrs. Cockerell, Larpent, & Co. had by letter engaged to hold the bills " as collateral security, to be returned to you on receipt of remittances for that amount." The learned counsel concluded by designating the transaction as one which, if participated in by the bankrupt ought to draw down upon him the punishment of the Court.

[In justice to Messrs. Cockerell, Larpent, & Co., we quote the following extracts from two of their letters—one to Mr. Grant and the other to Messrs. Cockerell & Co., of Calcutta, both dated September 7th, 1847:—" Aware that no positive permission is given to negociate these bills, although we consider, from the circumstances of the case and the communications received from Messrs. Cockerell & Co., that we are authorized to adopt such a course, we have written fully to those gentlemen upon the subject, and have given them such instructions as to the rate of exchange and the aid they may afford in payment of the said bills, if required, on our account, as will, we trust, be satisfactory to you and the Union Bank, and prevent any inconvenience to either party. As the communication between the two countries is now so frequent and rapid, we wish operations upon so large a scale and of so unusual a character not to be undertaken without previous communication with us, and upon our assent being given. Otherwise we are placed in the very unpleasant predicament of having to choose between refusing bills drawn upon us by parties like yourself, or of apparently going beyond the letter of our instructions. The evils of the former preponderating, in our judgment, we trust that this matter will be satisfactorily arranged between you and our friends, Messrs. Cockerell and Co." The above letter is addressed to Mr. Grant. The letter of which the following is an extract is addressed to Messrs. Cockerell:—"As a security for loans available in relief of your account, the notes of the Union Bank of Calcutta are useless, and we know that the Union Bank has overdrawn its account largely with Glyn & Co., and that although the remittances per Bombay mail were considerable, the bills were also large, and they told me this morning that if the account was not put square, they (Glyn & Co.) should be put to the alternative of refusing the bills of the Union Bank, and, indeed, were chiefly deterred from such a course by knowing the engagement of your house and ours with that concern. Under these circumstances, we have no alternative but either to refuse acceptance or negociate the said Union post-bills. We have reluctantly adopted the latter course and sold them to the amount of 410,000 rupees."]

Mr. Newcomen, the bankrupt, was examined. He joined the firm of Cockerell, Larpent, & Co. in January, 1847, but did not enter the office until March. Was no party to the transaction in question, and knew nothing whatever of it until it had been concluded, when he expressed his disapproval of it. The transaction was conducted and concluded solely by the senior partners, Sir George Larpent and Mr. Cockerell. When the bills were received they were put into the strong box, of which witness never had the key. Believed the bills so received from India were disposed of in the month in which the house stopped payment.

Mr. James.—Were not some of those bills disposed of on the 24th of September?

Bankrupt.—Yes, I believe so.

Mr. James.—Did not the house stop payment on the 27th of September?

Bankrupt.—No, on the 26th. The 27th was Sunday.

Mr. James.—Was not the stoppage in contemplation on or before the 24th?

Bankrupt.—I do not believe it was. There was considerable difficulty, no doubt, and a question rose as to whether or no the house would be able to go on

Mr. James.—Do you then state that it was not determined on the 24th that the house should stop payment?

Bankrupt.—Not that I am aware of. I believe not.

Mr. James said, that he did not feel bound to press the matter any further against Mr. Newcomen, to whom it appeared there was no blame due.

Commissioner.—I quite agree with you—*Reus inter alios.* As far as the balance-sheet is concerned, I have seldom seen a more satisfactory case. I feel pleasure, Mr. Newcomen, in granting to you your certificate.

Mr. Reyroux said he could, if his Honour would permit him, completely vindicate the course pursued by the senior partners. The learned gentleman was proceeding to do so, when

The Commissioner said, the question of their conduct was not before the Court and he could not entertain the subject.

Certificate granted accordingly.

[No dividend has yet been paid in on this estate.]

Messrs. REID, IRVING, & Co.,

East and West India Trade.

A meeting of creditors, numerously attended, took place on the 9th October, 1847, under the estate of Messrs. Reid, Irving, & Co., to receive the following statement of their affairs, prepared by Mr. J. E. Coleman, the accountant called in upon the occasion.

September 17, 1847.

Debtor.	£	s.	d.	£	s.	d.
To sundry creditors				633,239	11	5
Total amount of acceptances outstanding on the 17th of September, 1847	793,782	7	5			
Of these there were in the hands of Messrs. Reid, Irving, & Co. (having been remitted to them for their own account)	103,967	12	0			
With the public........	689,814	15	5			
Carried over				633,239	11	5

Brought over....		£689,814 15 5	£633,239 11 5
Of these there are included in the above sum of 633,239 11s. 5d.		341,885 0 10	
Leaving amount of acceptances which ought to be taken up by other parties than Reid, Irving, & Co.		347,929 14 7	
(The liabilities which may attach to Messrs. Reid, Irving, & Co. from these acceptances cannot be estimated)			
To sundry creditors holding securities	229,522 17 5		
Amount of cost of securities held by them.. 348,966 5 2			
Estimated to produce 261,827 0 0	261,827 0 0		
Surplus carried to credit side of statement	32,304 2 7		
To liabilities on bills receivable		493,869 7 1	
Of which it is expected there will be duly honoured as they arrive at maturity		461,185 7 6	
		32,683 19 7	
Balance at the Bank of England and at the bankers' (as per contra), which will be retained against liabilities		5,491 8 11	
			27,192 10 8
			£660,432 2 1

CREDITOR.	Amount to which they stand to debit or cost.	Amount which it is estimated they will produce.
By sundry debtors (good)	9,153 8 6	9,153 8 6
Ditto, partly secured and partly doubtful	125,634 1 10	56,200 0 0
Ditto, in the West Indies, partly secured by mortgage and otherwise	67,797 4 10	39,939 16 7
By various estates in Trinidad, Tortola, Nevis, and St. Kitts	194,496 15 7	109,833 8 1
By sundry debtors in the Mauritius	465,964 1 4	465,964 1 4
By various estates in the Mauritius, and shares in the Mauritius Bank	91,184 18 10	91,184 18 10
By sundry assets of produce, &c.	13,176 16 11	13,176 16 11
By value of premises in Tokenhouse-yard (less mortgage upon it)	4,000 0 0	4,000 0 0
By surplus of property deposited with creditors as per contra	119,443 7 9	32,304 2 7
By cash balance at the Bank of England, and at the bankers, which will be retained against liabilities as per contra	5,491 8 11	
By surplus from the separate estates	25,000 0 0	25,000 0 0
	£1,121,342 4 6	£846,756 12 10

[NOTE.—The above item of £465,964 1s. 4d. is subject to a deduction for the cost of cultivation of estates in the Mauritius, the accounts of which are not yet received.

Up to the time of their suspension, Messrs. Reid, Irving, & Co. had reason to expect that the property in the Mauritius might substantially realize what it stands at. The failure of houses in the Mauritius trade will no doubt injuriously affect this property, but to what extent cannot be estimated.

Messrs. Reid, Irving, & Co. sent a special agent to the Mauritius in August last, to press the liquidation of their accounts there, and from him they will receive detailed information on all points connected with it.]

From this statement there would appear a surplus of £186,324, but it will be observed that owing to the absence of any precise or recent estimate of what the Mauritius debts and estates are likely to yield, the total of those assets (£557,149) is put down without deduction. Upon this total it may be feared, looking at the results of such realizations of property as have lately been made in the island, the ultimate difference will prove enormous, and it must also be noticed that a liability of £347,929, exists on the part of Reid, Irving, & Co., on bills of exchange, which, although the firm are not primarily responsible for them, may, through the default of other parties whose names they bear, involve considerable loss. The liabilities on "bills receivable" are, moreover, extremely large, and it is to be apprehended that the loss on that head (£32,683) may, from the disasters now continually occuring, ultimately prove to be under-estimated.

"In explanation of the accounts" says a report of the proceedings, "Mr. Freshfield entered into a variety of details, showing, that with the assets at present available, and expected remittances, there will be sufficient funds to pay a dividend, before any considerable period shall elapse, of 5s. in the pound, in addition to the proceeds remaining to be realized from the properties belonging to the firm in the West Indies and the Mauritius. With reference to these it was mentioned, that although the estimates of their value had been made upon the best information that could be obtained, still their value, when submitted for sale, would depend upon contingencies, especially in the case of the Mauritius estates, as other large failures had occurred in connexion with that island. It appeared that the West India property was estimated on the information supplied by an agent who visited it last year. That gentleman was now at the Mauritius, where his presence, with the instructions he held, would, it was believed, operate beneficially for the interests of all parties concerned. Mr Freshfield also stated, that in consequence of the requirements of the firm, both in the shape of advances and securities to creditors, the private property of the partners had latterly undergone considerable reduction,"

A feeling being unanimously expressed in favour of winding up the estate by the partners under inspection, the annexed resolutions were proposed by Mr. Turner, of the firm of Sands, Turner, and Co., Liverpool, and Mr. Warren, of D. and J. K. Warren, & Co., London, and at once adopted and embodied in the following form for circulation :—

"At a meeting of the creditors of Messrs. Reid, Irving, & Co., held at Moorgate-street, in the city of London, this 9th day of October, 1847, Mr. W. Cotton in the chair, an account of the debts and assets of the house was submitted to the creditors.

"Resolved,—That it is the opinion of the creditors that it will be for the benefit of all parties interested in the estate of Messrs. Reid, Irving, & Co., that the property should be for the present administered by the partners, under inspection.

"That Mr. Baring, Mr. Blyth, and Mr. M'Chlery, be requested to act as inspectors of the affairs of Messrs. Reid, Irving, & Co., with power to employ an accountant if they shall see fit, and to report from time to time to the creditors as they shall see occasion, and further, that a monthly account shall be made out for the inspection of the creditors during the liquidation.—Carried unanimously.

W. COTTON, *Chairman.*"

Early in the month of June, 1848, the firm, in a review on affairs, issued the annexed circular.

London, 6th June, 1848.

Sir,—Under the sanction of our inspectors, Thomas Baring, Esq. M.P., James Blyth, Esq., and M. M'Chlery, Esq., we propose to make an immediate dividend of 1s. in the pound upon our debts, and we take the opportunity of offering some explanations upon the state of our affairs.

At the time of the meeting of our creditors on the 9th of October last, it was uncertain what might be the result upon our Mauritius assets of the failure of our own and other houses connected with that Island; but Mr. Comrie had then recently gone out to that Island, and we expected from him a report upon that subject. This gentleman having returned to England by the last Overland Mail, we take the earliest opportunity of laying before you the information we have obtained through him. You are aware, that the news of our failure caused the suspension of Messrs. Henry Adam & Co., our correspondents in the Mauritius. We had hoped that those gentlemen, having the greater part of the crop in their hands at the time the intelligence reached them, would have been enabled to withstand the pressure upon them;

but the general want of confidence, occasioned by the simultaneous failure of so many houses connected with the Island, rendered this impossible. Messrs. Henry Adam & Co., in the first instance, offered to their creditors a composition of 30 per cent., payable by instalments, and they proposed that our claim should be postponed till the other creditors had received their composition. This proposition was negatived. Messrs. Henry Adam & Co. then put their affairs into trust, and Mr. Comrie thought it for our interest to take estates and debts in payment of a considerable part of our claim; and having done this, Messrs. Henry Adam & Co's debt to us is reduced to about £110,000, on which we have to claim dividends from their estate.

Mr. Comrie obtained cash for some of these debts to the amount of about £6,000, and beyond this the probable recoveries from the Mauritius may be estimated as follows:—

Presumed dividend from H. Adam & Co.		£28,000	
Mortgages taken over estimated at their present reduced value		35,000	
Seven sugar estates in our own name, producing 5,000,000 lbs. of sugar, and estimated at	£155,000		
Less claims on them existing before they came into our hands	37,000		
		118,000	
			£181,000

independently of various minor items, the value of which cannot be exactly specified. In the present state of Mauritius, paralysed by the low price of sugar and the failure of the houses there and here who sustained the greater part of its cultivation, there are no buyers for estates, and it becomes therefore necessary to wait for a time when they may become realizable. Sufficient funds exist in the island, without aid from hence, to sustain the cultivation until the next crop shall become available for that purpose. The preservation of this large asset, therefore, will not cost anything to our general estate, while it will be maintained in a position for sale, for the benefit thereof, whenever circumstances admit. While Mr. Comrie holds out the most confident expectation that we may expect to receive the proceeds of the Mauritius asset if our affairs are left under our own administration, he expresses the most unqualified conviction that if our house were to become bankrupt the creditors would not receive one shilling from our estates in that island, as the prior liens would immediately be exacted, and would, by the properties being brought to a forced sale, swallow up the whole.

The same observation applies in its degree to the property in the West Indies, where there is the same necessity of present preservation for the purpose of ultimate benefit. There is no immediate means of converting the property into money, and the alternative is, the maintaining it in the way we have pointed out, or abandoning it.

All the Mauritius, and the most important West India estates, are in the highest order and condition, and would some years ago have readily fetched very large sums in the open market; but successive governments have, by their negligence, waywardness, and legislation, brought colonial property to the condition which we have to deplore at the present day. If however there be, by any means, a revival of colonial affairs, they will become saleable at a price proportioned to such improvement.

Under these circumstances, it is so obvious that a liquidation under inspection is the best mode of obtaining the most from the estate for the benefit of our creditors, that we have not felt at liberty to contemplate any other course.

In the collection of our general assets we regret to say we have met with much disappointment and delay, as may be supposed in such disastrous times. They may be stated in round numbers as follows:—

Funds in hand or nearly collected, about............	£45,000
Collections to be made hereafter estimated at........	60,000
Mauritius asset, as above	181,000
West India ditto, estimated	90,000
	£376,000

While our liabilities have diminished, in some instances, by more favourable results than we calculated on, they have increased in others by depreciation of property and other unforseen causes, and principally by the Mauritius bills now becoming a charge against our estate.

Amount of liabilities assumed 9th October, 1847		£660,000
Deduct loss on bills receivable *less* than then supposed ..	£3,000	
Acceptances which will be met by special funds under legal advice..	33,000	36,000
		624,000
Add Mauritius acceptances, as explained above.........	96,000	
Claims arising from deficiencies in proceeds of produce and securities held by creditors	36,000	132,000
		£756,000

besides some further claims undecided.

We have made arrangements for payment of a first dividend of 1s. in the pound on the 1st July, upon signature of our deed of inspection. The dividend will be paid at our counting-house, Tokenhouse-yard, between the hours of 12 and 3 o'clock, on the 1st July or any subsequent day to the creditors on production of their securities. Forms of Powers of Attorney will be delivered to creditors who are unable to attend.

We are, respectfully,
Sir,
Your most obedient servants,
REID, IRVING, & CO.

Another dividend of 6d. in the pound has since been declared, making the gross amount now paid, 1s. 6d. in the pound.

Messrs. BARCLAY, BROTHERS, & Co.,

Mauritius Trade.

A meeting was held on the 2d of November, 1847, of the creditors of Messrs. Barclay, Brothers, & Co , whose failure took place on the 13th October. Mr. J. A. Arbuthnot was in the chair, and the following is the statement of the debts and assets:—

TOTAL LIABILITIES.	£	*s.*	*d.*
Total amount of acceptances £244,678 6s. 2d., of which secured specially, £60,120, total to claim upon the estate	184,558	6	2
Sundry creditors uncovered	162,684	5	0
Sundry creditors partially secured; deficit in value of security ..	34,262	4	11
Liability in respect of bills on third parties, bearing our endorsements.—Total amount of such bills £158,259 6s. 10d., of which, bad, £3,000; doubtful, £3,000	6,000	0	0
	387,504	16	1
Sundry small accounts to be paid in full......................	2,000	0	0
	£389,504	16	1
TOTAL ASSETS.			
Bills of exchange £11,491 7s. 4d. of which doubtful value, say £2,000..	9,491	7	4
Produce and shipping documents in hand	9,000	0	0
Sugar expected to have been shipped from Mauritius before receipt of news of failure, say..........................	35,000	0	0
Bills of Exchange upon houses that have failed £11,881 13s. 9d., valued at	4,000	0	0
Carried over	£57,491	7	4

	£	s.	d.
Brought over	£57,491	7	4
Balance of account with correspondents in India	7,000	0	0
Surplus of securities in the hands of certain creditors, say	3,000	0	0
Remittances expected from Mauritius in next five months, say ..	5,000	0	0
Balance at bankers', who are creditors for an unsecured loan £1,900			
Sundry debtors	4,000	0	0

MAURITIUS ACCOUNT.	£	s.	d.
Total of debit of agents	420,200	0	0
Ditto of sundry planters and others	110,000	0	0
Cost of one-half share in three estates	88,000	0	0
	£618,200	0	0

This item is now represented by the following properties:—

	£	s.	d.
1. Seven estates in the island, which, by agreement with the Mauritius agents, made on the 1st of June last, are now Barclay, Brothers, & Co.'s property; these have been taken at the value of about £340,000. Estimated to realize, at 50 per cent.	170,000	0	0
2. Sundry claims, good, but not immediately realizable, amounting to about £58,000. Estimated value at 80 per cent...........	46,000	0	0
3. Claims still held in joint accounts with agents, standing at about £77,000. Estimated value	5,000	0	0
4. Proximate balance to be accounted for according to the terms of the agreement of the 1st of June	98,000	0	0
	£395,491	7	4

"The above account," says a report of the proceedings, "exhibits a nominal surplus of £8,987, but explanations were given which showed that the liquidation would be a very unfavourable one. It appears that in June, 1847, Messrs. Barclay, Brothers, & Co. entered into an arrangement with their agents in the Mauritius to divide the estates in which they were interested, and which, up to that time, had been held equally by the two firms. By that means the items in the above 'Mauritius account,' came into their possession. There are creditors, however, who hold drafts of the Mauritius agents upon the London firm to the amount of about £100,000, (and it does not appear certain but that that sum may be increased,) who will, of course, not permit the transfer to be completed without provision being made for the satisfaction of their claims. To secure that object it was accordingly suggested to the meeting that all the estates, &c., which, prior to the said agreement, belonged to the two firms, should be conveyed to trustees, subject to the payment of the Mauritius bill-holders, and afterwards that the property should be disposed of on the basis of the contemplated plan. On the other hand, as a consideration to the general creditors of Barclay, Brothers, & Co., for this step, it was agreed that the Mauritius bill-holders should be required to allow the sugars of the crop of the present year, and all the other assets of Barclay, Brothers, & Co., except the Mauritius assets, to be realized, and that they should forego all participation in the proceeds. The scheme was suggested in order to prevent unnecessary law proceedings in the island, and it was agreed by the meeting that it would be desirable, if possible, to carry it out."

"The settlement of the claims thus described would reduce the assets of the estate to about 14s. in the pound, and when the contingencies connected with the future prospects of realizations in the Mauritius are taken into account, the dividend that will be ultimately obtained must be expected to fall considerably below that amount.

"At the conclusion of the meeting, it was agreed that the affairs of the house should be wound up under inspection, Messrs. John Gurney Hoare, John Henry Pelly, and Kirkman Daniel Hodgson being the parties appointed. It is proper to add, that with regard to the item in the list of liabilities of 'sundry creditors uncovered,' amounting to £162,684, it was explained that nearly the whole of this total consists of debts to various branches of Mr. Barclay's family."

[A dividend of 2s. 6d. in the pound has been, up to the present date, paid.]

Messrs. A. A. GOWER, NEPHEWS, & Co.,

Mauritius Trade.

A meeting of the creditors of Messrs. Gower, Nephews, & Co., whose failure took place on the 11th September, was held the 23d October, 1847. Mr. L. P. Wilson, the Governor of the London Assurance Company, took the chair, and the following statement, prepared by Quilter, Ball, & Co., was submitted for consideration :—

DEBTOR.	£	s.	d.	£	s.	d.
To creditors uncovered				300,982	18	6
To creditors partially covered £85,798 7s. 8d.						
The amount by which the claim exceeds the estimated value of the securities				10,768	2	4
Total claims which ought to come against the estate				311,751	0	10
To sundry liabilities, viz. :—						
On our acceptances, which should be retired by the drawers, as per statement, fo. —, £248,720 3 11						
Of which it is estimated there will be claimed upon this estate	129,911	0	0			
On bills receivable 257,765 0 1						
Of which it is estimated there will be claimed upon this estate	17,817	1	5			
	147,728	1	5			
Deduct sundry balances due from surplus securities in the hands of persons holding the above bills which they claim to retain	8,646	13	4			
				139,081	8	1
Probable amount which will be claimed on the estate				£450,832	8	11

CREDITOR.				Ledger balances. £	s.	d.	Present valuation. £	s.	d.
By bills receivable on hand—									
Considered good				1,373	3	4	1,373	3	4
Considered doubtful				4,074	19	8	3,100	0	0
Considered bad				222	12	0			
By sundry debtors—									
Considered good				32,848	19	5	32,848	19	5
Considered doubtful				212,003	11	11	37,000	0	0
Considered bad				42,727	8	9			
By sundry property				15,907	2	2	15,907	2	2
Surplus value of property in the hands of creditors				616	0	4	616	0	4
By Henry Barlow & Co., Mauritius—									
For the amount of cash advances at the debit of this account				246,456	7	4			
Ditto, Giguel & Co.'s account				20,285	6	0			
In addition, A. A. G. & Co. are under acceptances for account of H. Barlow & Co., included in liabilities per contra £76,925 9 1									
N.B. It has not been deemed prudent to make an estimate of what may be forthcoming from the Mauritius beyond the estimated value (after deducting a lien thereon) of the portion of the sugar crop which, it is believed, will be shipped before the stoppage of the house is known in the Mauritius							25,000	0	0
				576,515	10	11	115,845	5	3
Deduct—									
Sundry creditors in full	£1,013	12	4						
Estimated expenses of liquidation	2,000	0	0						
				3,013	12	4	3,013	12	4
				£573,501	18	7	£112,331	12	11

Quoting a report of the proceedings, it is stated "that the assets, according to the present estimate, are equal to a dividend of 5s. in the pound, exclusive of the proceeds that may be derived from the realization of the Mauritius estates. On the subject of these properties it transpired, that the direct ownership of four plantations has been transferred by Messrs. Barlow & Co. to Messrs. Gower & Co., as the result of the progress of the heavy advances made by the latter firm on their account.

" In reference to one considerable item of assets, viz., £25,000, calculated as likely to be derived from sugar, it was stated that Messrs. Gower & Co., previous to their stoppage, with the view of taking the necessary measures for providing, in some degree, against the liabilities incurred by their Mauritius connexion, sent out several vessels to take in cargoes of the new crop. As these vessels would arrive before the month of December, the period at which at the earliest the intelligence of the failure could be received there, and as orders had been given to ship sugar with all possible despatch, it was reasonably concluded that at the lowest estimate the quantity thus secured would produce the amount named. With respect to the ultimate disposal of the Mauritius properties themselves, it was stated that much will depend upon the position of affairs when the announcement of the late severe disasters shall reach the island, and that, under these circumstances, it had been deemed most prudent not to put a value upon them. A special agent, despatched some time since by Gower & Co. to arrange their concerns in that place, would pay due regard to the interests of the creditors, as he was fully empowered to act in any emergency that might occur. Were it possible to hope that property would not be seriously depreciated by what had taken place on this side, then a reasonable prospect might be entertained that these estates would, on the *data* of recent sales, have reimbursed nearly, if not the whole of the advances.

" Several of the creditors, anxious to obtain full information respecting the shipments of sugar, suggested that in every probability they had already been drawn against—in that case they would constitute " specialty debts." In reply, it was remarked, that the firm possessed every assurance that such was not the case. In answer to other questions, it was stated that the partners' private property had been completely absorbed in supporting the house, even to the extent of an insufficiency remaining to provide for certain annuities stipulated by the the terms of the will under which they became entitled to it; and that, as regarded the transactions of the firm in railways, these having been chiefly in foreign undertakings had produced a profit, which, instead of injuring, had benefited the estate. The reason of so iarge an amount of doubtful debt being valued at so small a sum was said to result from the condition of several other firms with whom Gower & Co. held dealings. For instance, the three following cases were cited in illustration of the kind of accounts included in the estimate:—Alison, Cumberlege, & Co., £33,404; a claim upon a house at Naples for nearly £70,000; and another upon a house in Glasgow for £18,000; neither of which, it was believed, would yield scarcely anything. It was also further explained that the absence of a cash balance at the bankers' from the face of the accounts was occasioned by the bankers having in their own right retained the £3,000 or £4,000 in their hands, to cover, as far as it would go, loans they had advanced to the house; and that the bills accepted by the partners subsequently to their suspension on account of a New York incorporated company were accepted by them under the advice of Mr. Maynard, who considered himself justified in recommending such a course, to save the credit of the company, by preventing the return of protested paper, as it was known that arrangements had been made for the provision of its bills by remittances, and that it was in a perfect solvent state. A fact which came out in the course of the proceedings, and which seemed to take the creditors by surprise, was the extensive drawings made on the Mauritius account, especially within the last few years, seeing that so lately as 1840 they stood at the moderate amount of £11,000.

" At the termination of the discussion a proposal was made to allow the partners to wind up the firm under the management of inspectors, the three gentlemen named to act in the latter capacity being Mr. Gruning, Messrs. Huth & Co., Mr. R. Grant, of Messrs. Bell and Grant, and Mr. C. Joyce, of Messrs. Joyce, Thurburn, & Co., which was agreed to; Mr. M'Clelland, who represented the Scotch banks, supporting the proposition."

Messrs. Barlow & Co. having since failed, and Mauritius property having experienced great depreciation, the creditors will not it is anticipated realize the estimate presented by the accounts.

A dividend of 1s. 6d. in the pound has been paid under this estate.

MESSRS. LYALL, BROTHERS & Co.

EAST INDIA TRADE.

A meeting of the creditors of MESSRS. LYALL, BROTHERS, & Co. whose stoppage took place on the 30th September, was held 17th October, 1847, when the following statement of affairs, prepared by Messrs. Quilter, Ball, & Co., was submitted for consideration:—

DEBTOR.	£	s.	d.
To sundry creditors	120,837	14	6
To sundry creditors, partially secured, £122,414 13s. 7d., less the estimated value of securities held by them, £86,324 11s. 7d.	36,090	2	2
Total amount due to creditors	156,927	16	6
To liabilities on bills payable, which include the drafts of Lyall, Matheson, & Co., amounting to 107,422 1s. 1d. and which may be claimed on this estate by the holders, £125,635 1s. 6d.; to liabilities on bills receivable, amounting to £447,029 8s. 3d., of which are estimated to prove claims on the estate, £57,824 17s. 4d.	183,459	18	10
	£340,387	15	4

CREDITOR.	Ledger balances. £	s.	d.	Estimated to realize. £	s.	d.
By bills receivable on hand	1,056	10	11	1,056	10	11
By book debts—Considered good	40,834	15	2	40,000	0	0
Considered doubtful	57,112	19	3	5,000	0	0
Considered bad	5,409	19	9			
By counting-house furniture	845	16	7	500	0	0
By Lyall, Matheson, & Co. Calcutta—Balance due from them on cash account, £33,753 5s. 9d.; for our liability on their drafts, £107,422 1s. 1d.; for our liability on bills received from them, £12,500; for our capital in that house, £50,000	203,675	6	10	60,000	0	0
By private property belonging to partners ..	50,000	0	0	45,000	0	0
Total amount estimated to be realized......	..	..		151,556	10	11
By liabilities—For amount estimated to be claimed on the estate per contra, £183,459 18s. 10d.; less, on account of Lyall, Matheson, & Co., included above, £119,922 1s. 1d.	63,537	17	9			
	£422,473	6	3	£151,556	10	11

[Messrs. Lyall, Brothers, & Co. have not thought it prudent to make an estimate of what may be forthcoming from Calcutta beyond the actual amount of remittances already received, and what will come to hand by the three following direct mails—viz., £60,000, as it is impossible to form anything like a correct opinion of what may be realized from this source, although it is hoped that Messrs. Lyall, Matheson, & Co. will be able to meet all their engagements by the sacrifice of the partners' capital in that house, which amounted at last stock-taking to about £110,000.]

"These accounts" says the report of the meeting "show a deficiency of £188,831, and a dividend of not quite 9s. in the pound; but it will be observed, that, with commendable care to guard against expectations that may prove fallacious, the firm have excluded all estimate of the sums that may be received from the estate of Lyall, Matheson, & Co., except such as are actually looked for by the next three mails. Hence a claim of £203,675 figures in the assets at only £60,000. Messrs. Lyall appear to think that the Indian house 'will be able to meet all their engagements by the sacrifice of the partners' capital,'* in which case the dividend would be increased to about 17s.; but, taking the much more probable supposition, that that house will not pay more than 10s. or 15s. in the pound, the dividend from the present estate would then range from about 11s. to 14s. The concern is to be wound up under inspection."

Commenting on the balance-sheet, The *Times* remarks—" The most striking features in the foregoing statement are the large proportion of bad and doubtful debts, the lock-up of capital in India, the amount of acceptances, the enormous total of indirect liabilities, and the complete unpreparedness of the firm, as regards the amount of its capital, to meet the slightest casualty. We have here another illustration of the description of business which would have been bolstered up for a short period only to spread wider ruin ultimately if the cry for 'relief,' always raised in every time of pressure, had in the present instance been attended to."

A dividend of 1s. in the pound has been realized for the creditors up to this date.

Mr. G. T. BRAINE,

East India Trade.

A meeting of the creditors of this house was held at their offices, in New Exchange-buildings, on the 6th of July, 1848. Mr. Horsley Palmer, of the firm of Palmer, M'Killop, Dent, & Co., 11 King's Arms-yard, merchants, was called to the chair.

The chairman said that it was not necessary for him to say more than a few words. They all knew the disasters of 1846 and 1847, and also what passed in the early part of the present year, and the disastrous state of trade during these years was the cause of the stoppage of this respectable house. Mr. Braine started with a large capital, but what capital could withstand the calamitous events that occurred—events which baffled all foresight, and which no man could guard against. The recent occurrences on the Continent, too, had paralyzed our export trade—the silk trade, the indigo trade, and those other articles in which East India merchants traded. However, the house, though obliged to stop, from the pressure of circumstances, was not only solvent, but would, he thought, have a large surplus after paying all their creditors principal and interest. The accounts were the clearest that could possibly be presented, and, indeed, nothing could be more creditable to the house, or more satisfactory to the creditors, than the balance-sheet which he would submit to them. The Bank had been requested to assist Mr. Braine with an advance of £170,000, but, although the most unexceptionable security had been offered, it had refused to do so. The Bank of England had, however, assisted one or two large houses, and had not been successful in doing so, which was perhaps the reason of its refusal in this instance. For his own part, he must say that he thought the conduct of the Bank was unwise in this refusal; there could have been no sort of risk in making this advance, from the unquestionable nature of the guarantees, and had it complied, it would have been the means of retrieving an honest and respectable house from its temporary embarrassments, without its being subjected to the humiliation of the present proceeding. He thought the Bank ought to take an interest in the maintenance of such sound establishments, and not suffer them to fall for want of a little aid which might be afforded without any risk. Mr. Braine, finding that the Bank would not assist, called in the accountant and arranged for bringing his creditors together. He would read for the meeting the statement of the affairs of the house, which had been drawn up by the accountant.

DEBTOR.

	£	s.	d.
To total amount of acceptances out	£300,205	17	2
Of which part are drawn against goods hypothecated			

* The firm of Lyall, Matheson, & Co. stopped with the majority of the other Calcutta houses and will, it now appears, pay eventually a dividend of 8s. in the pound.

Invoice amount of goods hypothecated	£73,374 0 0		
Acceptances held against same	56,399 0 1	56,399 0 1	
Surplus carried to credit side		£16,974 19 11	
Acceptances to Messrs. Dent & Co. against goods shipped to Mr. Braine. These parties hold property of Mr. Braine's to a large amount		54,527 10 5	
Acceptances uncovered		189,279 6 8	189,279 6 8
		£300,205 17 2	
To sundry creditors on open accounts			32,632 18 7
To sundry creditors holding security on goods arrived and to arrive—			
Estimated value of securities held		179,388 0 0	
Amount of claims		134,979 0 0	
Surplus carried to credit side		£44,409 0 0	
To liability on bills receivable under discount		43,009 1 5	
Of which it is expected there will be duly honoured		41,009 1 5	2,000 0 0
To shipments to Dent & Co.		66,630 8 10	
Balance of capital and proceeds of goods to come from China		71,000 0 0	
		137,630 8 10	
Less advances on same	£31,206 11 6		
Acceptances of G. T. Braine to the drafts of Dent & Co. which the latter will deduct	54,527 10 5		
		85,734 1 11	
Surplus carried to credit side		£51,896 6 11	
To sundry ships and tradesmen's bills about			2,500 0 0
			£226,412 5 3

CERDITOR.

By bills receivable		8,869 10 9
Sundry debts and proceeds of goods in course of remittance from Mauritius, Madras, and Bombay		51,842 8 1
By amount to be recovered on policies of insurance		11,500 0 0
By shipments outwards to Bombay and Madras		13,362 19 6
By surplus from hypothecated goods, as per contra	£16,974 19 11	
By do. from goods upon which advances have been made	44,409 0 0	
		61,383 19 11
By surplus from capital and shipments to China, as per contra		51,896 6 11
By goods on hand	£6,438 0 0	
By goods to arrive	5,582 0 0	
By goods in Havre	6,000 0 0	
		18,020 0 0
By ships afloat, and securities in Calcutta		27,224 1 11
By debts in Calcutta, secured on indigo estates and blocks		21,750 0 0
By debts in England (good)		1,000 0 0
By debts secured on estates in the Mauritius		5,400 0 0
Sundry dividends to be received on dishonoured acceptances of various parties		1,500 0 0
Balance at bankers'	£1,293 4 11	
Carried over		£273,749 7 1

By debts in Calcutta, estimated to be good— Brought over..				£273,749	7	1
Mutty Loll Seal	£7,000	0	0			
T. Mookerjee & J. Ferguson	4,500	0	0			
Rockaldan Mookerjee	2,200	0	0			
J. Collee	1,200	0	0			
				15,600	0	0
By debts from Oswald, Seal, & Co., and sundry persons in Calcutta and Ceylon, about				122,000	0	0
				£411,349	7	1

The chairman, commenting on the statement, said that a portion of the unrealized assets consisted of silk, and he apprehended that there would be no loss whatever in the realization of it, and, in confirmation of what he stated, appealed to a creditor who was present.

Mr. Durrant fully confirmed the chairman's statement, but observed that there was a small portion of the silk that had not yet arrived.

The chairman next observed that there was another asset, £5,400, secured upon an estate in the Mauritius. They all knew what a deplorable state the Mauritius was in. However, if the estate in question was good for anything, it was good for £5,400. He thought it right to add that £7,400 was the sum originally advanced upon it, £1,800 had been paid, but another instalment, which was due, had not yet been paid. The chairman finally observed that the total of the assets of the house, exclusive of a claim upon the house of Oswald, Seal, & Co., of Calcutta, was £273,000. He did not think there would be much depreciation upon this sum, and if not, there would be a clear surplus, after paying 20s. in the pound, of £61,000. Supposing even they were to allow £10,000 or £11,000 loss by realization, there would still be a considerable surplus after paying the creditors in full. There was a claim of £122,000 upon the house of Oswald, Seal, & Co., of Calcutta, which was in jeopardy. The sum of £15,000 upon the same house was secured. In concluson, Mr. Palmer again observed that it was a very hard thing this house should have been obliged to stop for want of that aid which the Bank of England could have well afforded.

Mr. Dewhurst said, he considered the proceeding of the Bank to have been most iniquitous. Here was certainly 20s. in the pound, with a large surplus shown, and yet the house was allowed to drop, and call its creditors together.

Resolutions were then put to the meeting and carried, having the following objects in view:—

That affairs of Mr. Braine should be wound up under a deed of inspection; that persons should be appointed by the inspectors to conduct the affairs of the house at home, whilst Mr. Braine proceeded to India for the purpose of doing what he could to recover the debts due to him there, and that a dividend should be paid at the earliest time the inspectors thought suitable; the first dividend not to be less than five per cent.

In reply to questions, the chairman said that by letters recently received from India it appeared that the house of Oswald, Seal, & Co. was upon the verge of insolvency, and about to betake itself to the Insolvent Court there. Mr. Braine's bookkeeper was present, and also the accountant, who would answer any questions which the creditors might wish to put.

Mr. Freshfield stated that the assets offered peculiar facilities for realization, consisting mostly of money, and goods easily converted into money. The greater proportion of it would be realized in six months; the whole of it certainly realized within twelve months.

Mr. Thomas Dent, of the firm of Palmer, M'Killop, & Co., of King's Arms-yard, inquired if the chairman meant to state that there would be a surplus, after paying all creditors in full, of £60,000, exclusive of the claim of 122,000, which Mr. Braine had upon the house of Oswald, Seal, & Co., in Calcutta?

The chairman replied that was the case.

It was then agreed that the following gentlemen should be appointed inspectors:— Mr. Thomas Dent, of the firm of Palmer & Co.; Mr. E. W. Daniels, who represented a large interest in Bombay; and Mr. W. Bowman, of the firm of Horrocks, Miller, & Co., who represented the Manchester creditors.

Mr. Dewhurst, as a large creditor, felt bound to say, that the accounts were most satisfactory, and reflected great credit upon Mr. Braine, whose conduct throughout had been unexceptionable. He believed that when the accountant was called in, the books of the house were in a most clear and perfect state. But the accountant himself could best answer that question.

Mr. Coleman, the accountant, said it was impossible that any books could be in a more perfect state than Mr. Braine's were, and not merely the books, but the whole correspondence of the house was laid before him, enabling him to see how it stood almost at a glance.

Mr. Dent.—I believe that in one day you were enabled to get up a perfect statement of Mr. Braine's affairs for the Bank of England, in consequence of the accurate manner in which the books were kept?

Mr. Coleman.—That is so, sir.

Mr. Dent.—Then I would venture to say that no other house in London could have done the same thing.

A resolution of the high approval of the creditors at the conduct of Mr. Braine, and their entire confidence in him, was then passed, after which the meeting separated.

Mr. Coleman, of Coleman-street, the eminent accountant, prepared the "statement." Mr. J. Freshfield was Mr. Braine's solicitor.

A dividend of 5s. in the pound has already been declared, and a further large distribution is shortly anticipated.

Messrs. RICKARDS, LITTLE, & Co.,

East India Trade.

A meeting of the creditors of Messrs. Rickards, Little, & Co., whose stoppage occurred on the 9th October, was held on the 3d November, Mr. K. D. Hodgson in the chair. The subjoined figures show the state of their affairs :—

DEBTOR.	£	s.	d.
To sundry creditors unsecured	129,283	18	2
To sundry creditors fully secured. Value of securities, £35,516 8s. 11d., less amount of claims £29,762 12s. 1d.; taken as an asset per contra, £5,747 16s. 10d.			
To sundry creditors, partially secured; amount of claims, £14,101 9s. 9d.—Less value of securities, £11,510	2,631	9	9
To liabilities on acceptances £32,222 14s. 3d., of which it is estimated there will be claimed on this estate	9,211	7	7
To liabilities on endorsements £51,886 18s. 4d., of which it is estimated there will be claimed on this estate	3,500	0	0
	£144,626	15	6

CREDITOR.	£	s.	d.
By bills receivable on hand	1,845	8	10
By sundry debtors: considered good £31,677 15s. 7d.; Doubtful, £51,110 12s. 9d.: estimated at 7,000 (Bad, £17,939 16s. 1d.)	38,677	15	7
By losses on produce, and by bad debts written off since the 1st of January, 1845, £50,552 2s. 9d.			
By sundry property	2,164	15	8
By sundry consignments	2,338	18	8
By surplus securities in the hands of creditors, per contra	5,747	16	10
By litigated claims, about £20,000, not valued.			
	50,774	15	7
Deduct sundries, to be paid in full	344	5	5
	£50,430	10	2

With reference to the large amount of losses exhibited in the above statement, it was explained, in answer to a creditor, that of that sum £10,000 arose from losses in Ceylon coffee in the years 1845, 1846, and 1847, and £15,000 from speculations in iron; the remainder being made up " by bad debts, &c." It was further stated that the house had suffered losses to the extent of £50,000 within the last eighteen months, irrespective of recently accruing liabilities. Connected with the establishment of Messrs. Ford & Co., of Calcutta, engaged in transactions with Rickards & Co., it was said that the partners in that firm had some property, but at the same time it was recommended that the holders of such acceptances should temporarily retain them, as it was desirable to prevent Messrs. Ford & Co. from being forced into the Insolvent Court, to the injury of the general body of claimants.

It was then finally proposed and carried, that the partners should be allowed to liquidate the affairs of the estate under an inspectorship, composed of Mr. J. Gurney Hoare, Mr. J. J. Cummins, and Mr. W. Prinsep.

No dividend has at present been paid under this estate.

Messrs. PERKINS, SCHLUSSER, & MULLENS,

East India Trade.

A meeting of the creditors of Messrs. Perkins, Schlusser, & Mullens, whose stoppage took place on the 28th of September, was held on the 20th October, 1847. Mr. Joseph Tritton was in the chair, when the annexed statement was submitted for consideration:—

DEBTOR.		£	s.	d.
To sundry creditors uncovered		43,513	1	11
To creditors partially covered, £27,094 3s. 1d.; less, recoverable from third parties, £10,248 15s. 7d., and value of goods held by them on their account, £377 17s. 9d.		16,467	9	9
To creditors wholly covered:—Value of goods consigned to them, or held on their account, £28,545 8s. 4d.; recoverable by them from third parties, £40,199 2s. 4d.	£68,744 10 8			
Amount of claims	65,727 0 1			
	3,017 10 7			
Retained against liabilities	739 13 7			
Taken as an asset per contra	2,277 17 0			
To liabilities on acceptances outstanding in respect of Shearman & Co.'s drafts		64,013	17	1
Ditto expected to be honoured by the drawers	£76,554 11 2			
To liabilities on bills receivable:— Considered good, £172,577 9s. 10d.				
Considered bad	4,526 19 4			
Deduct amount retained by Bank of England, and Barclay, Bevan, & Co.	1,193 11 8			
		3,333	7	8
To liabilities on bills negociated— Considered good	26,994 9 9			
		£127,327	16	5

CREDITOR.	£	s.	d.
By cash on hand	2,011	18	4
By bills on hand, considered good	22,646	14	4
By sundry debtors, considered good, £30,029 3s. 5d.; doubtful, £5,617 2s.; estimated at 5s. in the pound, £1,404 5s. 6d.	31,433	8	11
Bad . . . £2,584 9s 1d.			
Carried up	£56,092	1	7

	£	s.	d.
Brought up......	£56,092	1	7
By stock of goods:—In England, £7,461 7s. 1d.; in Calcutta, £6,400 0s. 10d.	13,861	7	11
By surplus securities—per contra	2,277	17	0
By shares in ships:—for one-quarter share in *Unicorn*, £750; for ditto in *Hamlet*, £1,250	2,000	0	0
By capital:—In the house of Perkins, Smith, & Mullens, estimated to realize	5,000	0	0
By freights, interest, commission, paid for or chargeable to sundry parties in account current, not made up	11,133	0	0
By Shearman & Co., Calcutta:—For claim on balance of account, £3,546 11s. 5d.; on liability, per contra, £64,013 17s. 1d. £67,560 8s. 6d. Estimated to arrive in remittances and consignments, £30,000, at 10s. in the pound, on £37,560 8s. 6d., £18,780 4s. 3d. ..	48,780	4	3
	£139,144	10	9
Deduct, sundry creditors to be paid in full, £595 12s. 4d.; expenses of liquidation, £2,500	3,095	12	4
	£136,048	18	5
Realized since:—Bills become due about	£7,500	0	0

A report of the meeting says—"A surplus is here shown, after deducting all estimated amounts of loss, of £8,721; and thus far, therefore, the expectations held out at the date of suspension bid fair to be realized. At the same time, it will be perceived that the liabilities on bills receivable are very large, and that much will consequently depend upon the absence of any casualties that may bring the holders of them as claimants on the estate. After some discussion, from which it was evident that the communications made to the meeting were considered, on the whole, to be very satisfactory, it was resolved, that the estate should be wound up by the firm, under inspection; Mr. Joseph Tritton, Mr. W. E. Few, and Mr. Edmund Brandt, (of whom the two latter represent foreign creditors), being the parties named." It has since transpired that the liquidation will not prove so satisfactory as was at first anticipated.

Dividends to the extent of 8s. in the pound have been distributed.

Messrs. SAMUEL PHILLIPS & Co.,

East India Trade.

A meeting of the creditors of Messrs. Samuel Phillips & Co., whose failure took place on the 30th September, was held on the 4th November, 1847, Mr. Gouger in the chair. The following statement prepared by Mr. Samuel Notley, was submitted for consideration:—

DEBTOR.				£	s.	d.
To creditors unsecured				32,756	10	0
Ditto partly secured:—						
Claims	£88,594	9	4			
Securities held by them	63,454	18	1			
Ditto wholly secured:—				25,139	11	3
Securities held by them	19,374	8	0			
Claims	8,030	0	9			
Surplus carried as asset, per contrà	11,344	7	3			
Liabilities on account:—						
Bills payable	136,828	19	9			
Deduct to be provided for by other parties ..	93,250	11	3			
				43,578	8	6
				£101,474	9	9

CREDITOR.

		£ s. d.
By sundry debtors :—		
Considered good		35,896 3 10
Considered doubtful and bad, £5,353 14s. 8d.		
Estimated at		478 4 8
By surplus securities in the hands of creditors, as per contrà		11,344 7 3
By property as per statement		54,936 0 0
		102,654 15 9
Deduct sundry debts to be in full as per statement	£79 3 5	
Expenses of management	2,500 0 0	
		2,579 3 5
		£100,075 12 4

N.B. The contingent liabilities through bills receivable discounted, amount to £133,286 7s. 7d., and although several of the above bills are on firms that have suspended payment, still, through other parties to the bills, it is confidently expected that the whole amount will be provided for. At the present date (November 4th) upwards of £46,000 of the above amount will have run off, supposing all the bills on India to be paid, of which there is no reason to doubt.

"The above statement," says the report, "shows nearly 20s. in the pound. At the same time it transpired in the subsequent discussion, that among the assets stated as 'good,' one item of £23,000 is a litigated claim at Madras (the recovery of which, although a verdict is certain, will depend upon the ultimate position of the house from which it is to be collected); while it was also mentioned that among the liabilities, bills to the amount of £28,000 will possibly have to be paid in full, a lien in connexion with them, existing upon the Santipore sugar estate.

"At the close of the proceedings, it was agreed that the estate should be liquidated by the partners under inspectorship, five gentlemen being selected from the body of creditors present to fill that office. These were, Mr. Gouger, Mr. Dent, Mr. Bagshaw, Mr. Davis, and Mr. Cowell, the services of the latter being secured with the view of obtaining his attention to the realization of the property in India on his return to that country in the course of the next few months.

"The principal heads of this schedule are as follow :—

Goods consigned to foreign parts in safe hands		£6,761
Moiety of a sugar estate at Santipore, viz. original cost	£14,850	
Estimated value of rum and sugar in course of consignment and on hand at Santipore	16,700	
		31,550
Sundries, consisting of ships' charters, commission to receive from sundries on consignment, &c.		7,625
Private property of Mr. Samuel Phillips		9,000
		£54,936

"The Santipore estate is put down at its original cost, from its having been greatly improved by increased outlay, and particularly from the circumstance of the proposed railway communication with the part of the country in which it is situated, which will tend materially to enhance its value, rendering it one of the most desirable properties of the kind in India.

The amount paid under this estate, to the present time, is 1s. in the pound.

Messrs. LAURENCE PHILLIPS & SONS,

East India Trade.

The creditors of Messrs. L. Phillips and Sons met on the 10th of November, when the subjoined statement, prepared by Mr. J. E. Coleman, was submitted :—

DEBTOR.		£ s. d.	£ s. d.
To sundry creditors on account current, provided they take up the acceptances of Laurence Phillips & Sons, which are drawn for their account to the extent of £15,551 8s. 10d.		..	8,824 1 8
To sundry creditors partly secured		10,594 8 5	
Estimated value of securities in their hands		5,732 10 0	
To sundry creditors wholly secured—			4,861 18 5
Estimated value of securities in their hands		32,689 0 5	
Claims		30,338 16 8	
Surplus to credit as per contra		2,350 3 9	
To amount of acceptances outstanding on the 15th October, 1847		71,136 11 11	
Of which there are on account of creditors as above	15,551 8 10		
Of this amount it is estimated there will come against this estate £4,000 13s. 3d.	..	..	4,000 13 3
And credit is given for acceptances of Laurence Phillips and Sons, to various parties who are debtors (and which such debtors ought to meet) to the extent of	55,585 3 1		
		71,136 11 11	
To liabilities on bills receivable		46,291 5 11	
Of which it is expected there will be claimed against this estate		..	682 3 0
To liabilities on acceptances given for the account of correspondents which are covered by real securities, and therefore will not rank on this estate		6,000 0 0	
			£18,368 16 4

CREDITOR.	Amount to which they stand to debit or cost. £ s. d.	Amount which it is estimated they will produce. £ s. d.
By sundry debtors, (good)	17,855 17 1	17,855 17 1
Ditto debtors (doubtful)	7,344 6 4	2,337 0 1
By bills receivable.........................	10,994 3 8	10,781 5 0
Of this amount £7,105 11s. 1d. is secured by bills of lading (and policies of insurance on same) and other good securities.		
By produce on hand, and bills of lading of produce to arrive, estimated to yield	4,210 0 0	4,210 0 0
By consignments to Calcutta, Madras, Colombo, New York, and other parts	8,038 0 7	6,000 0 0
By surplus of securities held by creditors as per contra	2,350 3 9	2,350 3 9
By coffee plantation at Ceylon, known as "The Kaataboola estate"	8,698 11 7	8,698 11 7
By debt due from the Concessionaires of the Brillon Spelter Mines, in Prussia	12,607 2 9	12,607 2 9
A company for the carrying out the working of these mines has lately been formed, the necessary authority of the Prussian Government is in course of completion, and it is expected the whole of this amount will be paid.		
Carried over......	£72,098 5 9	£64,840 0 3

Brought over......				£72,098	5	9	£64,840	0 3
There is a balance of debt from the late firm of Barrow & Co., (which is now in course of liquidation) of................	£5,000	0	0					
There is also some property consisting of land and houses in America, of the estimated value of	5,000	0	0					
	£10,000	0	0					
				£72,098	5	9	£64,840	0 3

The above two items form the residue of the outstanding estate of the late firm of Jonas Phillips and Sons, and whatever proceeds are derived therefrom, will be divisible equally between Mr. Laurence Phillips and his brother, Mr. Samuel Phillips.

Mr. Barnet Phillips has London Dock stock of the value of £1,000.

" All that was stated at the time of the suspension with respect to the solvency of Messrs. Laurence Phillips, and the extreme hardness of their case, is fully borne out," says the report of the proceedings, " by the facts detailed, without reserve or exception to the parties interested, and which were to the effect that against liabilities of £18,000, there are assets valued at £64,000. The acceptances out amount to £71,000, but only £4,000 are expected to come upon the estate. The chairman, Mr. Bonar, represented friends in India, and expressed himself in high terms in favour of the statement submitted, which was the most creditable he had seen during his experience. There would probably be £20,000 to £23,000 available for a dividend within a few months; and if the parties indebted to the estate continued solvent, and met the claims upon them, there would be even within that short period, one-third of the assets got in, equal to 20s. in the pound upon the assumed liabilities, and leaving a handsome surplus for subsequent collection. There was a contingency, however, as regarded the amounts due from two houses in India. Mr. Coleman entered into various explanations, and remarked that there was produce coming forward, that the coffee plantation was excellently situated, having been selected by Captain Galway, the Government commissioner, who superintended its cultivation; that the merchandize sent out was expected to realize its value.

" A creditor suggested that the bills coming forward should be accepted by Messrs. Phillips, in order to protect the Indian houses indebted to them, and upon whose solvency the partial realization of the assets must depend. Strong objections were, however, very fairly urged to such a course, even supposing it to be practicable, for it was considered that no one would take the acceptance of a suspended firm, and as to the houses in India, if so inclined, they would stop the shipment of produce from their side, whether the bills were accepted by Messrs. Phillips or not. Mr. Cotterill, the solicitor to the estate, explained the difficulty of any arrangement of the kind proposed, and the danger of the assets of the firm becoming depreciated if further liabilities were incurred. Eventually the matter dropped, and Mr. Haes, Mr. E. H. Palmer, and Mr. Bonar, accepted the office of inspectors, to wind up the estate, after some very complimentary remarks had been made relative to the proceedings and position of Messrs. Phillips, whose suspension appears to have been the result of the mistrust abroad, and not of inherent weakness."

The amount already paid under this estate is 5s. in the pound.

Mr. A. A. LACKERSTEEN,

East India Trade.

When Messrs. Lackersteen & Co. first failed, which was in November, 1847, an attempt was made to " wind up" under inspection, but that process not proving successful, their estate was placed under the administration of bankruptcy.

Annexed is the balance-sheet of AUGUSTUS ALEXANDER LACKERSTEEN, one of the partners of Lackersteen, Crake, & Co., bankrupts, on which he passed his final examination before Mr. Commissioner Fane. The Fiat was dated the 10th day of April, 1848.

Commencing the 1st January, 1843, and ending the 10th day of April, 1848.

DEBTOR.	£	s.	d.
To creditors	78,720	15	10
To liabilities	66,550	14	5
To creditors holding security	40,259	9	2
To capital	9,034	2	6
In addition to the amount of capital inserted, A. A. Lackersteen possesses letters of credit from Messrs. John Lackersteen and Brothers, of Calcutta, on bankers and mercantile houses in England, to the extent of from £30,000 to £40,000.			
To profits	14,486	3	2
	£209,051	5	1
CREDITOR.			
By sundry debtors, Good	4,112	1	4
Doubtful	15,336	17	4
Bad	7,567	13	5
By cash balance handed to the official assignee	72	5	8
By property given up to the assignees	2,882	18	3
By property in the hands of consignees abroad	10,479	7	4
By property in the hands of creditors holding security per contra	59,909	17	1
By liabilities per contra	66,550	14	5
By losses on merchandize	29,770	19	9
By charges of trade	3,422	13	7
By expenses, domestic and personal	8,945	16	11
	£209,051	5	1

A dividend of 6d. in the pound has been paid under this estate.

MESSRS. LACKERSTEEN, CRAKE, & Co.,

EAST INDIA TRADE.

The balance-sheet of the estate of Messrs. LACKERSTEEN, CRAKE, & Co., was as follows:—

Commencing 1st day of July, 1847, and ending the 10th day of April, 1848.

DEBTOR.	£	s.	d.
To creditors	28,865	6	10
To liabilities	103,826	12	10
To creditors holding security	400	0	0
	£133,091	19	8
CREDITOR.			
By sundry debtors, Good	19	4	9
Doubtful	18	18	6
Bad	9,626	19	10
By bills of exchange, given up to the official assignee, viz.:—			
Good	13,099	18	9
Bad	3,500	0	0
By property in the hands of consignees abroad	538	10	10
By property in the hands of creditors holding security	400	0	0
By property claimed and in dispute	1,475	0	0
By liabilities per contra	103,826	12	10
By losses	586	14	2
	£133,091	19	8

Both of the partners subsequently applied for and obtained their certificates.

A dividend of 10½d. in the pound has been paid under this estate.

Messrs. THURBURN & Co.,

East India Trade.

The creditors of Messrs. Thurburn & Co., East India merchants, whose failure was announced on the 8th March, 1847, held a meeting on the 29th, Mr. Thomas Dent in the chair, when the following statement of affairs was submitted for consideration —

DEBTS.	£.	s.	d.	£	s.	d.
The house is under acceptances for	..			252,807	0	0
Part of these acceptances are against consignments of produce, of which the bills of lading are in the hands of the holders to the amount of	65,734	0	0			
Further part of these are against sundry securities, either held by the holders of the acceptances, or by their correspondent in Calcutta, to the amount of	66,254	0	0			
				131,988	0	0
Balance uncovered..............				£120,819	0	0
N.B. Of the above amount of £65,734 against produce, it is moreover probable that the sum of £47,116 will be provided for by third parties						
Of the above uncovered acceptances it is expected that there will be retired by third parties the sum of	..			16,380	0	0
				104,439	0	0
Liability on bills receivable bearing Thurburn & Co.'s endorsement, £86,000, of which there will be claims on their estate	..			4,700	0	0
Total debts	..			109,139	0	0

[The house has no book-debts with the exception of small sums amounting together to £25.]

ASSETS.	£	s.	d.	£	s.	d.
Amount due by the correspondents of the house in Calcutta to Thurburn & Co. upon the various accounts is	163,016	0	0			
A further sum due by them for funds remitted to Calcutta, for returns in bills unconnected with Thurburn & Co.'s general account, about ..	4,000	0	0			
	167,016	0	0			
Deduct amount of acceptances upon securities other than produce per contra	66,254	0	0			
				100,672	0	0
Amount of balance at bankers' and due by various debtors, all good and in the course of early realization........................				7,074	0	0
Amount of bills receivable	30,893	0	0			
Deduct amount of loan....................	27,966	0	0			
				2,927	0	0
Balance of account due by another firm in Calcutta	..			7,000	0	0
Remittances to Calcutta to other parties	..			4,431	0	0
Balance due on consignments to France about	..			17,500	0	0
N.B. It is probable that there will be a heavy deficit on this sum, in which case the difference would have to go to the debit of the shippers in Calcutta.						
Total assets	..			£139,604	0	0

The separate estates of the partners will be available, subject to the payment of the private debts. It is also stated that there will be a further alteration in the debit of the current accounts, and an increase of the above assets for interest and commission not charged.

It is likewise stated that Thurburn & Co. hold a deed of assignment of the indigo properties of the Calcutta house, executed by one of the partners while in this country, and which are valued at £90,000.

A special agent of Thurburn & Co. proceeded to Calcutta with full powers by the steamer of the 20th of October, to protect the interests of the firm, and was furnished with the deed of assignment of the properties in question.

Thurburn & Co. have a right also to receive, in the course of the season, the surplus over outlay of the indigo crop of the season, which at a very low estimate would be about £25,000.

They may also naturally expect, in the usual course of business, to receive in remittances from Calcutta before their failure could be known there, about £55,000. Of this sum they have received by last mail £10,000, and £5,000 is expected by next.

The *Times*, analyzing the accounts remarked—" It will be noticed that the above account shews a surplus of £30,465, but as the assets chiefly consist of the large claim upon the Calcutta firm of Hickey, Bailey, & Co., it must be ascertained in what position that establishment stands before any just estimate can be formed of the ultimate liquidation.* The assets immediately available, and which it is said can be collected and divided within three or four months, amount to between £35,000 and £40,000.

" In the course of the explanations which followed, mainly on trivial points, it appeared to be the general feeling that the liquidation of the estate would be best effected under the superintendence of inspectors, and on the motion of Mr. J. A. Smith, M.P., supported by the unanimous voice of the creditors present, the annexed resolution was passed.

" That it is expedient that the affairs should be liquidated under the direction of inspectors, and that the following gentlemen be requested to act as such inspectors: Mr. Alexander Matheson, M.P., Mr. Thomas Dent, and Mr. C. Joyce; and that a dividend be paid as soon as funds can be realized, and that a proper deed be prepared under the direction of the inspectors, containing such clauses and provisions as are usual, to be submitted to the creditors for signature. That Mr. Thurburn, sen., having come over only temporarily from Egypt, and having hitherto taken no active part in the business, be allowed to return to Egypt, and that the liquidation be conducted by Mr. Thurburn, jun."

A dividend of 2s. in the pound has been paid to the creditors.

MESSRS. JOHNSON, COLE, & Co.,

EAST INDIA TRADE.

A meeting of the creditors of MESSRS. JOHNSON, COLE, & Co., East India merchants, of Great Winchester-street, was held on the 20th November, 1847, when the following statement of their affairs was submitted. " It will be observed," said The *Times*, " that the liabilities were stated at £112,666, while the probable assets amount to £71,844 only, from which, unless the realization of the latter should turn out more than usually fortunate, the creditors can hardly expect a larger dividend than 10s. in the pound. It will be observed, however, that the Mauritius property is estimated at less than half its cost, and the debts due to Mr. John Johnson are valued at a little more than a third their actual amount. After some discussion the creditors considered it advisable to wind up the estate under inspection; and Messrs. G. H. de Russett and D. Davidson were appointed inspectors."

TOTAL LIABILITIES.	£	*s.*	*d.*
Total amount of acceptances	132,301	19	3
Of which secured specially, £18,327 18s. 10d.; secured partially £5,806 16s. 9d., say to the extent of £2,900	21,227	18	10
Carried over	£111,074	0	5

* The firm of Hickey, Bailey, & Co., of Calcutta, subsequently failed.

Brought over......			£111,074	0	5
Sundry creditors in open account uncovered			1,592	2	8
			112,666	3	1
Sundry creditors fully covered:—					
Amount of claims	£91,145 8 0				
Amount of securities..................	106,821 0 0				
Surplus of securities credited per contra ..	£15,675 12 0				
Liability in respect of bills receivable endorsed by us:—					
Total amount of such bills due in London £184,119 12s.					
Of which upon fallen houses £41,096 0 8					
Less amount detained by the holders £850 0 0		..	40,246	0	8
			£152,912	3	9

Several of these bills have good endorsements, and it is therefore hoped that they will not be proved against the estate.

Bills upon India purchased and resold by us with our endorsement, equivalent to £19,300, all of which it is expected will prove eventually to be good.

TOTAL ASSETS.

Sundry debtors	5,168	10	5
Estimated balances due by correspondents in India, supposed to be safe	29,800	0	0
[This amount may be subject to reduction to the extent of £14,000 owing to our acceptances going back to our correspondents, and being set off by them against our property in their hands.]			
Surplus securities in the hands of certain creditors, estimated as per contra	15,675	12	0
Bill of exchange in our hands upon houses that have failed, £6,000.			
Balances to John Johnson, old account, viz.:— Sundry debtors £31,011 14s., estimated to produce about £11,200; mortgage on sugar refining machinery in the Mauritius, £22,884,—estimated to yield, £10,000	21,200	0	0
	£71,844	2	5

The deed of inspectorship breaking through, the partners subsequently sought the Court of Bankruptcy, where they filed fresh accounts, which are annexed—

The balance-sheet, commences Jan. 1, 1846, and ends Dec. 31, 1847.

DEBTOR.	£	s.	d.
Creditors	113,501	16	6
Capital of Johnson	51,904	17	0
Profit and loss in 1846	3,096	16	5
Ditto in 1847	4,992	3	3
	£173,495	13	2

CREDITOR.			
By debts due, estimated to produce....................	55,988	0	8
Ditto due to John Johnson	51,904	17	0
Expenses 1846, 1847	8,219	9	7
J. W. Cole	1,698	4	1
John Johnson (private debts of).......................	54,838	7	0
Losses in 1846	846	14	10
	£173,495	13	2

The bankrupts have since obtained their certificates. Their estate has not yet paid a dividend, but it is expected to realize about 4d. in the pound.

It will be perceived by the annexed report of the proceedings in the Court of Bankruptcy, on December the 26th., before Mr. Commissioner Fonblanque, when the bankrupt John Johnson applied for his certificate, that the question of the regularity of their trading was fully entered into and discussed.

"Mr. Roy opposed on behalf of the assignees, assisted by Mr. Wryghte, as accountant; Mr. Lawrance supported.

"Mr. Cole obtained his certificate some months ago, during the present bankrupt's absence in India, with which country they chiefly traded. Mr. Johnson is a native of Calcutta, and for some years carried on a prosperous business in India. Mr. Cole was a confidential clerk in the employ of Messrs. Forbes, large East India merchants. Cole returned from Bombay in the beginning of 1846, when Johnson took him into partnership with him. Cole had no capital. Johnson puts down his capital at that period as £13,000, or thereabouts. Johnson went to India soon after the formation of the partnership in order to manage the business of the concern there. The house stopped payment during the crisis at the close of 1847. They traded under the designation of 'Johnson, Cole, & Co.' The fiat was issued on the petition of the bankrupt. It bears date May 6, 1848.

"Mr. Roy said, the assignees felt it to be their duty, through him, to place the facts of the case before the Court. The liabilities were immense, the assets extremely small, and the conduct of the bankrupt, as a trader, in their opinion, improper. The assignees were not actuated by any vindictive or personal feeling; they acted entirely from a sense of public duty, and, conceiving this case to be one of great importance to the commercial public, they had felt it to be their duty to examine into it as far as they were able, and to lay the result of their inquiries before his Honour. The first item that must strike the Commissioner was the enormous amount of liabilities (£262,000,) although the partnership only commenced on the 1st of January, 1846, and ended in November, 1847. He had, with the official assignee, been engaged in investigating the nature of the assets, and must say that in this respect the prospect was lamentable. They consisted, in a great measure, of debts due to the estate; and one reason why the certificate ought not now to be granted was that the bankrupt might leave the country, and give his creditors no further assistance in the collection of such debts. The bankrupt had begun with (taking his own version) only £13,000 capital, and ended, after the short space of 18 months, with the sum of £262,540 on the debit side of his balance-sheet. He had taken £52,000 out of the joint concern to pay his own old debts, which conduct the creditors of the late firm must regard with great displeasure. It was a most mischievous course of trading, and such as he felt assured that the Court would not lightly pass over. But there was another singular feature in this case. The bankrupt had been with Mr. Lackersteen, of the firm of Lackersteen and Crake, engaged in bill transactions to a large amount—transactions, he must say, of a very questionable nature, and showing, at least, the utter recklessness of Johnson. Some of these bills were drawn in India, with blanks for the date and amount, and filled up in London, and the bankrupt admitted that he had accepted those bills, although they purported to be made in London, whereas he knew they were made in Calcutta. But some of those bills, one of which he produced, were in every sense, even to the signature, made in London, although purporting to be made in Calcutta. Scarcely the Court would not sanction such a proceeding. He admitted that the books of the bankrupt were generally well kept; but in one respect there was a most culpable error, for the bankrupt's clerk had admitted that he had entered those London-made bills in the bill-book under the head of 'Receipt of advice' from Calcutta, although they were never advised at all. He laid these matters before his honour, on whose decision, whatever it might be, he should rest perfectly satisfied."

"Witnesses having been examined in support of the above statement.

"Mr. Lawrance addressed the Court on behalf of the bankrupt. The bills in question were good and legal bills, and the remitting of bills from India to this country with blanks to be filled up here was in accordance with the custom of the East India trade. Neither the drawer nor the acceptor had repudiated any of the bills. Mr. Lackersteen, who had filled them up, had passed through this court without one word of opposition, and it was admitted upon all hands that the conduct of that gentleman had been fair, open, and honourable. This was the state of the case:—Mr. Lackersteen carried on business in this city with Mr. Crake, under the firm of Lackersteen and Crake. Mr. Lackersteen's brothers had a house in Calcutta, and traded under the firm of Lackersteen Brothers. It was the custom of the East India houses to make advances upon goods transshipped, but as, from the distance, many months must elapse between the purchase of the goods and their transshipment, it was necessary for the shipper to obtain advances upon the goods. Accordingly, Lackersteen Brothers made remittances to Lackersteen and Crake of bills blank in amount and date, trusting to the latter honestly to fill up the blanks according to the exigency. The latter bills having been accepted by Johnson were discounted at a London banker's. There was nothing morally or legally wrong in all this. The bills were *bonâ fide* bills, drawn, accepted, and negociated in good faith, and nobody was deceived by them. It was true Messrs. Johnson and Cole had failed; but their failure was not attributable either to recklessness or dishonesty. They were crushed in the terrible wreck of the East India houses in 1847, and could not have been expected to survive when such houses as Cockerell, Larpent, & Co., Reid, Irving, & Co., and Barclay Brothers, sank. To show the Court how the bankrupts were effected by the failures of those eminent houses, he would read the following list:—Mr. Lawrance then read a list, from which it appeared that the bankrupt had bills upon the above mentioned three houses and upon 11 other first-rate East India houses to the amount of £126,921, and these 14 houses had failed for no less a sum than £3,816,413. Surely in such general misfortune it was too bad to single out Mr. Johnson for punishment. Mr. Johnson, as soon as he learned the embarrassment of his house, returned from India and voluntarily placed himself at the discretion of this Court. Was he blameable for relying upon the stability of such houses as Cockerell, Larpent, & Co., and Barclay Brothers? One might as well blame a man for taking the bills of Baring Brothers or Rothschilds; for up to the crisis the former were deemed quite as solvent as the latter. Was it not but too notorious that the railway speculation of 1845, the famine of 1846, and, above all, as regarded the East India trade, the alteration in the sugar duties, had produced deep, wide-spread, terrible distress? It was said that the capital of the bankrupt was disproportionate to his liabilities, but in point of fact his capital depended upon the solvency of those first-rate houses with whom he dealt, and if a providential visitation or an act of Parliament crushed the latter, it was too bad to expect Mr. Johnson to hold his position. He dealt like others upon confidence, that upon which the prosperity of this country as a trading country was, in a great measure, based; and to say that he ought to be punished for so doing was to say that confidence ought to cease in mercantile affairs. He had neither rashly speculated nor been personally extravagant; his profits had been large, and but the unfortunate occurrence which had taken place, and for which he was not answerable, his trading would upon the whole have been prosperous. The books were extremely well kept, and in this respect the official assignee had reported most favourably. If Mr. Roy could point out a single item which had not been duly registered in the books, he would consent to the entire refusal of the certificate. For all the bills which Johnson had accepted he had received full value. No creditor came forward to say he had been cheated or deceived. There had been no malversations of assets; no fraudulent misrepresentations; and, taking all the circumstances into account, he felt sure that the Court would not for one day delay the certificate.

" The Commissioner said he wished to know something about the custom of the East India trade in respect to the transmission of bills partly in blank, and filled up in London.

" Mr. Roy denied that there was any such custom.

" Mr. Lawrance positively affirmed that such was the custom.

" The Commissioner asked if he had any witness to establish it?

" Mr. Lawrance replied in the negative; and added, that from peculiar delicacy of the subject it was found impracticable to obtain competent testimony.

" The COMMISSIONER said, it struck him as being a very irregular practice. But for the objections arising out of those bill transactions, there would be very little difficulty in dealing with the case, for there were no charges of undue speculation, or fraud, or concealment. The bankrupt's house had fallen in a storm which had crushed many stronger ones. There were many other meritorious features in his case. The official assignee reported most favourably of the mode in which the books were kept, and his personal expenses had been most moderate. Instead of launching out into that expenditure which some of the 'merchant princes' had indulged in, he had lived frugally, and he had come over here from India, and voluntarily placed his affairs under the administration of the Court of Bankruptcy, for which he was to be commended. Therefore, had the case been divested of those bill transactions, the certificate would not have been for a moment delayed. In this respect, however, his conduct was irregular, for it was clear that he had accepted those bills knowing them to have been drawn in London, although they purported to be drawn in Calcutta, and in one instance a bill of this sort was accepted by Johnson which he knew to have been made, in every sense of the word, even to the signature, in London. But, after all, the bills, as appeared from the report of the official assignee, really represented value, and that there was nothing fictitious in them. Had they been worthless, mere kite-flying transactions between two London houses, he would have felt it to be his duty to mark his decided disapprobation of such conduct; but, as it was not so, as this was the only censurable part of the bankrupt's mercantile career, as there were many meritorious features in the case, and as he had been before the Court since May, he would grant the certificate at once. At the same time he must say, that Mr. Roy and the assignees had acted most properly in bringing the case before the Court, and had only discharged their duty in an able and impartial manner."

MESSRS. SCOTT, BELL, & Co.,

EAST INDIA TRADE.

At a meeting of the creditors of Messrs. SCOTT, BELL, & Co., who suspended on the 23d of October, 1847, held on the 24th of the following month, it was agreed, on the presentation of the annexed account, to liquidate the estate under the process of inspection.

LIABILITIES.	£	s.	d.	£	s.	d.
1. Under acceptances, which are covered by consignments to India and elsewhere, for returns to them	102,760	10	2			
2. Ditto covered by consignments on hand or in transit, and partly by bill remittances	81,761	16	7			
3. Ditto which will be retired for account of, or paid by the drawers, all of whom are of undoubted stability	43,665	19	11			
4. Ditto in our own account, and to be claimed on our estate	..			23,678	13	11
5. To creditors fully covered—						
Amount of securities	33,256	11	10			
Amount of claims	31,729	11	8			
Excess to be taken as an asset	£1,527	0	2			
6. To creditors partially covered	30,000	0	0			
Amount of securities	26,909	13	5			
				3,090	6	7
7. To creditors uncovered				72,860	8	8
To bills bearing our endorsement, but which it is expected will be paid by the acceptors, drawers, or endorsers £121,428 5s. 7d.						
				£99,629	9	2

ASSETS.	£	s.	d.
1. By sundry debtors, all considered good	111,975	7	5
2. By sundry debtors, doubtful, covered by life insurance, amounting to £11,507 17s. 10d. The whole are in gradual liquidation, and expected to be ultimately realized with interest; meanwhile valued at	8,630	0	0
Carried over	£120,605	7	5

Brought over		£120,605 7 5
By 1-8th share of sugar-works at Aska, in the East Indies, the plant of which (1-8th share) has cost £2,400, but is now valued at	£1,200 0 0	
By 1-8th share of produce manufactured and purchased, now in course of shipment to England, and expected to realize cost	3,836 12 6	
		5,036 12 6
3. By bills on suspended firms, amounting to £35,926 15s. 11d. of which £6,964 14s. 5d. are on Scott, Bell, & Co.'s account, valued at about 10s., are		3,500 0 0
By excess in creditors, fully covered		1,527 0 2
By bills receivable		2,226 17 11
By office furniture, annually reduced, now valued at		270 0 0
By cash		83 0 10
N.B. Balance with bankers, £1,309 6s., liable to separate claims.		
By growing commissions and interest to be charged on the accounts current, valued at		10,000 0 0
		£143,248 18 10

Written off—

On sundry debtors, doubtful	£2,877 17 10
On Aska account	1,200 0 0
On produce on hand................	1,060 0 0
On bills on suspended firms	3,464 14 5
	£8,602 12 3

"We, the undersigned, having gone through the foregoing accounts with the partners of the firm, and having received their explanation of the several items, feel no doubt of the correctness of the statements; and from our personal knowledge of these gentlemen, are of opinion, that the creditors of the firm would run no risk, by entrusting the winding up the affairs to the partners, under inspection; and we think there is reasonable ground to expect, that they would ultimately realize the full amount of 20s. in the pound on their debts.

ARCH. HASTIE. J. A. ARBUTHNOT.
London, 24th Nov. 1847. R. C. L. BEVAN. JAMES WEBSTER."

Subsequently the firm issued the annexed circular proposing an arrangement for the payment of 20s. in the pound, with interest, which was most cordially assented to by their creditors.

"London, 11th December, 1847.

"We beg to hand you a statement of our liabilities and assets, which has been submitted to the careful examination of the gentlemen who have certified their approval of the correctness of these accounts.

"Encouraged by our friends, and entertaining a confident belief in the solvency of our firm, we have to submit to the creditors the following plan for the liquidation of our estate:—

"1st. That all our creditors be asked to concur in allowing their debts to be paid as follows:—

"5s. in the pound on the 30th of June next; 5s. in the pound on the 31st of December next; 5s. in the pound on the 30th June, 1849; 5s. in the pound on the 31st of December, 1849, with interest.

"2nd. That we be authorized, in the mean time, to pay all debts not exceeding respectively £100, the aggregate amount of such small debts being about £5,000.

"3rd. That a deed be prepared by which the partners covenanting to pay at the above periods, the creditors will covenant not to sue unless default be made in payment.

"4th. That in the mean time we be allowed to announce to our friends abroad, and to the public, our resumption of business.

"5th. That, as the condition on which we are allowed to resume, we covenant not to enter upon any new business, whereby any additional claims are capable of being thrown upon the existing assets.

"6th. That there be inspectors appointed to whom we shall report periodically the progress of the realizations, and the general state of our business; and the following gentlemen have already consented to act as such inspectors, if agreeable to the creditors, viz.—Archibald Hastie, Esq., M.P., R. C. L. Bevan, Esq., and James Webster, Esq.

"7th. That the four partners be allowed, during the liquidation, to receive an allowance not exceeding in the aggregate, £ ——— per annum.

"8th. That, if the inspectors shall certify at any time, that the house ought not longer to continue its business, that it shall at once cease.

"9th. That, if contrary to expectation it shall appear that funds will not be realized sufficient to pay in full, or to pay the instalments within the periods proposed, that we shall make over to trustees all existing assets, and thereupon shall be discharged from the remainder of our debts.

"10th. That, if required by any of the creditors, the firm be authorized to give their acceptances or promissory notes for the above four instalments, such acceptances or notes, when paid, being in satisfaction of the instalments for which they are given.

"11th. That the firm be authorized to pay their acceptances of the drafts of parties whose property shall be in the hands of the firm, out of such property, or to give up such property on being relieved from all their acceptances of the drafts of the parties to whom the property belongs.

"12th. That we respectively engage to make our private property available when required by the inspectors, after payment of our private engagements.

"Previously to making this proposition to our creditors, we have been anxiously engaged in the most thorough investigation of the accounts, the result of which has been submitted to the gentlemen whose names are attached to the statement, and we have not ventured to make the proposition until we were satisfied ourselves that we could duly fulfil our proposed engagements.

"The time occupied in making these investigations has necessarily delayed us in bringing our accounts before the parties interested, and we have not, under the circumstances, deemed it necessary in the mean time to have a meeting of creditors.

"We were most anxious to pay the first instalment at an earlier date, but the remittances in hand, and to be expected, being of long dates, we have thought it better to fix our instalments at periods of certainty, than to run the risk of any irregularity in their payment. We shall however, be most desirous, if sufficient funds are in hand, to pay the proposed instalments at earlier periods, and we engage to do so with the sanction of the inspectors.

"We shall feel obliged by your informing us as early as convenient, whether we may consider you as an assenting party to the above proposals.

"We are,

"Your most obedient servants,

"Scott, Bell, & Co."

The payment of the 20s. in the pound was carried out within the period specified as announced in the appended circulars:—

"Sir, "London, 23d June, 1848.

"The first instalment of 5s. in the pound, under our deed of arrangement, will be payable at our office here, on or after Friday, the 30th instant. And we have much pleasure in adding that the second instalment, of a like amount, fixed for the 30th December next, will be anticipated and paid at the same time.

"We are, Sir,

"Your most obedient servants,

"Scott, Bell, & Co."

"No. 2, Alderman's Walk, New Broad-street,

"London, 23d November, 1848.

"We have the pleasure to inform you that the two remaining instalments of 5s. each, fixed for payment under our deed of arrangement for the 30th June and 31st

December, 1849; and being in full of 20s. in the pound, will be anticipated and held at your disposal, with arrears of interest, on or after the 1st January next, at our office here; or carried to your credit in new account with us.

"Thanking you for the great confidence and forbearance which you have kindly shewn to us during a period of unprecedented commercial difficulty.

"We remain,

"Your most obedient servants,

"Scott, Bell, & Co."

Mr. WILLIAM TULLOH FRASER,

East India Trade.

A meeting of the creditors of Mr. William Tulloh Fraser was held on the 5th of November 1847, when the annexed statement of his affairs was submitted. After a preliminary discussion, it was agreed to wind up the estate under inspection in the usual form, and the following gentlemen were appointed as inspectors,—Mr. Mackay, Mr. Felgate, and Mr. Blackmore:—

DEBTOR.	£.	s.	d.
To bills payable, partially secured, £37,390 6s. 6d.; to open accounts, £13,874 15s. 10d. Total £51,265 2s. 4d.—Less the value of the securities held by the auditors, £26,248 19s. 8d.	25,016	2	8
To bills accepted by Mr. Fraser for the accommodation of parties who cannot pay them	4,750	0	0
To bills receivable, discounted, amounting to £24,133 9s. 10d., of which it is supposed will be dishonoured and claimed on this estate, about	2,500	0	0
To liability on bills endorsed by Mr. Fraser, amounting to £10,400; secured by shipping documents deposited by him, valued at £9,000 9s. 11d.	1,399	10	1
To liability upon a bill accepted by Mr. Fraser for the accommodation of a party who it is presumed will pay it when due £400.			
	£33,665	12	9

CREDITOR.	£.	s.	d.
By shipments to India, £36,885 18s. 10d.; less claims thereon £26,248 19s. 8d.	10,636	19	2
By book-debts amounting to £34,646 3s. 9d., valued at	22,216	11	6
By bills of exchange on hand	1,069	7	7
By shares in insurance companies, &c.	3,760	0	0
By household and counting-house property, cost 3,600, valued at £2,000; less lien thereon, £500	1,500	0	0
By interest in a shipment to China, assigned to Mr. Fraser by a debtor	1,500	0	0
By policy on the life of L. H. Bodelio, Esq., of Calcutta, for £3,000; one premium paid of £118; age 43. Held as security against his debt of £9,445 10s. 9d.			
	40,682	18	3
Less rent, salaries, &c.	375	0	0
	£40,307	18	3

This estate has paid, at present, 4s. in the pound.

Messrs. RYDER, WIENHOLT, & Co.

East India Trade.

At the meeting of creditors held in the month of November, 1847, of Ryder, Wienholt, & Co., whose failure took place on the 29th October, it was resolved that the affairs of the estate should be liquidated under an inspectorship composed of Mr. F. Newsam (a director of the National Bank of Ireland, who accepted office, not as a party interested, but simply to oblige the creditors,) Mr. J. Skilbeck, and Mr. L. Roussel. It was distinctly asserted that the difficulties of the house were solely attributable to the receipt of remittances on fallen establishments and the depreciation of produce. According to the subjoined statement prepared by Mr. W. C. Wryghte, the accountant employed in the case, it would appear that the assets show about 14s. in the pound.

CLAIMS.	£ s. d.	£ s. d.
To sundry creditors unsecured	..	24,768 10 11
To sundry creditors partly secured	7,299 11 2	
Present estimated value of securities	5,981 12 3	
		1,317 18 11
To sundry creditors, fully secured,—		
Value of securities in their hands	9,149 4 4	
Subject to the claims of creditors, amounting to	8,792 0 10	
Surplus securities, carried as an asset per contra	357 3 6	
To liabilities on bills receivable—		
Total amount unpaid, £47,617 5s. 1d.		
Of which it is expected the claims on this estate will be	7,000 0 0	
On bills for which other parties have engaged to provide	1,501 5 7	
		8,501 5 7
		£34,587 15 5

ASSETS.		Ledger balances.	Estimated to realize.
By total amount of cash, bills of exchange, and remittances in hand	..	9,865 0 9	7,865 0 9
By book debts—			
Good	..	13,918 17 11	13,918 17 11
Doubtful	430 10 10		
Bad	6,685 0 9		
		7,115 11 7	
By property, merchandize, and counting-house furniture	..	1,529 3 4	1,529 3 4
By surplus securities per contra	..	357 3 6	357 3 6
		£32,785 17 1	23,670 5 6

This estate has been wound up, and the assets have realized 2s. 3d. in the pound for the creditors.

MESSRS. LYSAGHT, SMITHETT, & Co.,

EAST INDIA TRADE.

The creditors of Messrs. LYSAGHT, SMITHETT, & Co., who failed on the 9th of December, 1847, held their meeting the 18th of February, 1848. An arrangement for a composition would have been accepted if Messrs Lysaght & Co. could have offered 12s. 6d. in the pound with security, but as they did not feel themselves justified in proposing more than 10s. in the pound, owing to the uncertain value of debts due by parties abroad, it was agreed that they should wind up under inspection. The subjoined statement laid before the creditors was prepared by Mr. J. Jackson, the accountant:—

LIABILITIES.	£	s.	d.	£	s.	d.
Acceptances of Messrs. Lysaght, Smithett, & Co.	..			45,289	5	8
Deduct, specially secured by shipping documents	7,997	11	3			
Deduct, to be paid by the drawers	17,513	9	4			
Securities held by creditors, valued at	16,262	8	9			
Deduct their claims thereon..................	13,670	0	0			
Surplus taken as an asset	2,592	8	9			
Creditors who are partly secured	9,000	0	0			
Deduct estimated value of their securities......	6,915	16	11			
Amount to be claimed upon this estate	..			2,084	3	1
Creditors who do not hold securities	..			4,537	14	9
Bills receivable in circulation, £20,540 8s. 4d., of which the amount expected to claim on this estate is	..			2,958	9	0
				£29,358	11	11

ASSETS.	£	s.	d.	£	s.	d.
Cash in the house	..			342	0	9
Bills receivable in the hands of Messrs. Lysaght, Smithett, & Co...........................	3,127	11	9			
Deduct bills on Messrs. C. de Bruyn & Co., which since the 9th of December have been delivered to the persons for whom they were received by Messrs. Lysaght, Smithett, & Co. .	1,797	5	1			
Bills remaining in their hands	2,030	6	8			
Of these bills, £1,401 10s. 11d. are on Messrs. T. & H. Murray, of Liverpool, and £200 on A. A. Lackersteen; the whole are estimated to produce to this estate	..			1,335	19	5
Sundry debtors, considered good..............	..			10,556	19	1
Sundry debtors, bad and doubtful, £8,243 11s. 4d. estimated value	..			2,158	7	5
Surplus securities in the hands of creditors	..			2,592	8	9
Estimated proceeds of produce of which shipping documents are in hand....................	..			5,412	19	0
Consignments to India and other places, for part of which it is expected remittances are now in transmission, estimated value	..			2,470	12	11
Office furniture and sundries	..			162	14	0
Total assets	..			25,032	1	4
Deduct rent and sundries to be paid in full	..			1,331	9	2
				£23,700	12	2

MESSRS. BIRLEY, CORRIE & Co.

EAST INDIA TRADE.

When MESSRS. BIRLEY, CORRIE, & Co., of Manchester, suspended in April, 1848, in asking the consent of their creditors to a liquidation by inspection, which it is understood was granted, they issued the subjoined statement of their affairs in the shape of a circular.

"LIABILITIES.				£	s.	d.
Acceptances				35,919	2	8
Ditto secured	£14,184	7	6			
By securities estimated at present value	14,694	7	6			
Excess, carried below to 'surplus of securities'	£510	0	0			
Creditors secured	7,923	12	10			
By securities, estimated at	12,065	12	6			
Excess, carried below to 'surplus of securities'	4,141	19	8			
Sundry creditors	32,333	9	9			
Less secured	2,000	0	0			
				30,333	9	9
Liabilities on bills on failed houses, expected eventually to claim				3,118	7	8
Liabilities in respect of which no claim is expected to be made on our estate, £23,837 0s. 6d.						
Balance of accounts due from Calcutta house to correspondents				15,462	9	0
Bills on failed houses, remitted to ditto, expected eventually to claim				6,725	0	0
Bills bought and resold with Calcutta house endorsement, expected eventually to claim				4,375	0	0
Ledger accounts				758	19	1
				£96,692	8	2
ASSETS.						
Cash and bills				2,131	14	9
Bills of lading, &c., present value				3,865	9	8
Stock of goods in Calcutta, as per invoices				32,576	5	5
Surplus of securities from above				4,651	19	8
Estimated dividends on failed houses				10,324	18	6
Ledger accounts				1,257	10	5
Sundry assets in Calcutta, but which are chiefly of doubtful realization, £32,455 7s. 4d.						
Surplus of private estates, estimated at				4,500	0	0
				£59,307	18	5"

"The inference to be drawn from this statement," remarked Messrs. Birley, Corrie, & Co., "is that our present unfortunate position is attributable to the severe losses we have sustained upon our East India trade, to the present difficulty of finding a market for our large stock remaining there on hand, and, above all, to the dishonour of a very large proportion of our remittances; and it will be observed that our means of satisfying our creditors substantially depend upon our shipments not being sacrificed by forced sales, and upon the amount of dividend we may receive from the dishonoured remittances."

Messrs. CRUICKSHANK, MELVILLE, & Co.,

East and West India Trade.

The affairs of this firm, involving two partnerships—one, Cruickshank, Melville, & Co., the other, Melville & Co.—having been placed under the administration of bankruptcy, the Bank of England being the petitioning creditor, the annexed balance-sheets, representing the position of the respective partners interested, were filed in the Basinghall-street Court on Tuesday, March 13th, 1849, preparatory to taking their final examination: Cruickshank, Melville, & Co. were announced to have failed in October, 1847; and Melville & Co. stopped in the following month of November. Mr. Wryghte was the accountant who prepared the balance-sheets, which extend from 1st of January, 1845, to the 19th of December, 1848.

DEBTOR.		£	s.	d.
To creditors		40,741	12	3
To creditors secured		142,243	0	5
To capital, P. Cruickshank:				
1st January, 1845	£12,400 16 11			
Added since	12,622 9 3			
		25,023	6	2
To J. Melville:				
1st January, 1845	7,625 17 1			
Added since	10,245 7 2			
		17,871	4	3
To W. F. Street:				
1st January, 1845	8,213 17 11			
Added since	1,161 5 7			
		9,375	3	6
To R. Ramsay, deceased:				
1st January, 1845		4,887	9	7
To profits		27,016	10	11
To cheques on bankers, never presented		67	0	1
To difference in books		2	3	3
	Total	£267,227	10	5

CREDITOR.		£	s.	d.
By good debts	£377 6 8			
By doubtful	2,224 2 7			
		£2,601	9	3
By bad, carried to losses £35,363 18s. 6d.				
By property given to assignees	..	100	0	0
By balance of Bank of England	..	13	1	10
By property in the hands of creditors secured, consisting of ships, West India plantations, &c.:				
Originally assigned	£168,084 0 0			
Realized since	18,619 0 0			
		149,465	1	0
By losses		101,990	6	8
By charge of trade		7,277	16	8
By partners drawings:				
P. Cruickshank		2,234	19	4
J. Melville		1,133	6	1
W. F. Street		1,014	19	6
R. Ramsay		1,396	10	1
	Total	£267,227	10	5

Firm of MELVILLE & Co., from 1st July, 1846, to 19th December, 1848.

DEBTOR.	£	s.	d.
To creditors	25,367	17	1
To creditors holding security	23,544	7	3
To liabilities	38,224	9	4
To capital advanced by H. H. Oddie, as part of intended capital, but claimed on this estate by the executors of H. H. Oddie	14,635	8	9
To John Melville	247	14	0
To W. F. Street	242	14	11
To John Oddie	250	0	0
To profits	3,560	3	10
	£106,072	15	2

CREDITOR.	£	s.	d.
By good debts	£296	7	1
By doubtful ditto	4,403	7	9
By property given up to the assignees	2,914	2	7
By property in the hands of creditors holding security	31,099	12	8
By trade charges	1,650	13	10
By losses	12,984	0	9
By ditto (bad debts)	14,351	6	10
By partners drawings	148	14	4
By liabilities per contra	38,224	9	4
	£106,072	15	2

Separate Balance-sheet of PATRICK CRUICKSHANK.

DEBTOR.	£	s.	d.
To creditors	£32,291	15	4¾
To creditors secured	27,704	6	0
To liabilities	20,871	16	1
To capital	27,380	4	6
To profits of West India estates	8,853	3	0
To amount drawn from the firm of Cruickshank & Co.	2,234	19	4
To mortgage account, ships paid off	3,871	19	2
To rental of Scotch estates	1,203	0	0
To National Provincial Bank shares, agency, public company's director's fees, &c.	3,537	8	8
To marriage settlement	191	2	11
	£128,139	15	0¾

CREDITOR.				£	s.	d.
By debtors				0	0	0
By property given up				112	17	0
By property in the hands of creditors				26,675	8	0
By losses				44,965	10	5
By domestic expenses				8,658	3	7¾
By charges of trade				1,833	1	11
By liabilities per contra				20,871	14	1
By capital in the firm of Cruickshank, Melville, & Co., January 1, 1845	£12,400	0	0			
Added since	12,623	0	0			
				25,023	0	0
				£128,139	15	0¾

Separate Balance-sheet of J. MELVILLE, from 1st Jan., 1845, to 19th Dec., 1848.

DEBTOR.	£	s.	d.
To creditors	5,138	9	7
To liabilities	9,000	0	0
To creditors secured	28,380	14	2
To capital, 1st January, 1845	2,790	10	4
To wife's income	1,790	7	10
To amount drawn from partnership	1,133	6	1
To further amounts	1,019	3	4
To dividends on ships	819	2	4
To fees as director of public companies	1,155	7	5
	£51,227	1	1

CREDITOR.	£	s.	d.
By bad debts	89	1	10
By liabilities	9,000	0	0
By property given up to the assignees	1,429	2	10
By property in the hands of creditors	14,262	12	6
By losses	3,858	7	3
By expenses	7,101	2	2½
By interest	5,382	6	2½
By capital in the firm of Cruickshank & Co.	7,527	14	9
By ships since transferred	2,576	13	6
	£51,227	1	1

Separate Balance-sheet of WM. FAUNTLEROY STREET.

DEBTOR.	£	s.	d.
To creditors	£31,535	5	9
To holding security	1,280	0	0
To liabilities	7,009	12	7
To capital	482	19	2
To amount drawn from Cruickshank, Melville, & Co.	1,014	19	6
To ditto, from Melville & Co.	148	14	4
To insurance	2,441	13	7
To income	702	1	8
To ship's dividend, &c.	1,161	5	7
	£45,776	12	2

CREDITOR.	£	s.	d.
By good debts	£123	12	1
By bad ditto	12,083	9	5
By property given up to assignees	1,499	9	4
By property with creditors	1,280	0	0
By liabilities per contra	7,009	12	7
By losses	10,848	16	10
By expenses	3,556	8	5
By capital in the firm of Cruickshank, Melville, & Co. 1st Jan. 1845	9,375	3	6
	£45,776	12	2

No dividend has yet been paid, and the prospects of ultimate realization are extremely uncertain.

MESSRS. BOYDS AND THOMAS,

EAST INDIA TRADE.

The creditors under this estate, the partners in which failed in October, 1847, received the following statement of affairs prepared by Mr. J. E. Coleman, the accountant employed on the occasion. A distribution to the extent of 2s. in the pound has already been announced, and the firm is in course of liquidation by the process of inspection.

DEBTOR.		£ s. d.
To creditors on open accounts		14,029 11 3
Do. on our acceptances		19,739 8 8
Do. partly secured	£69,182 15 4	
Less securities held	64,267 5 1	
	£4,915 10 3	4,915 10 3
		£38,684 10 2
To creditors wholly secured—		
Amount of securities held	60,614 19 8	
Claims	51,010 17 9	
To credit	£9,604 1 11	
To capital		28,945 5 2
To liability on account of George Ackland	7,500 0 0	
Supposed to be fully secured, and therefore will not claim on this estate.		
To amount of bills receivable under discount	34,685 1 2	
The whole of which are expected to be paid by the acceptors.		
		£67,629 15 4

CREDITOR.	
By debtors, good	3,845 11 0
Do. doubtful, £23,431 3s. 8d., estimated to produce 3s. 4d. in the pound	3,905 3 11
By bills receivable on hand	2,240 19 5
By surplus to come from estates as per contra	9,604 1 11
By surplus to come from other estates	8,198 7 0
By debts due from other estates	1,750 0 0
	£29,544 3 3
By balance at Bank of England which will be retained by it against bills under discount	24 8 10
By debt due from Ackland, Boyd & Co.	6,552 4 3
Exclusive of debt on estate account £5,000.	
By Losses	31,508 19 0
	£67,629 15 4

MESSRS. THOMAS, SON, AND LEFEVRE,

RUSSIA TRADE.

A meeting of the creditors of Messrs. THOMAS, SON, AND LEFEVRE, was held on the 20th of October, 1847, Mr. Bonamy Dobree in the chair, at which the following statement was submitted:—

DEBTOR.

			£ s. d.
To sundry creditors			55,751 2 5
To acceptances, viz.—			
On account of De Jersey & Co		£180,099 1 8	
On account of J. Thomas & Co., St. Petersburgh, viz., their drafts	26,057 17 10		
De Jersey & Co.'s drafts	74,610 7 0		
Drafts of other parties	15,329 5 8		
		115,997 10 6	
On account of sundries		49,912 14 9	
			346,009 6 11
			401,760 9 4
To balance,—surplus			40,212 10 0
			£441,972 19 4

CREDITOR.

By cash in hand and at bankers'		2,892 18 5
By bills receivable, in hand		27,064 19 4
By De Jersey & Co., debtor on balance, provided we pay our acceptances		183,129 1 9
By John Thomas & Co., of St. Petersburgh, debtor on balance, provided we pay our acceptances		180,766 18 3
By sundry debtors, good		48,119 1 7
By ditto, doubtful and bad	£6,589 8 6	
		£441,972 19 4

"In connexion with the above," says a report of the proceedings, "the meeting were informed that remittances to the amount of about £40,000 have been received from the St. Petersburgh house since the 4th instant, (the date of suspension, and to which the account is made up), thus forming a total of £67,000 in bills receivable, &c., which will shortly be applicable for a dividend. The ultimate liquidation in full will depend, it will be observed, upon the ability of De Jersey & Co., of Manchester, and of the St. Petersburgh firm, who figure jointly for £363,000, to meet their engagements; but as it is known that De Jersey & Co. have made arrangements by which they are likely to sustain themselves, and as it is believed also that the St. Petersburgh house (from whom a balance-sheet was received about March last, showing a surplus of £80,000,) will be able to hold its ground, the prospect is certainly much more favourable than had been anticipated. No accounts have yet arrived from St. Petersburgh of the effect produced by the news of the stoppage on this side, and hence, as it is too early to form a definite calculation, the meeting was adjourned for a few weeks. The debt of the St. Petersburgh house, it should be mentioned, appears to be for goods which were chiefly shipped in July and August last, and which, it may be presumed, are in course of realization." At a subsequent meeting, the accounts were fully tested, and found to be correct.

This estate has paid 20s. in the pound, and the firm has since resumed business.

Messrs. H. CASTELLAIN, SONS, & Co.,

General Merchants.

A meeting of the creditors of Messrs. Castellain, Sons, & Co., whose suspension took place on the 23d of August, 1847, was held on the 18th of October, when the following statement prepared by Messrs. Quilter, Ball, & Co., was submitted by Mr. Maynard, of the firm of Crowder & Maynard, solicitors to the estate.

The failure of the house was mainly attributable to the default of Messrs. Fraser's, of Antwerp, indebted to them for about £30,000.

DEBTOR.		£ s. d.	£ s. d.
To sundry creditors, on accounts current		37,001 2 3	
To holders of H. C. S. and Co.'s acceptances, of Fraser & Co.'s drafts	£17,225 17 10		
Less balances due by sundry holders	932 16 6		
		16,293 1 4	
			53,294 3 7
	Liabilities.	Estimated as Claims.	
To liabilities on acceptances to be retired by the drawers	57,680 13 0		
Estimated as probable claims ..	..	4,000 0 0	
To liabilities on bills receivable, discounted	214,052 3 1		
Estimated to prove claims	..	3,000 0 0	
To liabilities on foreign bills negociated	248,740 13 3		
Estimated to prove claims	..	10,606 16 10	
Total	520,473 9 4	17,606 16 10	
Deduct—			
Cash and bill at Bank of England held against liabilities .	819 9 6		
Balances due by sundry holders..	429 16 4		
		1,249 5 10	
			16,357 11 0
To liabilities on confirmed credits (disputed) £4,000.			
			£69,651 14 7

CREDITOR.		£ s. d.	£ s. d.
By cash in hand, viz.			
In the house		156 11 6	
At Robarts & Co.'s		3,478 19 7	
			3,635 11 1
By bills receivable, on hand, considered good ..		7,297 0 11	
Do. doubtful	£34 9 4		
Estimated at		18 11 4	
Remitted for collection for other parties......................	6,376 13 4		
Subject to this amount due by the parties to H. C. S. & Co.		919 3 8	
			8,234 15 11
By sundry debtors, considered good		20,756 17 7	
Do. doubtful........	17,579 0 2		
Probable value at 5 per cent.	..	878 19 0	
Considered bad	55,485 13 2	..	21,635 16 7
By sundry property		..	2,100 0 0
By sundry foreign (good) debts attached by parties having doubtful claims on this estate; if the attachments are sustained this amount will go in reduction of liabilities per contra; if not, they become available as assets		1,419 7 9	
By H. Castellain, Sons, & Co., of Liverpool—			
Amount at our credit as capital in that firm ..		6,600 0 0	
Balance in our favour on account current		2,605 2 9	
		9,205 2 9	
Carried over			£35,606 3 7

Deduct :—	Brought over	£35,606	3	7
Clerks' salaries, rent, taxes, and small creditors, to be paid full	503 2 7			
Expenses of liquidation, say	1,500 0 0			
		2,003	2	7
		£33,603	1	0

"We have here" says the *Times*, "a deficiency of £36,048, and a probable dividend of 9s. 8d. in the pound. In connexion with the large amount of indirect liabilities running upon the firm at the time of their suspension, and which appear in the above statement, Mr. Maynard informed the meeting that a total of about £300,000 had already run off, and that under these circumstances there was every reason for confidence that the estimates now given would be fully borne out. Of the assets about £24,000 have been realized and invested in Exchequer-bills. Much considerate feeling was expressed for the members of the house, and a proposition to wind up under inspection met with general approval. The inspectors named were Mr. Furse, Mr. Meinertzhagen, and Mr. Bordier, all of whom represent foreign creditors."

This estate has paid 10s. in the pound.

Messrs. SANDERSON & Co.

Bill Brokers.

A meeting of parties interested in the affairs of Messrs. Sanderson & Co., was held on the 20th September, 1847.—Present, Mr. S. Jones Loyd, in the chair; Prescott & Co., per Mr. Prescott; Masterman & Co., per Mr. John Masterman; London Joint Stock Bank, per Mr. Pollard; Barnard, Dimsdale, & Co., per Mr. Barnard; Lubbock & Co., per Mr. Forster; Union Bank of London, per Mr. Scrimgeour; Coutts & Co., per Mr. Robinson; Dennison & Co., per Mr. Kennard; Provincial Bank of Ireland, per Mr. Hewat, when the following statement was submitted to the meeting :—

Total amount of bills running on the evening of the 13th inst., for which Sanderson & Co. are responsible	£1,725,000
Amount paid up to this evening, the 18th of September, £194,400, still running, £1,530,000	£1,725,000
Money held at call, and for which securities are lodged with the parties, £622,569; money at call, and for which the parties have no security, £168,420	790,989
Total amount owing by Sanderson & Co., not covered by equivalent security	168,420
Against this uncovered debt, and also the general responsibility on the bills running, the following assets are held by Sanderson & Co. (as per schedule submitted to the meeting), viz.	259,000
In addition to the above, the separate property of the partners amounts (as per schedule submitted to the meeting), to	188,000

After the above statement had been fully examined, it was resolved unanimously,—

"1. That from the statements laid before this meeting, and the explanations afforded by Mr. Sanderson, it appears that there is sufficient ground for confidence in the solvency of the concern, and that the resumption of its operations may be practicable at no distant period.

"2. That, with the view of watching the progressive realization of the bills, and the collection of the other assets of the partnership, and thus being prepared to determine with more confidence on the propriety of resuming the business, this meeting be adjourned to Tuesday, the 28th inst., at one precisely, at the office of Messrs. Sanderson & Co., 83, King William-street.

"3. That a copy of these resolutions be transmitted to every creditor accompanied with the assurance that the statements and explanations afforded by Mr. Sanderson, as well as his general conduct in the present emergency, so far as it has come under the knowledge of the meeting, has been correct, and highly satisfactory in all respects."

"It will be seen," remarked The *Times*, "that the total amount of assets to meet the unsecured debts of the firm (£168,420,) and the contingencies upon the bills bearing their endorsement, is £447,000. The valuation of these assets, it is to be mentioned, has been made with great care, and it is likewise stated that a large proportion of the bills on which the house is liable are of the most unquestionable description, while at the same time the amount of those which are bad is less than has been generally supposed. Under these circumstances, there can be little doubt of an early resumption."

Business by the house has since been resumed, the creditors having received 20s. in the pound.

Messrs. TRUEMAN & COOK,

Colonial Brokers.

The meeting of creditors of Messrs. Trueman & Cook, whose failure took place on the 15th of November was held on the 23d of December, 1847. Mr. Henry Kingscote was called to the chair, when the following report of Mr. Coleman, the accountant appointed by the Bank of England to investigate the affairs of the house, together with the annexed balance-sheet, was laid before the meeting. The report of Mr. Coleman is addressed to the Bank's solicitors, and from its importance we give it without abridgment, as follows:—

"Having, agreeably to the instructions that I respectfully received from you, investigated and ascertained the state of the affairs of Messrs. Trueman & Cook, of Mincing-lane, on behalf of the governor and directors of the Bank of England, I now have the honour to hand you the result of my inquiry.

"My examination has been directed to the various points that I considered requisite from the 1st January, 1844, to the day that the house suspended payment, viz., the 16th November last, and I must here observe that the suspension so promptly determined on was an act of great discretion, and one of infinite benefit to the creditors generally; for, although the resources of the house would have enabled them to have struggled on for a month or two, yet if such a course had been adopted, it would have been attended with material loss to all parties interested.

"I find that the capital of the firm on the 1st of January, 1844, was £127,755 15s. 11d., and at the date of suspension it amounted to £156,463 9s. 11d., showing an increase amounting to £28,707 14s. on this item. The drawings of the several partners throughout the whole period have been very moderate, but the losses sustained each year as against the gross profits have been heavy.

"As the termination of my inquiry presents so favourable a view for all parties concerned, it precludes the necessity of my entering into such details, that otherwise might have been deemed requisite. I will, therefore, now turn to the general statement of the liabilities and assets of the house, and offer some suggestions which bear upon the subject of liquidation.

"The total amount of liabilities is £379,104 16s. 5d., and the joint assets I estimate to realize (after payment of charges attendant upon the liquidation) £381,835 8s. 8d., and which in my opinion may be marshalled and converted for distribution as follows: one-fourth in cash within three weeks from this time; one-fourth by the 1st of May next; one-fourth by the 1st of October next; one-eighth by the 1st January, 1849; and the remaining eighth by the 1st March in the same year. In order to meet the first instalment, it will be requisite to obtain an advance of 75 per cent. on about £50,000 produce, which is valued at the present low market prices, and I think such an advance would be extremely beneficial, both as regards the interests of the estate as well as the interests of all parties connected with colonial produce, as it would prevent the pressure of too much commodity on the market at one time, and thus probably enhance its value.

"The contingencies upon the realization of the assets of this estate are very limited, and they can only be effected to any extent by the account with Messrs. Reid, Irving, & Co. and the securities held by Messrs. Trueman and Cook, for their debt against the firm of Messrs. Cruickshank, Melville, & Co. As regards the first, it is now ascertained beyond doubt, that sugars have been shipped, and are coming forward to the extent of one-half of the whole sum dependent upon the balance; and as to the latter, should it only realize one-half of the amount the securities are estimated to produce, that deficiency is amply provided for by the assets that will arise from the separate estate of Mr. Cook, and which are not included in the before-mentioned sum of £381,835 8s. 8d.

"Should you think proper to advise any suggestions as to the liquidation, the same can be carried out under such supervision as you may think proper to recommend.

"The books and accounts have been kept in the most correct manner, and all losses incurred within each year have been regularly passed off to the debit of profit and loss prior to the balances being carried to each partner's accounts, and the losses, amounting in all to nearly £154,600 (made and estimated), have been incurred in the present year.

"The transactions between Messrs. Trueman and Cook, and Mr. A. A. Lackersteen, having formed a subject for public comment, I have directed particular attention to the same. The facts of which are as follows:—

"Mr. Lackersteen called upon Messrs. Trueman and Cook with a letter of introduction from a house of great respectability, in January last. The object he had in view was to get them to make some speculative purchases of sugar and coffee. Messrs. Trueman and Cook having satisfied themselves, by inquiry, as to the respectability of Mr. Lackersteen, consented to execute his orders, and to make purchases for him. Mr Lackersteen was not in a position to pay the cash at the time the prompt became due; viz., on the 6th March, upon which Messrs. Trueman and Cook gave to him their acceptances for £16,000; and Mr. Lackersteen handed to them a like amount on the 5th and 6th March, to cover the payments made by them for the produce purchased, amounting in all to £16,236 19s. 8d.

"The value of the produce that had been purchased having declined considerably, Messrs. Trueman and Cook called upon Mr. Lackersteen to pay a further deposit; he did so by handing to them two acceptances amounting to £2,000, one of which for £800 has been honoured, but the remaining one is accepted by a firm since suspended.

"A further purchase, amounting to £4,109 15s. 4d., was made by Messrs. Trueman and Cook on account of Mr. Lackersteen, the prompt of which was due on the 19th of June, and for which Mr. Lackersteen paid them £3,600 cash on the 14th. Some minor transaction took place, which brought the cash matters to nearly a balance.

"The acceptances of Messrs. Trueman and Cook become due on the 18th of August, and as Mr Lackersteen was still desirous of holding on his produce, Messrs. Trueman and Cook assented to again give their acceptances, which they accordingly did on the 16th of August, to the amount of £18,000, for which Mr. Lackersteen handed them cash on the 16th and 17th, amounting to £13,500, towards meeting the acceptances for £16,000 which fell due on the 18th, and on the 27th of August Mr. Lackersteen paid Messrs. Trueman and Cook £5,000 to cover the remaining amount of the £18,000 acceptances.

"Interviews took place from time to time after this date, and Mr. Lackersteen, with much persuasion, assented to some sales being made. Accordingly two sales of coffee were made on the 2d and 4th of October amounting to £5,178 18s. 6d, the prompts of which fell due on the 23d and 30th of October.

"Immediately after these sales prices of produce further gave way to a considerable extent, and rumours were abroad that Mr. Lackersteen, was in difficulties. Messrs. Trueman and Cook became extremely desirous of closing the account, in order to protect themselves against their acceptances for £18,000, which were approaching maturity (viz., the 19th of November,) and after several interviews and conversations between all parties, at which times Messrs. Trueman and Cook strongly urged the necessity of the sales being made, the following letter was addressed by Messrs. Trueman and Cook to Mr. Lackersteen:—

"'Dear Sir, "'Mincing-lane, October 28th, 1847.

"'With reference to our interviews respecting the sale of your Java sugar, and to your desire to limit the price to 45s. per cwt., we beg to inform you, that we believe that price to be quite unobtainable; and as your bill upon us will become due next month, it is necessary that an immediate course of action should be adopted. Of course it is our desire that the sale should be conducted without undue precipitation, as it would be if driven to the last moment. A sale effected to-day would scarcely be available by the maturity of the bill, as time is required for the payment of the duty, for the delivery of the sugar, and for the regulation of the accounts of the buyers (to whom we continue to give every facility which we know insures an offer on the best terms,) while if the matter is protracted a forced sale for cash would entail further serious loss upon you.

" ' To show our readiness to afford you every opportunity to realize the full market price, we are quite ready to permit any other broker to procure a purchaser, and we will further even allow him ½ per cent. of our brokerage upon the sale; but this must be done at once, or we shall proceed to protect our own interest by effecting a sale upon the best obtainable terms. It is much to be regretted that you declined selling when we could have obtained 48s. per cwt., and when we urged you to allow us to go on; but in the present position of affairs, we cannot submit to any further delay, and therefore must beg your reply to this by to-morrow morning, when we shall feel it our duty to place the cargo on the market for sale.

" ' We are, dear sir, your obedient servants,

(Signed) " ' TRUEMAN AND COOK.'

" To A. Lackersteen, Esq.' "

" After the receipt of this letter, Mr. Lackersteen consented to the disposal of the remainder of the sugars, and accordingly Messrs. Trueman and Cook passed a contract on the 1st of November, of which the following is a copy :—

" ' London, 1st November, 1847,—Sold for account of Mr. A. A. Lackersteen, per Maria Jacoba Cornelia (D V K N M); 1,205 baskets Java Sugar, at 43s. per cwt., duty paid or allowed, prompt 13th January, 1848.—Usual conditions. ' "

" It so happened, that the buyers required delivery of the goods, prior to which, they, in the ordinary course of dealing, would have to pay the amount of purchase; and accordingly they did (voluntarily and without any application) pay to Messrs. Trueman and Cook the following amounts :—On the 2d November, £3,500; 9th November, £1,150; 12th November, £1,770.

" It will therefore be seen that the whole course of these transactions was in accordance with the customary proceedings of the trade, and the moneys so received merged into the general assets of Trueman and Cook in the same manner as other receipts of precisely the like nature did (on that very day, and in fact almost every succeeding one, up to the time of their suspension being made known.)

" The state of account between Messrs. Trueman and Cook and Mr. Lackersteen, on the day of the suspension of the former firm, was as follows :—Provided Messrs. Trueman and Cook paid their acceptances, amounting in all to £20,000 (one of £2,000 being out, in respect of some indigo sold for account of Mr. Lackersteen,) there was a balance in their favour of £1,492 17s. 8d., by having given him credit for various bills paid by him to Messrs. Trueman and Cook; but as a portion of those bills, amounting to £2,136 10s. 9d., are upon houses since suspended, and which will not be honoured at maturity, the balance against Mr. Lackersteen will be increased to the sum of £3,629 8s. 5d.

" I cannot conclude this report without expressing my obligations to the several partners and their establishment for the proffered and full information given to me, as well as the assistance that they have rendered during my investigation.

" Should there be any other points which I have not noticed, where further information is required, I will most cheerfully furnish it.

I am, gentlemen,

" Yours very faithfully and much obliged,

JAS. EDW. COLEMAN.

" 36, Coleman-street, Dec. 14, 1847."

Statement of affairs of Messrs. Trueman and Cook, 15th November, 1847—

LIABILITIES.	£	s.	d.	£	s.	d.
To amount of acceptances out	360,835	13	2			
Less a sum of £500 off one bill for £3,500 with the London Joint Stock Bank, upon which they advanced only £3,000	500	0	0			
	£360,335	13	2	360,335	13	2
To sundry creditors on open balances........				18,769	3	3
To sundry creditors for produce sold, the proceeds of which will be paid to them so soon as it is received by Trueman and Cook	42,330	18	8			
To sundry creditors holding security :—						
Estimated value of securities held by them....	90,500	0	0			
Amount of their claims	68,749	5	0			
Amount available to the estate, as per contra	21,750	15	0			
To liabilities on bills receivable under discount	87,362	10	0			
Ditto guarantee	1,000	0	0			
	88,362	10	0			
The whole of these bills will be duly honoured by the acceptors, and proceeds are expected to cover the guarantee, in which case there will be no claim on the estate in respect of the above sum of £88,362 10s.						
				£379,104	16	5

ASSETS.	£	s.	d.	Amount which they stand to debit. £	s.	d.	Amount which they are estimated to produce. £	s.	d.
By sundry debtors (good)....	£112,420	0	4						
Less amount to be paid over to creditors as per contra	42,330	18	8						
	70,389	1	8	70,089	1	8	70,089	1	8
By ditto, partly secured				360,519	19	6	220,609	6	3
By ditto doubtful, unsecured				9,899	14	3	4,650	10	1
By bills receivable in hand				15,157	12	11	13,561	6	6
By cash, balance at bankers ..	£1,048	17	3						
Ditto, in hand	1,300	0	0						
				2,348	17	3	2,348	17	3
By produce in hand				52,825	11	11	52,825	11	11
By surplus balance of securities, as per contra				21,750	15	0	21,750	15	0
				£532,591	12	6	385,835	8	8
Less salaries and charges to be paid	1,500	0	0						
Charges of sending an efficient person to the West Indies, and other expenses of liquidation	2,500	0	0						
							4,000	0	0
							£381,835	8	8

Estimated proceeds of Mr. Cook's separate estate £22,000.

The balance at the bankers was £11,048 17s. 3d., but they wrote off a sum of £10,000 to the loan account, which has increased the surplus balance arising from securities, upon which advances were made, to the sum of £21,750 15s., as stated above.

In addition to the preceding, showing the debts and assets as existing on the day of the stoppage, a supplemental statement was presented, showing the amount at the present time, which upon the result of these statements, appeared as follows:—

LIABILITIES.

Total acceptances				£297,435	13	2
Creditors on open balances				22,345	2	0
Creditors secured fully	£68,449	5	0			
With surplus	21,750	15	0			
Liabilities on bills under discount and on guarantee, all good	89,362	10	0			
Total liabilities	£319,780	15	2			

ASSETS.

Good debts	£70,089	1	8
Debts secured	177,815	5	10
Cash balance in hand and at bankers	2,348	17	3
Produce	36,108	11	11
Doubtful debts, valued at	4,650	10	1
Bills on hand	13,561	6	6
Surplus balance of securities	21,750	15	0
Total assets	£326,324	8	3

The surplus of the private property, after payment of the private liabilities, would be also available.

It was then stated to the meeting that the house would be prepared to pay 20s. in the pound, by three instalments of 5s. each, and two of 2s. 6d. each, as follows:— The first instalment of 5s. in the pound to be paid on the 18th day of January, 1848; the second, on the 18th day of May, 1848, and the third, on the 18th day of September, 1848. The two instalments of 2s. 6d. in the pound each to be paid on the 18th day of January, and the 18th day of April, 1849. After this statement had been discussed, the following resolutions were agreed to:—

"1. That it is expedient for the creditors to concur in allowing the house to proceed with the administration of its affairs under inspectors, and that the following gentlemen be requested to act as such inspectors,—Mr. Joshua Bates, Mr. Henry D. Blyth, and Mr. Erie Erickson.

"2. That the house be authorized to pay small debts not exceeding in the aggregate £1,500.

"3. That a deed be forthwith prepared by which the partners shall covenant to pay 20s. in the pound, according to the proposals, viz.—5s. in the pound on the 18th January, 1848; 5s. in the pound on the 18th May, 1848; 5s. in the pound on the 18th September, 1848; 2s. 6d. in the pound on the 18th of January, 1849; and 2s. 6d. on the 18th April, 1849.

"4. That such deed shall contain covenants by the creditors not to sue, and an ultimate release on payment of the instalments, but with such provisions as the inspectors shall deem necessary for assigning all the outstanding assets to trustees, in case there shall be any default in payment of the instalments, or in case they shall otherwise deem it necessary.

"5. That the deed shall in other respects be prepared in such manner as the inspectors on behalf of the creditors shall approve, and with such clauses as are usual in deeds of inspectorship.

"6. That the house shall be at liberty to give its promissory notes or acceptances for the several instalments, such notes or acceptances when paid being in satisfaction of the instalments for which they are given, and the parties taking the same being bound by the terms of the deed of inspectorship.

"7. That creditors acceding to this arrangement shall not be prejudiced as to their rights against third parties, or upon their securities.

"8. That the private property of the partners, after payment of their separate liabilities, be made available for the payment of the instalments, or otherwise applied in the administration as the inspectors may direct.

"9. That Mr. Trueman, sen., and Mr. Trueman, jun., and Mr. William Cook, be relieved from attending to the administration, and that the same be conducted by Mr. Cook and Mr. Windsor, under the inspectors."

It having been stated to the meeting that the partners would require no allowance during the liquidation—

"It was further resolved, That any of the partners should be at liberty to transact business as brokers on their covenanting not to use either directly or indirectly any of the existing assets of the firm, and to incur no new engagements, which could by any possibility be thrown on the existing assets. But such business shall be discontinued if the inspectors shall certify that it ought not to be continued."

(Supplementary Statement.)

TRUEMAN & COOK, IN LIQUIDATION. 36, COLEMAN ST. LONDON, Sept. 21, 1848.

In accordance with your request I beg to forward the several particulars relating to the past and present position of the affairs of this estate.

	£	s.	d.	£	s.	d.
The amount of LIABILITIES stated upon the 15th of November last was				379,104	16	5
Which has been reduced by the following items:—						
By various acceptances retired by the drawers, and sets off in account	£75,420	1	8			
By proceeds of produce paid to various parties who were entitled to the same	20,778	9	1			
By sundry bills drawn against and on account of West India estates, taken up as they arrived at maturity	4,324	0	2			
By cash paid for the two instalments of 5s. each in the pound	131,320	15	1			
By portions of securities obtained from Messrs. Reid, Irving, & Co., in order to procure a discharge on their liability of £50,000 of their drafts on Trueman and Cook	4,166	13	4			
By sundry small creditors and balances of accounts to release goods for the benefit of Messrs. Trueman and Cook's estate	7,725	0	3			
By proceeds of sugar received by the Bank of England from the estate of Gower Nephews, eventually to come in reduction of Trueman and Cook's liability to them	4,026	19	3			
By payments made to the London Joint Stock Bank and the London and County Bank, to get per Cruickshank's release in respect of his liability on drafts held by them, in order to obtain produce for the benefit of Trueman and Cook's estate	875	0	0			
				248,636	18	10
Thus reducing the total liabilities of this estate at the present time to	..			£130,467	17	7

The periods for the payment of the several instalments were fixed by me, and I therefore think it but right to state the sources from which I calculated the proceeds to arise, and the non-receipt of which has caused the postponement of the instalments now due, viz:—

	£	s.	d.	£	s.	d.
By proceeds of produce taken in November, 1847, in the assets available for the general estate, but since given up to various parties entitled	20,778	9	1			
Proceeds of Gower's sugars	4,026	19	3			
				24,805	8	4
By deficiency in sugars that were to have arrived from the Mauritius from Reid, Irving, & Co.'s estates, but which were not shipped, in consequence of the unfounded rumour of their suspension being made before the fact did occur				23,010	13	10
Carried forward				£47,816	2	2

	£	s.	d.
Brought forward	47,816	2	2
The like deficiency in Gower's	2,562	16	11
By deficiency of produce from Boyds and Thomas's estate in Ceylon, in consequence of the failure both of that firm, and also of the firm of Ackland, Boyd, & Co., of Colombo	7,000	0	0
By amounts calculated to have been received from Bombay, Madras, and Sydney, in respect of securities assigned to Trueman and Cook by Cruickshank, Melville, & Co.	8,000	0	0
By sundry balances (secured) but not yet paid	3,800	0	0
	69,178	19	1
To this may be added—			
Cash balance and produce in hand	9,700	0	0
	£78,878	19	1

A further addition to a large amount might also be added for depreciation of produce.

The amount required for the payment of the forthcoming instalment is £69,457 16s. 1d. therefore the calculation as to the means was quite ample to meet the same provided they had been realized as anticipated.

I may also mention that up to the present time the only losses to any extent really ascertained are the balances of Reid, Irving, & Co., and of Gower, Nephews, & Co., which amount in round numbers to £25,000.

The assets available for the general estate are as follows :—

		£	s.	d.
Bills receivable of which the greater portion are the promissory notes of Regulus, Pardo, & Co. which fall due in various periods between May, 1849, and July, 1850, (amounting to £5,894 10s. 2d.)		7,595	7	2
Cash at Bankers'		4,144	5	3
Produce in hand		5,570	6	6
Sundry good debts partly secured, and partly unsecured, considered good but requiring time for payment		16,026	0	0
The amount of debts due from Messrs. Cruickshank, Melville, & Co. to Messrs. Trueman and Cook in November, 1847, was	£132,289 12s. 4d.			
Against which various securities were assigned by Messrs. Cruickshank, Melville, and Co. to Messrs. Trueman and Cook, amounting according to the estimate of the former firm (in value) to	98,220 10 1			
In the statement that I prepared to Nov. 1847 I estimated the same at	45,000 0 0			
And to this period there has not been received on account of such securities more than....	5,000 0 0			
Leaving to recover		40,000	0	0
Balance due from the estate of Boyds and Thomas secured by assignment of coffee crops, and mortgages on their various estates at Ceylon		27,768	16	10
Estimated surplus of securities held by Messrs. Glyn & Co. but which cannot be made available until the remaining securities with them are disposed of........		10,000	0	0
The separate estate of Mr. Cook, consisting principally of Spanish passive bonds and shares in the Paris and Lyons and Paris and Strasburg railways, taken in November, 1847		22,000	0	0
Total assets available		£133,104	15	9

In reference to the securities held from Messrs. Cruickshank, Melville, & Co. they consist of various descriptions of properties, as follows:—partly entire and partly of portions of some estates in Demerara and St. Vincent's, and it was found necessary to dispatch a competent person to those islands to protect the interests of Messrs. Trueman and Cook, to negociate either for the purchase or sale of the interests of others as circumstances might best dictate, to test the validity of certain claims that were put forward, and finally to obtain possession. The gentleman selected for this purpose has, after several expensive and protracted suits in the various local Courts of the islands, succeeded to a great extent in accomplishing the above named purposes, and the late manager of the different estates is at this time in London, with whom I hope to be enabled to come to an arrangement of all unsettled matters so as to leave the estates clear, and enable their disposal to be accomplished.

Powers of attorney have been forwarded to Sydney to convert the properties and collect the debts there without delay.

Parties at Madras and Bombay, whose debts formed a portion of the assignment, are now in London, and negociations are being made for settlement.

Claims on parties in Hong-Kong, for which a chancery suit has been pending for some time, is in the course of compromise; and the like observation will apply to some claims on the Underwriters at Lloyd's.

In regard to the estates in Ceylon, the like precaution has been used in intrusting a power of attorney to a gentleman in every way qualified to protect the interests of Messrs. Trueman and Cook, and to carry on the cultivation of the estates. The reports of these properties are decidedly favourable, taking into consideration the present prices of produce.

As I am unable to define the time of the realization of these assets I cannot fix the date for the payment of the instalments.

I have, so far as my judgment prompts me, given such details as I hope will prove satisfactory; and I trust this explanation will show that every exertion is being made for the benefit of the creditors. It would be unjust towards Mr. Cook if I were not to bear testimony to his unwearied and persevering energy from the time that the arrangement was made down to the present moment, and it is only by a continuance of his able assistance that I can look forward to that favourable result of this estate which I have from the commencement anticipated, and in the fulfilment of which you may rest assured no exertion shall be spared on the part of

Your obedient servant,

J. E. Coleman.

Dividends, under this estate, to the extent of 12s. have been declared.

Messrs. FRY, GRIFFITHS, & Co.

Colonial Brokers.

A meeting of the creditors of Fry, Griffiths, & Co., the colonial brokers, whose failure took place in September, was held on the 28th of October, 1847. The chair was taken by Mr. Chambers, and the annexed statement prepared by Messrs. Quilter, Ball, & Co., the accountants, was submitted for consideration.

DEBTOR.	£	s.	d.
To creditors unsecured	62,309	14	3
To creditors partially secured, amount of claims £100,869 3s. 5d.; less value of securities held, £78,657 16s, 3d.	22,211	7	2
To creditors fully secured—value of securities held, £12,025; amount of claims thereon, £10,635 13s. 11d.; surplus, taken as an asset per contra, £1,389 6s. 1d.			
To liabilities on acceptances expected to be provided for by the drawers, £126,361 15s. 7d.			
To liabilities on bills receivable, £30,872 2s. 2d., of which the amount estimated to prove claims on the estate is	6,458	4	4
	£90,979	5	9

DEBTOR.

By sundry debtors considered good, £7,564 1s. 4d.; ditto doubtful, £15,891 9s. 8d.; estimated as 5s. in the pound, £3,972 15s.; (ditto bad £49,762 6s. 9d.)	11,736	16	4
By sundry property, viz., surplus securities in the hands of creditors as per contra, £1,389 6s. 1d.; surplus securities, £3,632	5,021	6	1
By estimated surplus of separate estates	3,000	0	0
	19,558	2	5
Deduct many payments in full, rent, salaries, &c.	326	16	3
	£19,231	6	2

[This account shewed about 4s. 3d. in the pound.]

At an adjourned meeting of creditors, a report on the affairs of the suspended firm was read, accompanied by a case laid before Sir Fitzroy Kelly and Mr. Lloyd relating to the exchange of securities with Messrs. Overend, Gurney, & Co., respecting which the creditors required explanation. These documents, as they throw much light on the transactions of Messrs. Fry, Griffiths, & Co , are subjoined :—

"The report of James Alexander Simpson, of No. 62, Moorgate-street, London, solicitor, who was appointed at a meeting of the creditors of Messrs. Fry, Griffiths, & Co., held on the 28th day of October, 1847, to investigate the accounts and affairs of the insolvents, and report the result of his inquiries to a meeting of creditors, to be held by way of adjournment, on Thursday, the 11th of November."

"In pursuance of the resolution of the creditors, I have proceeded to inquire into the accounts and affairs of Messrs. Fry, Griffiths, & Co., and in doing so every facility has been most readily afforded to me by Mr. M'Leod and Mr. Jay, the books and papers of the firm have been laid before me, and the parties themselves have readily answered all my inquiries.

"I have directed my attention in the first instance to the state of their cash account for a fortnight previous to their stoppage of payment, and it appears to me that their books have been regularly kept; and I find that they kept daily balances of their banker's account. Upon going through their cash transactions, I observe nothing worthy of notice until the 25th of September, on which day I find that Messrs Fry, Griffiths, & Co., paid Messrs. Overend, Gurney, & Co. a cheque for £3,905, dated the 27th of September, being in repayment of advances made by the latter to them on the deposit of certain securities which Messrs. Overend, Gurney, & Co. had permitted Messrs. Fry, Griffiths, & Co. to withdraw during the course of that week, it being their custom to allow Messrs. Fry, Griffiths, & Co. to pay at the end of each week the amount of advances made to them on the securities taken away during that week, instead of paying the advance on each security at the time of taking them out of their hands. On the 27th of September Messrs. Fry, Griffiths, & Co. had not the means of meeting their cheques, and on being informed of that fact, Messrs. Overend, Gurney, & Co., on the same day, gave them a cheque for £4,000, to meet the one they held for £3,905, which was never afterwards repaid.

"I find, also, that on the morning of the 28th of September, Messrs. Fry, Griffiths, & Co. had a balance to their credit with their bankers, of £847 19s. 5d., and that in the course of the day they paid in various sums, which appear to have been received in the ordinary course of their business, amounting to £831 17s., making in all £1,679 16s. 5d.; and that on the other side they paid an acceptance in favour of Messrs. Lyall, Brothers, for £1,500, and another sum of £100, in favour of the same parties, though, as it appears to me, Messrs. Fry, Griffiths, & Co. must have known on the morning of the 28th of September that their situation was hopeless, and that stoppage of payment was inevitable.

"I also find, that on the 28th of September, Messrs. Fry, Griffiths, & Co. (having previously obtained from a party certain bills of lading, or warrants, on which the same party had advanced a sum of £1,600) executed in favour of that creditor a security for the same sum of £1,600 and upwards; the exact particulars and circumstances of which I have not been able to ascertain, nor have I thought it material to do so, as I am led to believe that the share assigned will not prove of any considerable value.

"I then proceeded to inquire into the history of the transaction which took place between Messrs. Fry, Griffiths, & Co. and Messrs. Overend, Gurney, & Co. on the 29th of September, and, as the facts of it are detailed in the case laid before Sir Fitzroy Kelly and Mr. Lloyd, I refer to the case submitted to them without recapitulating them here. I have had an interview with Messrs. Overend, Gurney, & Co. upon the subject; and these gentlemen offered me, on behalf of the creditors, every information which it was in their power to supply. They laid before me all the securities which they held, and expressed their desire to retain nothing to which they had not both a legal and moral right. It appears to me that nothing can be more regular and straightforward than have been the whole of their dealings with Messrs. Fry, Griffiths, & Co. Every transaction is kept distinct; and whenever an advance was made, a separate memorandum was taken from Messrs. Fry, Griffiths, & Co., signed by them, specifying the particulars and value of the property pledged, and the amount advanced upon it. These memoranda speak for themselves. At the end of every week the accounts were balanced; and, as may be expected, in most cases there was a balance due to Messrs. Overend, Gurney, & Co., which was carried on.

"I have further to report, that having made myself acquainted with the transaction, I deemed it advisable to take the opinion of Sir Fitzroy Kelly and Mr. Lloyd as to whether the transaction can be considered as a preference, and whether the securities could be recovered for the benefit of the creditors. That case, and the opinion of the learned counsel upon the subject, will be read to the meeting.

"I have further to report that, in the event of the creditors acceding to any arrangement, I think that they must not calculate on receiving as large a dividend as 4s. in the pound, for certain liabilities which, at the time of preparing the statement, were considered good, have since turned out to be bad, and the amount of such extra claims will be between £9,000 and £10,000.

"Nov. 10. "J. A. SIMPSON."

"CASE.

"The firm of Fry, Griffiths, & Co., colonial brokers of Fenchurch-street, which consisted of Joseph Fry, Rhys Barker Griffiths, Thomas Gouger Merridew, and — Fry, junior, stopped payment on the 29th of September last, or rather it may be more properly said, that they did not pay after the 28th of September.

"This firm possessed but small capital, but it was well known from Mr. Fry's connexion with Mr. Gurney, of the firm of Overend, Gurney, & Co., that they had great command of means through that firm, and thus carried on a very extensive business

"Previously to the 28th of September, Messr. Fry, Griffiths, & Co., had been in expectation of receiving from a gentleman of the name of Stewart, and other parties, a sum of money amounting to about £12,000, but being disappointed in the receipt of it on that day, they became pretty sure that they could not continue their payments. They accordingly on the morning of the 29th of September sent for their solicitor to consult with him as to the best course to pursue. Upon his arrival, and making enquiry into their affairs, he discovered that they had pledged with Messrs. Overend, Gurney, & Co., certain securities which had been intrusted to their care by parties who were not indebted to them, to cover loans to the amount of £11,462. Upon their solicitor being made acquainted with this fact he pointed out to them that, although the pledge might be good in law as against the owners of the securities, the transaction might subject them to an indictment for a misdemeanour under the Factor's Act, and in consequence of this intimation an application was made to Messrs. Overend, Gurney, & Co., to exchange those securities for others. At this time, viz. the 29th September, Messrs. Fry, Griffiths, & Co. had in their possession other securities to the amount of £22,594. Upon some of these latter securities Messrs. Fry, Griffiths, & Co., had either made no advance, or, at all events, had not advanced to their full value. Messrs. Fry, Griffiths, & Co. accordingly made application to Messrs. Overend, Gurney, & Co. to deliver up the securities for £11,462, and to receive in exchange for them those for £22,594, it being distinctly understood that the latter gentlemen were only to hold the securities for £22,594 for the amount of the £11,462, and no more, or whatever the latter might realize. Messrs. Overend, Gurney, & Co., thinking that they had not been well used by Messrs. Fry, Griffiths, & Co. at first declined to accede to the proposal, but ultimately, upon being advised by their solicitors that they could do so with safety, determined to accede to the proposal, and the securities for £11,462 were on the

29th of September returned to Messrs. Fry, Griffiths, & Co., who in their stead delivered over to them the securities for £22,594, which Messrs. Overend, Gurney, & Co. now retain. Upon the occasion of this arrangement being made a memorandum, of which the following is a copy, was signed:—

" 'Messrs. Overend, Gurney, & Co., in consideration of your delivering up to us the warrants mentioned in the first schedule hereunder, and on which you have advanced us sums of money amounting to £11,462, we hereby lodge and deposit with you, as security for that amount and interest, the bills of exchange, promissory notes, policies of insurance, and other securities named in the second schedule, and also agree to make all necessary transfers for perfecting such securities.'

[Here follow the schedules mentioned.]

" The securities £11,462, when received by Messrs. Fry, Griffiths, & Co., were by them returned to the parties to whom they belonged. It is not pretended by any one that by this arrangement Messrs. Overend, Gurney, & Co. were placed in any better position than they were in before the exchange, for the probability is that they could have retained the securities for £11,462 against all the world; so that what they did was in reality an act of kindness towards their connexion, which would save him from a prosecution; but the effect of the arrangement is a damage to the estate to the extent of £11,462, or in round numbers of 1s. 9d. in the pound to the creditors.

" Supposing Messrs. Overend, Gurney, & Co. to be entitled to the securities for £22,594, and they should all prove good, they will retain their £11,462. £7,500 will have to be accounted for by the estate to the owners of the securities, and the remaining £3,632 will be assets for the creditors; whereas had Messrs. Overend, Gurney, & Co. retained the securities for the £11,462, the owners of them would have been creditors of the estate for the amount, and the debts due by the firm would have been increased so much; but the amount of the £22,594 (deducting the £7,500 short advanced upon them) would have been assets for the creditors.

" Messrs. Fry, Griffiths, and Co. did not pay after the 27th of September; indeed one of their cheques for £4,000, which they had given to a customer, and which was dated that day, was not presented for payment, at their request, there not being assets to meet it.

" It may not be unimportant to state, that when Messrs. Fry, Griffiths, & Co., handed over the securities for £22,594, they left themselves without anything excepting certain debts due to them, the surplus of certain securities held by a class of creditors, and their small private property.

" By the statement submitted to the creditors, it is estimated that the estate may pay rather more than 4s. in the pound.

" Under the circumstances stated, you are requested to advise the creditors of Messrs. Fry, Griffiths, & Co. whether, in the event of their affairs being driven into bankruptcy, the exchange of securities with Messrs. Overend, Gurney, and Co. would be considered a preference? and whether, in the same event, the assignees of Messrs. Fry, Griffiths, and Co., would be entitled to recover back the securities for £22,594, for the benefit of the general creditors?

" OPINION.

" We are of opinion that the exchange of one set of securities for another, whereby Messrs. Overend, Gurney, & Co. obtained no advantage whatever, is not such a transaction as could be impeached by the general creditors in the event of a bankruptcy. It was a *bonâ fide* contract, founded on a present and sufficient consideration, which, no act of bankruptcy having then taken place, could not be disturbed. It has nothing in it of the character of a fraudulent preference of a creditor by an insolvent trader on the eve of bankruptcy, because here the creditor relinquishes what was to him an exact equivalent for the new securities deposited. We think, therefore, that, under any circumstances, Messrs. Overend, Gurney, & Co. can retain these new securities against the general creditors to the extent of their original lien for £11,462. " FITZROY KELLY.

" Temple, Nov. 8. " S. H. LLOYD."

" In the course of the proceedings," says The *Times*, "Mr. D. Chapman, who represented the firm of Messrs. Overend, Gurney, & Co., entered into explanations concerning the dealing of that house with Fry, Griffiths, & Co., in all of which he was supported by the statement made by Mr. Simpson. He at the same time volunteered to go into any detail that the creditors might desire, as it was his object to dispel any impression of his firm having acted mysteriously, or of having availed themselves of more than they had morally and legally a right to possess. Although the creditors generally appeared to regard the result of the investigation as completely satisfactory so far as Messrs. Overend, Gurney, & Co. were concerned, especially when Mr. Chapman positively asserted that they were really unacquainted with the true position of Fry, Griffiths, & Co., and that they had considered them, up to the latest moment, a thriving and prosperous establishment, not in any way likely to deposit securities which were not their own, still, the conduct of the insolvent firm was again severely animadverted upon, and it was strongly contended, that an estate of this description ought properly to be subjected to the rigour of the law as administered in bankruptcy. One professional gentleman present, while acquitting Messrs. Overend, Gurney, & Co. from all charge of seeking a preference, and expressing his conviction of their desire to deal in a thoroughly straightforward manner, questioned much the policy of advancing extensively on warrants. Finally, it was attempted to pass a resolution exonerating not only Messrs. Overend, Gurney, & Co. from blame in the transaction, but also Messrs. Fry, Griffiths, & Co., but it was suggested that it would not be prudent to adopt any such step. At length a further adjournment was consented to, with the view of affording Fry, Griffiths, & Co. an opportunity of coming forward with an offer for a composition."

At the subsequent meeting no offer of composition was made, and the creditors then consented to the liquidation of the estate under inspection, the assets to be realized for the best amount they would bring.

This estate has paid 4s. in the pound.

Messrs. SARGANT, GORDON, & Co.,

Colonial Brokers.

This firm failed in November, 1847, and the creditors agreed to a liquidation by inspection. Mr. J. E. Coleman was the accountant. A first payment of 2s. 6d. in the pound has been made, and some further small dividend is anticipated.

DEBTOR.	£	s.	d.	£	s.	d.
To creditors on open balances	..			2,888	13	5
To bills payable	74,759	19	8			
Less secured in all or part	37,560	0	0			
To amount likely to claim, say	..			42,000	0	0
To liabilities on bills receivable	40,327	1	2			
Less expected to be duly paid at maturity	21,611	11	0			
	18,715	10	2			
Less covered by R. Hemingway	6,000	0	0			
				12,715	10	2
Amount of creditors holding security	90,659	3	1			
Less securities and bills held	83,009	5	3			
				7,649	17	10
				£65,254	1	5

CREDITOR.	£	s.	d.	£	s.	d.
By debtors (good)				£1,976	17	11
By ditto (doubtful), estimated to produce				936	7	4
By surplus available from property held by parties who have made advances, &c.				519	0	0
By debtors on produce	£2,738	9	5	999	7	8
By produce on hand	..			953	0	0
By balances estimated to come from shipments on which advances have been made by us				5,500	0	0
				10,884	12	11
Less rent, &c. to be paid in full				232	10	0
				£10,652	2	10

ROUGEMONT, BROTHERS,

GENERAL MERCHANTS.

Mr. George Rougemont, the surviving partner in the firm of ROUGEMONT, BROTHERS, passed his final examination in the Bankruptcy Court on the 26th of January, 1848, and the subjoined is an abstract of the balance-sheet presented.

The balance-sheet of George Rougemont (trading as Rougemont, Brothers), as to the partnership transactions of himself and his brother, Francis Frederick Rougemont, (who died on the 26th of July, 1847), and also of the subsequent transactions of George Rougemont in continuing the business under the same firm.

From the 1st of January, 1847, to the 30th of November, 1847, (date of fiat.)

DEBTOR.

	£	s.	d.
To creditors	28,042	18	1
Creditors (private) of George Rougemont	136	8	5
Creditors holding security	30,540	3	0
Liabilities, as per contra	30,658	8	9
	£89,377	18	3
To surplus on the 1st of January, 1847, as per statement of affairs	20,073	13	8
Money received, dividend on property of George Rougemont's creditors	233	0	0
Profits	4,549	12	7
	£114,234	4	6

CREDITOR.

				£	s.	d.	£	s.	d.
By debtors—									
Good				£11,077	6	8			
Doubtful, £7,882 16s., valued at				4,882	16	0			
							15,960	2	8
Bad, carried to losses below	£14,919	17	7						
By Liabilities, as per contra				..			30,658	8	9
Property				..			7,096	6	5
Property in the hands of creditors				..			14,579	16	7
Cash and bills given up to official assignee—									
Cash				2,757	7	7			
Bills				5,938	3	11			
				£8,695	11	6			
Deduct bill considered bad, carried to losses below				290	0	0			
							8,405	11	6
Private property of George Rougemont				6,904	2	9			
In hands of creditor				5,700	0	0			
							1,204	2	9
							£77,904	8	8
By trade expenses				..			2,409	15	6
Losses				14,727	14	3			
On bills receivable, taken as bad	£290	0	0						
On doubtful debts above	3,000	0	0						
Bad debts	14,919	17	7						
	£18,209	17	7						
Less taken as bad Dec. 30, 1846	1,168	0	4						
				17,041	17	3			
							31,769	11	6
By amounts drawn out by partners—									
George Rougemont				1,007	17	11			
F. F. Rougemont				1,142	10	11			
							2,150	8	10
							£114,234	4	6

Mr. Geo. Rougemont subsequently obtained his certificate without the least opposition. The estate has paid 8s. in the pound.

MESSRS. LESLEY ALEXANDER & Co.,

CORN TRADE.

The proceedings in the Court of Bankruptcy before Mr. Commissioner Goulbourn, when these bankrupts applied for their certificates, April 8th, 1848, furnishes a succinct history of their failure.

Mr. Lawrence appeared for the bankrupts.

The solicitor for the assignees said he had no opposition to offer.

The Commissioner asked Mr. Follett, the official assignee, if he had anything to say respecting the conduct of Messrs. Alexander and Bardgett?

Mr. Follett replied, that he was perfectly satisfied with their conduct since the issue of the fiat. Mr. Bardgett was most unremitting in attendance at his office, and had spared no pains in making up his accounts and assisting the creditors. He then presented the following report, in which the whole facts of the case are clearly stated:—

"The fiat is dated January 12th, 1848.

"The house suspended payment on the 7th of August, 1847, and on the 28th of that month a general meeting of the creditors having been called, it was resolved to wind up the affairs under a deed of inspection. Messrs. J. G. Hubbard, J. Pittman, and J. Ashlin, were appointed inspectors, and these three gentlemen are the creditors' assignees under the fiat.

"The proceedings of the inspectors appear to have been conducted with great regularity, distinct accounts of the receipts and expenses kept, the assets invested from time to time in exchequer bills, and on the fiat being issued I consequently received from the bankers upwards of £40,000 in cash and securities.

"Up to the period of the stoppage of the house, it does not appear that any profit and loss account had been taken since the year 1840, although trial balances were regularly made each year, and as the object of the inspectors was liquidation they took notice of claims and assets alone.

"An account from the books as set out in the proceedings was made subsequently to the 1st of July, 1846, when the balance-sheet commences, showing the then situation of the house; this presents a deficiency of £21,613 12s., with a marginal note that Mr. Alexander's private property, estimated at £93,509 1s. 1d., was liable to make it good.

"A profit and loss account has now been taken to July 1, 1847, which shows a balance in favour of the house £38,914 9s. 6d., thereby redeeming the deficiency of the former year.

"The balance-sheet now presents—				£	s.	d.
Creditors				190,388	14	4
Creditors fully secured	£59,740	2	6			
Deduct securities	24,906	4	0			
				34,833	18	6
Creditors fully secured, £2,991 15s. 1d., the estimated value of the property being £7,019 3s. 2d., the difference £4,027 8s. 1d., being taken as an asset.						
Liabilities on acceptances by the firm				227,132	10	2
Liabilities upon the drafts of the firm upon persons who failed				120,833	4	8
Total claims upon the estate				£573,188	7	8
"The assets disclosed are—						
Good debts	£29,504	8	3			
Property	80,042	3	10			
Property,—surplus in the hands of secured creditors	4,021	8	1			
				113,575	0	2
Deficiency	..			459,613	7	6
"To which must be added— Net profits from July 1, 1846, to July 1, 1847	..			38,914	9	5
"To be accounted for ..	..			£498,527	16	11

Which is thus explained—

	£	s.	d.	£	s.	d.
Liabilities upon acceptances..............	£218,754	11	8			
Liabilities upon bills drawn upon other parties	47,048	17	9			
Losses between July 1, 1847, and 12, 1848..	107,561	7	2			
Bad debts between July 1, 1847, and Jan. 12, 1848	66,683	10	10			
				440,048	7	5
" Depreciation between the cost price and value of corn at the date of the fiat, as estimated				25,453	17	5
Drawn out by Mr. Alexander to pay mortgage				5,000	0	0
Personal expenses since the 1st of July, 1846				2,159	15	11
Payment to creditors since June 1, 1846				2,000	0	0
Repairs of premises				619	6	9
Personal expenses since July 1, 1846				1,632	17	5
Deficiency July 1, 1847................................				21,613	12	0
				£498,527	16	11

" The losses on this estate involve so large an amount that I have thought it right to investigate their character, and I find they have arisen in a great measure as follow :—1. Upon goods shipped by the house for parties who have since been unable to pay for them. 2. On sales of produce for which Alexander & Co. accepted bills at its then value, but the net proceeds fell far short of that sum. 3. On acceptances in part payment of cargoes contracted for, but which contracts the foreign house declined to complete. 4. On grain shipped from London to foreign parts, and, from bad weather, not arriving at the stipulated period—then thrown on the market and sold at a ruinous loss, in some cases not paying freights and charges. 5. On cargoes shipped to outports by parties, on whose account remittances were promised, but the consignees retained the proceeds. 6. On shipment to foreign ports, the proceeds of which were absorbed by the failure of the parties, and the holders of Alexander & Co.'s acceptances having proved there, now seek to obtain the balance from this estate.

" In justice to the house, I beg to add, that by far the greater proportion of the above-mentioned losses have arisen on account of correspondents, who, by the sudden and unforeseen depreciation in the corn trade, have been unable to meet their engagements."

The Commissioner then gave judgment, he said—" This is a case of considerable importance, from its intrinsic nature as well as from circumstances connected with it. I therefore propose to say a few words upon it, not only regarding the application immediately before the Court, but also with reference to the conduct of this case from the issue of the fiat up to the present moment. I think this case is a very fair illustration of the benefits which result from the administration of the bankruptcy laws, when worked in the efficient way in which it has been done by those who have had the management of this case. It appears that the fiat against the bankrupts is dated so recently as January in the present year—the 12th of January, so that not quite three months have elapsed from the first stage to the last. It appears that both the bankrupts assisted the official assignee to the utmost, and laboured with unceasing diligence at their accounts, so as to have them ready on the day fixed for the last examination—an unusual occurrence, especially where, as in this case, their accounts were necessarily so complicated and extensive, and the failure so large. The debts and liabilities of this firm amount to more than half a million of money, and the assets to between £120,000 and £130,000. All the accounts are made out with great regularity and clearness, indeed so much so as not to call for opposition from a single creditor on the day fixed for the last examination, and they passed without a single objection being raised. The affairs of this estate could never have been wound up so rapidly if the books of the house had not been most regularly kept; and I must be permitted to say that this case completely demonstrates the use and value of book-keeping, for it shows that concerns, however vast and intricate, may be by it accurately and truthfully delineated, and it satisfies the creditors, who go away without entertaining any ill-feeling or doubts against the bankrupts. There seems to me to have been another peculiarity about this case. It was this; that on the day fixed for passing the last examination—the earliest which the present state of the law permitted—a dividend was declared; not perhaps a very large one; but still a dividend of about £40,000 or £50,000, or 2s. 2d. in the pound upon all the debts proved; and I understand there will be yet a further dividend of the same amount or something more. The official assignee is unwilling to pledge himself to the exact amount, as a good deal depends upon the sum which Mr. Alexander's private property may realize; but I should say at a rough estimate the estate will pay 5s. in the pound. In the course of the short period which intervened between the issue of the fiat and the last examination meeting, proofs of debts were placed upon the files of this Court amounting to between £400,000 and £500,000. I will now make two observations upon the Bankruptcy Law of a general nature. The one is, that it gives the creditors a prompt and immediate remedy, and distributes the assets at as early a period as possible; the other is, that it gives the bankrupts the opportunity of having their conduct immediately inquired into and protection extended if their conduct be, as it is on this occasion, honest and honourable. These gentlemen seem to have been the victims of misfortune, and to have been borne down by events over which they could not have any control, and which the most prudent man alive could not have foreseen or guarded against. It would therefore be hard if they could not obtain that protection from this Court which their conduct as traders eminently entitled them to. They stand acquitted in the face of the commercial world of all misconduct, and their position so far from deserving any blame attracts sympathy and kindly feeling, as I am sure will be extended towards them. (His honour then went into the circumstances of the case, and the course of trading pursued by this house since the date at which the balance-sheet commences, attributing their misfortunes wholly to the sudden fluctuations which took place in the price of corn in 1846 and 1847, and concluded by saying)—I do not see what steps the bankrupts could have taken to prevent the great misfortune which has befallen them. I do not see anything culpable in their conduct: I think it is one of those visitations which often occur in extensive trading which is greatly to be lamented, but which it would be cruel to punish the bankrupts for. I feel deeply for these gentlemen; they are suddenly reduced from the high position of British merchants in affluenced eminence to one in which they have nothing left but their good name and their spotless reputation. They leave this court without the slightest reproach of any kind. They carry with them my sincere sympathy, and I believe I may add, the sympathy, the kind feeling, and the good wishes of the whole body of their creditors. I have great pleasure in granting to these gentlemen their certificates."

Mr. Lawrence.—" On behalf of my clients I desire to return to your honour my sincere gratitude, and they wish me to assure you that they prize most highly this expression of your honour's opinion, and that they will entertain a warm sense of your kindness to the end of their lives."

The creditors have received 2s. 8d. in the pound.

Messrs. W. R. ROBINSON & Co.,

Corn Trade.

A meeting of the creditors of Messrs. W. R. Robinson & Co., was held to receive the report of Messrs. Quilter & Co., the accountants appointed at the former meeting to investigate the books, and the following very satisfactory statement of affairs was exhibited :—

DEBTOR.	£	*s.*	*d.*
To sundry creditors unsecured..............................	71,123	14	11
To sundry creditors, partially secured £33,253 13s. 9d., less estimated value of securities £22,839 9s. 10d..............	10,414	3	11
To sundry creditors, wholly secured: estimated value of securities £59,150 3s. 1d., less amount of claims £42,464 4s. 3d.; taken as an asset per contra £16,685 18s. 10d.			
Carried up	£81,537	18	10

	£	s.	d.
Brought up	£81,537	18	10
To liabilities on bills receivable, £60,420 9s. 4d., of which those estimated bad amount to £13,695 10s., less balance with Messrs. Prescott & Co. £3,920 18s. 6d.	9,774	11	6
To sundry liabilities	3,050	0	0
	£94,362	10	4

CREDITOR.

	£	s.	d.
By cash and bills in hand	5,996	10	8
By sundry debtors, considered good, £7,092 7s. 6d.; doubtful, £2,178 15s. 4d., estimated at 6s. 8d., £726; bad, £8,135 8s. 11d.	7,818	7	6
By stock on hand, £19,720 9s. 10d.; add surplus security in the hands of creditors, as per contra, £16,685 18s. 10d.	36,406	8	8
By probable dividends, recoverable from liabilities	5,000	0	0
By surplus, from the private estates of W. R. Robinson, after paying all claims, £43,000; T. M. Robinson, £1,000; M. G. Cotton, £1,500	45,500	0	0
	100,721	6	10
Deduct sundry creditors to be paid in full......	330	17	5
	£100,390	9	5

[Here a surplus is shown to the amount of £6,000.]

This estate it was agreed should be liquidated under inspection, and 20s. in the pound have since been realized for the creditors.

MESSRS. GILES, SON, & Co.,

CORN TRADE.

The following is the statement of affairs of MESSRS. GILES, SON, & Co. presented at the meeting of their creditors:—They suspended on the 13th of August, 1847.

DEBTOR.	£	s.	d.
To sundry creditors, £215,616 18s. 9d.; of which the amount unsecured is	138,659	16	10
To liabilities on bills receivable; of which those considered bad amount to	11,164	18	7
To sundry liabilities	3,000	0	0
	£152,824	15	5

CREDITOR.

	£	s.	d.
By sundry debtors—considered good, £35,694 16s. 8d.; considered doubtful, £7,277 16s. 8d., and estimated at 5s. in the pound, £1,819 9s.	37,514	5	8
By stock in hand, estimated at £44,936 3s. 4d.; surplus stock, &c., in the hands of creditors, £5,076 12s. 5d.	50,012	15	9
By sundry property, valued at	8,975	12	1
	£96,502	13	6
Deduct—sundry creditors, payable in full	5,591	11	8
	£90,911	1	10

Inspectors were immediately chosen to liquidate the estate, which, upon realization, distributed to the extent of 12s. in the pound.

Messrs. W. & J. WOODLEY,

Corn Trade.

The following is the statement of affairs of Messrs. W. & J. Woodley, whose suspension took place on the 27th August, 1847. The assets fell short of the liabilities to the extent only of £9,000, and it was resolved to wind up affairs under inspection.

DEBTOR.	£	s.	d.
To sundry creditors unsecured	87,139	19	4
To creditors, partially secured, £26,210 16s. 9d.; deduct estimated value of securities, £18,000 16s. 6d.	8,210	0	3
To creditors wholly secured—estimated value of securities, £14,986 19s. 5d.; deducting amount of claims, £6,526 7s.; taken as assets per contra, £8,460 12s. 5d.			
To liabilities on contracts	4,159	3	11
To liabilities on bills receivable, considered good, £11,703 2s. 1d.			
	£99,509	3	6

CREDITOR.			
By cash on hand	1,089	3	4
By bills on hand—considered good	2,285	13	7
Doubtful, £1,157 14s. 2d.; and estimated to produce	578	17	1
By sundry debtors—considered good, £18,874 15s. 11d.; and considered doubtful, estimated at £356 10s. 10d.	19,231	6	9
By stock of American and other wheat, flour, &c.	54,292	9	11
By sundry property	9,418	18	11
By surplus securities per contra	8,460	12	5
By life's policies—amount insured on J. W.'s own life £4,000.			
	95,357	2	0
Deduct—Creditors to be paid in full, and expenses of liquidation	4,511	15	0
By amount expected to be paid by J. Fuller towards his share of loss on the American, £5,000.			
	£90,845	7	0

The dividends paid to the creditors made in gross 17s. 7d. in the pound.

Messrs. THOMAS USBORNE & SON,

Corn Trade.

At a meeting of the creditors of Messrs. Thomas Usborne & Son, whose suspension took place at the end of September, 1847, the following was the statement presented:—

DEBTOR.	£	s.	d.
To sundry creditors	56,543	2	0
To liability on acceptances	250	0	0
To T. M. Usborne, £18,346 4s. 3d.; less securities, £16,681 10s.	1,664	14	3
To liabilities on bills receivable	1,000	0	0
	£59,457	16	3

CREDITOR.	£	s.	d.
By cash on hand	9,714	14	5
By bills on hand, viz.—Good, £2,232 8s. 5d.; doubtful, estimated at £2,904 10s. 9d.	5,136	19	2
By sundry debtors:—Good, £9,112 19s. 11d.; doubtful, £8,842 7s. 2d., estimated at £2,210 11s. 9d.	11,323	11	8
By stock	7,549	12	0
By sundry property	1,526	9	0
	35,251	6	3
Deduct—Creditors in full, and expenses of liquidation	1,723	7	5
	£33,527	18	10

The above statement showed a dividend of 11s. 3d. in the pound, and Messrs. Usborne having made a proposition to pay 11s. in the pound in the following manner, namely, 7s. on the 15th of November, 2s. on the 15th of February, and 2s. on the 15th of May, the meeting agreed thereto.

Messrs. HASTIE and HUTCHISON,

Corn Trade.

On the 20th of September, 1847, a meeting was held of the creditors of Messrs. Hastie and Hutchison, whose stoppage took place on the 10th of September; and the following statement, prepared by Messrs. Quilter & Co., the accountants, was exhibited:—

DEBTOR.	£	s.	d.
To sundry creditors unsecured	44,339	7	9
To liabilities on bills receivable as per statement, £24,509 7s. 8d., of which the amount estimated to prove claims is £11,371 14 1, less balance in the Union Bank 5,259 9 1	6,112	5	0
	£50,451	12	9

CREDITOR.	£	s.	d.
By bills receivable on hand, considered good, viz.:—Jones & Co., £79 4s.; Goddard, L., £1,171 17s.; Cox & Co., £18	1,269	1	0
By sundry debtors:—considered good, £26,156 6s. 6d.; considered doubtful, £10,513 5s. 11d., and estimated at £2,000; considered bad, £9,518 18s. 11d.	28,156	6	6
By stock of grain, &c.:—At present prices, on hand	5,564	17	0
By Robert Hastie:—For estimated surplus of his estate, cost £9,004 1s. 1d., and estimated at	5,000	0	0
	£39,990	4	6
Deduct—Creditors to be paid in full, as per statement, £693 15s. 11d.; estimated expenses of liquidation, £500	1,193	15	11
	£38,796	8	7

This statement exhibited a deficiency of only £11,655, and a consequent dividend of 15s. in the pound. This amount Messrs. Hastie & Co. proposed to pay by four instalments, viz.—5s. down, 5s. in four months, 2s. 6d. at nine months, and 2s. 6d. at fifteen months; to which the meeting agreed. It transpired that the firm had sustained bad debts, since the commencement of the corn panic, to the extent of £28,000.

Messrs. NEVINS and ALLEN,

Corn Trade.

The following is the balance-sheet, prepared by Quilter, Ball, & Co. accountants, of the estate of Nevins and Allen, corn factors, whose failure took place, on the 11th August, 1847. It showed about 2s. 3d. in the pound, but the creditors were informed that some of the items had improved since the account was made up. The estate was ordered to be liquidated under inspection:—

DEBTOR.	£	s.	d.	£	s.	d.
To creditors uncovered	..			2,229	6	8
To creditors partially covered	23,223	18	5			
Less value of securities	9,936	13	0			
				13,292	5	5
To creditors wholly secured	12,741	1	2			
Value of securities	21,359	10	8			
Asset per contra	8,618	9	6			
To creditors in respect of endorsements on bad bills receivable	71,237	1	3			
Less securities in hands of holders	18,051	7	5			
				53,185	13	10
To claims in respect of unfulfilled contracts				1,200	0	0
				£69,907	5	11

CREDITOR	£	s.	d.	£	s.	d.
By cash in hand				3,285	0	0
By debtors—considered good	477	14	2			
Estimated produce of £1,204, doubtful debts	301	4	9			
				778	18	11
By stock of wheat, &c.				1,168	10	0
By surplus securities in hands of creditors, per contra	8,618	9	6			
Liable further to holders of bills on failed houses	6,000	0	0			
				2,618	9	6
By sundry property	..			800	0	0
By corn, &c., in the hands of other parties claimed by Nevins and Allen	7,513	0	1			
				8,650	18	5
Deduct rents to be paid in full and expenses of liquidation				524	15	3
				£8,126	3	2

This estate has realized 1s. 10½d. in the pound.

MESSRS. REAY & REAY,

WINE TRADE.

This firm failed in November, 1847. After endeavouring to make a composition in which they were unsuccessful, they gazetted themselves in February, 1848.

The following is a copy of the balance-sheet prepared by Mr. Croysdil; it commences January 1, 1843, and ends April 6, 1848.

DEBTOR.

		£	s.	d.
To creditors		17,692	6	9
Ditto holding securities		11,049	17	11
Ditto liabilities holding securities	15,255 0 11			
Ditto liabilities	21,494 0 0			
		36,749	0	11
		£65,491	5	7
Capital, January 1, 1843		12,013	16	7
John Reay, jun.—				
Office value of policies deposited with Glyn & Co.	3,052 15 0			
Amount borrowed on deposit of policies and brought into the firm in October last	1,800 0 0			
		4,852	15	0
Craven Arms at Coventry, made over to us by J. J. Hart, on granting him an annuity, and which he survived but a short period		2,557	7	10
Profits on trading		69,236	3	1
		£154,151	8	1

CREDITOR.

		£	s.	d.
By debtors—				
Good		3,651	1	3
Doubtful and bad	18,541 19 10			
Estimated to realize	2,250 0 0	2,250	0	0
Losses	£16,291 19 10			
Property taken under fiat	..	10,558	5	9
Property held by creditors—				
Policies on John Reay's (jun.) life	3,052 15 0			
Sundries	12,143 9 2			
		15,196	4	2
Bills of exchange held by creditors as collateral security		2,706	0	7
Liabilities		36,749	0	11
John Reay, jun.—Amount drawn out by him		15,407	11	9
Henry Reay—Amount drawn out by him		3,957	7	5
Expenses in trade		29,179	4	2
Losses	18,204 12 3			
Amount deducted from doubtful and bad debts	16,291 19 10			
		34,496	12	1
		£154,151	8	1

Since passing their final examination, they have obtained their certificates, notwithstanding the opposition of several creditors. The estate, since its administration in bankruptcy, has already produced 4s. in the pound.

MESSRS. JOHN KINGSTON & Co.,

WEST INDIA TRADE.

It was agreed at a meeting of the creditors of Messrs. JOHN KINGSTON & Co., West India merchants, whose failure took place on the 8th February, 1848, that the estate should be liquidated by the process of inspection. From the annexed statement submitted by Mr. Wryghte, the accountant, it would appear that the assets of the firm greatly exceed its liabilities; and although these assets, which chiefly consist of property in the West Indies, may not realize near their estimated amount, it seems certain that the liquidation will, under any circumstances, prove favourable.

CLAIMS.

	£ s. d.	£ s. d.
To sundry creditors		24,953 12 9
Capital to credit of Mr. John Kingston	£47,897 0 5	
	£72,850 13 2	
To liabilities	7,266 13 4	
Of which it is expected will come upon this estate		291 13 4
		£25,245 6 1

ASSETS.

		Ledger balance.	Estimated to realize.
By total amount of cash and bills of exchange in hand		7,196 15 2	6,396 15 2
By book debts—			
Good		3,639 1 6	3,639 1 6
Doubtful	240 9 5		
Bad	3,312 4 9		
		3,552 14 2	
By property in West India estates and mortgages		57,093 13 7	32,033 6 5
By ditto in life policies, &c.		1,368 8 9	553 6 7
		72,850 13 2	42,622 9 8
Private property belonging to Mr. John Kingston—			
Household furniture, plate, and effects		750 0 0	
25 shares in the National Provincial Bank		700 0 0	
50 shares in the Demerara railway—cost		250 0 0	
4 shares in the Colonial Bank		60 0 0	
			1,760 0 0
			£44,382 9 8

No dividend has yet been realized under this estate.

MESSRS. BENSUSAN & Co.,

MOGADOR TRADE.

Appended is the joint balance-sheet of the bankrupts, prepared by Mr. J. HUTTON, creditors' assignee, and accountant to the estate, filed in the Court of Bankruptcy, October the 24th, 1848.

From 1st of January, 1841, to the 24th November, 1847 (date of fiat.)

DEBTOR.

	£ s. d.
To Creditors for cash	32,061 3 0
Creditors for merchandise	14,998 1 10
Carried up	£47,059 4 10

Brought up		£47,059 4 10
To Creditors for trust-monies who have proved on the separate estates of S. L. Bensusan and Jacob Levy Bensusan, as trustees		7,335 2 11
Liabilities on bills drawn by us on our correspondents, or guaranteed		1,416 8 1
Liability for the trust-estate of A. L. Bensusan, and for which we received no value, the estates of S. L. Bensusan and Jacob Levy Bensusan being separately liable for the trusteeship ..		2,151 8 1
Capital on the 1st of January, 1841, as per statement of affairs		1,345 0 6
Profits as under :—		
Merchandize and produce	£36,369 15 6	
Commission	20,948 3 2	
Sundries	1,571 3 9	
		58,889 2 5
		£118,196 6 10

CREDITOR

By debtors :—		
Good	336 19 10	336 19 10
Doubtful	1,024 15 11	1,024 15 11
Bad, carried to losses below	55,598 17 1	
	£56,960 12 10	
Property in the hands of creditors	..	48 4 0
Property realized by Official Assignee	516 4 10	
not disposed of (to September, 1848)	392 12 3	
		908 17 1
Liabilities on bills	..	1,416 8 1
Liability, as per contra	..	2,151 8 1
Trade expenses	..	26,081 9 10
Losses	5,094 19 1	
Bad debts, above	55,598 17 1	
		60,693 16 2
Amount drawn out by partners :—		
M. L. Bensusan	1,556 10 8	
Jacob L. Bensusan	8,564 9 5	
S. L. Bensusan	8,428 15 0	
Joshua L. Bensusan	6,884 12 9	
		25,534 7 10
		£118,196 6 10

The question of the bankrupts' certificates has been decided, so far as the surviving partners are concerned, adversely, as will be perceived by the annexed report of Mr. Commissioner Fonblanque's judgment.

"Court of Bankruptcy, April 18, 1849, before Mr. Commissioner Fonblanque.

"The bankrupts in this case failed in the panic period of 1847, and to-day was named by the Commissioner for giving his judgment on the question of certificate. Messrs. Rixon & Son appeared for the assignees; Mr. Lawrance for the bankrupts.

"His honour, in giving judgment, said—That this fiat was issued in 1847 against the four bankrupts, Moses L. Bensusan, Jacob L. Bensusan, Samuel L. Bensusan, and Joshua L. Bensusan. With respect to the first-named bankrupt, who had died since the fiat was issued, there was little to say, but it might be stated that, from what could be ascertained, there appeared every reason to believe that the management of business, considering his age and infirmities, was past his control. It ought, also, to be noticed, that his expenses had been exceedingly moderate; and, under such circumstances, it might be some consolation to his family and friends to know that the Court, had he lived, would in all probability have granted him his certificate immediately. He was sorry, however, to say, that with regard to the position of the firm generally, the Court could not come to so satisfactory a conclusion. He (the Commissioner) had looked carefully over the voluminous proceedings which had taken place under this estate, and he found that, in January, 1841, the business of this firm with four partners was based upon a nominal capital of £1,345 only,—he said a nominal capital, because, in reality, they then possessed no capital at all, but were, in fact, insolvent, since, included in this estimate of capital were three debts, one of £6,000, due from the old firm of Bensusan and Brandon; a second of £4,000, from the house of Hassan; and a third of £8,000, from Pariente, making a total of what shortly proved to be £18,000, bad debts. Viewing, then, their situation in this respect, and giving them credit for their assumed amount of £1,345, they were in truth upwards of £16,000 worse than nothing. From 1841 up to the time of their bankruptcy, the amount of profits was stated at £58,000; but then the item of trade expenses and losses was put down at no less a sum than £86,000, so that there was a deficiency on that account of £27,000; and yet, in spite of that deficiency, the partners had managed to absorb, in the shape of private expenses, the immoderate sum of £25,000. The result of such a course of trading might be easily conceived. This estate, with debts and liabilities to the extent of £58,000, possessed assets, from which not more than £1,200 would be realized; and therefore, allowing for the costs of investigation, it was impossible that the joint estate could be estimated to pay 4d. in the pound. And now to enter more minutely into their conduct as traders. Their books were carelessly kept, so much so, that it had been found utterly useless to depend upon them, and hence since the bankruptcy it had been deemed necessary to raise new accounts, for the purpose of elucidating their affairs. The bankrupts, associated as they were in family, could not, therefore, be exonerated on that ground, and must take the consequences of that dereliction of duty which attached to rendering insufficient accounts. But there was another objection in relation to accounts which weighed in the mind of the Court, and that was a certain secrecy and mystery which had been observed in keeping the books. One of the brothers complained of not having been allowed to see the accounts, notwithstanding his urgent representations, and he (the Commissioner) must express his opinion that whenever such secrecy was practised, it must be regarded as a badge of misconduct. The reputable manner of keeping books was to keep them in such a manner that every body interested might be well acquainted with their contents, in order that, if error or misstatement arose, it might at once receive correction, and that they might (if ever it were required) reveal to creditors, in a clear and straightforward course, the whole of the trader's transactions. Having considered the way in which the books were kept, attention might properly be directed to the question of capital when the bankrupts commenced their business. If at that date they really considered themselves in a solvent condition, that delusion, if they ever entertained it, was soon dissipated, for in that year Bensusan and Brandon, who owed them £6,000, failed, and their affairs were wound up. This large loss, compared with their estimated capital of £1,300, should have proved a warning to them, and had they acted prudently then, they ought to have made a strict inquiry into their position, and called in their creditors, or, on the other hand, reduced considerably their dealings. But this first warning was not enough—there was a second, for Hassan, with whom they appeared to be connected, failed in 1843, £4,000 in their debt—another warning, which it might have been thought, would have induced discretion, but no heed was taken of it. A third warning followed, and Pariente, owing the firm £8,000, failed in the year 1843 or 1844. Large as the gross amount of these three losses was, it had apparently created little effect upon the bankrupts. Their duty at such a juncture, especially after the third warning, was to have suspended payment and distributed their estate, whatever might have remained, and, blameable as their conduct might have been considered after the second warning, they would have been less liable to severe condemnation than they were now. On this point alone two years' suspension would scarce be adequate punishment. But, having looked at their conduct with respect to the joint estate, to carry the inquiry throughout it was requisite to look at their conduct independently in connexion with their separate estates. He (the Commissioner) had already stated that £25,000 had been drawn out of the firm in the shape of private expenditure. Referring to figures, it seemed that Samuel had taken out £8,400, Jacob, £8,600, and Joshua, £6,800. According to these amounts, Samuel had lived at the rate of £1,100 a year, and Jacob at £1,600 a year, sums quite unjustifiable. Joshua's expenditure was more moderate, and much beneath his brothers.

"Mr. Lawrance.—And he has in addition given up £1,500 to his separate estate.

"Mr. Commissioner Fonblanque.—The dividends are as follows:—Jacob pays 6d. on his separate estate, Samuel pays 1s. 5d., and Joshua 10s. in the pound, with probably in the latter case a further distribution. The father's expenditure was moderate in the extreme, not being at the rate of more than £250 a year, and his separate estate would pay 15s. in the pound. He (the Commissioner) looking at these facts, could only come to the conclusion that the private expenses of every one of the surviving bankrupts were wholly unjustifiable; Joshua's least so, Jacob's most so. The application of trust funds was a painful topic to advert to, and Samuel stood in that respect condemned, for he had misappropriated between £4,000 and £5,000 which belonged to his wife and children. In another breach of trust connected with the family of Abraham Levi Samuel and Jacob were each identified, and their conduct deserved strong reprehension. Whenever cases of breaches of trust came under his (the Commissioner's) notice he was inclined to exercise the administration of the law with severity. It was not only the serious evil inflicted upon the parties properly entitled to the funds misappropriated that was to be considered, but also the means such acts afforded for raising fictitious credit, and he would never suffer breaches of trust to go unpunished, because persons when reduced to extreme exigencies of the kind must be fully aware of the desperate nature of their position. Reviewing, therefore, the conduct of the bankrupts, so far as concerned their joint estate, and also their separate estates, and taking into consideration that Joshua, although as culpable as the rest with regard to the joint estate, stood the lowest in the scale of private expenses, and was not implicated in the breaches of trust, and regulating his decision in that direction, he should award (recollecting the length of time which had elapsed since the issue of the fiat) a suspension of his certificate for 10 months; Jacob, whose expenditure was the most excessive, and who had been a party to the breaches of trust, his certificate must be suspended 18 months; and Samuel, who among other misconduct, stood most implicated in breaches of trust, must be adjourned for two years. His honour concluded by saying that as, with the exception of the breaches of trust, he did not find frauds to have been committed on creditors, he should give the bankrupts protection; but he added that when his mind was first brought to bear upon the question he had doubted the propriety of this course, or whether he ought not to have refused granting certificates, particularly in the case of Samuel, altogether."

Messrs. LEAF, BARNETT, SCOTSON, & Co.,

Warehousemen.

A numerous meeting of the creditors of Messrs. Leaf, Barnett, Scotson, & Co., whose failure was announced on the 27th of November, took place on the 15th of December, 1847, Mr. Twentyman in the chair; when the subjoined statement, prepared by Quilter, Ball, & Co., was submitted for consideration:—

DEBTOR.

	£	s.	d.	£	s.	d.
To sundry creditors—						
On trade account	47,926	15	6			
On cash ditto	26,157	3	4			
Sundries under £20 each	1,151	8	1			
				75,235	6	11
To liabilities on bills receivable, £50,164 19s. 6d., of which the amount estimated to prove claims on the estate is	11,598	4	10			
Less balances owing by persons holding the above bad bills	1,258	4	4			
				10,340	0	6
				£85,575	7	5

CREDITOR.

	£ s. d.	£ s. d.
By cash and bills on hand—		
Cash at Lubbock & Co.'s	1,129 18 6	
Do. at Bank of England	2 9 7	
Do. at house	42 11 2	
Bills considered good	2,864 7 8	
Do. doubtful, £1,316 3s. 9d., estimated at	658 1 10	
		4,697 8 9
By sundry debtors—		
Considered good	26,337 9 8	
Do. doubtful, £8,592 17s. 8d., estimated at	4,296 8 10	
		30,633 18 6
By stock in trade as per statement at cost	..	49,660 6 6
By estimated dividends to arise from bad debts, already written off	1,194 11 4	
Ditto, from bad liabilities, amounting to £11,598 4s. 10d., after providing for the payment in full to the holders thereof, say	2,500 0 0	
		3,694 11 4
By George Sharpe & Co., Dublin:—		
Balance remaining owing by them, secured by leases of premises in Grafton-street, Dublin, estimated at	..	1,000 0 0
By surplus security with W. West	..	764 4 0
By furniture, wine, &c., estimated at	..	352 12 6
		90,803 1 7
Less sundries having priority, rents, salaries, &c.	..	1,723 19 8
		£89,079 1 11

"It will be perceived," says a report of the meeting, "that the account here presented shows 20s. in the pound, with a surplus of £3,500; but it was explained by Mr. Lloyd, the professional representative of the suspended firm, that a considerable allowance would have to be made for depreciation in realizing the stock, as well as for a large amount of bad debts incurred since the books had been adjusted. Under the circumstances of the case, the offer Leaf, Barnett, & Co. felt themselves competent to make, should the creditors not manifest a disposition to pursue any other course of liquidation, was 15s. in the pound, payable by equal instalments, with security for the last, at three, six, and nine months. As this proposal did not meet with the approval of the meeting, a long discussion ensued upon the real position of the house, and the expectation recently held out of the discharge of all claims in full, in the course of which a variety of questions were asked relative to the connexion of Captain Carnegie with the firm. It was stated that this gentleman was formerly a partner, but that a dissolution occurred in 1846, although it was not regularly gazetted till the middle of the present year. It further appeared, that he is a claimant against Leaf, Barnett, & Co., for £12,000, on which he is entitled to rank equally with all other creditors, and it seemed to be a question whether he would consent to a delay in the receipt of his dividends to accommodate the other parties having claims on the estate. After much conversation on the best means to be adopted for obtaining a better distribution than 15s. in the pound, a creditor suggested that the shortest way of coming to a definite understanding on the point was to reject that offer, and at the same time to intimate that 17s. 6d. would be accepted. With the view of consulting the partners on this amended proposition, a committee of four of the creditors was constituted, and after an interview with Mr. Barnett, who was in attendance, they returned, and stated as the result, that having carefully weighed the whole circumstances, they were of opinion that Leaf, Barnett, Scotson, & Co. should be permitted to arrange at the rate of 16s. in the pound. It being understood that this amount would be paid in the same manner and at the same dates as the 15s., and that the committee would pursue the necessary steps to obtain, if possible, security for the last instalment. Resolutions were passed authorizing proceedings for a compromise on the terms stated. In conclusion it is to be mentioned, that testimony was borne by the creditors to the correctness of the whole of the business transactions of the suspended firm, while at the same time, justice was rendered them for having at once submitted their affairs to investigation, when they found that their solvency could not be relied upon."

Messrs. JAMES and WILLIAM MORLEY,

Warehousemen.

A meeting of the creditors of Messrs. James and William Morley, whose failure took place on the 14th October, 1847, was held on the 26th of the same month. Mr. Ainsworth, on behalf of certain Manchester creditors, took the chair, and the following statement was read:—

DEBTOR.	£	s.	d.	£	s.	d.
To trade creditors	62,749	13	4			
To cash creditors	30,558	18	11			
				93,308	12	3
To bills accepted for Messrs. J. & W. Morley's accommodation				9,196	8	11
To bills accepted by J. & W. Morley for the accommodation of other parties, which will be claimed on this estate				2,463	7	10
To bills receivable, discounted, drawn upon parties who have failed, £17,061 7s. 4d.—Deduct cash and securities held by bill-holders £2,298 10s. 11d.				14,762	16	5
(To liability upon bills receivable, considered good £55,542 8s. 11d.)						
				£119,731	5	5

CREDITOR.	£	s.	d.
By stock in trade at cost	35,948	7	4
By book debts, good	44,856	0	2
Doubtful and bad, £3,421 10s. 9d.; estimated at	562	17	0
By cash in house	367	17	4
By bills of exchange in house	644	18	6
By value of railway shares	60	0	0
By policies on customers' lives	447	17	9
By improved rental of a house in Friday-street	200	0	0
By bills of exchange, amounting to £20,474 2s. 2d., deposited as collateral security for cash advances of £13,843 7s. 10d., supposed will realize the estate above the advances	2,723	12	9
By leases of premises in Carey-lane, valued at £9,500,—mortgaged for £8,000	1,500	0	0
By furniture, fixtures, &c.	1,689	3	0
By freehold and leasehold property, mortgaged to creditors and deducted from their debts £3,300.			
	89,000	13	10
Less rent, salaries, taxes, &c.	983	8	0
	88,017	5	10
By value (above the mortgage) of premises No. 3, Nassau-place, Commercial-road	1,200	0	0
By debt due from the estate of W. Morley, sen. (amount not stated)			
	£89,217	5	10

"The result of a discussion, which did not conclude without angry comments escaping from some of the creditors" says the report, "elicited from Messrs. Morley a proposal for the arrangement of their affairs, and it was intimated on their behalf that, allowing for deductions to the extent of nearly £19,000 on the collection of debts, realization of stock, &c., grounded on their own conviction that the statement laid before the meeting gave much too favourable a view of their estate, they thought they could offer 11s. in the pound, payable at three, six, and nine months' date, loan creditors to the extent of £1,500 having consented to enter into a bond not to receive payment until all other claims were satisfied. After a little consideration the proposition was acceded to, and resolutions were passed for its confirmation. It is stated that this estate includes nearly 400 creditors."

Messrs. TANNER & WARD,

Leather Factors.

These parties, who failed in November, 1847, it will be observed, passed through the ordeal of the Court of Bankruptcy, an attempt to pay a composition having failed. Their certificate sitting before Mr. Commissioner Shepherd, was on the 8th April, 1848.

Mr. Lane opposed on behalf of the assignees. Mr. Lawrance supported.

The balance-sheet which commences January, 1844, and ends February, 1848, contains the following items:—

DEBTOR.	£	s.	d.
Creditors	19,846	8	6
Gross profits	13,382	12	5
J. Ward, capital account	1,818	11	6
Liabilities	4,343	0	4
Error in balance	10	0	0
	39,100	12	9

CREDITOR.	£	s.	d.
By debts	6,107	17	5
Property	3,258	12	8
Expenditure	12,129	19	8
Loss by railway shares	6,381	1	11
Loss by the realization of property	571	2	3
Amount due by Tanner to the firm in January, 1844	4,396	10	8
Drawn out by Ward	1,899	16	6
Liabilities	4,343	0	4
Balance	12	11	4
	£39,100	12	9

The grounds of opposition urged by Mr. Lane were, fraudulent preference, extravagant expenditure, speculating in railway shares, erroneous accounts, sales to their principals, and the smallness of the profits.

The first ground was not proved, as there is an action pending for the recovery of the amounts paid to creditors, whom the assignees say were unlawfully favoured; the second was established, and so was the third; the fourth fell to the ground; and the fifth was admitted.

Mr. Lawrance, in reference to the objections which had been maintained, said, the business in which his clients had been engaged almost inevitably entailed heavy losses and great expenditure upon them. They received large consignments of leather from the manufacturers, who drew upon them, the consignees, and the consignees were obliged to honour their drafts, whether the goods respecting which they were drawn were sold or not. As to the main charge—dealing in railway shares—he acknowledged that his clients in common with all other persons, high and low, rich and poor, were swept into the vortex of railway speculation during the period of the mania in 1845. His honour well knew that the whole community was mad after railway shares. His clients held a large number of shares at the period when The *Times*—which every honest man must admit had done good service to the country—opened a battery upon the unfortunate system, which fell to the ground, in short when the public had, through the exertion of The *Times*, been brought to their senses. From that period such speculation was crushed, and his clients, who held shares to the amount of more than £5,000, were obliged to hand them over to the official assignee, who sold them for about £300. The learned gentleman concluded by saying that the estate had already paid 5s. in the pound, and would pay something more, and hoping that the court would not deem it necessary to suspend the certificate for any lengthened period.

His honour suspended the certificate for six months.

Messrs. HUGHESDON and MACKAY,

East India Trade.

The annexed report of the proceedings under the Fiat in Bankruptcy issued in London against this firm, will furnish a succinct narrative of their affairs. The bankrupts, Joseph Hughesdon and Alexander Mackay, were East India merchants, having places of business in Calcutta and in Chandernagore. Their failure took place in December, 1847, and the fiat was issued in April, 1848. This was a last examination meeting. Mr. Lawrance supported, Mr. Roxborough opposed; Mr. Coleman attended as accountant on behalf of the Messrs. Henderson, for whom Mr. Murray was solicitor.

Court of Bankruptcy, April 17, 1849, before Mr. Commissioner Fane.

" The bankrupts traded under the firm or style of Hughesdon, Brothers. Their London correspondents were Messrs. Henderson. It was stated that the immediate cause of Messrs. Hughesdon's bankruptcy was their holding and remitting, in September, 1847, bills on Cockerell, Larpent, & Co., to the amount of between £20,000 and £30,000. The bills arrived here by the mail of the 24th of September, 1847, the very day on which Messrs. Cockerell stopped payment; and that latter event induced Messrs. Henderson to refuse acceptance of Hughesdon's drafts, and Messrs. Henderson, fearing the downfall of the house of Hughesdon, Brothers, in the following month sent out a gentleman named Heugh, to India, to protect their interests. The refusal of Messrs. Henderson to accept Messrs. Hughesdon's drafts, and the stoppage of Messrs. Cockerell, at once paralysed the operations of the house of Messrs. Hughesdon, and in November, 1847, meetings of their creditors were held in Calcutta. The creditors, finding it impossible to agree to a private arrangement with the bankrupts, proceeded against them in the Calcutta Insolvent Court, and an adjudication against them was advertised on the 17th of December. Mr. Hughesdon passed through the Calcutta Insolvent Court, but not without a reprimand from the judge, who said that Mr. Hughesdon had been guilty of secrecy and suppression in his transactions with Mr. Heugh, the agent of Messrs. Henderson.

" The following is a copy of the joint balance-sheet on the files of the Court. It commences January 1, 1847, and ends April 1848.

DEBTOR.	£	s.	d.
To creditors	69,857	19	7
,, Creditors on account, as yet unadjusted, and holding securities, their right to retain which is disputed by the assignees	27,870	11	9
,, Hughesdon, Brothers, (late firm), amount introduced into new firm	8,303	19	1
,, Profits	11,291	1	10
,, Balance	275	5	5
	£117,598	17	8

CREDITOR.	£	s.	d.
By debtors, English, (bad)	49	13	7
,, Property in hands of assignees in London	5,258	14	5
,, Debtors, foreign (good)	300	0	0
,, Do. (doubtful)	4,420	17	6
,, Property in hands of assignees in India	2,735	4	10
,, Property in the hands of creditors, claimed by assignees	23,553	17	10
,, Goods in Calcutta and cash in Bank of Bengal, proceeds of such goods claimed by creditors	16,553	19	9
,, Expenses of business	1,513	10	1
,, Interest	1,636	12	9
,, Brokerage	973	3	8
,, Commission	1,552	1	1
,, Insurance on ship " Sir R. Seppings"	475	0	0
,, Partners' drawings:—			
J. Hughesdon	1,289	6	3
A. Mackay	1,331	4	4
,, Losses	55,955	11	7
	£117,598	17	8

" And the separate balance-sheet of Joseph Hughesdon is as follows :—

DEBTOR.	£	s.	d.	CREDITOR.	£	s.	d.
To creditors	21,923	1	5	By debtors :—			
,, Capital, 1st Jan. 1847	8,600	0	0	Good	30	0	0
,, Drawings from firm	1,289	6	3	Doubtful	150	16	10
,, Gifts from relations	250	0	0	Bad	82	16	10
				,, Property	1,195	0	0
				,, Debtor, on unadjusted account	978	3	7
				,, Amount paid into new firm	8,303	19	1
				,, Commission	810	6	6
				,, Interest	332	12	9
				,, Private expenses	707	0	0
				,, Losses	19,471	12	1
	£32,062	7	8		£32,062	7	8

" Mackay's separate balance-sheet shows debts and liabilities £260, the drawings from the firm £1,331; and the assets are—furniture £450, share in Calcutta insurance office £50; and personal expenses, £891.

" The principal creditors are the Messrs. Henderson, and it is in respect to their claim and the mode they took of securing it, that so much discussion and delay has occurred. Messrs. R. and J. Henderson, who carry on business in Mincing-lane, appear upon the balance-sheet as creditors for £27,870. These gentlemen seized upon two vessels of the bankrupts, the Sir Robert Seppings and the City of Palaces. It is alleged that the cost of these two vessels was nearly £22,000. Messrs. Henderson sold them for £15,600. They also seized upon and sold certain sugar consigned to them by the bankrupts in liquidation of their claim, and which realized £1,659. The Messrs. Henderson claim a further amount in respect to a balance standing in their favour in the books of a former firm, the liabilities of which the present bankrupts took upon themselves, and also in respect of losses upon the realization of produce.

" The Commissioner observed, that the Messrs. Henderson had contrived to get hold of the lion's share of the estate, whilst the creditors had but the jackal's. He thought the account between Messrs. Henderson and the bankrupts ought to be further inquired into, and did not at all wonder that the body of the creditors were dissatisfied with the conduct of the Messrs. Henderson.

" The property consists of cash in the Bengal Bank amounting to 552 rupees, and rum, sugar, and saltpetre. There is also a large quantity of other goods in Calcutta, of the estimated value of £18,000, which Messrs. Henderson also claim.

" Lawrance contended that the bankrupts had made out the best accounts in their power, and that the differences or litigation between Messrs. Henderson and the body of the creditors ought not to prevent their passing.

" Mr. Whitmore, the official assignee, said he believed the bankrupts had furnished just and true accounts, and the best that under the circumstances they could render, their books being in India, and they not having the means of copying them.

" The Commissioner allowed them to pass, but at the same time acceded to the request of Mr. Roxborough that an accountant should be appointed to investigate into and report upon the transactions between Messrs. Henderson and the bankrupts.

" Passed accordingly."

LIST OF FAILURES,

ALPHABETICALLY ARRANGED,

Commencing with August, 1847, *and concluding with December*, 1848;

EXHIBITING AT ONE VIEW

The Description of the several Firms, the Nature of their Trading, and the Locality of their Operations.

A.

Alexander, L. & Co.,	Corn Trade,	London.
Alison, Cumberlege, & Co.,	South American Trade,	Do.
Abbott, Nottingham, & Co.,	Warehousemen,	Do.
Abbott, W.,	Stock Exchange,	Do.
Arkell, A.,	Stock Exchange,	Do.
Alston, Bevan, & Co.,	Mediterranean Trade,	Do.
Ashburner, T.,	Leather Factor,	Liverpool.
Atherton, W.,	Merchant,	Do.
Ainsworth, D.,	Warehouseman,	Manchester.
Armstrong, J. A.,	Merchant,	Do.
Anderson, J. & Co.,	South American Trade,	Glasgow.
Anderson, McGregor, & Co.,	West India Trade,	Do.
Ayrshire Iron Company,	Iron Trade,	Do.
Abingdon and Wantage Banking Company,	(H. Knapp),	Abingdon.
Adams, Warren, & Co.,	Bankers,	Shrewsbury and Market Drayton
Ackland, Boyd, & Co.,	Merchants,	Ceylon.
Adam, H. & Co.,	Merchants,	Mauritius.
Adan, A. J.,	Banker,	Brussells.
Aubin, R.,	Banker,	Marseilles.
Arbid, L. & Co.,	Merchants,	Leghorn.
Alessio, E. & Co.,	Corn Merchants,	Genoa.
Arnemann and Son,	Bankers,	Altona.
Albert, F. X.,	Banker,	Madrid.

B.

Booker, Sons, & Co.,	Corn Trade,	London.
Bensusan, M. L. & Co.,	African Merchants,	Do.

Burnell & Co.,	Coal Trade,	London.
Bernoulli, E.,	Levant Trade,	Do.
Barclay, Brothers, & Co.,	Mauritius Trade,	Do.
Barnes, F. & Co.,	Hardwaremen,	Do.
Boyds and Thomas,	East India Trade,	Do.
Bruce, Buxton, & Co.,	Bill Brokers,	Do.
Brightman, J. & Co.,	East India Trade,	Do.
Braine, G. T.,	East India Trade,	Do.
Brown, Todd, & Co.,	Provision Trade,	Liverpool.
Brooke and Wilson,	Shipowners,	Do.
Barton, Irlam, & Higginson,	E. & W. India Merchants,	Do.
Berey, Young, & Co.,	Cotton Brokers,	Do.
Blain & Co.,	Corn Dealers,	Do.
Branckner, J. B. & Son,	Brokers,	Do.
Brownrigg & Co.,	East India Trade,	Do.
Byrne, A. E.,	Merchant,	Do.
Blake, G. & J.,	Soap Boilers,	Do.
Burts, Watson, & Co.,	Merchants,	Manchester.
Birley, Corrie, & Co.,	East India Trade,	Do.
Brodie, W. B. & Co.,	Bankers,	Salisbury.
Brodie and King,	Bankers,	Shaftesbury.
Buchan, R.,	Broker,	Glasgow.
Baillie, Honeyman, & Co.,	Merchants,	Do.
Bertram and Parkinson.	General Merchants,	Newcastle-upon-Tyne.
Bartley & Co.,	Manufacturers,	Halifax.
Barlow, H. & Co.,	Merchants,	Mauritius.
Birley, Corrie, & Co.,	East India Trade,	Calcutta.
Baudon & Co.,	Bankers,	Paris.
Bechet & Co.,	Bankers,	Do.
Bourget & Co.,	Discount Bankers,	Do
Bass, M.,	Banker,	Do.
Bruyn & Sons,	Sugar Refiners,	Amsterdam.
Breebart, N.,	Merchant,	Do.
Bleecker and Toosting,	Money Dealers,	Do.
Beeldsnyder, M.,	Money Dealer,	Do.
Boissevain, J.,	Money Dealer,	Do.
Beyfus, Brothers,	Bankers,	Frankfort.
Baert, A.,	Merchant,	Do.
Braasch & Co.,	Merchants,	Hamburgh.
Benet, L. & Co.,	Engineers,	Marseilles.
Badetti, M.,	Greek Trade,	Do.
Busse & Co.,	Bankers,	Berlin.
Bertrand, N. & Co.,	Merchants,	Courtray.
Briard, H.,	Banker,	Mons.
Boutaux, De la Hante, & Co.,	Bankers,	Lyons.

Barthlingth, J. H.,	Merchant,	St. Petersburgh.
Bonaffé & Co.,	Merchants,	Havre.
Barnwell & Co.,	Merchants,	New York.
Bogart, E.,	Commission Merchant,	Do.
Ballard, Vale, & Co.,	Dry-goods Trade,	Boston.

C.

Coventry and Sheppard,	Corn Trade,	London.
Castellain, Sons, & Co.,	Merchants,	Do.
Cockerell, Larpent, & Co.,	East India Trade,	Do.
Cockburn & Co.,	Bankers & Army Agents,	Do.
Cockburn & Co.,	Wine Merchants,	Do.
Coppers Miners (The Company of, in England),	Miners, &c., &c.,	Do.
Clagget, W. T.,	American Trade,	Do.
Cruickshank, J. P. & Co.,	E. & W. India Trade,	Do.
Coates and Hillard,	American Trade,	Do.
Curtis, L. S.,	Hide Factor,	Do.
Cohen, Judah, & Sons,	West India Trade,	Do.
Cotesworth, Powell, & Pryor,	Brazilian and Spanish American Trade,	Do.
Clay, Wm. & Co.,	Warehousemen,	Do.
Capper, G. and Nephew,	Irish Trade,	Do.
Cornthwaite & Co.,	Tea Dealers,	Liverpool.
Carter and Baines,	Merchants,	Do.
Coleman and Todd,	Share Brokers,	Do.
Campbell, J. G., & Co.,	W. India & Mexican Trade,	Do.
Cooper, E. M. & Co.,	Manufacturers,	Manchester.
Coates, Hillard, & Co.,	Warehousemen,	Do.
Cowrill, P.,	Calico Printer,	Do.
Cargill, Headlam, & Co.,	East India Trade,	Newcastle-upon-Tyne.
Clarke, J. P.,	Merchant,	Leicester.
Cowan, Smith, & Co.,	Corn Agents,	Glasgow.
Campbell and Batty,	Agents,	Do.
Campbell, Harvey, & Co.,	Silk Merchants,	Do.
Caird & Co.,	Steam Ship Builders,	Greenock.
Cockerell & Co.,	East India Trade,	Calcutta.
Church, Lake, & Co.,	East India Trade,	Do.
Colville, Gilmore, & Co.,	East India Trade,	Do.
Crooke, H. & A.,	East India Trade,	Do.
Carr, Tagore, & Co.,	East India Trade,	Calcutta.
Collomb and Iselin,	Merchants,	New York.
Cohen, Julius,	Banker,	Paris.
Chedaux, O. I. & Co.,	Bankers,	Do.

Continental Flax Co.,	Manufacturers,	Boulogne.
Crozet, Nephew, & Co.,	Merchants,	Marseilles.
Chataud, Sons, & Desages,	Merchants,	Do.
Cucurney, Uncle, & Co.,	General Merchants,	Do.
Chancel, Brothers,	Drysalters,	Do.
Commercial Bank of Antwerp,	Bankers,	Antwerp.
Carp & Co.,	Money Dealers,	Amsterdam.
Courant & Co.,	Merchants,	Havre.
Cochetaux & Co.,	Manufacturers,	Lisle.
Cohn, L. B.,	Banker,	Berlin.
Conte, F. A.,	Banker,	Cadiz.
Calcagne, G.,	Money Broker,	Genoa.
Custe & Co ,	Merchants,	Do.
Cropp and Marchand,	Merchants,	Hamburgh.

D.

Douglas, C. & Son,	Corn Trade,	London.
De Mattos and De Leon,	General Merchants,	Do.
Duffell, J.,	Stock Exchange,	Do.
Durand and McKenzie,	American Trade,	Do.
Day, Binns, & Co.,	Provision Trade,	Do.
Dalgleish & Co.,	Merchants,	Liverpool and Glasgow.
De Jersey & Co.,	Merchants & Manufacturers,	Manchester.
Downie, A. & J.,	Wool Trade,	Glasgow.
Denny, D. & A.,	Corn Trade,	Do.
Dickson, A. & Co.,	Corn Trade,	Belfast.
Dennison & Co.,	Provision Trade,	Limerick.
Deaves, Brothers,	Russia Trade,	Cork.
Darncott, Adams, & Co.,	Merchants,	Trinidad.
Danger & Co.,	Bankers,	Paris.
De la Chaume, E. & Co.,	Bankers,	Do.
De la Hante & Co.,	Bankers,	Do.
D'Eichthal and Son,	Bankers,	Do.
Devot & Co.,	Merchants,	Havre.
De Pierre, J.,	Merchants,	Do.
Dubois & Co.,	Havre Commercial Bank,	Do.
Defosse and Noete,	Bankers,	Antwerp.
D'Andouard & Co.,	Seed Crushers,	Marseilles.
Delvaux & Co.,	Bankers,	Mons.
De Court, I. F. & Co.,	Merchants,	Dordt.
Dirks, Brothers,	Commission Agents,	Hamburg.
De Costa,	Money Dealer,	Amsterdam.
De Haan & Co.,	Money Dealers,	Do.
Durand, Delapanche, & Co.,	Commercial Jt.-stock Bank,	Rouen.

Dervieu, Sen. & Co.,	Corn Trade,	Algeria.
Darby, G. F. & Co.,	Merchants,	New York.
Dale & Co.,	Produce Merchants,	Do.
De Castro & Co.,	West India Trade,	Porto Rico.

E.

Evans, T. H.,	Stock Exchange,	London.
Eykin, W.,	Stock Exchange,	Do.
Edwards & Co., J.,	Wool Brokers,	Liverpool.
Ewing, Anderson, & Co.,	East India Trade,	Manchester.
Eccles, Burnley, & Co.,	West India Trade,	Glasgow.
Ewing & Co.,	East India Trade,	Calcutta.
Enet, G. R. & Co.,	General Merchants,	Hamburg.
Elliott, W. & Co.,	Merchants,	Do.
Ewald & Co.,	Commission Merchants,	Do.
Excels & Co.,	Corn Trade,	Venice.
Emanuel and Van Clief,	Produce Merchants,	New York.

F.

Fraser, Neilson & Co.,	West India Trade,	London.
Fry, Griffiths, & Co.,	Colonial Brokers,	Do.
Farrand, R.,	Corn Factor,	Do.
Fraser, W. Tulloch,	East India Trade,	Do.
Froske & Co.,	Shipowners,	Liverpool.
Farbridge, R. & S.,	East India & Russia Trade,	Manchester.
Farthing, Son, & Co.,	Merchants,	Hull.
Flood & Co.,	Bankers,	Honiton.
Ferguson, Watson, & Co.,	Silk Merchants,	Glasgow.
Forrestor, R.,	Warehouseman,	Ditto.
Ford, B. T. & Co.,	East India Trade,	Calcutta.
Fourchon, Philip,	Banker and Money Dealer,	Paris.
Fraser & Co.,	Merchants,	Antwerp.
Forbin, Janson, & Co.,	Sugar Refiners,	Marseilles.
Flersheim, L. H.,	Banker,	Frankfort.
Fonvent, M. & Co.,	Bankers,	Namur.
Fetschow and Son,	Bankers,	Berlin.
Fox and Livingstone,	Merchants,	New York.
Fales and Dana,	Dry-goods Trade,	Boston.

G.

Gower Nephew, A. A. & Co.,	Mauritius Trade,	London.
Giles, Son, & Co.,	Corn Trade,	Do.
General Maritime Association,	Insurance Brokers,	Do.

Gates, Coates, Bartlett, & Co.,	Warehousemen,	London.
Gabain & Co.,	German Trade,	Do.
Gouger and Stewart,	East India Trade,	Do.
Gregg, H. and G.,	Corn Trade,	Liverpool.
Gazebrooke & Co.,	Merchants,	Do.
Gardner, R.,	Spinner,	Manchester.
Gael & Co.,	Spinners,	Do.
Glover, F. H.,	Merchant,	Manchester.
Gibson and Sturt,	Bankers,	St. Alban's.
Grundy & Co.,	Bankers,	Bridport.
Gellows & Co.,	Spinners,	Preston.
Gales, J.,	Ship Builder,	Sunderland.
Gemmel Brothers,	East India Trade,	Glasgow.
Gilmour and Kerr,	Spinners,	Do.
Gray and Roxburgh,	Merchants,	Greenock.
Gibson, Read, Davidson, & Co.,	Mill Proprietors and Merchants,	Ceylon.
Green & Co.,	Merchants,	Do.
Gouin & Co.,	Bankers,	Paris.
Ganeron's Joint Stock Bank,	Bankers,	Do.
Gontard, S. F. and Sons,	Bankers,	Frankfort.
Goldschmidtson & Co.,	Bankers,	Amsterdam.
Guerro & Co.,	Spanish Trade,	Marseilles.
Grosjean, Nephews,	Bankers,	Brussells.

H.

Heilbut, Rubens, & Co.,	American Trade,	London.
Hanbury and Wright,	Stock Exchange,	Do.
Hadden & Sons,	Worsted Spinners,	Do. and Aberdeen.
Hawkins, J. H.,	Stock Exchange,	Do.
Howard & Co.,	Colonial Brokers,	Do.
Hadlow, W. S.,	Stock Exchange,	Do.
Hastie and Hutchison,	Corn Trade,	Do.
Hemingway & Co.,	African Trade,	Liverpool.
Hargreaves & Co.,	Merchants,	Do.
Higgins, V. and Sons,	Iron Trade,	Do.
Hamilton, W. S. & Co.,	West India Trade,	Dublin.
Henry & Co.,	Calico Printers,	Do.
Hughesdon, Brothers,	East India Trade,	Calcutta.
Hawarth, Hardman, & Co.,	East India Trade,	Do.
Hickey, Bailey, & Co.,	East India Trade,	Do.
Heine, J. and Sons,	Stock Brokers,	Hamburg.
Heuss and Mencke,	Merchants,	Do.
Hirschfield and Wolff,	Bankers,	Berlin.

Heyman, M.,	Banker,	Berlin.
Henry Brothers,	Merchants,	Marseilles.
Hurlbut, E. D. & Co.,	Merchants,	New York.
Henshaw, Ward, & Co.,	Drug Trade,	Boston.
Hays, La Fontaine, & Co.,	Merchants,	Constantinople.

I. & J.

Johnson, Cole, & Co.,	East India Trade,	London.
Jones, W. & Co.,	Merchants,	Liverpool.
Jevons, Sons, & Co.,	Iron Trade,	Do.
Just, Z.,	Manufacturer,	Manchester.
James, Nephew, & Co.,	Merchants,	Do.
Imreay, R.,	Alkali Manufacturer,	Newcastle.
Jaeger, W. T.,	Banker,	Frankfort.
Iselin, W.,	Merchant,	Havre.
Jacobs, L. W. A.,	Merchant,	Hamburg.

K.

Kelsall & Co.,	East India Trade,	London and Manchester.
Kingston, John, & Co.,	West India Trade,	London.
King, Melvil & Co.,	Corn Trade,	Do.
Kirkpatrick, & Co.,	Provision Trade,	Liverpool.
Kershaw, Hilliard, & Co.,	Manufacturers,	Manchester.
Kaye, W. H.,	Merchant,	Huddersfield.
Kilgour and Leith,	West India Trade,	Glasgow.
Kewney & King,	Bankers,	Grantham.
Kelsall & Co.,	East India Trade,	Calcutta.
Königswater, L. S.,	Merchant & Money Dealer,	Paris.
Klecks & Co.,	Bankers,	Breslau.
Kirchheim, Firmin,	Banker,	Berlin.
Kantzow and Biel,	Merchants,	Stockholm.
Kramer and Son,	Merchants,	Amsterdam.

L.

Lyall, Brothers,	East India Trade,	London.
Lackersteen, A. A.,	East India Trade,	Do.
Lackersteen and Crake,	East India Trade,	Do.
Leaf, Barnett, Scotson, & Co.,	Warehousemen,	Do.
Lysaght, Smithett, & Co.,	East India Trade,	Do.
Leys, Masson, & Co.,	Flax Spinners,	Do. and Aberdeen.
Liverpool Banking Co.,	Bankers,	Liverpool.
Lyon and Finney,	General Merchants,	Do.

Lake, Calrow, & Co.,	East India Trade,	Liverpool.
Livingstone & Co.,	East India Trade,	Do.
Logan, J. & Co.,	Canada Merchants,	Do.
Losh, Spiers, & Co.,	West India Trade,	Trinidad.
Lacey, J.,	West India Trade,	Glasgow.
Lyall, Matheson, & Co.,	East India Trade,	Calcutta.
Lackersteen, Brothers,	East India Trade,	Do.
Lake, Hammel, & Co.,	East India Trade,	Do.
Livingston & Co.,	East India Trade,	Do.
Layard, H. L. & Co.,	Merchants,	Ceylon.
Levett, Norison,	Manufacturer,	Hull.
Lafitte, Blount, & Co.,	Bankers,	Paris.
Luuyt, M. L. & Co.,	Bankers,	Paris.
Lantelme, Senior, & Co.,	Bankers,	Marseilles.
Laubon & Co.,	Bankers,	Do.
Lavison, Novach, & Co.,	American Trade,	Do.
Labile D.,	Merchant,	Havre.
La Maison, Bouwer, & Co.,	Money Dealers,	Amsterdam.
Legrelle & Co.,	Bankers,	Brussells.

M.

Merchant Trader's Ship—Loan and Insurance Association,	Insurance Brokers,	London.
McMullen, J. C.,	Stock Exchange,	Do.
Morley, J. and W.,	Warehousemen,	Do.
McDonald, A. & Co.,	South American Trade,	Do.
McTear, Hadfield, & Co.	Ship Brokers,	Liverpool.
Molyneux and Hulbert,	Tea Brokers,	Do.
Murray, T. and H.	East India Trade,	Do.
Maury, W.,	American Trade,	Do.
Mocatta and Son,	Spanish American Trade,	Do.
Martin and Hartwright,	Yarn Merchants,	Manchester.
Marsland, J.,	Cotton Spinner,	Do.
Marsland, Veltman, & Co.,	Manufacturers,	Do.
Mitchell & Co.,	Canada Trade,	Glasgow.
McKenzie, D., Jun.,	East India Trade,	Do.
McGregor, Brownrigg, & Co.,	Merchants,	Do.
Mc Phails & Co.,	Spinners,	Do.
Molley and Mergin,	Cattle Dealers,	Dublin.
Murphy, T.,	Provision Merchant,	Waterford.
M'Clelland, R.,	Linen Trade,	North of Ireland.
Muir, Taylor, & Co.	Merchants,	New York.
Martyrt, C.,	Merchant,	Vienna.

Morfeurgo and Tedeschi,	Merchants,	Leghorn.
Melum & Co., Widow,	Merchants,	Havre.
Mantricher & Co.,	American Merchants,	Marseilles.
Mendes, De Leon, & Co.,	Money Dealers,	Amsterdam.

N.

Nevins and Allen,	Corn Trade,	London.
Nash, W.,	Warehouseman,	Do.
North and South Wales Bank,	Bankers,	Liverpool.
Newcastle Joint Stock Bank,	Bankers,	Newcastle.
Napier, D.,	Iron Founder,	Glasgow.
Neilson & Co.,	Spinners,	Kirkland.
Naegly and Escher,	Merchants,	Marseilles.

O.

Oakley, R.,	Stock Exchange,	London.
O'Neal, J. and F.,	Corn Trade,	Liverpool.
Oldham Banking Co.,	Bankers,	Oldham.
Oakes and Jones,	Iron Trade,	Kingswinford.
Oak Farm Co.,	Iron Trade,	Do.
Ogilvie, Clarke, & Co.,	Agents,	Glasgow.
Owen, Allhusen, & Co.,	East India Trade,	Calcutta.
Oswald, Seal, & Co.,	East India Trade,	Do.
Oczle & Co.,	Mill Proprietors,	Venice.
Oxnard and Choix,	American Trade,	Marseilles.
Oeder & Co.,	Bankers,	Aix-la-Chapelle.

P.

Preece, R. M.,	Stock Exchange,	London.
Pemberton, Wm.,	Canada Trade,	Do.
Phillips, Lawrence, and Sons,	East India Trade,	Do.
Phillips, Samuel, & Co.,	East India Trade,	Do.
Perkins, Schlusser, & Mullens,	East India & Baltic Trade,	Do.
Pearce, W., & Co.,	Merchants,	Liverpool.
Platt, Hammill, & Co.,	East India Trade,	Do.
Perrin and Sons,	Corn Trade,	Do.
Pindleton, J. T. H.,	Manufacturer,	Manchester.
Potter, E. & Co.,	Agents,	Do.
Pearson, Wilson, & Co.,	Merchants,	Glasgow.
Perston, M.,	Merchant,	Do.
Pattison and McGibbon,	Calico Printers,	Do.
Planters Bank,	Bankers,	Jamaica.

Paccard, Dufour, & Co.,	Bankers,	Paris.
Pagny, C.,	Banker and Money Dealer,	Do.
Post Jacob,	Merchant,	Amsterdam.
Pieterse & Co.,	Money Dealers,	Do.
Pluym and Bakker,	Bankers,	Do.
Pehmoller and Tollens,	Merchants,	Hamburg.
Pegra, Guttiers, & Co., D.,	Merchants,	Leghorn.
Poppe and Co.,	Bankers,	Berlin.
Perret, F., and Sons,	Bankers,	Neufchatel.
Plitt, J. C.,	Merchant,	St. Petersburg.
Parangue and Sons,	Bankers,	Marseilles.
Patengat & Co.,	Corn Trade,	Bayonne.
Pacifico, Salvador,	Merchant,	Trieste.
Prime, Ward, & Co.,	Merchants,	New York.

Q.

Quertier and Godefroy,	Merchants,	Havre.

R.

Robinson, E. (deceased)	Mauritius Trade,	London.
Robinson, W. R., & Co.,	Corn Trade,	Do.
Reid, Irving, & Co.,	Mauritius Trade,	Do.
Rougemont, Brothers,	Continental Merchants,	Do.
Rickards, Little, & Co.,	East India Trade,	Do.
Ryder, Wienholt, & Co.,	East India Trade,	Do.
Reay, J. & H.,	Wine Merchants,	Do.
Roberts, Mitchell, & Co.,	East India Trade,	Do.
Ridge, S.,	Stock Exchange,	Do.
Rowett & Co.,	Merchants,	Liverpool.
Royal Bank of Liverpool,	Bankers,	Do.
Ricardo and Harding,	Merchants,	Do.
Rowand and Dunlop,	Australian Trade,	Liverpool and Glasgow.
Render and Milner,	Agents,	Manchester.
Ridehalgh & Co.,	Worsted Spinners,	Halifax.
Rogers and Brierley,	Cotton Spinners,	Blackburn.
Reid, Robinson, & Co.,	Merchants,	Glasgow.
Rankin, A.,	West India Trade,	Do.
Rankine & Co.,	Warehousemen,	Do.
Roux & Co.,	Merchants,	Paris.
Rutgers and Rosenberg,	Money Dealers,	Amsterdam.
Ruys, T. D.,	Money Dealer,	Do.
Roseboom M.,	Money Dealer,	Do.
Roothan & Co.,	Bankers,	Do.
Rupe, J. H. and Son,	Sugar Refiners,	Do.

Riewit and Langevelt,	Merchants,	Rotterdam.
Rouffaer and Sons,	Merchants,	Do.
Robinow, M. and Sons,	Bankers,	Hamburg.
Richer & Co.,	Manufacturers,	Prague.
Riley and Reussner,	Bankers,	Magdeburg.
Reinach, Jacques, & Co.,	Bankers,	Mentz.
Rosing & Co.,	Merchants,	Bremen.
Riva, C., & Co.,	Merchants,	St. Petersburg.
Reese, J., and Sons,	Merchants,	Philadelphia.

S.

Sanderson & Co.,	Bill Brokers,	London.
Shewell and Sons,	Stock Exchange,	Do.
Soares, M. J.,	Portuguese Trade,	Do.
Scott, Bell, & Co.,	East India Trade,	Do.
Sutherland, C. & Co.,	Colonial Brokers,	Do.
Sargant, Gordon, & Co.,	Produce Brokers,	Do.
Schwartz, H. W.,	Merchant,	Do.
Shaw and Caffary,	Merchants,	Do.
Secretan and Capper,	Stock Exchange,	Do.
Speir & Co.,	East India Trade,	Do.
Steele and Son,	Soap Boilers,	Liverpool.
Synnot, M. S.,	Ship Owner,	Do.
Sands, T. and J.,	Merchants,	Do.
Stocks and Tait,	Bleachers,	Manchester.
Scholes & Co.,	Bankers,	Do.
Story, & Co.,	Bankers,	St. Alban's.
Southam & Co.,	Cotton Spinners,	Ashton.
Sampson, Langdale, & Co.,	Corn Trade,	Stockton on Tees.
Saunders, May, Fordyce, & Co.,	East India Trade,	Calcutta.
Shearman, Mullens, & Co.,	East India Trade,	Do.
Smith, Cowell, & Co.,	East India Trade,	Do.
Schmidt, H. C.,	Belgian Trade,	Hamburg
Spengel, J. B.,	Merchant,	Do.
Samson, Brothers, & Co.,	Dealers in Manufact. Goods,	Do.
Sontag, G. H. & Co.,	African & West India Trade,	Do.
Schultza, W. J. C.,	Sugar Refiner,	Do.
Sigart, Tercelin,	Banker,	Mons.
Serret, M. G. & Co.,	Bankers,	Valenciennes.
Schaafhausen, A.,	Banker,	Cologne.
Sigrist, Jacob,	Banker,	Amsterdam.
Schrieber and Sons,	Bankers,	Breslau.
Seligman, I. & Co.,	Merchants,	Amsterdam.
Schrœder & Co.,	West India Trade,	Porto Rico.

T.

Trueman and Cook,	Colonial Brokers,	London.
Trueman, Charles & Co.,	Silk Merchants,	Do.
Tanner and Ward,	Leather Factors,	Do.
Thomas, Son, & Lefevre, (John)	Russia Trade,	Do.
Thurburn & Co.,	East India Trade,	Do.
Turner, T.,	Stock Exchange,	Do.
Thorne, W.,	Canada Trade,	Do.
Tomlinson, W. and T.,	Corn Trade,	Liverpool
Taylor, R.,	Soap Boiler,	Do.
Taylor, W. and A.,	Manufacturers,	Glasgow.
Thurneyssen, M. & Co.,	Bankers,	Paris.
Theunissens F. de Kinder,	Banker,	Antwerp.
Thompson, J., Jun.,	Merchant,	New York.

U. & V.

Usborne, T. and Son,	Corn Trade,	London.
Vanzeller, F. J.,	Portuguese Trade,	Do.
Union Bank of Calcutta,	Bankers,	Calcutta.
Venay, Cardoza, & Co.,	East India Trade,	Madras.
Van den Bogaerts, M.,	Merchant,	Antwerp.
Van der Beek, J. C.,	Manufacturer,	Elberfeldt.
Viet, Brothers, & Co.,	Bankers,	Berlin.
Von Haber and Sons,	Bankers,	Frankfort.
Von Haber, Baron de J.,	Banker and Manufacturer,	Carlsruhe.
Van Harpen, A. L., & Co.,	Money Dealers,	Amsterdam.
Valentin, J. L., & Co.,	Merchants,	Leghorn.
Vernein and Giells,	Manufacturers,	Courtray.
Vermechren & Co.,	Merchants,	St. Petersburg.
Vanzeller, J. and Sons,	Merchants,	Lisbon.
Ventura, M. & Co.,	Merchants,	Venice.
Van Sennep, J. & Co.,	Merchants,	Smyrna.

W.

Woodley, W. and J.,	Corn Trade,	London.
Weber & Co.,	East India Trade,	Do.
Whitmore, H.,	Stock Exchange,	Do.
Williams, J., Jun.,	Stock Exchange,	Do.
Wright, Job & Co.,	Russian Trade,	Do.
Watson, Brothers, & Co.,	Merchants,	Liverpool.
Wilson, Nash, & Co.,	Merchants,	Do.
Warden & Co.,	Merchants,	Do.

Wotherspoon, Stewart, & Co.,	Share Brokers,	Liverpool.
Westlake & Co.,	Corn Trade,	Southampton.
Watson, Elder, & Co.,	Manufacturers,	Manchester.
Wilson and Eber,	Merchants and Spinners,	Do.
Watson, M'Knight, & Co.,	Merchants,	Glasgow.
Wingate, A. and I.,	Calico Printers,	Glasgow.
Walker, M.,	Flax Spinner,	Leeds.
White & Co.,	Corn Trade,	Waterford.
Wienholt, John & Co.,	East India Trade,	Calcutta.
West India Bank,	Bankers,	Barbadoes.
Windmuller, Brothers, & Co.,	Merchants,	Hamburg.
Warburg, E.,	Banker and Bill Broker,	Do.
Wittenstein & Co.,	Spinners,	Elberfeldt.
Westerndorp & Co.,	Money Dealers,	Amsterdam.
Wilcox, Maris, & Co.,	Merchants,	Philadelphia.
Wells, Brothers, & Co.,	Merchants,	New York.
Wilder, M. P.,	Wholesale Grocery Trade,	Boston.

Y.

Young, C. B.,	Stock Exchange,	London.
Young, G. & Co.,	Calico Printers,	Glasgow.

FINIS.

TABLE OF DIVIDENDS.

The appended table of dividends shews the results, as far as can be ascertained, of Forty-five of the principal firms, the whole of which with the exception of Messrs. Harman & Co., were compelled to suspend payment during the memorable Crisis, 1847–48. It will be perceived that in cases where estates have been administered in Bankruptcy, or composition accepted, the circumstance is recorded—in all others it may be generally assumed that the process of liquidation by inspectorship was adopted.

NAME OF FIRM.	DESIGNATION OF TRADING.	DATE OF SUSPENSION.	AMOUNT OF LIABILITIES.	ESTIMATED ASSETS.	GROSS AMOUNT OF DIVIDEND PAID UP TO APRIL, 1849.
			£	£	
Alexander, L. & Co	Corn trade	August, 1847	573,188	125,000	2s. 8d. in the pound—further dividends expected. Estate administered in Bankruptcy.
Barclay, Brothers, & Co.	Mauritius trade	October, 1847	389,504	395,491	2s. 6d. in the pound—further dividends expected.
Booker, Sons, & Co.	Corn trade	September, 1847	40,000	Amount not known	2s. 6d. in the pound.
Bruce, Buxton, & Co........	Bill Brokers	October, 1847	347,000	61,000	1s. in the pound—further dividends expected.
Bensusan & Co.	Mogador trade	September, 1847	57,961	2,316	No dividend yet paid—estimated realization about 4d. in the pound. Estate administered in Bankruptcy.
Braine, G. T.	East India trade	July, 1848	226,412	411,349	15s. in the pound, and every prospect of the remaining 5s. being shortly distributed.
Boyds and Thomas..........	East India trade	October, 1847	38,684	29,544	2s. in the pound, and a further distribution anticipated.
Cockerell, Larpent, & Co. ...	East India trade	September, 1847	619,393	809,254	No dividend yet paid—estimates respecting probable realization extremely uncertain.
Castellain, Sons, & Co.	General Merchants	August, 1847	69,651	33,603	10s. in the pound—probably a small further distribution.
Cotesworth, Powell, and Pryor	Brazilian and Spanish American trade	December, 1847	350,000	Amount not known	Arrangements made for 20s. in the pound. The Firm have resumed business.
Cruickshank, Melville, & Co...	East & West India Trade	October, 1847	182,984	152,179	No dividend yet paid—prospects of realization extremely uncertain.
Coventry and Sheppard	Corn trade	August, 1847	200,000	Amount not known	5s. 6d. in the pound.
Douglas, C. and Son	Corn trade	August, 1847	250,000	Amount not known	5s. in the pound.
Fraser, W. T................	East India trade	September, 1847	33,665	40,307	4s. in the pound—further dividends anticipated.
Fry, Griffiths, & Co.	Colonial Brokers	September, 1847	90,979	19,231	4s. in the pound.
Gower, A. A. and Nephews ..	Spanish and Mauritius trade	September, 1847	450,832	112,331	1s. 6d. in the pound—further dividends anticipated.
Giles, Son, & Co.	Corn trade	August, 1847	152,824	90,911	12s. in the pound.
Harman & Co.	Russia trade	October, 1846	541,439	110,194	3s. in the pound. The Estate is closely estimated to realize 3s. 3d.
Hastie and Hutchison	Corn trade	September, 1847	50,451	38,796	A composition accepted of 15s. in the pound.

Johnson, Cole, & Co.	East India trade	November, 1847	122,666	71,844	No dividend yet paid—expected to realize about 4d. in the pound. Estate administered in Bankruptcy.
King, Melvil, & Co.	Corn trade	August, 1847	200,000	Amount not known	8s in the pound.
Kingston, J. & Co.	West India trade	February, 1848	25,245	44,382	No dividend yet paid.
Lackersteen, A. A.	East India trade	November, 1847	185,529	100,355	6d. in the pound—a further small dividend anticipated. Estate administered in Bankruptcy.
Lackersteen and Crake	East India trade	November, 1847	133,091	26,257	10½d. in the pound—a further small dividend anticipated. Estate administered in Bankruptcy.
Leaf, Barnett, Scotson, & Co.	Warehousemen	November, 1847	85,575	89,079	A composition accepted of 16s. in the pound.
Lyall, Brothers, & Co.	East India trade	September, 1847	340,387	151,556	1s. in the pound—further dividends anticipated.
Morley, J. and W.	Warehousemen	October, 1847	119,731	89,217	A composition accepted of 11s. in the pound.
Nevins and Allen	Corn trade	August, 1847	69,907	8,126	1s. 10½d. in the pound.
Perkins, Schlusser, & Mullens	East India & Baltic trade	September, 1847	127,327	136,048	8s. in the pound—a further dividend expected.
Phillips S. & Co.	East India trade	September, 1847	101,474	100,075	1s. in the pound—further dividends expected.
Phillips, L. & Co.	East India trade	October, 1847	18,368	64,840	5s. in the pound—further dividends expected.
Reid, Irving, & Co.	West India and Mauritius trade	September, 1847	660,432	846,756	1s. 6d. in the pound—further dividends expected.
Rickards, Little, & Co.	East India trade	October, 1847	144,626	50,430	1s. in the pound—the estimates respecting the ultimate realization of the Estate uncertain.
Rougemont, Brothers, & Co.	General Merchants	October, 1847	109,450	77,900	8s. 3d. in the pound—further dividends anticipated. Estate administered in Bankruptcy.
Robinson, W. R. & Co.	Corn trade	August, 1847	94,362	100,390	20s. in pound.
Ryder, Wienholt, & Co.	East India trade	November, 1847	34,587	23,670	2s. 3d. in the pound.
Reay and Reay	Wine trade	November, 1847	47,788	16,459	4s. in the pound—further dividends anticipated.
Scott, Bell, & Co.	East India trade	October, 1847	99,629	143,248	20s. in the pound—the Firm have resumed business.
Sargant, Gordon, & Co.	Colonial Brokers	November, 1847	65,254	10,652	2s. 6d. in the pound—further dividends expected.
Sanderson & Co.	Bill Brokers	September, 1847	168,000	447,000	20s. in the pound—The Firm have resumed business under a new partnership.
				139,604	2s. in the pound—further dividends expected.
Thurburn & Co.	East India trade	November, 1847	109,139	441,972	20s. in the pound. The Firm have resumed business under a new partnership.
Thomas, Son, & Lefevre	Russia trade	October, 1847	401,760		
				381,835	12s. in the pound up to the present date. Further dividends anticipated. The Firm have separated and new partnerships have been formed.
Trueman and Cook	Colonial Brokers	November, 1847	379,104		
Usborne, T. and Son	Corn trade	September, 1847	59,457	33,527	A composition accepted of 11s. in the pound.
Woodley, W. and J.	Corn trade	August, 1847	99,509	90,845	17s. 7d in the pound.